CW00933194

The Illustrated History of

LMS

STANDARD
COACHING STOCK

II: General Service Gangwayed Vehicles

David Jenkinson and Bob Essery

(OPC)
Oxford Publishing Co.

'Patriot' Class 5XP 4-6-0 No. 45508 climbing Shap early in BR days with a typical mixture of LMS carriages, some of them already repainted in the new BR crimson and cream livery. The first five coaches can be identified as Period III Corridor Brake Composite (D1932 or D2010), Period III ('all-steel' porthole) Corridor Composite (D2159), Period I (LNWR style) Composite Dining Car (D1743), Period II Vestibule Third (D1897) and Period III Corridor Brake Third (D2123). All but one of the remaining seven coaches are Period III – specific types uncertain but mostly third class — but the train itself is unidentified. (Authors' Collection)

A Catalogue record for this book is available from the British Library.

ISBN 0 86093 451 9

Oxford Publishing Co., is an imprint of Haynes Publishing
Sparkford, near Yeovil, Somerset, BA22 7JJ

Printed in Great Britain by Butler & Tanner Ltd, Frome and London
Typeset in Times Roman Medium

Publisher's note: Although there are references to Volume III of *The Illustrated History of LMS Standard Coaching Stock* this is to be published at a later date.

Contents

A mixed LMS/GWR formation leaving Bristol in 1936 behind Stanier 'Jubilee' Class 5XP 4-6-0 No. 5609 *Gilbert and Ellice Islands.* The LMS portion contains all three periods of LMS design, five variants being present: Period III (shallow window ventilator) Corridor Brake Third (D1852), Period III (deep window ventilator) Corridor Third (D1899). Period II (fully panelled) Vestibule Third dining car (probably D1721 ex-FO D1722, but possibly D1795), Period I (steel panelled) Kitchen Only Car (D1697), Period I (panelled twin window) Vestibule Composite (D1744). The latter car has the only first class accommodation in the LMS portion (12 seats!) but the second GWR coach is a 4F + 3T corridor composite which would offer another 24. The train is not identified but the nature of the accommodation suggests a holiday type working. (Soole Collection — NRM)

List of Line Drawings and Diagrams

Note: Except where stated otherwise and/or obvious in context, all drawings and diagrams in the book should be assumed to be at a scale of 4mm = 1ft

List of Summary Tables

Authors' Introduction to the Third Revised Edition, Volume II

We were delighted at the reception given to the first volume of our revised and enlarged survey of LMS Coaching Stock. We now continue the story in this volume with comprehensive coverage of the LMS general service gangwayed fleet. In this context, though we include sleeping and dining cars, we have not covered any of the gangwayed articulated stock built for general services as we feel that this development is more appropriate to Volume III, where we shall deal with it in association with the closely related non-corridor and "Coronation Scot" variants.

As with Volume I we have included a great number of drawings and official pictures not previously present in the original single volume survey, along with those which were, of course. Also, where they are the only known pictures of the type, we have thought it helpful to repeat a few views from the introductory section of Volume I, this time in association with their appropriate diagram(s). Lastly, the extra space has again enabled us to give the full pre-1933 LMS carriage number series (where applicable) which had, hitherto, only appeared in 'sample' form.

Once again, we should state that this data (including the official pictures) mostly stemmed originally from the PR&PO's office of the London Midland Region during the 1960s. Since we obtained our copies, the bulk of the official picture collection has been rehoused at the National Railway Museum, York, to which interested readers should refer for any copies they might require, although we cannot say if all have survived. The pre-1933 numbers come from one of very few known full copies of the official LMS list which has survived and which is happily still in our possession.

This volume is structured broadly as before–i.e. a general introductory section to each chapter followed by a detailed analysis of each vehicle type rather than chronologically by age. Readers of our earlier survey will, of course, find much that is familiar – rather inevitable in the circumstances – but we reckon that some two thirds of the offered material is new in terms of not having been published before. We have tried to prepare a fully illustrated version of the complete LMS carriage diagram book as far as sources render this feasible and have made full use of the real diagrams wherever possible, though we must also make the point that one or two are missing. From the 1930s onwards the issued diagrams deteriorated considerably in both quality and information (we guess because of economies in the drawing office), so we have supplemented several diagrams with detailed drawings which we hope will give sufficient extra data to enable the somewhat basic original material to be more easily interpreted. Concerned about the poor quality of the later LMS diagrams we consulted others (interested modellers) and their view was that upon the basis of historical accuracy they should be included. Furthermore the general opinion was that, whenever possible, they should be reproduced to 4mm scale. Accordingly, we have accepted their advice.

We should also, perhaps, point out that ours is not an overtly technical survey. Rather, it is an overview of the vast variety of passenger rolling stock which our biggest private railway managed to put into service during its relatively brief existence. Such technicalities as seem relevant in context have already been covered in Volume I, and although we add some information in this volume, readers who wish to 'dig deeper' in this respect will find ample to reward them in such sources as contemporary issues of the *Railway Gazette* and *Locomotive* magazines, copies of which should be available in many good reference libraries and reference to which is certainly possible at the NRM.

For ourselves, we are content to let the story speak for itself. The LMS was undoubtedly the most significant provider of long distance passenger stock in these islands during the company era. It derived design inspiration mainly from its two large English constituents, the LNWR and MR, both of whose influence can be seen in the pre-1930 carriage designs. But from 1930 onwards it established its own distinctive way of doing things and in the final Stanier designs, we do not think we are exaggerating if we state that ordinary railway passengers (especially those who bought a third class ticket) were offered the finest long distance stock ever to be seen up to that time – and rarely, if ever, equalled since. This is our story of those carriages and we hope you enjoy reading it.

DJ
Easingwold
1994

RJE
Rolleston-on-Dove
1994

Explanation of Terms

DIAGRAMS AND LOTS

LMS coaches were built to various *Diagrams*. Basically the Diagram was a drawing which defined the precise type of coach which was to be built although not, in itself, a working drawing. The various Diagrams have identifying numbers, not necessarily in consecutive sequence through the years, and in this book will be referred to throughout as Dxxxx. Several Diagrams were current for a number of years and each separate batch of coaches built to a particular diagram was given an identifying *Lot Number*. In general, Lot numbers, while not always consecutively numbered on a particular Diagram, were in ascending order as the years went by. Thus Lot 954 of D1915 would represent later coaches than Lot 843 of the same Diagram.

Whenever a design was changed–even to a minor extent–a fresh Diagram was almost always issued. As far as can be ascertained there were very few exceptions to this policy and these have been noted. Diagrams have been used extensively as illustrative material in this book.

PLATING

This term will be used to refer to the LMS practice of putting works plates on the coach. These were carried on the solebar and on the coach end. The solebar plate generally gave details of the works where built and the date of building, including Lot numbers from 1934/5, while the plate on the coach end was a dimension plate giving length, width and tare weight, to the nearest ton. Sometimes the plates were slightly at variance with the official Diagram version. The policy in this book will be to give the Diagram version drawing attention where necessary to any discrepancies in the coach plating details as observed in traffic.

DIMENSIONS

Unless otherwise stated, basic coach dimensions will be given as follows:

Height: Rail level to top of roof, not counting roof ventilators.

Length: Over Headstocks–with LMS coaches, which almost always had flat ends, this dimension was some 1in to 1½ins less than the body length of the coach.

Width: Over projections–i.e. a coach with a 9ft 0in wide body but with projecting handles would be quoted as 9ft 3in if this dimension was the width over the handles.

STRUCTURAL TERMS

The following definitions have been adopted as a standard for this work.

Beading: Raised wooden strips covering the panel joints on wood panelled stock.

Cantrail: The point at which the coach side meets the roof.

Cornice: The moulding, often of slightly ornamental nature, which was frequently found along the line of the cantrail.

Chassis: The complete underframe together with bogies, buffing and draw gear &c.

Gutter: The rainwater channel along the top of the cornice.

Headstock: The end section of the underframe which carried the buffing and draw gear.

Light: A generic term for a carriage window, sub-classified as follows:

Droplight: An opening window which moves in the vertical plane–usually wood framed but there were aluminium frame and frameless variants.

Fixed Light: A window which will not open.

Quarterlight: The small fixed light flanking the doors of all compartments which had outside doors.

Toplight: A small window situated between the cantrail and the top of the main carriage window.

Panelling: A generic term relating to the method of covering the exterior of the coach–e.g. wooden panelling, steel panelling, flush panelling &c. The following principal sub-classifications should be noted:

Eaves Panel: The section of the body panelling located between the window top and the cantrail.

Flush panelling: Used to refer to any coach which did not have any form of raised body projections in the form of wooden beading.

Matchboarding: The name used in reference to the type of coach end panelling which consisted of a series of tongue and groove boarding running vertically from roof level to headstocks. This was a technique generally confined to coaches with an 'all wood' exterior finish.

Tumblehome: The incurving portion of the bodyside panelling as it approaches the solebar.

Waist Panel: The portion of the body panelling situated immediately below the windows and on LMS coaches, having a depth of some 8in. Waist panelling was generally confined to high waisted fully beaded coaches of wood panelled style.

Roof Types: The LMS, for the most part, adopted two types of roof as follows:

Rainstrip roof:	This was of wood and canvas construction with a continuous rainstrip from end to end and on each side of the roof.
Ribbed roof:	This was the Stanier pattern metal clad roof with a series of strengthening ribs from one side of the coach to the other, rainstrips if present at all, being generally confined to the section of the roof immediately above the doors. Some coaches had flush welded roof panels without external transverse ribs.

Semi-elliptical: This is a term used to refer to the roof profile above the cantrail when in the form of a semi-ellipse.

Solebar: The heavy section forming the main side members of the coach underframe. On LMS design coaches this was a steel channel section, generally with the channel facing outwards.

Truss-rods: The angle section fixed underneath the underframe between the bogies, giving additional strength to the underframe itself and acting as a support for some ancillary fittings.

Underframe: The supporting frame of the coach on which the body was mounted, but not counting the bogies, buffers, ancillary fittings &c.

Ventilators: The following principal sub-classifications should be noted:

Door ventilators:	These were the ventilators situated on outside doors above the droplight, either hooded or louvred.
Hooded ventilators:	External ventilators (generally on doors or above windows) which were covered by a plain metal 'hood'.
Louvre ventilators:	External ventilators (usually mounted over door drop-lights) which consisted outwardly of a series of horizontal wooden louvres, usually three.
Shell and Torpedo ventilators:	The two types of roof ventilator generally used by the LMS. Torpedo ventilators were of several styles and the differences are best appreciated by comparing pictures of the various types.
Sliding ventilators:	The type of ventilator used in the upper part of the big side windows of Stanier pattern gangwayed coaches.
Stones ventilators:	These were ventilators generally placed above the main windows of coaches in the eaves panel. They had swivelling glass vanes (six or nine elements) which could be adjusted by the passenger to 'face' or 'trail' the airstream past the coach.
Dewel ventilators:	Similar to Stones ventilators but even shorter (five moving vanes).

TYPES OF COACH

The following definitions will be adopted throughout:

Corridor coach:	A coach with a side corridor for all or part of its length and with gangway connections to adjacent vehicles.
Dining Car:	A vestibule coach containing a kitchen as well as passenger seating accommodation.
Vestibule coach:	An open coach with gangway connections to adjacent vehicles. Note that a vestibule coach used exclusively for dining purposes but *not* having a kitchen was referred to as a 'vestibule dining coach' and was *not* called a dining car.
Non-corridor coach:	Any coach without gangway connections.
Lavatory coach:	A non-gangwayed coach with toilets serving individual compartments either directly or from a short side corridor.

The nomenclature of other types of coaches is self explanatory.

COACH CODING

Where it seems appropriate, the standard British Railways coach codes have been adopted for ease of reference. These are, in fact, based on the old LNER system but the familiarity of present day usage will, it is felt, make them easier to understand for most readers than the official LMS codes. Full details are given on page 10, together with the old LMS code letters.

COACH NUMBERING

Until 1932, new standard LMS coaches were numbered somewhat haphazardly in the gaps available between the various batches of pre-group coaches which themselves, apart from the ex-MR vehicles, had been numbered in blocks in 1923. The ex-MR coaches retained their pre-group numbers except for the M&GSW and M&NB Joint Stock vehicles which were given vacant numbers in the ex-MR allocation, generally at the end of this series.

    From 1933, the whole coaching stock (pre-group and standard) was renumbered systematically by generic vehicle types and these 1933 numbers are the ones which are used throughout this book. Details of the renumbering principles are given on pages 10 and 11. At nationalisation, LMS coaches generally retained their numbers and newly built coaches to LMS/LMR diagrams were given numbers in the appropriate LMS series. From 1948 until 1951, the LMS number was prefixed by a letter 'M' to denote the company/region of origin of the design. At about the time of the introduction of BT standard coaching stock, the prefix/suffix system was introduced. The prefix letter now denoted the region of allocation the suffix letter was introduced as the identification of the vehicle's origin. Thus, for example, LMS coach No. 1234 would first have become M1234 in 1948 and then, if allocated to, say, Scotland, would have finally become Sc1234M. For the sake of consistency, it will be the policy in this book to omit the prefix/suffix letters in all references to LMS/LMR coaches–even those which entered service carrying such prefix or suffix letters.

Basic Dimensions and Assumptions

IN the chapters following this, the various generic types of coach built by the LMS are described and listed. Because of the high degree of standardisation of LMS coaches it is possible to take as read many basic features of the designs and thus confine the description of the types and the tabulated data to those aspects peculiar to the coaches under discussion. It is hoped that this will simplify the understanding of the subject.

Dimensions
The following basic table of dimensions can be taken as standard for all coaches of the lengths specified:

Length over Headstocks	69′	68′	65′	62′	60′	58′	57′	54′	51′	50′
Bogie Type	6wh	6wh	4wh	4wh	4wh	4wh	4wh	4wh	4wh	4wh
Bogie wheelbase	12′6″	12′6″	9′0″	9′0″	9′0″	9′0″	9′0″	9′0″	9′0″	9′0″
Bogie centres	46′0″	45′0″	48′0″	45′6″	43′6″	41′6″	40′6″	37′6″	34′6″	33′6″
Buffer type Oval (O) or Round (R)	O	O	O	O	R	R	R	R	R	R

Because of this standardised pattern, the only dimensions quoted in the summary tables will be length over headstocks, width over projections and height from rails to rooftop.

Typical window and panel dimensions of all three periods of design are given in Volume I, page 6.

Assumptions
Unless stated otherwise it may safely be assumed that the following styling and other features were common to all LMS coaches to be described:

Period I coaches:	Body:	High waisted, wood panelled, fully beaded sides and matchboard ends.
	Roof:	Wood construction with canvas covering and carrying an end to end longitudinal rainstrip at each side.
	Roof vents:	Torpedo pattern.
	Door vents:	3-element louvre type, but hooded metal on coaches built with MR locks/handles &c.
	Corridor connections:	British standard (scissors type).
	Livery when new:	Fully lined out, original insignia styles and placings, grey and black roof, red coach ends.

Period II coaches:	Body:	a. Gangway stock:	Low waisted, 'square windowed', wood or steel panelled. The type of panelling and presence or absence of beading will be specified in the narrative.
		b. Non-corridor:	High waisted, steel panelled, 'square' windows.
	Roof:	Wood/Canvas/Rainstrip.	
	Roof vents:	Torpedo pattern.	
	Door vents:	Hooded metal (steel panelling), louvre type (wood panelling).	
	Corridor connections:	British standard (scissors type).	
	Livery when new:	Fully lined out but without waist panel, stretched scroll figures and later insignia placing, grey and black roof, red coach ends.	

Period III coaches:	Body:	Totally flush clad without raised window mouldings, rounded window corners, steel panelled.
	Roof:	Metal clad 'ribbed' pattern.
	Roof vents:	Shell pattern.
	Door vents:	Hooded metal.
	Window vents:	Sliding type with *two* moving elements.
	Corridor connections:	British standard (suspended gangway type).
	Livery:	Simplified lining, shaded block style figures and later insignia placing, metallic roof finish (pre-war), grey roof finish (post-war), black ends from late 1936, 'straw' lining from 1946.

The principal exceptions to the above summary were the early Stanier coaches. Some of these came out in full livery and some had the earlier sliding ventilator with one moving element. A few had torpedo ventilators and there were other slight points of difference. All these aspects are covered in the summary tables. Stanier coaches in full livery generally carried unshaded block style figures.

In all subsequent chapters, the various coaches are listed in the form of standardised summary tables at the end of the narrative. These give all details supplementary to those which may be deduced from the above list of assumptions. The tables themselves are, in most cases, supplemented by diagrammatic plans of the coaches themselves to show the interior layout of the vehicle.

In most summary tables, the first and last withdrawal dates for each coach 'lot' are given. The dates are London Midland Region four-week periods and relate to the normal planned coach withdrawals. They do not generally take account of premature withdrawals due to accident or wartime enemy action.

Standard Codes for Coaching Stock

The BR system of coding coach types is based on the old LNER system and following parts of it are relevant to LMS standard coaches discussed in this book, the LMS codes being given for comparison:

Dining and Kitchen Vehicles	BR Code	LMS Code
First Class Kitchen/Dining car	RF	1st RKC
Composite	RC	Compo RKC
Third Class	RT	3rd RKC
Unclassified	RU	Common RKC
Kitchen/Buffet car	RB or RKB	BRC
Kitchen only car	RK	KC
First Class vestibule dining coach	RFO	QL (Dining)
Composite	RCO	VC (Dining)
Third Class	RTO	QF (Dining)
Unclassified	RUO	—

Sleeping Cars		
First Class	SLF	SC
Composite	SLC	CSC
Third Class	SLT	SCT
.. .. (twin berth)	SLT (T)	—

Vestibule Stock		
Vestibule First Class	FO	QL
.. Composite	CO	VC
.. Third Class	TO	QF
.. Third Class Brake	BTO	VH
Semi-open First Class (Corridor Vestibule)	Semi-Fo or Semi-RFO	CQL
Semi-open Third Class (Corridor Vestibule)	Semi-TO or Semi-RTO	—

Corridor Stock	BR Code	LMS Code
First Class	FK	CL
.. .. Brake	BFK	E
Composite	CK	CBC
.. Brake	BCK	CBB
Third Class	TK	CF
.. .. Brake	BTK	CH

Non-corridor Stock		
First Class	F	L
.. .. (with lavatory)	FL	LM
Composite	C	BC
.. (with lavatory)	CL	L&C
Third Class	T	F
.. .. Brake	BT	H
.. .. .. (with lavatory)	BTL	LH

Other Coaching Stock		
Passenger full brake with gangway	BG	CBR
6 wheel passenger full brake with gangway	BGZ	CR
.. .. without gangway	BZ	R
Post Office Sorting Van	POS	POR
Post Office Tender (Stowage Van)	POT	PPR

Note: 1. Articulated stock is prefaced by the word 'Twin' or 'Triple' in the BR system.
2. Codes exist for multiple unit stock but have not been employed in this book.

A Note on the 1923 LMS Coaching Stock Numbers

When the LMS was formed in 1923, the ex-Midland carriages mostly kept their old numbers and the former M&GSWR/M&NB Joint stock was eventually assimilated into this series in 1923 and 1928 respectively. The other pre-group companies were then allocated blocks of new numbers following on in sequence, each company being kept together before going on to another company. Thus, for example, the LNWR/WCJS carriages were allocated the 4301-10700 block, followed by the LYR etc. Non-passenger coaching stock was numbered in a separate series with the ex-MR vehicles again at the head of the list (retaining their numbers) followed by the other pre-group fleets.

For the most part, new LMS carriage numbers for pre-group carriages were allocated in ascending diagram page order and the coaches on any particular diagram were usually numbered in pre-group number order. Although this system was not particularly refined it did, in most cases, collect all coaches of any particular type and diagram into one consecutive number series – often for the first time, given the somewhat random numbering principles followed by most LMS constituents. The basic fault was that inadequate provision was made for the numbering of newly built LMS standard coaches.

The general principle was to use appropriate gaps in the pre-group lists but this was not wholly successful. Where a complete series of old pre-group carriages had been scrapped, this would normally, of course, vacate a fully consecutive LMS number series (given the 1923 renumbering principles) but even when this was added to the existing gaps in the sequence, the blocks of numbers selected in 1923 were frequently too small to absorb the sheer numbers of new carriages. In consequence, the pre-1933 numbers of new coaches could either be found in short consecutive batches (existing gaps or replacing withdrawn pre-group stock) or randomly scattered anywhere in the whole LMS series where any gap (even one only!) was to be found. Even this did not suffice and the LMS itself eventually had to resort to an old LNWR principle of 'cyphering' the running numbers of still existing pre-group carriages. This was done by adding a 'O' prefix to many 1923 LMS numbers, thus freeing the originals for re-use.

By 1932/3, the situation had become so confusing that the LMS felt obliged to introduce a completely new and systematic numbering scheme whose principles are outlined below. It is felt that this may have been the main reason for introducing sans-serif carriage number insignia – mainly to allow easy differentiation of new from old numbers during the changeover.

The 1932/3 LMS Coach Renumbering Scheme

The 1932/3 renumbering scheme grouped all coaching stock (pre- and post-grouping) into systematic number blocks according to coach type. Within the pre-group allocations, the numbering order was generally as follows: LNWR (which carried the lowest numbers): MR: LYR: FR: CR: GSWR: HR (which carried the highest numbers). Generally speaking the LMS standard coaches were numbered consecutively upwards from the start of the block and the pre-group coaches were numbered backwards from the end of the block. The pre-group numbers were allocated in such a way that the complete pre-group block of coaches generally occupied the last and highest numbers in any series. This usually left a gap between the end of the LMS standard block and the start of the pre-group block which was available for new construction. In some cases the 1932 planners underestimated the size of the number blocks they would need and certain coaches overflowed into the other blocks – these are annotated below.

1-99 First Class Kitchen/Dining Cars
1-44   LMS Standard types
45-58   Vacant
59-99   Pre-group types

100-199 Third Class Kitchen/Dining Cars and Buffet Cars
100-148   LMS Standard types
147-199   Pre-group types (including first 147/8)

200-299 Composite Kitchen/Dining Cars
- 200-221   Ex-Pullman cars (mostly Scottish)
- 222-252   LMS Standard types
- 253-270   Sundry post-1947 cafeteria conversions of LMS coaches
- 241-299   Original pre-group allocation

300-499 First Class Sleeping Cars
- 300-402   LMS Standard types
- 403-437   Vacant
- 438-496   LNWR (with a few gaps)
- 497-499   Vacant

500-699 Third Class Sleeping Cars
- 500-599   LMS Standard SLT
- 600-624   LMS type SLT(T)
- 625-699   Vacant

700-799 Composite Sleeping Cars
- 700-724   LMS Standard types
- 725-789   Vacant
- 790-799   LNWR—note second 798 later given to HM The King's and HM The Queen's Saloons

800-999 Special Saloons—mainly pre-group varieties

1000-1199 Corridor Firsts and Semi Open Firsts
- 1000-1128   LMS Standard types
- 1128-1199   Pre-group types (including first 1128)

1200-3399 Corridor Thirds
- 1200-2516   LMS diagrams
- 2235-3399   Pre-group types (including first 2235-2516)

3400-3499 Push pull conversions of older gangwayed stock—both pre-group and LMS Standard types (some of the pre-group examples were built new as push pull vehicles)

3500-4999 Corridor Composites
- 3500-4514   LMS Standard types
- 4357-4999   Pre-group types (including first 4357-4514)
- 2nd 4800-4899   LMS Standard types

5000-5199 Corridor First Brakes and Open First Brakes
- 5000-5004   LMS Standard Lounge (open) brakes
- 5005-5077   LMS Standard BFKs
- 5078-5144   Vacant
- 5145-5199   Pre-group types

5200-6599 Corridor Third Brakes
- 5200-6038   LMS diagrams
- 5990-6599   Pre-group types (including first 5990-6038)

6600-7399 Corridor Composite Brakes
- 6600-6876   LMS Standard types
- 6877-6956   Vacant
- 6957-7399   Pre-group types

7400-7599 Vestibule Firsts (both FO and RFO)
- 7400-7575   LMS Standard types (Note: First 7465-89 were later downgraded and the numbers in part used again for later standard coaches)
- 7556-7599   Pre-group types (including first 7556-7575)

7600-9699 Vestibule Thirds (both TO and RTO)
- 7600-9518   LMS Standard types
- 9519-9561   Vacant
- 9562-9699   Pre-group types

9700-9799 Vestibule Composites (both CO and RCO)
- 9700-9758   LMS Standard types
- 9759-9791   Vacant
- 9792-9799   Ex-LYR

9800-9999 Vestibule Brake Thirds
- 9800-9970   LMS Standard types
- 9971-9999   Pre-group types—first coaches with these numbers.

Note: This concluded the initial allocation of numbers for passenger carrying non-articulated gangwayed stock. Extra batches built after the number series filled up were as follows:
Corridor Thirds: 12750-13184
Corridor Composites: 24500-24739
Corridor Brake Thirds: 26100-27095   } Some of these also orginally used
Vestibule Thirds: 27100-27449   } to re-number pre-group gangwayed
Vestibule Third Brakes: 27900-27956 } stock to clear the original series for standard construction.

10000-10699 Non-corridor Firsts
- 10000-10131   LMS Standard types
- 10132-10308   Vacant
- 10309-10699   Pre-group types

10700-15799 Non-corridor Thirds
- 10000-12267   LMS Standard types
- 12268-12277   Downgraded composites from 160xx series
- 12278-12283   Ex-MSJA trailers (converted 1954)
- 12284-13610   Vacant (12750-13184 used for overflow numbering of TKs and 13610 downwards used for various downgraded vehicles)
- 13611-15799   Pre-group types

15800-15999 Non-corridor Thirds—Motor Fitted
- 15800-15857   Pre-group types
- 15858-15906   LMS Standard types
- 15907-15996   Vacant
- 15997-15999   LMS Standard types (converted)

16000-17899 Non-corridor Composites
- 16000-16325   LMS Standard types (16000-16006 originally compo. seconds)
- 16326-16330   Vacant—allocated initially to 17900-4 (Push-Pull version)
- 16331-16796   LMS Standard types
- 16797-16876   GWR designs built post-1947 and given LMS series numbers
- 16850-16937   Originally part of the vacant series but later used in part (post-1947) for ex-CLC stock and marked down pre-group firsts
- 16938-17899   Pre-group types

17900-17999 Non-corridor Composites—Motor Fitted
- 17900-17942   LMS Standard types
- 17943-17957   Vacant but some later used for conversions
- 17958-17999   Pre-group types

18000-18199 Non-corridor Lavatory Firsts
- 18000-18029   LMS Standard types
- 18030-18161   Vacant
- 18162-18199   Pre-group types

18200-18999 Non-corridor Lavatory Thirds
- No LMS Standard designs built but 18614-18999 were pre-group coaches.

19000-19999 Non-corridor Lavatory Composites
- 19000-19199   LMS Standard types
- 19200-19386   Originally Vacant but 19377-86 were given to non-lavatory Cs to Lot 1450 (Motor fitted coaches—D1921A)
- 19387-19999   Pre-group types. also first 19385/6

20000-24399 Non-corridor Third Brakes
- 20000-21251   LMS Standard types
- 21252-22214   Vacant (22196-202 later used for ex-North London area LMS Standard brake seconds and 22203-14 for other down graded coaches)
- 22215-24399   Pre-group types (24317-31 later used again for Push-Pull driving trailers—1950)

24400-24499 Non-corridor Driving Trailer Thirds
- 24400-24459   LMS Standard types
- 24460-24499   Pre-group types and LMS standard conversions

24500-24799 Non-corridor Composite Brakes
- 24500-24717   Vacant (no LMS designs) but later used for overflow numbering of Period III CKs 24500-24739
- 24718-24799   Pre-group types (including first 24718-24739)

24800-24899 Non-corridor Driving Trailer Composites
- 24800-24895   Vacant (No LMS Standard types)
- 24896-24899   Ex-MR and Ex-LYR

24900-24999 Non-corridor Second Brakes
- 24900-24906   LMS Standard designs for North London sets—later downgraded and renumbered 22196-202
- 24907-24999   Vacant but 24989-99 later used for marked up BTs (pre-group) which were later marked down again

25000-25699 Non-corridor Lavatory Third Brakes
- 25000-25272   LMS Standard types
- 25273-25507   Vacant
- 25508-25699   Pre-group types

25700-25999 Non-corridor Lavatory Composite Brakes
- 25700-25777   Vacant (No LMS Standard designs)
- 25778-25999   Pre-group types

26000-27999 Pre-group four/six wheel passenger carrying coaches—all types
Note: Survivors of this block again renumbered 26000-99 when the 'overflow' numbering began

28000-29899 Electric Multiple Unit Stock
The number allocation in these blocks was a little complex and is best appreciated by studying Volume III.

29900-29999 Miscellaneous Railcars, etc.

30000-30199 Kitchen Cars
- 30000-30106   LMS Standard types
- 30107-30196   Vacant
- 30197-30199   Ex-LNWR

30200-30399 Post Office Vehicles
The numbers in this group were completely haphazard

30400-32899 Bogie Corridor Full Brakes
- 30400-32019   LMS Standard types and LMS built conversions from other coaches. There were vacant numbers.
- 32020-32899   Pre-group types built as full brakes

32900-33499 Six Wheel Corridor Full Brakes
- 32900-33019   LMS Standard types
- 33020-33441   Vacant
- 33442-33499   Pre-group types

33500-44999 Non-passenger carrying coaching stock

45xxx numbers Chairman's and Engineer's Saloons (total of 16 to LMS design)

50000 Upwards Articulated coaches

'Jubilee' No. 45598 *Basutoland* leaves St Pancras with a down express c.1950; note the third coach still in LMS colours. The presence of a 'dining pair' at the end of a train was quite typical of LMS practice as it allowed for the easy transfer of catering vehicles between trains in the days before fixed formations. The two types in this view are Period III First Class Dining Car (D1900) leading and Period III Vestibule Third (D1915A, note the welded underframe), used for dining in spite of its 2 + 2, 56-seat arrangement. (Authors' Collection)

A typical mixture of LMS stock forming an up express in Tring Cutting c.1947, the engine being Patriot No. 5543 *Home Guard*. A Period I (twin window) Vestibule Third (D1692) leads followed by a Period II (fully panelled) equivalent (probably D1795). These seem to be 'strengtheners' at the front of a mainly Period III set. The first four coaches behind the leading open thirds are Period III, the fourth one being a Period III First Class Dining Car (D1900). There then comes a Period II First Class Corridor Vestibule Car (D1719) followed by an unidentified Period II carriage and three more Period III vehicles (BR LMR).

Chapter 1 – Sleeping Cars

First Class coaches; Third Class coaches; Composite coaches; Summary Table; Survey by Diagrams

IN numerical terms, sleeping cars were among the less common standard coaches, only 253 being built to LMS designs and this total includes quite a number built after 1947. At the same time, the design phases are interesting especially since the early first class cars represent what might be called the 'final flowering' of the LNWR design ideas. Moreover, the first two varieties of third class coach were each responsible for introducing a new length of vehicle to the LMS.

FIRST CLASS COACHES

There were but four types of LMS first class sleeping car and only two really different styles. The first two types perpetuated the LNWR styling except for the depth of waist panel, while the last two types were Stanier pattern coaches. All were 12 wheel vehicles, the Period III coaches being 69ft long and the earlier ones 68ft long.

Towards the end of the pre-group era, the LNWR had built for itself and for the West Coast Joint Stock some massive 68ft long semi-elliptical roof sleeping cars (see Volume I) and the first two LMS types were logical developments of this final LNWR design. They were built in various batches between 1924 and 1930. Ten were to D1739 while the remainder were to D1705. There was little difference between the two diagrams but the distinguishing aspects may have been significant. Both versions had 12 berths but the earlier coaches had the attendant's and the lavatory compartment both at the same end and 'outside' the entrance vestibule. In D1705, the attendant was placed 'inside' the vestibule entrance adjacent to the sleeping compartments and at the opposite end of the coach to the lavatory, which remained 'outside'.

Plate 1 This is the pioneer LMS first class sleeping car to D1739 from which the more numerous D1705 was derived. Coach No. 10389, later No. 308. Note the smaller than usual descriptive lettering.

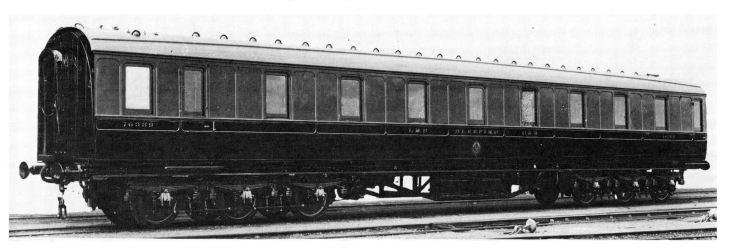

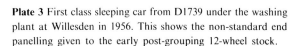

Plate 2 Passenger compartment of the pioneer LMS first class sleeping car, No. 10389 to D1739. Note the heavy timber veneers and the hinged toilet fixture against the right hand wall of the compartment.

Plate 3 First class sleeping car from D1739 under the washing plant at Willesden in 1956. This shows the non-standard end panelling given to the early post-grouping 12-wheel stock.

Plate 4 LMS Car No. 10370. This picture shows a D1705 car but note that between the windows the panels are now of double width compared with Figure 2. This coach became LMS 351 in 1932/3.

This re-positioning of the service areas seems to have represented a partial reversion to LNWR practice since this company, of course, always placed everything 'inside' the entrances. This policy was, as many will appreciate, traceable back to the original LNWR 12 wheel sleeping cars with very narrow vestibule entrances which left room for little more than the corridor connections. It is possible, therefore, that the predominantly LNWR staff of the early LMS sleepers objected to the new position of their compartment. It separated them from their passengers and, being over the bogie, may have given a less comfortable ride. Moreover, the 'outside' location of the attendant was more of a Midland idea which may, in the circumstances have given rise to its own particular problems—Wolverton exterior styling notwithstanding! At all events, D1705 went back to the earlier LNWR arrangement as far as the attendant was concerned. Many more of these were built than the D1739 version and the design remained current for some five years or more.

The detail differences between the two types were more subtle. Both had fully beaded exteriors but later examples of D1705 introduced a single panel of double width between the windows rather than the characteristic double panels of the earlier coaches. Neither type had door ventilators but D1705 did have a small panel above the droplight which suggests that a door ventilator may, originally, have been intended.

Inside the coaches there were again small differences. Both had heavily wood panelled interior finishings, probably mahogany, and contemporary illustrations reveal the ornate finish of these elegant sleeping cars. The sleeping berths themselves were alternately right and left handed when entering via the corridor door and the bedheads were positioned against the corridor wall. Within the compartments, the later versions were fitted with corner handbasins below the window as opposed to the combination toilet cabinets against the compartment wall in the D1739 cars. The later cars also had hinged flap shelves above the berths and extra luggage shelves adjacent to the vestibule entrance.

These coaches represented almost exactly half the total of LMS design first class sleeping cars. Lot 341 was additionally interesting as its cars were built for the M&NB joint stock in 1927. After this stock was divided between the LMS and LNER in 1928, both the cars eventually came to the LMS but during the first year or two of their life it must have seemed a little strange to observe an almost pure Wolverton coach in M&NB livery.

These early sleeping cars were robust coaches. They were refurbished inside to Stanier standards of comfort in the 1930s and in this form lasted well into BR days, ultimately succumbing to BR designs in 1962. Car 350 went to America in 1933 with the 'Royal Scot' train while car 342 achieved a certain amount of immortality by being used in the Prime Minister's train during the second world war—it was still in fully lined livery at the time.

Stanier pattern first class sleepers were introduced in 1935 to D1926 and saw an increase in length from 68ft to 69ft. Their interior arrangement was very similar to the earlier cars except that they went back completely to the old LNWR

Plate 5 LMS Car No. 352, the pioneer Stanier first class sleeping car to D1926, shown in simple livery. A similar car (377) was modified and repainted for the 1939 'Coronation Scot' tour of America. Note the recessed door handles to allow for a slight increase in body width.

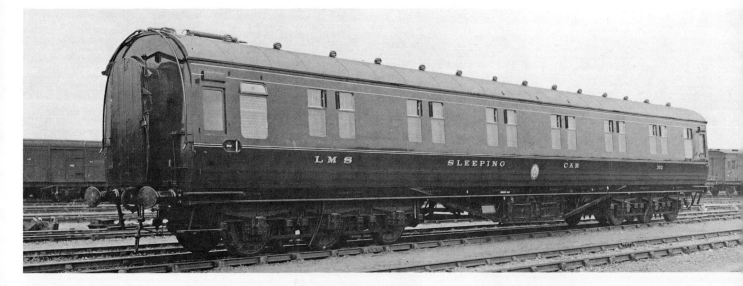

Plate 6 LM Region Car No. M387M, the post-nationalisation development to D2166 of the Period III sleeping car. This view was taken at Wolverton in 1968 and shows the BR blue/grey livery which most of this batch acquired. Note, compared with Plate 5, the absence of hooded door vents, completely flush roof, BR type vents and roof top air conditioning apparatus.

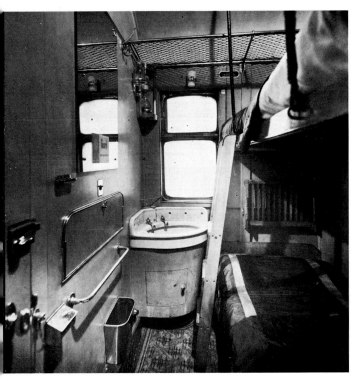

Plate 7 This picture shows a typical Stanier first class sleeping compartment. The upper berth was added in 1942 but other than this, the style of compartment hardly altered between 1935 and the final versions in 1952. The upper berth was removed in about 1949/50. The interior layout of post Nationalisation twin berth thirds was very similar.

Plate 8 A compartment of the convertible third class coaches (D1709) as made up for night use. The arrangement of berths in the fixed four-berth coaches was similar except there was no window to the corridor behind the heads of the berths.

Plate 9 LMS Car No. 8617 represents the later, steel-panelled version of D1709 from the corridor side. Note the single waist lining at the 'low waisted' level, the changed insignia placing and the 'stretched' scroll running numbers. The coach was renumbered 580 in 1932/3.

arrangement and the entrances were at the extreme ends of the car. Externally they were typical Stanier vehicles but, as with all Stanier sleepers, the lower edges of the compartment windows were at a higher level than those on the normal Stanier gangwayed coach. Door handles were recessed to enable a little extra body width to be obtained within the limits of the loading gauge. In relation to their size, they were not unduly heavy coaches, being of welded construction.

The LMS clearly regarded these new Stanier cars as the last word in sleeping car luxury. Special attention was paid to smooth and silent riding. The underside of the floor was sprayed with almost half an inch of asbestos to act as an anti-noise blanket, while the floors themselves were covered with layers of cork, felt, linoleum and carpet.

The usual compartment fittings were provided (hot and cold water, towel rails, clothes hangers, luggage racks, shelves and mirrors) and much use was made of plated metal fittings. The whole interior decor was considerably brighter than the earlier cars and four decorative schemes were utilised. Each compartment had a distinctive colour scheme (yellow, green, blue or beige) with rugs and bedcovers to match, the object of the designer being to make the compartment conform, within the limits of space, to the standard first class hotel bedroom. Timber finishes used were teak, sycamore or walnut.*

The compartment heating and ventilation was of the passenger controlled 'Thermotank' type with punkah louvres for each berth. These were of the 'Thermo-Reg.' pattern which gave passengers control, not only of the volume and temperature of the incoming air, but also the direction of discharge. They were located over the bed head.

The LMS seems to have referred to this system as 'air conditioning' and, as far as can be ascertained, fitted it to the earlier sleepers in place of the old rotary electric fans–see Figure 3.

In 1939, car 377 of the first Stanier series was refurbished and fully air conditioned and went to the USA with the 'Coronation Scot' special train to act as an accommodation car for the staff. For this visit it was repainted in the Crimson/Gold livery and given the streamlined fairings to conceal the underframe and match the special set of coaches. It returned to this country in December 1946.

From May 1942, some of these Stanier cars were experimentally converted to a two-berth arrangement in the end compartments. This was in order to increase the passenger accommodation to 14 without increase of train weight. A second berth was installed above the existing bed and access was via a short ladder. The LMS converted further coaches to this pattern in 1943 and the surviving records indicate that at least 36 cars were scheduled for this operation. If so, clearly it must also have involved some of the earlier cars, but which ones are not known. The first class twin berth arrangement was new to LMS sleeping cars and probably provided the idea for the post-war twin-berth thirds described on page 17. All reverted to single berth c. 1949/50.

The final design of first class sleeping car was to D2166 of which 25 were built. These did not appear until 1951/2, were almost identical to D1926, but were considerably heavier than their predecessors. The interiors were similar to D1926 and they represent the last complete batch of 12 wheel coaches to run in general service in this country. They were also the only first class sleeping cars to last long enough as a class to receive the latest BR blue and grey livery–but see remarks column of Table 1a (D1926).

THIRD CLASS COACHES

Third class sleeping cars were introduced to the British railway scene in 1928, by which time the single window design of coach was beginning to make its appearance on the LMS system. This design trend resulted in the externally rather attractive coaches to D1709 of which 85 were built at Derby between 1928 and 1931 in four batches. These cars introduced a 60ft underframe to LMS standard coaches and they were true Period I vehicles owing little to pre-group ideas.

They had a symmetrical end to end layout containing seven compartments with diagonally opposed toilets and lavatories at the four extreme corners of the car. The entrance vestibules divided these facilities from the compartment area. The corridor side exhibited the large single window styling of the 1928/9 period but the compartment windows were almost unique—at least for the LMS. They were of a triplet arrangement with two quarterlights separated by a single frameless droplight and without external door. There was a nine-element Stones pattern ventilator in the eaves panel above the droplight.

Inside the coaches the upholstery was in fawn velvet, the wood finish was mahogany and compartment floors were covered with grey mohair carpet. The compartments were, in essence, conventional four-a-side thirds but were convertible for night use. The lower seats were used as berths, being provided with a spring mattress, while an additional spring mattress, used as a daytime seat, provided the sleeping mattress for the upper berth. The seats were arranged to pull forward to give a wider berth for sleeping. The top berth was hinged to the compartment partition and in the lowered position was supported by brackets and fitted with two safety straps. When folded out of use, the underside of the top berth displayed mahogany panels with the usual pictures and mirrors, thus rendering it difficult to distinguish the coach from a normal day vehicle. Access to the upper berth was by a combined fold-away table and ladder. For night use, the four berths were provided with pillows and blankets only. They were illuminated by a dim blue light which was automatically switched on when the main lights were turned out.

The first 75 cars to this design were fully beaded with a high waist and matchboard ends in orthodox Period I style. The last 10, however, post-dated the change to steel panelling and came out with this style of treatment. They did, however, retain the high waist of the wood panelled version and were given a fully lined livery. However, this livery was applied without a waist panel and the waist lining was placed at the, now standard, low waisted level of the Period II coaches. This put the lining some 3in below the window level and, in consequence, made the coaches look rather peculiar.

None of the D1709 cars carried the legend 'Sleeping Car' since this branding seems to have been reserved by the LMS for single purpose sleeping coaches. In fact, the coaches were very similar to, if rather more spacious than the orthodox LMS corridor third of the day. They went into service on all the principal LMS overnight services in September 1928 and the charge to passengers was 6/- (30p) per berth.

*A fine model of one of these coaches is displayed in the National Railway Museum.

At a later stage, during the 1930s, many of the cars were altered to fixed berth although still, as far as is known, without the wording 'Sleeping Car' on the exterior. Some 40 of them were further converted into ambulance vehicles during the war and later still, after nationalisation, 17 re-appeared as cafeteria and buffet cars (see page 50), the remainder being reconverted to sleeping cars, some of which retained the convertible berths.*

Because of the large number of sleeping cars to D1709, the LMS itself only built 15 more third class coaches of the type. These were all Period III vehicles to D1863. Again there was introduced a new length of underframe, this time 65ft and the outcome was a more than usually handsome looking vehicle. Along with some 65ft open firsts (see page 14) they were the longest eight-wheel locomotive hauled coaches to be built by the LMS.

The coaches were built in one batch at Derby in 1933 and thus had the early Period III shallow window ventilators. They were also the first modern LMS thirds, having fixed berths from the outset. This may have been a Swindon-inspired Stanier importation from the GWR where fixed berth thirds had for some time superseded the convertible type. There were again seven compartments with corner sited toilets and lavatories. The extra length over the earlier cars was used to provide an attendant's compartment—at the right hand end of the compartment side. The exterior elevations of the coach presented a 'mirror' image with single windows on the corridor side exactly the same size as and directly opposite to those on the compartment side. All the batch had the fully lined livery when new. However, car 585 was given its number in the 'stretched' scroll figures for its trip to America with the 'Royal Scot'. It was probably the only one to have this particular livery variation.

Inside these 65ft sleepers, the compartments were finished in stippled brown rexine with mouldings and frames in matching finish. Ceilings were pale cream rexine, upholstery was fawn and brown shaded rep and mattresses were one of two types, either spring interior or rubber latex. Mirrors, racks and coat hooks were provided and there was a baggage recess over the corridor ceiling for the upper berth occupants. Window blinds were fitted with 'Zip' Flexide fasteners. The blue night light was again present but, in addition, each berth had a bell push and reading light. Ventilation was by 'hit and miss' floor level ventilator slides under passenger control and the floors themselves were covered with rubber mats.

Toilets and lavatories were duck egg blue with mahogany mouldings. They included water filtering equipment and drinking cups were provided to supplement the pantry facilities available in the attendant's compartment. To cut down noise, the floor was of 1¼in cork sheet laid over a dovetail steel sheet with a blanket of insulating material fitted to the underside of the floor.

These cars represented pretty lavish provisioning for the 1933 third class passenger and give further evidence, were such needed, that the LMS was making more than a little effort to cater well for this class of traveller on its long distance trains of that period.

The third and final design of LMS pattern third class sleeping car was to D2169 and post-dated nationalisation by some four years. The cars themselves were, however, very much in the LMS tradition, even more so than the corridor composites alluded to on page 18. British Railways built 25 cars of this pattern and, like both preceding third class types, they introduced a whole variety of new features, later developed for the standard BR-type cars. In this case it took the form of a standardised twin-berth compartment of the kind first introduced as a wartime expedient on the first class cars. These twin-berth third class cars retained the 65ft eight-wheel chassis of their predecessors but were rather more massive looking because the body width was increased to the first class dimension to take full advantage of the loading gauge. For the same reason they were fitted with recessed pattern commode handles. The new profile and exterior details, together with the 'paired' arrangement

*One or two survived in departmental stock as staff dormitory coaches into the 1970s and have been preserved for posterity, including one in almost original condition for the National Railway Museum collection.

Plate 10 LMS Car No. 585 was the first example of the 65ft Stanier pattern fixed berth third class sleeping cars to D1863, with the shallow window ventilators and full livery typical of very early Stanier vehicles. This coach went to America in 1933 with the 'Royal Scot' tour—hence the 1932/3 series running number in obsolete stretched type numerals. These coaches were the first fixed berth LMS thirds and the first third class sleeping cars to be so branded.

Plate 11 LMR Car No. M603 one of the post-nationalisation twin berth third class cars to D2169. Note the general similarity in style to the Stanier 12-wheel sleeping cars. The 65ft underframe was little changed from the earlier coaches but note the self-contained, double acting buffers, a post-LMS innovation, retrospectively applied to some of the pre-war 65ft sleeping cars.

of the compartment windows consequent upon the twin-birth interior, gave the cars a very strong resemblance to their contemporary 12-wheel first class partners.

In construction, there were one or two other new features for third class sleeping cars. Integral body structure was adopted, considerable use being made of welding in both body framing and outside panelling. The sound insulation was generally to the now standard first class specification, while the coaches were fitted with self-contained double acting buffers with rubber springs and strengthened heads. LMS standard screw couplings were fitted but the coaches had gangway adapters from the outset.

Apart from the double deck arrangement of the twin berths and the fact that there were only eleven instead of twelve compartments, the general layout and amenity of these cars was all but identical to the first class version. All the usual Period III luxury features were present and, for the first time, third class passengers were given the individually adjustable 'punkah louvre' type ventilation for each berth. Air ducts for these fitments were carried above the corridor ceiling.

The resemblance to first class cars went through to the corridor side where, instead of the full complement of windows of their third class predecessors, they had small windows in the manner of the orthodox Period III 12-wheel sleeping cars.

Finally, these coaches introduced fully made up beds into third class sleeping accommodation and the supplementary charge for their use was some 50 per cent greater than for the four berth third. In effect, they provided what might be termed 'second class' sleeping accommodation by comparison with the previous single and four berth variety.

The twin berth thirds (now seconds) remained in service to the mid-1970s.

COMPOSITE COACHES

Only two varieties of composite sleeping car were built by the LMS. The first were to D1781 and were introduced during Period II. As explained in Volume I, these coaches were distinctly atypical of LMS designs in general except for their overall dimensions. Their exteriors indicated that LNWR influences predominated in the styling but, not being built until 1930/31, they post-dated the change to steel panelling. Thus, apart from the heavy waist moulding strip, the exteriors were, to all intents and purposes, flush sided. They did not even have the normal Period II raised moulding round the window apertures.

Inside the coaches there was a marriage of style between the Period I first and third class sleeping cars. There were six single berth first class compartments in the centre, flanked each side by two convertible four berth thirds arranged like those of D1709. The similarities continued to the outside in that the thirds had Stones ventilators above the centre droplight which was flanked by quarterlights while the external windows in the first class area were of the normal 'paired' type

Plate 12 This view shows the corridor side of SLC No. 10637 (later 709) to D1781 as built. Note that the full livery was not applied symmetrically in relation to the windows in each 'panel' although there was an end-to-end symmetry on the whole vehicle.

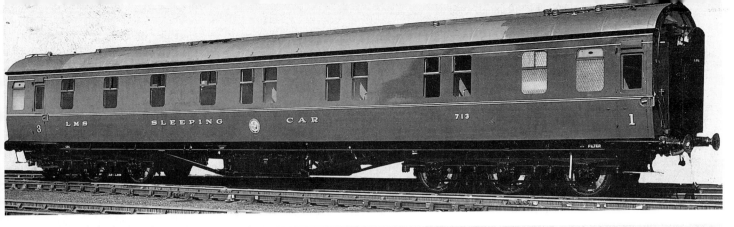

Plates 13-14 The Stanier composite sleeping cars to D1947 were very similar to their contemporary first class companions but, unlike the earlier composites, had all the third class compartments at one end. This pair of pictures shows both sides of the first vehicle of the type to be built, No. 713.

extended to cornice level. All the external windows had rather rounded top corners—again reminiscent of the LNWR—and there was the prominent waist moulding along the outside of the car to add to the effect. There was, however, no waist panel either real or simulated.

There were one or two internal details worthy of further comment in these cars. The wash basins in the first class compartments were of the 'swing out' type, being housed out of use under a glass top shelf. Metal fittings were oxidised silver. First class compartments were panelled in walnut and the thirds in mahogany. Third class upholstery was exactly as described for the 1928 built third class sleepers.

During the 1930s, the third class accommodation was reduced to 14 from 16 and the cars converted from convertible third class to fixed berth third class. The reduction in accommodation was effected by turning one third class compartment into a twin berth and altering the area occupied by the other two berths into a narrow lavatory compartment serving the first class section. This converted compartment was immediately to the left of the first class section when viewed from the compartment side. The conversion was to D1844 and at the same time it is thought that the first class compartments were refurbished to Stanier standards of comfort. In this form they lasted until the end of 1963.

The remaining composites were Stanier pattern cars to D1947. Like their first class equivalents to D1926, they were 69ft coaches. However, whereas the Stanier first class cars were little changed in layout from the earlier pattern, the Stanier composites showed a number of changes from the D1781 coaches just described. All the third class compartments were now brought together at one end of the coach and were of the fixed-berth type from the outset. There were three four-berth and one two-berth third class compartments. Outside windows were of the familiar 'paired' style at the first class end while the thirds had a single window, slightly larger than that of the firsts, between the pairs of berths rather in the fashion of the Stanier 65ft third class cars of 1933. The corridor side was very much like the first class sleeping cars except that the third class toilets were 'outside' the entrance vestibule.

All six first class compartments were arranged in inter-connecting pairs and were fitted-out in the same fashion as the contemporary full first sleeping cars. Three colour schemes were used, blue, beige and green, one for each pair of compartments. Wood finishes were either sycamore or walnut. The third class berths were similar to those described for D1865. They were finished in patterned rexine with cream rexine ceilings. Wood panelling was Philippine Walnut (upper panels) and mahogany (lower panels). The ventilation arrangements, however, showed an improvement over the pioneer Stanier third class sleepers.

The first class 'Thermo-Reg.' system was adopted but with louvres on the ceiling and arranged to diffuse the air so that no currents were perceptible by passengers. Air was extracted by a louvred opening at the foot of the compartment door and there was no recirculation, all incoming air being drawn from outside. The ducting for the ventilation was carried on top of the roof in order not to encroach upon the luggage space provided over the corridor ceiling at the third class end of the vehicle. The roof ducts were protected by a long external cowl which was carried the full length of the vehicle. From the outside, this cowl was a further distinguishing identification feature of these coaches.

Each third class berth had an attendant's bell push which, via a corridor mounted indicator, showed the attendant from which berth the call had originated.

Addenda

It eventually turned out that the longest lived passenger carrying vehicles to LMS design (other than special and Royal Saloons) were the post nationalisation sleeping cars. The twelve wheel firsts ran on well into the 1970s and the twin berth thirds (later seconds) were not finally withdrawn until the turn of 1975/6. Some of these cars have, happily, been privately preserved.

TABLE 1a: SUMMARY TABLE OF LMS STANDARD SLEEPING CARS

Note: This table should be read in conjunction with the list of standard dimensions and details on page 9

Type	Diag	Lot	Qty	Date	Built	Dimensions (L × W × H)	Weight	Period	Running Numbers	Withdrawals First	Withdrawals Last	Remarks
SLF	1739	62	10	1924	Wolverton	68' × 9'1½" × 12'4¾"	41T	See remarks	300-309	5/58	10/59	The first LMS version of the LNWR style —plated 9'2".
SLF	1705	146	10	1925	Wolverton	68' × 9'3" × 12'4¾"	42T	See remarks	310-319	10/58	2/60	The standard LNWR styled version with slight detail changes and more modern fittings. Lot 341 were built for the M&NB joint services later being absorbed into LMS stock. Car 350 went to America in 1933 with the Royal Scot train. Car 342 was used in the Prime Minister's train during the second world war. Car 347 plated 42T.
		297	10	1927	Wolverton		41T		322-331	8/58	2/60	
		341	2	1927	Wolverton		41T		320-321	2/59	6/60	
		381	5	1928	Wolverton		41T		337-341	12/60	1/61	
		401	5	1928	Wolverton		41T		332-336	12/60	6/62	
		441	5	1929	Wolverton		41T		342-346	4/61	1/62	
		489	4	1929	Wolverton		41T		348-351	6/60	11/62	
		521	1	1930	Wolverton		41T		347	—	12/60	
SLF	1926	876	20	1935/6	Wolverton	69' × 9'3" × 12'4⅞"	42T	III	352-371	8/64	11/66	Underframes were built at Derby. Car 377 to America in 1939 with 'Coronation Scot' train. One very late survival (376) because of a premature withdrawal of car 397 of D2166. 376 was given BR blue/grey livery, the only pre-war LMS coach to be so finished, except for odd departmental coaches.
		935	6	1936	Wolverton		42T		372-377	8/64	see remarks	
SLF	2166	1570	5	1951	Wolverton	69' × 9'3" × 12'4⅞"	47T	III	378-382	—	—	The post-nationalisation version of D1926. Much heavier cars and slight detail differences eg, no hinged ventilators above lavatory windows. All given crimson/cream livery when new. Postwar torpedo type ventilators. All withdrawn in mid-1970s.
		1584	20	1951/2	Wolverton		47T		383-402	8/66	—	
SLT	1709	418	25	1928	Derby	60' × 9'3" × 12'4¾"	29T	I	500-524	4/59	12/60	Convertible sleepers styled as for a Period I TK but no compartment doors. Lot 579 was flush clad and had no painted waist panel. Cars later converted to fixed berth and probably heavier on conversion. Many later conversions to RB & c—see p. 50.
		428	25	1928/9	Derby		29T		525-549	11/55	8/61	
		469	25	1929	Derby		28T		550-574	11/55	11/61	
		579	10	1931	Derby		30T		575-584	11/60	10/61	
SLT	1863	699	15	1933	Derby	65' × 9'3" × 12'4⅞"	37T	III (Shallow ventilator)	585-599	11/61	13/63	Full livery when new. 585 to America with Royal Scot in 1933. First LMS fixed berth SLTs.
SLT(T)	2169	1574	10	1951/2	Derby	65' × 9'3" × 12'4⅞"	40T	III	600-609	12/65*	—	Twin berth sleepers built after nationalisation. All BR crimson/cream when new and fitted Torpedo ventilators (postwar style) Pressure heating/ventilation. *Accident withdrawals—most others withdrawn 1975/6.
		1628	15	1952	Derby		40T		610-624	8/67*	—	
SLC	1781 (later D1844 —see remarks)	543	6	1930	Wolverton	68' × 9'2¼" × 12'4½"	42T	see remarks	700-705	2/61	12/63	Period II vintage but LNWR type styling. Third class compartments were originally convertible for day use but the cars were later altered to fixed berth losing two third class berths in process becoming 6F + 14T. Conversion to D1844.
		571	6	1931	Wolverton		42T		706-711	7/61	12/63	
SLC	1947	934	13	1936	Derby	69' × 9'3" × 12'4⅞"	43T	III	712-724	5/63	1/64	Bogies built at Wolverton. Fitted thermostat heating equipment.

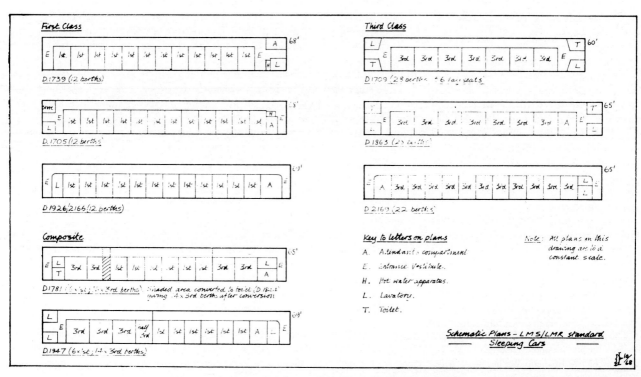

LMS standard sleeping cars—sketch plans (Drawn by D. Jenkinson)

Table 1b SLEEPING CARS–1933 RENUMBERING

D1739 (SLF)		D1709 (SLT) cont.	
New No.	*Old No.*	*New No.*	*Old No.*
300	10319	520	14245
301	10320	521	14246
302	10383	522	14247
303	10384	523	14248
304	10385	524	14249
305	10386	525	14419
306	10387	526	14420
307	10388	527	14421
308	10389	528	14422
309	10390	529	14423
		530	14424
		531	14425
D1705 (SLF)		532	14426
		533	14427
310	2768	534	14428
311	2769	535	14429
312	2770	536	14430
313	2771	537	14431
314	2772	538	14432
315	2773	539	14433
316	2774	540	14434
317	2775	541	14435
318	2776	542	14436
319	2777	543	14437
320	2778	544	14438
321	4031	545	14439
322	2785	546	14440
323	10371	547	14441
324	10372	548	14442
325	10373	549	14443
326	10374	550	80
327	10375	551	157
328	10376	552	206
329	10377	553	230
330	10381	554	270
331	10382	555	308
332	8412	556	714
333	8413	557	750
334	8414	558	846
335	8415	559	847
336	8416	560	855
337	10367	561	870
338	10368	562	884
339	10378	563	1396
340	10379	564	1810
341	10380	565	1815
342	3792	566	1816
343	3793	567	10651
344	4087	568	10654
345	4090	569	14708
346	8420	570	14758
347	8406	571	15252
348	2766	572	15253
349	10355	573	16148
350	10369	574	16965
351	10370	575	8609
		576	8611
		577	8612
D1709 (SLT)		578	8615
		579	8616
New No.	*Old No.*	580	8617
500	14225	581	8618
501	14226	582	8619
502	14227	583	8620
503	14228	584	8621
504	14229		
505	14230		
506	14231	**D1781/D1844 (SLC)**	
507	14232		
508	14233	700	10548
509	14234	701	10549
510	14235	702	10550
511	14236	703	10551
512	14237	704	10555
513	14238	705	10556
514	14239	706	10558
515	14240	707	10559
516	14241	708	10636
517	14242	709	10637
518	14243	710	10638
519	14244	711	10639

Plate 15. This corridor view shows the interior of the first LMS standard sleeping car design to D1739, probably No. 10389–see page 13. Its heavy and sombre interior finish was very characteristic of the LNWR design from which it was directly derived and was soon altered in the succeeding D1705 to the less oppressive version shown at Plate 18.

INTRODUCTION TO THE TYPE BY TYPE SURVEY

In the following pages we describe the vehicle diagrams in conventional LMS sequence (first, third, composite) and in most cases we are also able to provide the original diagram. However, the Stanier period diagrams are not very clear so we have also included more detailed drawings of two of them. We have also added extra pictures and other information, incorporated as close as possible to the diagrams to which they are relevant.

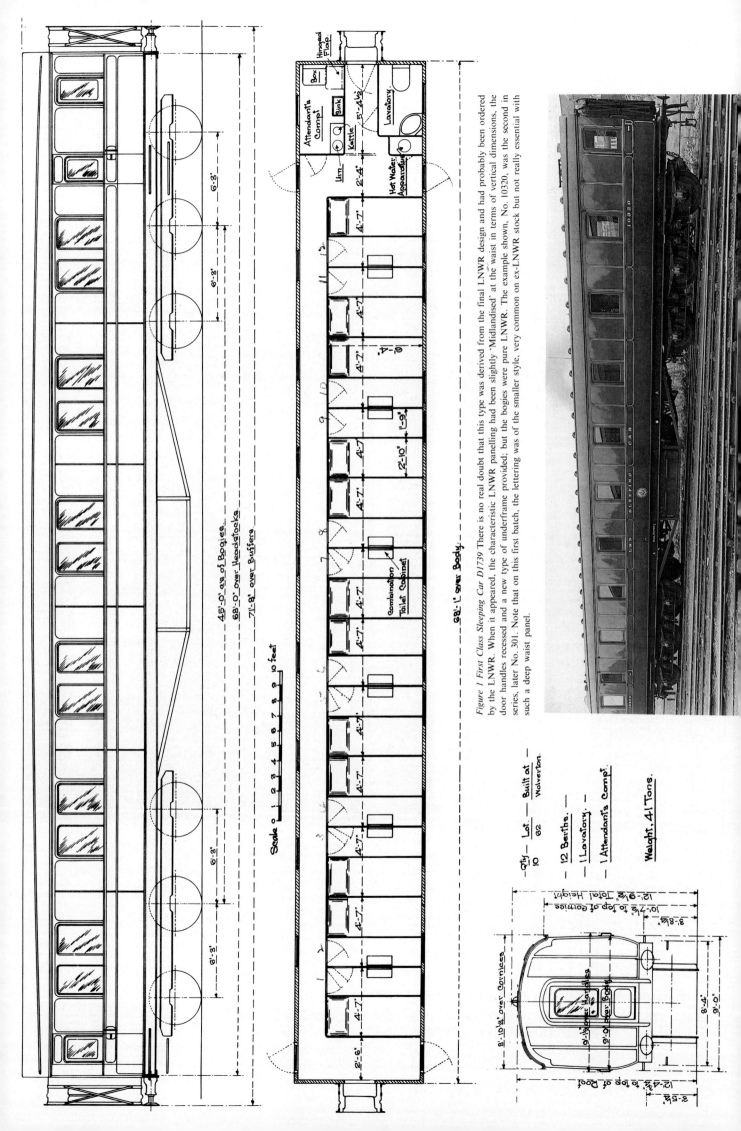

Figure 1 First Class Sleeping Car D1739 There is no real doubt that this type was derived from the final LNWR design and had probably been ordered by the LNWR. When it appeared, the characteristic LNWR panelling had been slightly 'Midlandised' at the waist in terms of vertical dimensions, the door handles recessed and a new type of underframe provided; but the bogies were pure LNWR. The example shown, No. 10320, was the second in series, later No. 301. Note that on this first batch, the lettering was of the smaller style, very common on ex-LNWR stock but not really essential with such a deep waist panel.

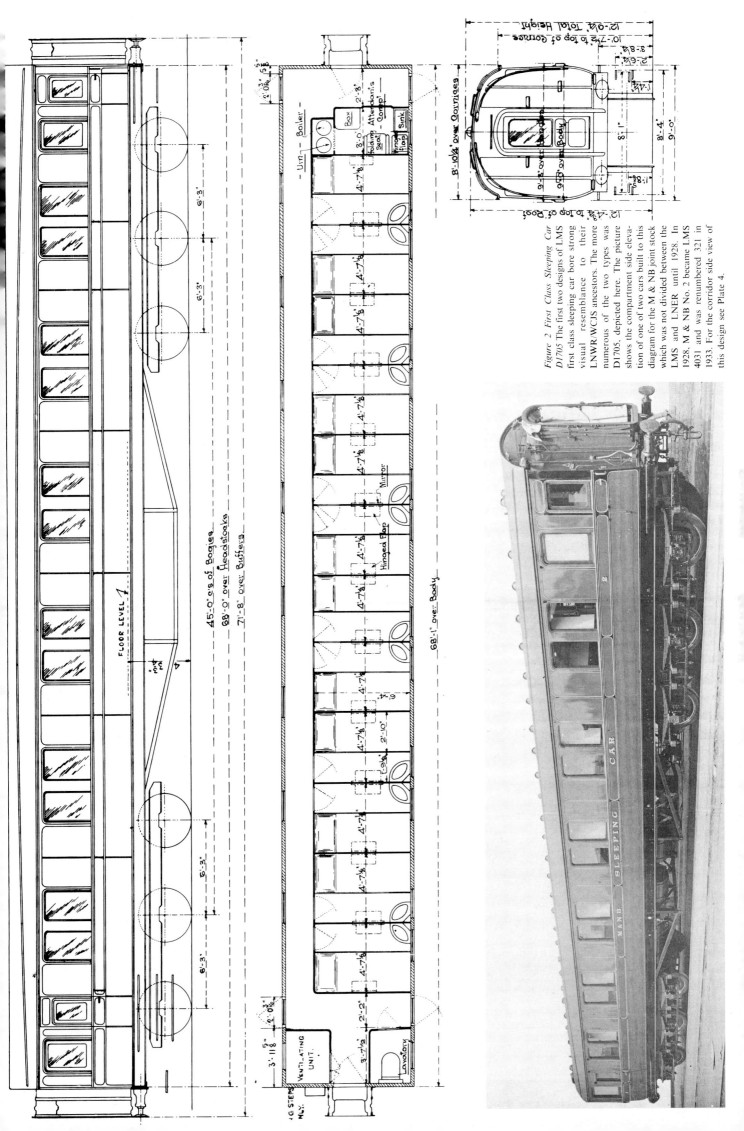

Figure 2 First Class Sleeping Car D1705 The first two designs of LMS first class sleeping car bore strong visual resemblance to their LNWR/WCJS ancestors. The more numerous of the two types was D1705, depicted here. The picture shows the compartment side elevation of one of two cars built to this diagram for the M & NB joint stock which was not divided between the LMS and LNER until 1928. In 1928, M & NB No. 2 became LMS 4031 and was renumbered 321 in 1933. For the corridor side view of this design see Plate 4.

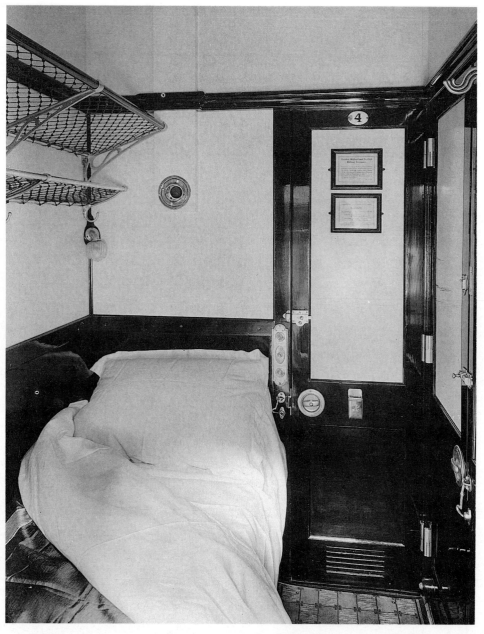

Plate 16. During the 1920s, some changes were made to the first generation LMS sleeping cars which were later adopted as standard in later construction. Most visibly obvious was attention to the interior finish, well exemplified by the appended view of a compartment interior from D1705, wherein the older dark wood panelling gave way above the dado to a light painted finish. It is not, however, thought that D1739 was retrospectively altered to match.

Figure 3A A more significant alteration which later became a routine design feature in the Stanier period was the introduction of 'Thermotank' ventilation equipment, first applied to a D1705 sleeping car in 1929. It took the form of a fan driven fresh air duct along the whole coach which drew fresh air from the outside and extracted stale air from the interior, each compartment having its own control to regulate the amount of circulation provided–none if required. This contemporary diagram shows the modifications to D1705 where it was located below the corridor ceiling.

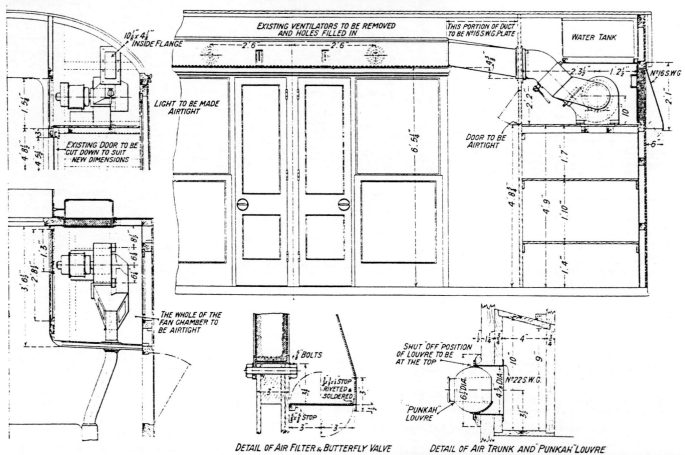

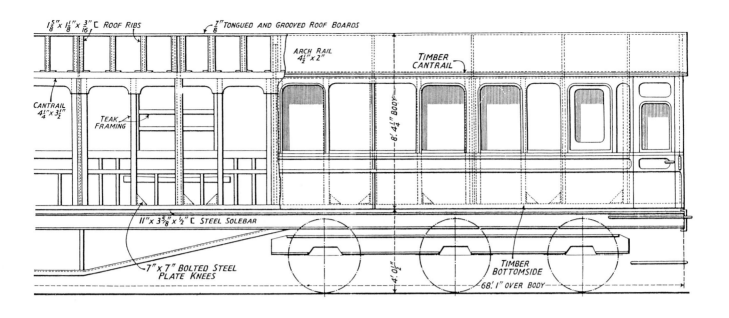

$1\frac{5}{8}'' \times 1\frac{1}{8}'' \times \frac{3}{16}''$ ⊏ ROOF RIBS

$\frac{7}{8}''$ TONGUED AND GROOVED ROOF BOARDS

ARCH RAIL
$4\frac{1}{2}'' \times 2''$

TIMBER
CANTRAIL

CANTRAIL
$4\frac{1}{4}'' \times 3\frac{1}{2}''$

TEAK
FRAMING

$8' \ 4\frac{1}{4}''$ BODY

$11'' \times 3\frac{5}{8}'' \times \frac{1}{2}''$ ⊏ STEEL SOLEBAR

$7'' \times 7''$ BOLTED STEEL
PLATE KNEES

$4' \ 0\frac{1}{2}''$

TIMBER
BOTTOMSIDE

$68' \ 1''$ OVER BODY

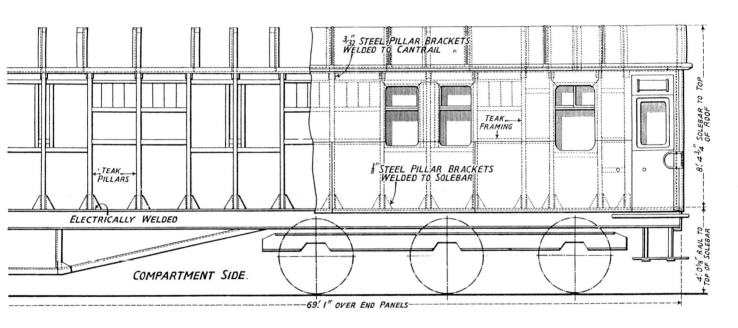

$\frac{3}{32}''$ STEEL PILLAR BRACKETS
WELDED TO CANTRAIL

TEAK
FRAMING

$8' \ 4\frac{1}{4}''$ SOLEBAR TO TOP OF ROOF

$\frac{1}{8}''$ STEEL PILLAR BRACKETS
WELDED TO SOLEBAR

TEAK
PILLARS

ELECTRICALLY WELDED

COMPARTMENT SIDE.

$4' \ 0\frac{7}{8}''$ RAIL TO
TOP OF SOLEBAR

$69' \ 1''$ OVER END PANELS

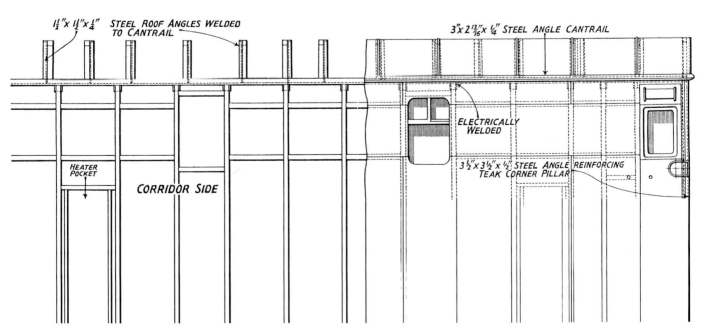

$1\frac{1}{2}'' \times 1\frac{1}{2}'' \times \frac{1}{4}''$ STEEL ROOF ANGLES WELDED
TO CANTRAIL

$3'' \times 2\frac{13}{16}'' \times \frac{1}{4}''$ STEEL ANGLE CANTRAIL

ELECTRICALLY
WELDED

HEATER
POCKET

CORRIDOR SIDE

$3\frac{1}{2}'' \times 3\frac{1}{2}'' \times \frac{1}{2}''$ STEEL ANGLE REINFORCING
TEAK CORNER PILLAR

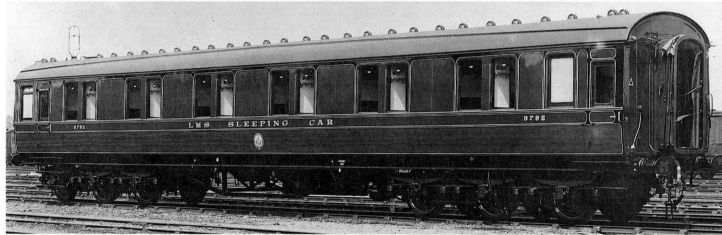

Plates 17-18. These two views show earlier (No. 10371, later 323) and later (No. 3792, later 342) examples of D1705. The main differences are in the panelling arrangements (simpler on No. 3792) and toilet window detail. The lighter interior finish is particularly noticeable on No. 3792. This was the first example of Lot 441 and probably marked the changed style. This car was additionally interesting in having been used in Winston Churchill's train during World War II.

Plate 19. This exterior view of No. 352 shows the opposite side to that given at Plate 5; note the continued use of Mansell wood-centred wheels.

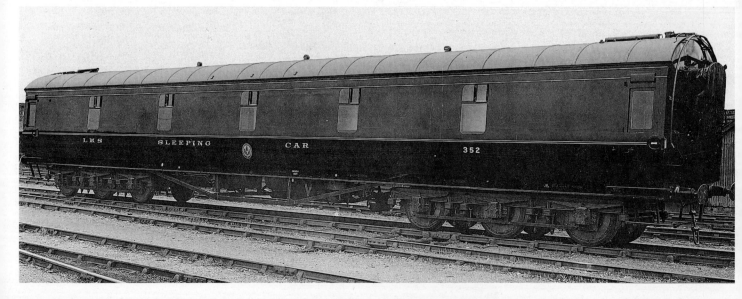

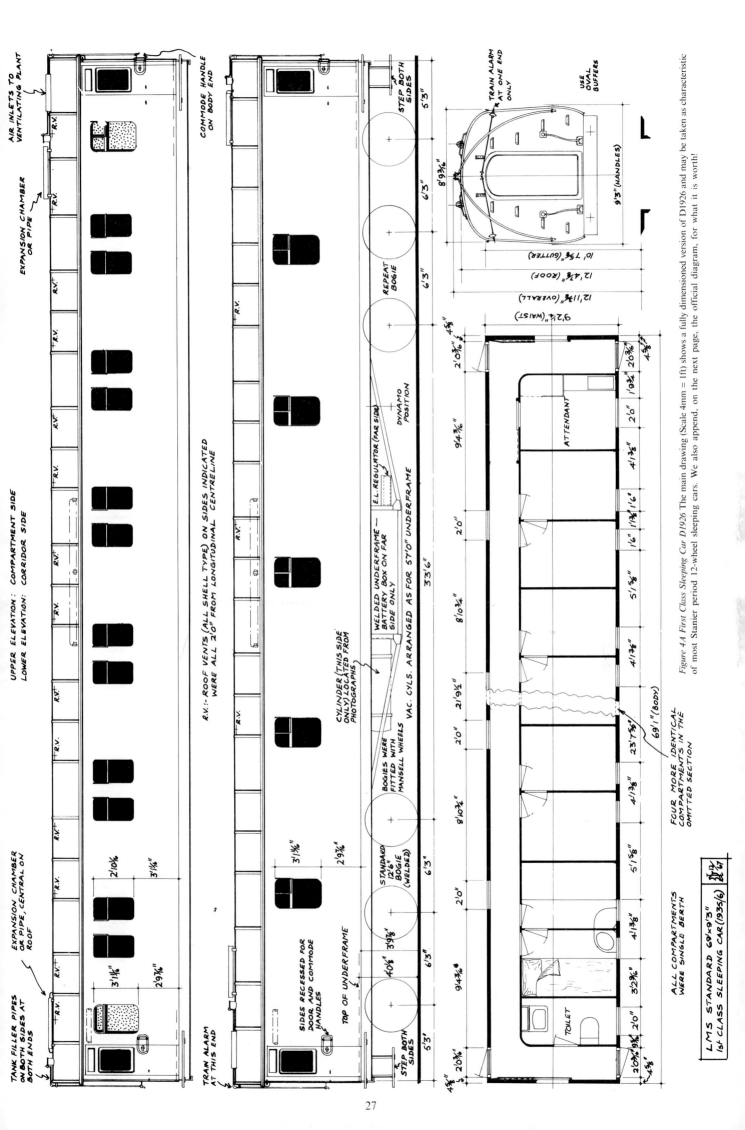

AIR INLETS TO VENTILATING PLANT

EXPANSION CHAMBER OR PIPE

R.V.

UPPER ELEVATION : COMPARTMENT SIDE
LOWER ELEVATION : CORRIDOR SIDE

COMMODE HANDLE ON BODY END

R.V. :- ROOF VENTS (ALL SHELL TYPE) ON SIDES INDICATED WERE ALL 2'0" FROM LONGITUDINAL CENTRELINE

TRAIN ALARM AT THIS END

SIDES RECESSED FOR DOOR AND COMMODE HANDLES

TOP OF UNDERFRAME

CYLINDER (THIS SIDE ONLY) LOCATED FROM PHOTOGRAPHS

BOGIES WERE FITTED WITH MANSELL WHEELS

WELDED UNDERFRAME — BATTERY BOX ON FAR SIDE ONLY

E.L. REGULATOR (FAR SIDE)

DYNAMO POSITION

VAC. CYLS. ARRANGED AS FOR 57'0" UNDERFRAME

REPEAT BOGIE

STEP BOTH SIDES

TANK FILLER PIPES ON BOTH SIDES AT BOTH ENDS

EXPANSION CHAMBER OR PIPE, CENTRAL ON ROOF

STANDARD 12'6" BOGIE (WELDED)

STEP BOTH SIDES

TRAIN ALARM AT ONE END ONLY

USE OVAL BUFFERS

8'9⅝"

9'3" (HANDLES)

10' 7⅝" (GUTTER)

12' 4⅞" (ROOF)

12' 11⅝" (OVERALL)

9'2¼" (WAIST)

ATTENDANT

TOILET

FOUR MORE IDENTICAL COMPARTMENTS IN THE OMITTED SECTION

ALL COMPARTMENTS WERE SINGLE BERTH

69'1" (BODY)

33'6"

6'3"

Figure 4A First Class Sleeping Car D1926 The main drawing (Scale 4mm = 1ft) shows a fully dimensioned version of D1926 and may be taken as characteristic of most Stanier period 12-wheel sleeping cars. We also append, on the next page, the official diagram, for what it is worth!

LMS STANDARD 69'×9'3"
1st CLASS SLEEPING CAR (1935/6)

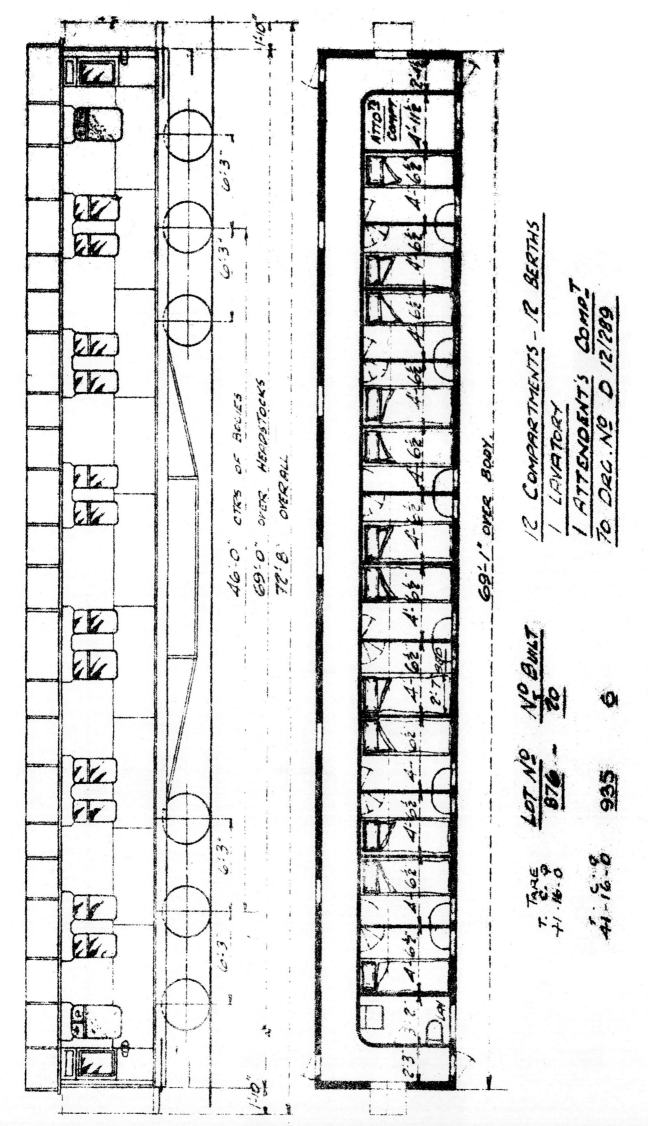

Figure 4B Official diagram of First Class Sleeping Car D1926.

Plate 20. The first example of Lot 876 under construction at Wolverton. The new style welded underframes were built at Derby and note how the body side panelling extends below the top of the solebar–see also Volume I Chapter 2. A very full account of the building of these innovative cars (including many diagrams) will be found in *The Railway Gazette* for 22nd November 1935.

Plates 21-22. These interior views show the original form of first class accommodation in a Stanier sleeping car and the experimental double-berth wartime arrangement first applied to No. 361–see also Plate 7. This latter conversion set the general style for post-war twin-berth third (later second) class sleeping car compartments.

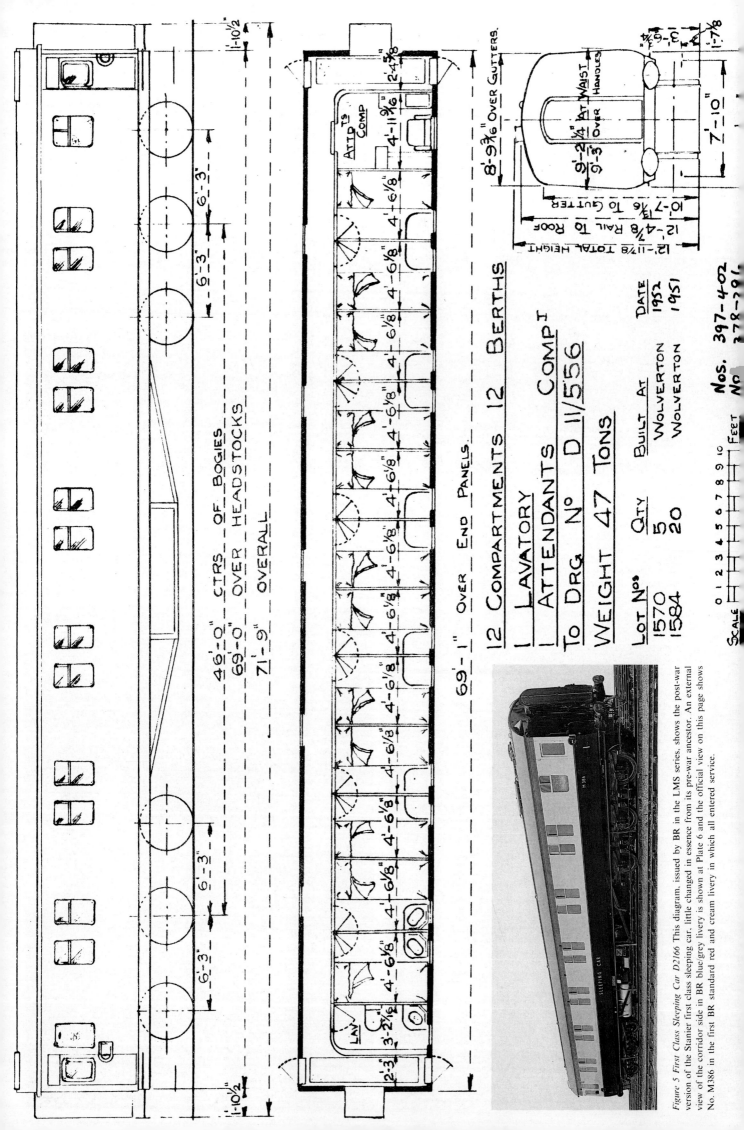

1'-10½"
1'-10½"

6'-3"
6'-3"
6'-3"
6'-3"

46'-0" CTRS OF BOGIES
69'-0" OVER HEADSTOCKS
71'-9" OVERALL

ATTD⁹ COMP⁷

2'-4⅛"
4'-11⅝"
4'-6⅛"
4'-6⅛"
4'-6⅛"
4'-6⅛"
4'-6⅛"
4'-6⅛"
4'-6⅛"
4'-6⅛"
4'-6⅛"
4'-6⅛"
3'-2½"
2'-3"

LAV⁷

69'-1" OVER END PANELS

8'-9⁹⁄₁₆" OVER GUTTERS.

9'-2¼" AT WAIST
9'-3" OVER HANDLES

4'-9"
3'-6¾"

10'-7⁷⁄₁₆" TO GUTTER
12'-4⅜" RAIL TO ROOF
12'-11⅞" TOTAL HEIGHT

7'-10"
1'-7⅞"

12 COMPARTMENTS 12 BERTHS

	LAVATORY		
	ATTENDANTS COMP⁷		
TO DR⁶ Nᵒ D 11/556			DATE
WEIGHT 47 TONS			1952
			1951
LOT Nᵒˢ	QTY	BUILT AT	
1570	5	WOLVERTON	
1584	20	WOLVERTON	

Nᵒˢ 397-402
Nᵒ 378-396

SCALE 0 1 2 3 4 5 6 7 8 9 10
FEET

Figure 5 First Class Sleeping Car D2166 This diagram, issued by BR in the LMS series, shows the post-war version of the Stanier first class sleeping car, little changed in essence from its pre-war ancestor. An external view of the corridor side in BR blue/grey livery is shown at Plate 6 and the official view on this page shows No. M386 in the first BR standard red and cream livery in which all entered service.

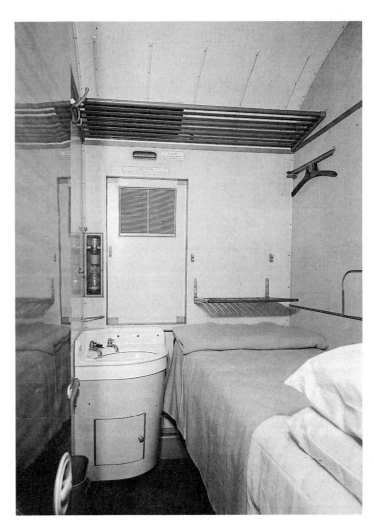

Plate 23. Close-up detail of No. M387M (see also Plate 6) at Wolverton in October 1968. Note, in particular, the replacement metal framed droplight, a common BR period alteration to many Stanier vehicles.

Plates 24-26. These three interior views of No. M386, taken when the car was new, show clearly that the basic interior arrangement of these BR-built cars showed little significant difference from those introduced before the war and illustrated on an earlier page.

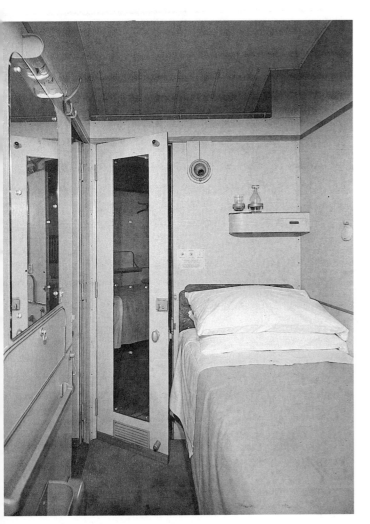

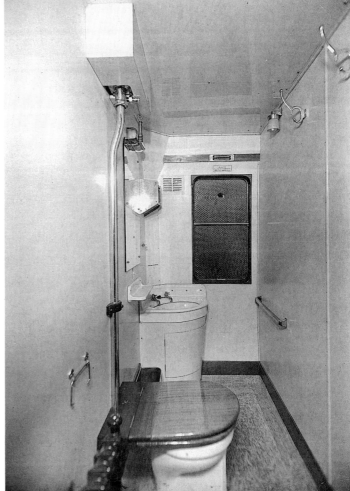

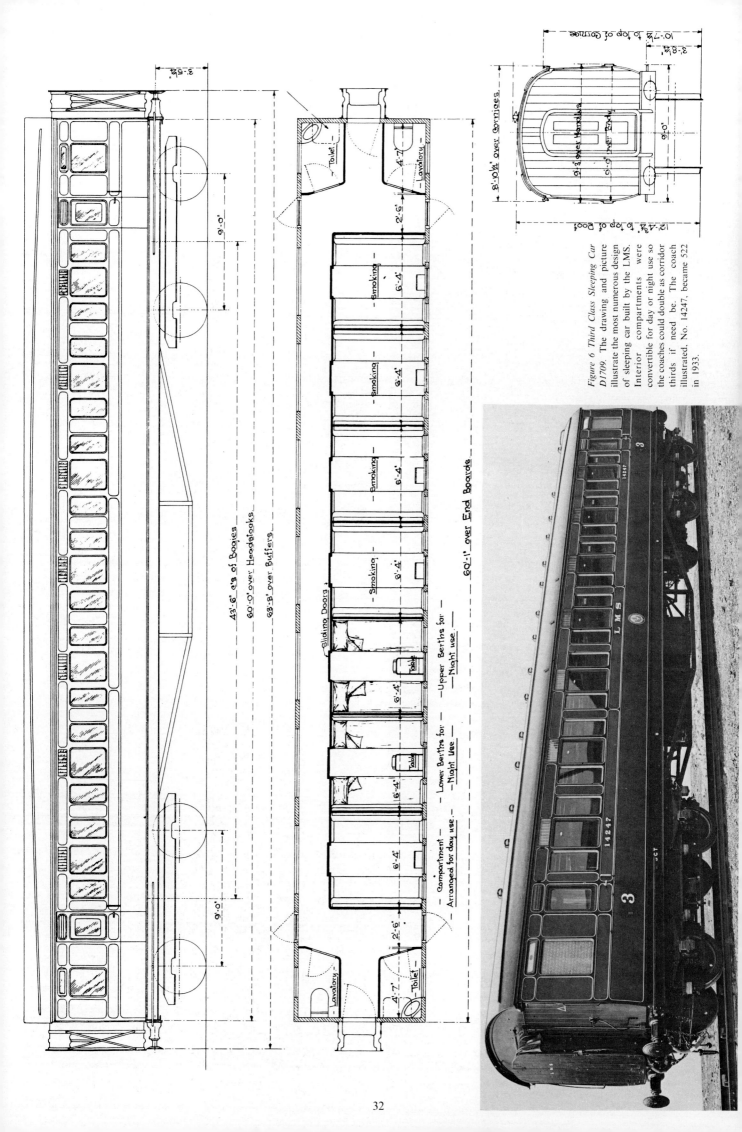

Figure 6 Third Class Sleeping Car D1709. The drawing and picture illustrate the most numerous design of sleeping car built by the LMS. Interior compartments were convertible for day or night use so the coaches could double as corridor thirds if need be. The coach illustrated. No. 14247, became 522 in 1933.

Plate 27. This second view from the compartment side of D1709 shows No. 14229 (later 504) in service. Observant readers will note that the emergency train alarm apparatus is fitted to the opposite end of the carriage.

Plate 28. This second view of D1709 No. 14247 shows how the corridor side body styling of these pioneer third class sleepers closely followed the 'big window' style of the final series of Period I open stock–see Chapter 4. Plate 9 shows the corridor side of the final steel panelled examples.

Plate 29. This interior view of D1709 made up for night use (see also Plate 8), shows the small table-like feature below the central droplight which also acted as the step ladder to the upper berths.

Plates 30-31. Modern though they may have been from outside, the D1863 sleeping cars still retained a somewhat sombre interior. These views were both taken inside No. 585 just prior to its American trip and presumably typified the series. Note that in the view showing the corridor door, one can see both the interior cover to the outside ventilation 'scoop' on the corridor wall–see Figure 7–and the left hand end of the associated floor level ventilator on the door itself.

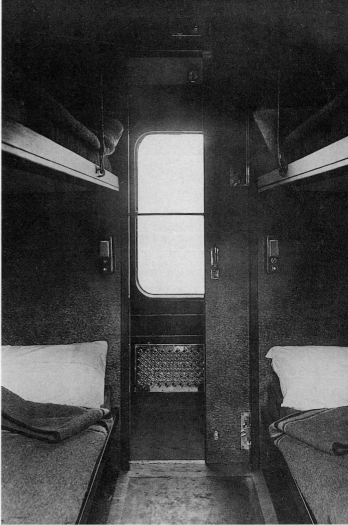

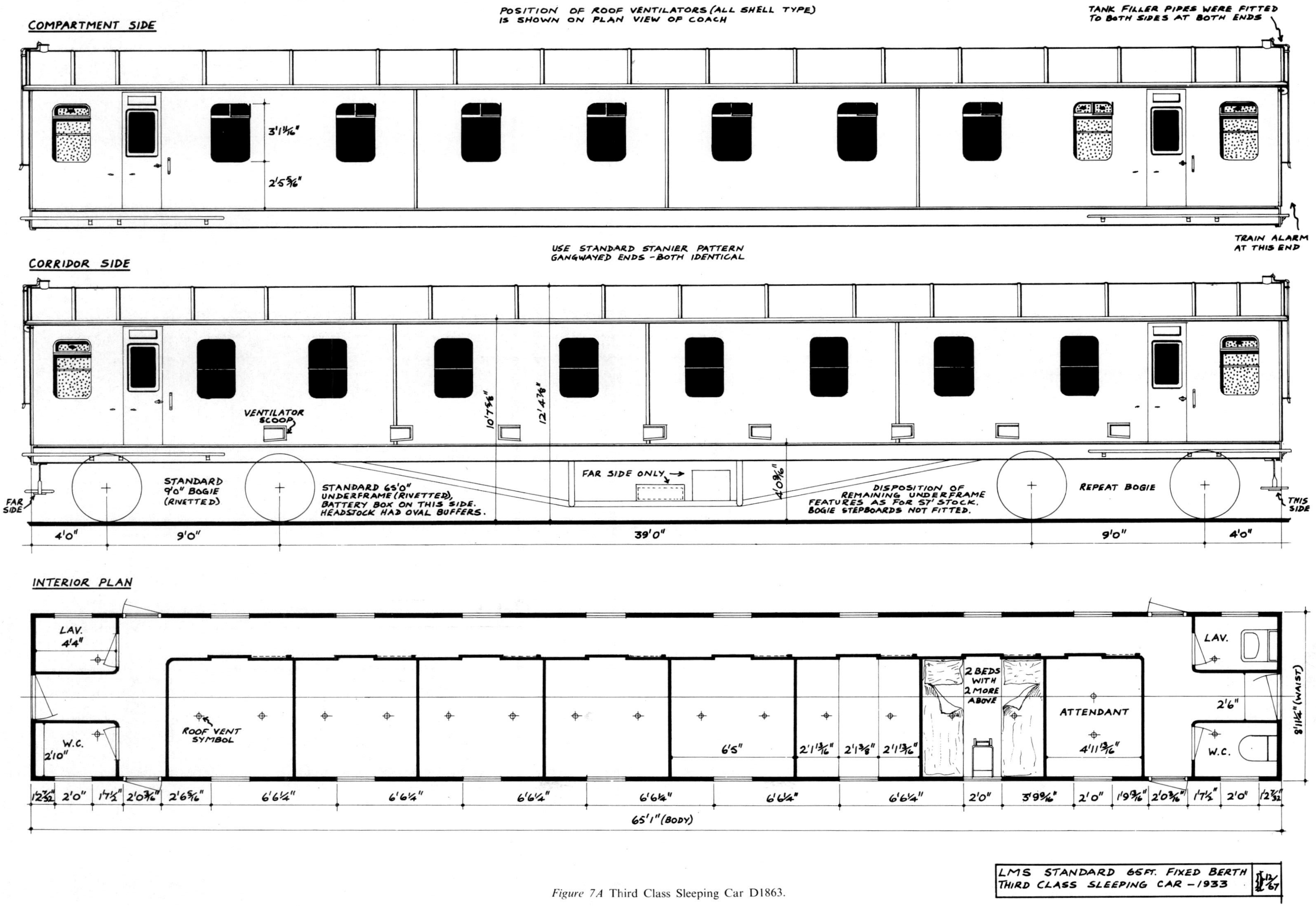

Figure 7A Third Class Sleeping Car D1863.

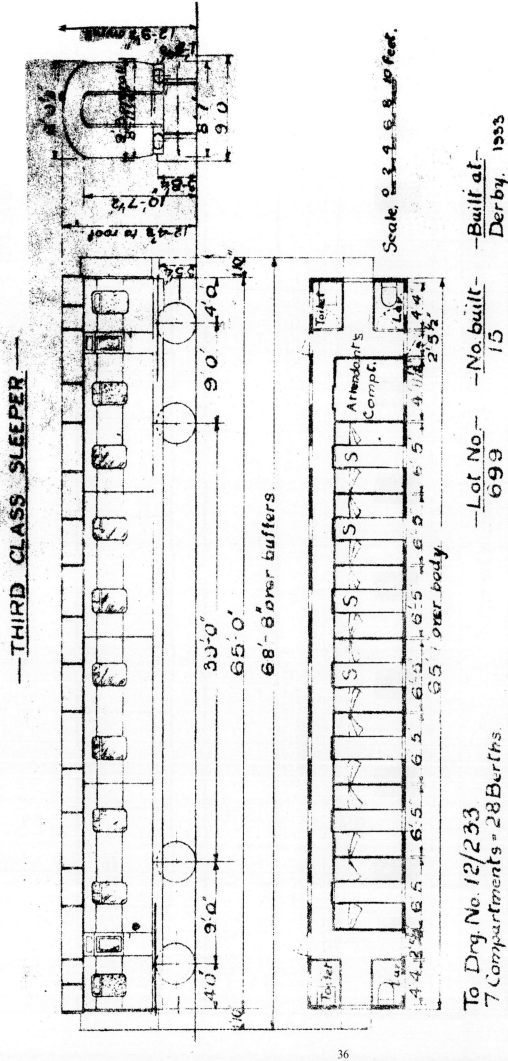

— THIRD CLASS SLEEPER —

To Drg No. 12/233.
7 Compartments = 28 Berths.
1 Attendant's Compt.
2 Toilets.
2 Lavatories.
'S' = Smoking.
Weight = 37 Tons.

—Lot No.—   —No. built—   —Built at—
699   15   Derby. 1953

Scale, feet.

Figure 7B *Third Class Sleeping Car D1863.* As with the previous Stanier design, the main drawing (Scale 4mm = 1ft) shows a fully dimensioned version of D1863. Once again we append the official diagram on this page for the sake of completeness. Exterior views of these cars are somewhat rare and Plate 10 is the only posed official view known to us.

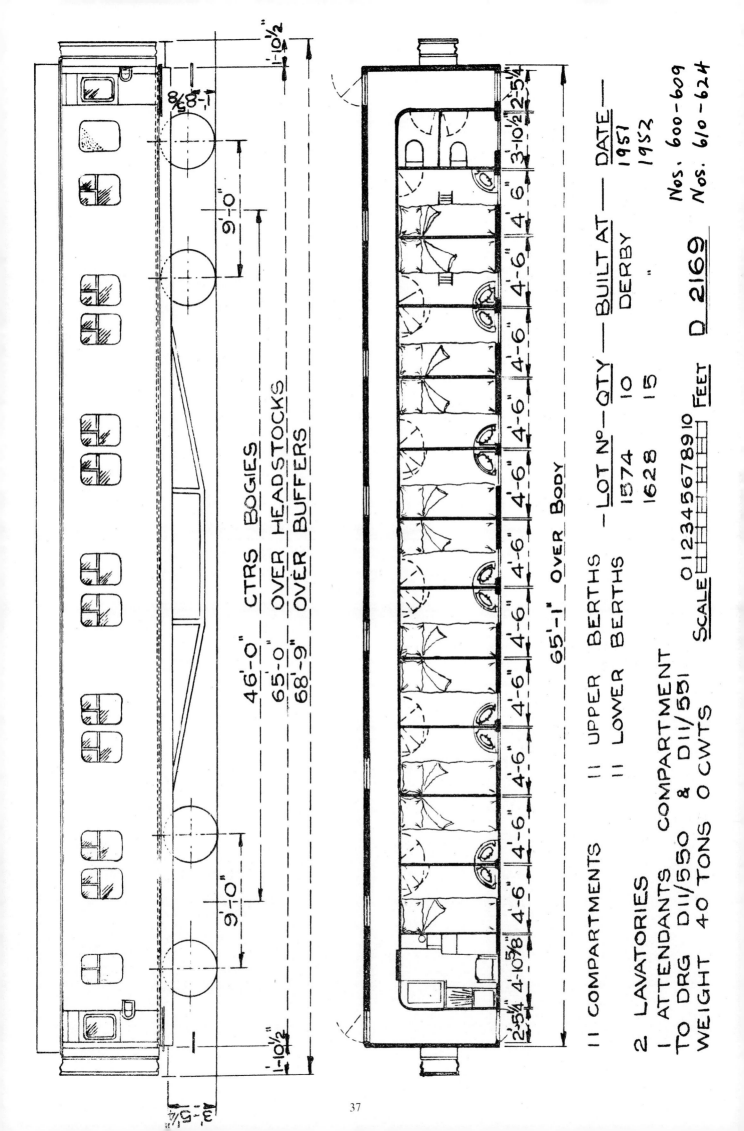

8'-8⅝"

1'-10½"

9'-0"

9'-0"

9'-0"

1'-10½"

3'-5¼"

46'-0" CTRS BOGIES
65'-0" OVER HEADSTOCKS
68'-9" OVER BUFFERS

2'-5¼" 3'-10½" 4'-6" 4'-6" 4'-6" 4'-6" 4'-6" 4'-6" 4'-6" 4'-6" 4'-6" 4'-6" 4'-6" 4'-5⅝" 4'-10⅞" 2'-5¼"

65'-1" OVER BODY

		LOT Nº	QTY	BUILT AT	DATE
11 COMPARTMENTS	11 UPPER BERTHS	1574	10	DERBY	1951
	11 LOWER BERTHS	1628	15	"	1952

2 LAVATORIES
1 ATTENDANTS COMPARTMENT
TO DRG D11/550 & D11/551
        D11/554 & D11/551
WEIGHT 40 TONS 0 CWTS

Nos. 600-609
Nos. 610-624

0123456789 10

SCALE ▢▢▢▢▢▢▢ FEET

D 2169

37

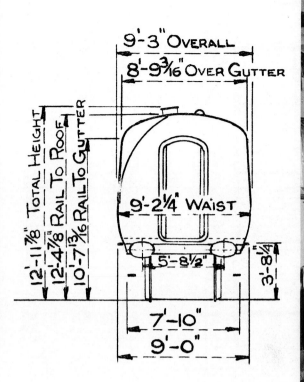

Above, right and previous page: Figure 8 Third Class Twin Berth Sleeping Car D2169 This diagram, also issued by BR in the LMS series, shows the post-war version of third class sleeping car. Apart from its shorter length it had far more in common with the Stanier first class cars than with the preceding D1863, both in terms of body styling (full width) and interior amenity–see appended view. The only known official exterior view is shown at Plate II and shows No. M603 in the BR standard red and cream livery in which all entered service.

Below and opposite: Figure 9 Composite Sleeping Car D1781 These distinctive coaches were built to D1781 and modified later to D1844. The original arrangement along with a corridor side elevation of the first example built (No. 10548, later 700) is shown. Comparison with Plate 12 will reveal a difference in roof ventilator style and a lack of roof mounted destination board brackets compared with later examples.

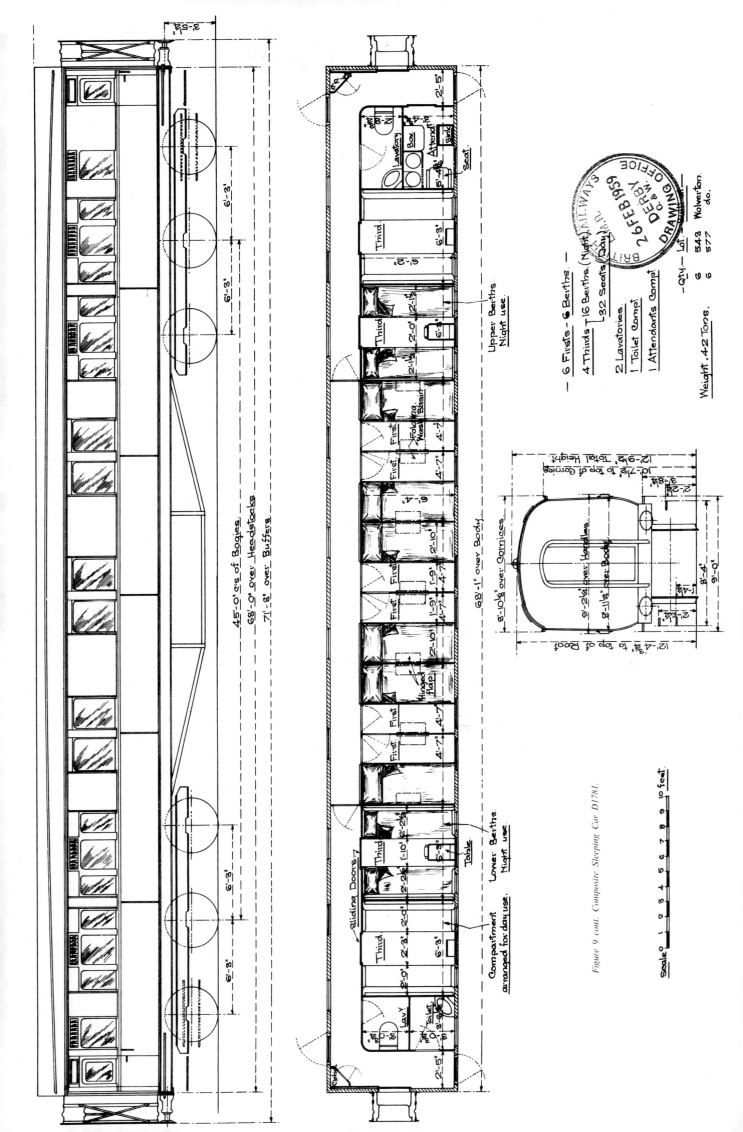

Figure 9 cont. Composite Sleeping Car D178L.

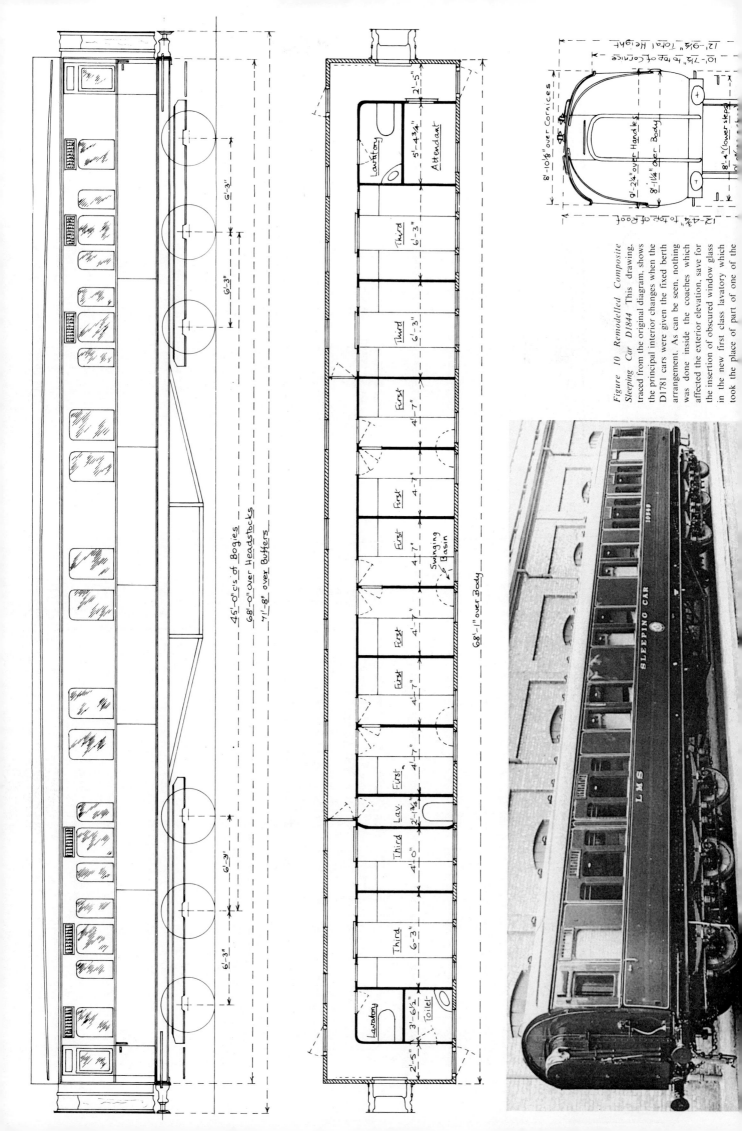

Figure 10 Remodelled Composite Sleeping Car D1844 This drawing, traced from the original diagram, shows the principal interior changes when the D1781 cars were given the fixed berth arrangement. As can be seen, nothing was done inside the coaches which affected the exterior elevation, save for the insertion of obscured window glass in the new first class lavatory which took the place of part of one of the

Plate 32. For convenience, this view of D1781 No. 10637 (later 709) is repeated from Volume 1. It again shows the compartment side, this time from the train alarm end and also emphasises the roof variation between the later and earlier examples. It is likely that the change came between the two lots–see Summary Table, page 20. Viewed from this angle, the residual 'Wolverton' characteristics of this design are particularly obvious.

Plates 33-34. These two interior views are believed to be of composite sleeping cars to D1947. The fixed four-berth third class interior is certainly that of No. 713 but the other cannot be positively identified.

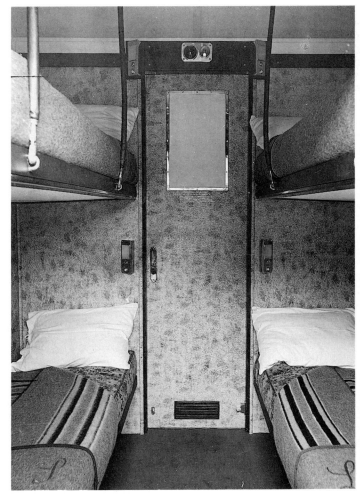

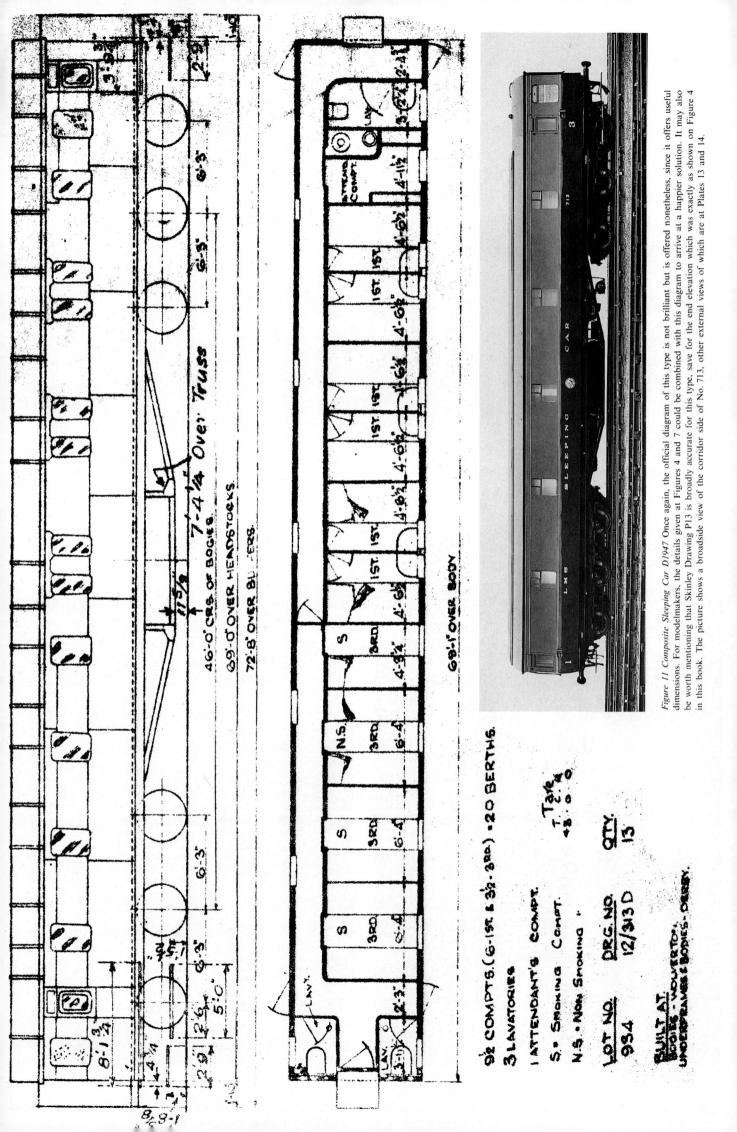

9½ COMPT5. (6·15T. & 3½·3RD) = 20 BERTH5.
3 LAVATORIE5.
1 ATTENDANT'S COMPT.
S = SMOKING COMPT.
N.S. = NON SMOKING "

TARE		
T.c.q.		
+3.0.0		

LOT NO.	DRG. NO.	QTY.
934	12/343 D	13

BUILT AT.
BODIE5 - WOLVERTON;
UNDERFRAME5 & BODIE5 - DERBY.

Figure 11 Composite Sleeping Car D1947 Once again, the official diagram of this type is not brilliant but is offered nonetheless, since it offers useful dimensions. For modelmakers, the details given at Figures 4 and 7 could be combined with this diagram to arrive at a happier solution. It may also be worth mentioning that Skinley Drawing P13 is broadly accurate for this type, save for the end elevation which was exactly as shown on Figure 4 in this book. The picture shows a broadside view of the corridor side of No. 713, other external views of which are at Plates 13 and 14.

Chapter 2 – Dining, Kitchen and Buffet Cars

Kitchen/Dining coaches; Buffet cars; Kitchen only cars; Post Nationalisation conversions; Summary Tables; Survey by Diagrams

THE LMS in 1923 assumed responsibility for the continuance of the strong dining car traditions established by the pre-group companies—particularly the LNWR and MR. True to these traditions, the new company continued to lay emphasis on good refreshment services and built a considerable number of comfortable and well-equipped dining vehicles. They can be conveniently divided into those with some form of cooking facility and those without. The latter were nearly all of the full open type, very similar in style to the general service open stock and as such, they are dealt with in Chapter 4.

KITCHEN/DINING COACHES

LMS design combined Kitchen and Dining coaches, hereafter referred to simply as dining cars or diners, were built during all three periods of LMS coach design, eventually totalling 119 vehicles of all three classes. All were 68ft, 12 wheel cars.

The first to appear were six rather ornate cars to D1743 in 1925. These were styled in LNWR fashion and can be compared with the contemporary sleeping cars to D1739. They seated 30 passengers in two saloons (12 plus 18) arranged in five seating bays. The seats were arranged singly on the corridor side of the coach and in pairs on the kitchen side. This 2 + 1 seating arrangement was universal in all LMS dining cars and will not, therefore, be alluded to again. The D1743 diners were regarded as being for first *or* third class passengers—nominally 12 first and 18 third—but variable by the dining car staff to suit the needs of the traffic. They were numbered into the composite series in 1932/3.

Why LNWR styling was preferred for these cars is no clearer than in the case of the contemporary sleeping cars. There seems no good reason why these six coaches could not have been given orthodox Period I features but they were not and, moreover, they were the only dining cars to appear during the first design phase. After nationalisation, they were converted as kitchen/buffet cars to D2180 and ran for several more years in this new role.

The relative lack of Period I dining cars was amply compensated in Period II when the LMS introduced 36 palatial cars in the short space of two years between 1930 and 1932. Of these, 24 were first class cars with four seating bays

Plates 35-36 These two pictures give an interior impression of the D1718 first class dining cars. The kitchen was a fairly typical LMS arrangement with the gas cooking range prominent in the foreground (car No. 2592, later 4). The passenger interior view is car No. 3129 (later No. 7) of the same batch. The elegant styling is reminiscent of contemporary Pullman Car design and the non-standard seat end design compared with most other LMS open stock is worthy of note.

Plate 37 LMS Car No. 2074 of the later Period II cars to D1810 from the corridor side exhibits some subtle differences from D1718. Note the changed position of the full lining to a position between the windows and the use of six-element Stones ventilators above the seating bays, unlike the five-element Dewel ventilators of the earlier cars. The passenger door was slightly further away from the end of the coach and opposite, the toilet window was surmounted by a Stones ventilator, not the 'fall-back' type as displayed on Car 2592. Car 2074 was to Lot 616 and became No.21 in the 1932/3 renumbering. The absence of the figure '1' on the entrance door was unusual.

accommodating 24 passengers (D1718, D1810).* The other 12 were composites with five seating bays but otherwise very similar in style (D1811). All the cars were steel panelled Period II designs. The two diagrams for the first class cars differed only in minor aspects like the precise size of the toilet and pantry areas and such detail matters as shelf design and linen cupboards. The most noticeable external difference between them when new was the livery. Both types were given full livery but the D1810 cars had lining between the windows whereas the D1718 vehicles had the lining at the edge of the windows. There were also slight variations in the ventilator design above the windows.

This 1930–32 period was the time when the LMS was actively experimenting with a variety of matters connected with the improvement of coach design and, as will be noted for some of the other Period II designs (e.g. the TOs to D1807 page 221), slight variations in detail were by no means uncommon within batches of coaches.

The Period II composite diners were, like their LNWR styled predecessors, neutral vehicles and did not carry class figures on the outside doors. They had detachable class indicator boards fitted in the window which could be changed, if need be, by the dining car staff.

In addition to the exterior innovations already mentioned, the LMS Period II diners seem to have been some of the few pre-Stanier coaches to depart from the traditional early LMS seat designs. The interior of the first class cars was quite different from the typical pattern as used in most Period I/II open stock. The Pullman-like decor was probably quite deliberate and in these elegant cars, the LMS certainly achieved a most harmonious design, fit to compare with any of their pre-group ancestors from either Derby or Wolverton. The Period II Semi-RFO's (page 181) were furnished in similar style.

The bulk of LMS standard dining cars were Period III coaches. Between 1933 and 1937 no fewer than 77 new cars were introduced divided into 20 first class, 13 composite and 44 third class vehicles. The firsts and composites were, fundamentally, Stanier versions of the aforementioned Period II coaches but the thirds were new designs.

*There is a large scale model of one of these cars in the South Kensington Science Museum.

Plate 38 LMS Car No. 10440, the Period II car to D1811, contemporary with the RFs to D1718/D1810. The detachable class boards in the windows enabled the seating to be altered to suit the dining car staff. Note also the lack of class figures on the door. This coach was renumbered 238 in 1932/3.

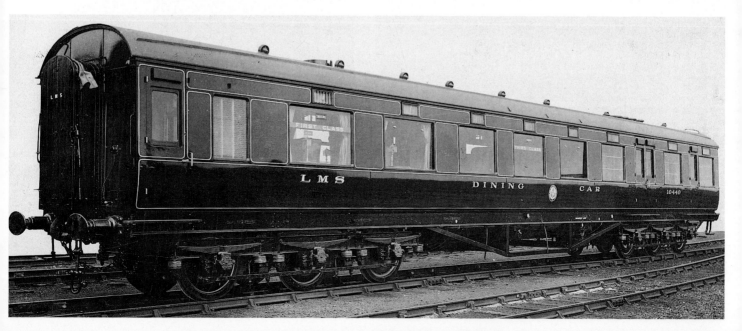

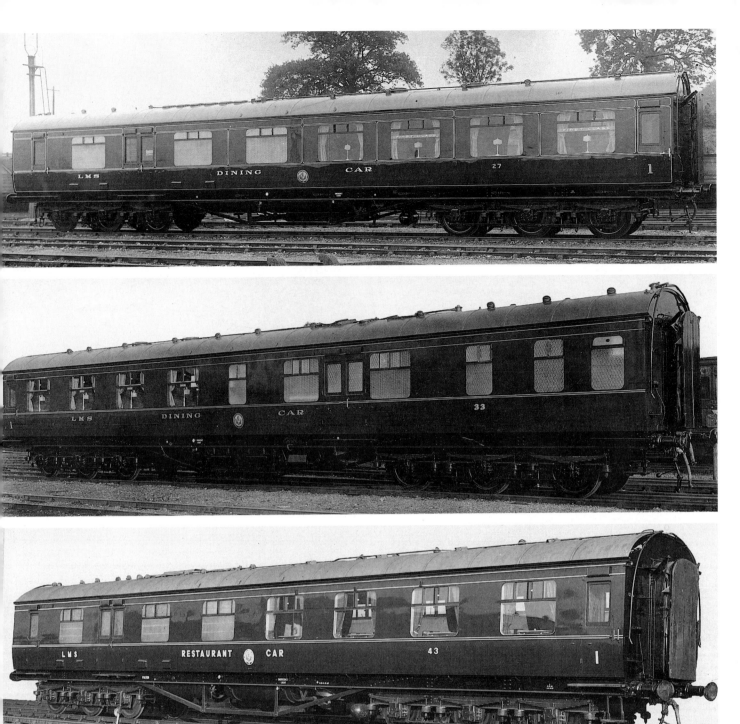

Plates 39-41 These three pictures show the evolution of the first class dining car during the Stanier period. Car No. 27 was one of four built in 1933 to D1857 with shallow depth window ventilators and full livery. There can be little doubt that from the exterior point of view, the adoption of the simpler livery produced a less elegant looking vehicle (Car 33 of the 1935 batch to D1900). After the war, one of these was refurbished with loose chairs and other interior changes and given the full 1946 livery, now branded 'Restaurant Car' (Car No. 43-see also Figure 16).

Chronologically, the first Stanier dining cars to appear were the four RFs to D1857 and 10 RTs to D1861. They were built at Wolverton and Derby respectively and probably entered service simultaneously. All 14 were early Period III cars with shallow window ventilators and full livery. The remaining Stanier diners were all of orthodox Period III style with deep ventilators and simple livery (16 RFs to D1900; 13 RCs to D1938; 34 RTs to D1901/D1923). The firsts, as before, seated 24 passengers in four bays but, unlike the Period II cars had no luggage or lavatory accommodation. The thirds had five bays and 30 seats, again without luggage or lavatory accommodation. Some 13 of the latter were used as wartime ambulances and some may never have returned to the dining car service, being withdrawn as early as 1953.

The five bay, 30 seat composites, differed from the Period III first and third class diners in having luggage and lavatory areas, compensated by a somewhat shorter kitchen portion. This was because the composites most commonly ran as single unit cars whereas the firsts and thirds usually ran with at least one extra vestibule dining coach, generally being paired RF + TO or RT + CO. This need to provide more meals than in a single car necessitated a larger kitchen area than in the composites.

After the war, one of the first class cars (No. 43) was the subject of an interesting conversion to D2120. This took the form of stripping the interior and refurbishing it with double glazed windows, individual chairs and tables. The car was one of the relatively few LMS coaches to be given the full 1946 livery utilising sans-serif characters throughout and being branded

Plate 42 Interior view of the post-war conversion of RF No. 43. This conversion exhibited a mixture of fixed and loose seating. The fixed seats on the right of the gangways were angled to the wall for ease of access.

'Restaurant Car' rather than 'Dining Car'. An open first (No. 7555) was similarly treated—see page 183—but no other like conversions of LMS dining cars took place although some of the Buffet and Cafeteria conversions (page 50) were given loose seats. Whether the idea was a great success is not known but the loose seating concept may have had some influence on the design of some of the BR standard diners.

Two of the Period III third class cars (105 and 117) were converted to kitchen/buffet cars after Nationalisation—these are considered on pages 49-50.

BUFFET CARS

The LMS did not seem enamoured of the Buffet Car idea (unlike the LNER) and built but five cars of the type. The prototype vehicle was a Period II coach to D1848 on a standard 57ft underframe (Car No. 100). It was followed some four years later by four similar Stanier pattern cars to D1948. There was nothing particularly remarkable about these coaches except to remark that their decor seemed to reflect all that was most hideous in the fashions of the 1930s! Both varieties seated 24 passengers in four bays.

Why the buffet car was not popular on the LMS is not clear. There may not have been enough medium distance services to necessitate large scale use of the type and, of course, the vogue for buffet type facilities was nothing like as strong in the pre-war years as it is today.

Plate 43 LMS Period III Composite dining car to D1938 No. 250. These cars were very similar in layout to their Period II predecessors (Figure 21), even to the extent of having courtesy table lamps at the first class end only.

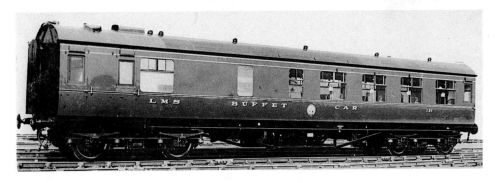

Plates 44-45 Exterior and interior views of the prototype Stanier buffet car to D1948 No. 131. Like the Period II example, the four Period III cars were numbered in the third class series. As far as can be deduced, these cars operated in paired circuits (i.e. one travelling in each direction daily). Known services in the late 1930s include a complex Manchester–York–Sheffield–Birmingham roster (extended to Worcester on Friday nights) and the afternoon Euston–Manchester service.

KITCHEN ONLY CARS

By contrast with dining cars, the LMS acquired but a handful of kitchen only cars from the pre-group constituents. Indeed this type of vehicle does not seem to have found favour amongst the LMS constituent companies except the LNWR—even in the latter case it was confined to the Euston-Liverpool (Riverside) services. However, the situation was to change radically during the 1924-28 period when some 73 kitchen cars were built to D1697.

They were all high-waisted Period I style cars but they had steel-panelled exteriors after the Period II style–possibly to reduce fire risk since they employed gas cooking and lighting. The full livery adopted for them included a painted waist 'panel' and from the outside, they matched the fully-beaded Period I coaches with which they at first ran. An odd single car of the same type (30072) was built in 1932 to replace an accident victim while another car (30034) was nominally 'rebuilt' with a Stanier body in 1938. Some of the Period I kitchen cars were converted to buffet cars in the early 1950s–see page 48.

Plate 46 Corridor side view of RK No. 312 (later 30002) to D1697. The kitchen side elevation of this particular car is at Plate 60, volume I.

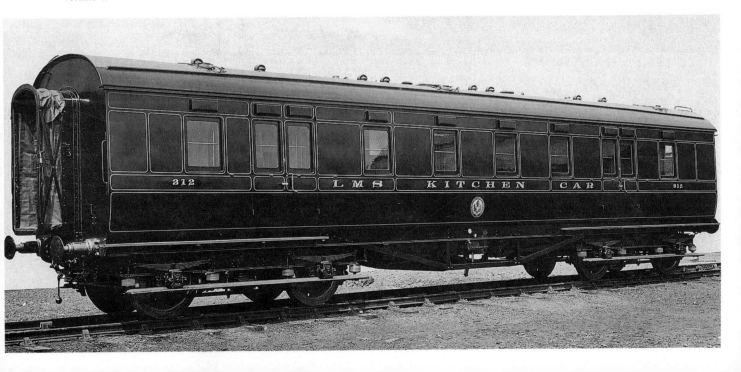

The large number of Period I kitchen cars may well have been a contributory reason for the relative paucity of newly constructed kitchen/diners during the first few years of the LMS. Together with the emphasis placed by the LMS on open coaches during the same period it would seem reasonable to conclude that there was a real need on many services for more dining space than could be achieved in an orthodox dining car. The wheel seemed to turn full circle after the war when many of the Period I kitchen cars were stored out of use for long periods.

In 1933, two 60ft, all-electric kitchen cars were introduced, the first one having early Period III styling. The extra length was to accommodate the diesel generating equipment and there is some evidence that the cars were introduced in connection with the 'Royal Scot' tour of America. The first of the pair (30073) did indeed go to America but the second coach was not completed until 1934 and the design was not multiplied. The all-electric idea did not find favour and the cars were not a great success, being stored out of use from 1942 until their withdrawal, still in LMS livery, in 1956. The LMS, unlike the LNER, reverted to gas cooking and lighting with the Stanier standard 50ft kitchen car to D1912.

These cars were, in all essentials, the Stanier equivalent of the Period I kitchen cars and 32 were built between 1934 and 1938 plus the nominal 'rebuild' of 30034 (page 47). In 1937, six Stanier cars were adapted for use with the blue/silver 'Coronation Scot' sets.

POST NATIONALISATION CONVERSIONS

After Nationalisation, the buffet-cum-cafeteria car concept received a great deal of attention and many vehicles of this kind were produced by suitable conversion of older coaches; 31 LMS standard coaches were involved in this exercise and this caused the insertion of no fewer than seven new diagrams into the refreshment section of the old LMS diagram book. Although these new diagrams were dignified by a number of different names (Party Car, Cafeteria Car &c), they basically fell into two types of coach. First were a group of kitchen/buffet cars (BR code RKB) all of which had started life as LMS 12 wheel dining cars. These cars retained sufficient kitchen facility to be able to serve meals to an adjacent open coach as well as to provide snacks at the buffet counter. The other conversions were true buffet cars (BR code RB) with a kitchen portion sufficient only to provide a service of light refreshments within the confines of the vehicle itself.

Plate 47 After the second world war, many LMS kitchen cars were redundant and a number were converted to Cafeterias–see Plate 53. Another interesting conversion was to a track recording coach. No. DM 395223 is seen in this guise at Wolverton in 1968, branded for dual heating and 100mph running. (D. Jenkinson)

Plate 48 The experimental Period III diesel-electric car to D1855 No. 30073. Note the full livery, shallow depth sliding window ventilators and 'stretched' type running numbers of this 60ft car. Car 30074 was similar but had deep window ventilators and simple livery.

Plate 49 The standard Period III 50ft Kitchen car to D1912 No. 30084 as altered for the 1937 Coronation Scot train. Five others were similarly treated. The general service version showed no significant external differences except for livery.

Kitchen/Buffet Conversions

Seven LMS standard dining cars were converted to RKBs during the 1952-5 period. Six were to D2180 and these involved the pioneer LMS standard diners, the RCs to D1743. The conversion took the form of removing all but the extreme end seating bay and utilising the space previously occupied by the other four bays for an open buffet area served by a counter which connected with the kitchen. The kitchen itself remained substantially unchanged from its original form. The new buffet saloon had narrow shelves against the walls and a sort of island shelf in the centre of the open area. The one residual seating bay of the original five bay layout seems to have been left substantially unaltered.

The other 12 wheel coach to be converted to RKB form was Period III RT No 105. It had all the seating removed and a buffet counter installed adjacent to the kitchen which remained unchanged. At the end of the car away from the kitchen in the space occupied by two of the old seating bays, four sets of tables and chairs were installed giving eight seats. It was at first rostered to run with open first No. 7555 (see page 183).

Plate 50 The saloon and bar counter of RKB No. M105M, photographed in late 1952. As can be seen, little remained of the original third class dining car interior, save for roof vents and light fittings. This was really quite a tasteful conversion compared with some contemporary efforts.

Plate 51 Car No. M105M, rebuilt from dining car No. 105 to RKB form (D2182). The large blank panel between the kitchen and the seating area was where the buffet counter was located.

Plate 52 Car No. M253M was ex-third class diner No. 117 as rebuilt to D2197. This rebuilt was a true Cafeteria car and the far end contained the three seating bays. (J. Alsop)

Buffet Conversions

Between 1953 and 1955, 24 buffet cars were produced from three types of LMS standard coach. One was from a 12 wheel RT, six were from Period I kitchen cars and the remainder from Period I 60ft third class sleepers of D1709 which had been in ambulance train service during the war. They probably never ran again as sleepers, being surplus to requirements. The kitchen cars were not renumbered but all the remainder were given numbers in the LMS composite dining car list (253-270). A feature of the utilisation of these cars after conversion was the considerable number which were initially allocated to other regions than the LMR. All the conversion work was done at Eastleigh in the Southern Region.

The first conversion was of the six kitchen cars which were turned into what were called 'party cars'. They were given a small central kitchen/pantry area and each end of the car was made into a buffet saloon with a longitudinal centre table. Each saloon had eleven bar stools grouped round this table, six on one side and five on the other. Some at least were allocated to the Western Region. The conversion was to D2184.

Plate 53 Car No. W30017M, a conversion of a Period I kitchen car to D2184 called a 'Party Car' although branded Cafeteria. (J. E. Cull)

Plate 54 Car No. W256M was the D2195 conversion of the 60ft sleeping cars. This one was originally third class sleeper No. 512 and the conversion was classified 'Party Car'. As seen, little, if any, of the original bodywork remained on these conversions. (J. E. Cull)

All the remaining conversions took place at about the same time and carried consecutive diagram numbers (D2195–8). The running numbers were mixed up amongst the diagrams. After 253 (ex-117) the numbers reflected the order of numbering as sleeping cars. Two basic kinds of coach were produced which were called either Party Cars or Cafeteria Cars. However, to confuse matters, all were branded 'Cafeteria' on the outside.

The party cars were all to D2195 and were all ex-Period I sleeping cars. They were basically a stretched version of the converted kitchen cars with larger kitchen/pantry area but no increase in seating capacity in the end saloons. The exterior window arrangement of these cars—indeed of all the former sleeping cars—differed considerably and with doors at the extreme ends in every case, it is difficult to see how any of the bodywork of the sleeping cars (except the ends) can have been retained.

All three cafeteria diagrams shared certain features in common: all had centre kitchens and all had one end of the coach given to a conventional three-bay 18 seat dining saloon with individual chairs. The opposite end of the car was similar to the saloons in the Party Cars with a centre table and bar stools. D2197 was the ex-12 wheel RT No. 117 and had a 12 stool saloon while D2196/D2198 were ex-sleeping cars with nine-stool and seven-stool saloons respectively.

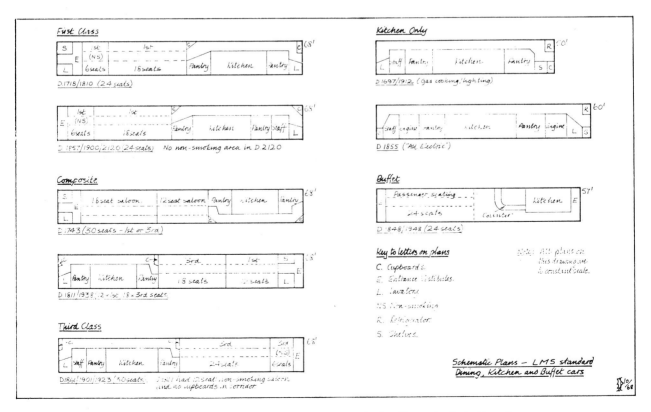

LMS standard dining, kitchen and buffet cars—sketch plans (Drawn by D. Jenkinson)

TABLE 2a: SUMMARY TABLE OF LMS STANDARD DINING, KITCHEN AND BUFFET CARS

Note: This table should be read in conjunction with the list of standard dimensions and details on page 9

Type	*Diag*	*Lot*	*Qty*	*Date*	*Built*	*Dimensions* (L×W×H)	*Weight*	*Period*	*Running Numbers*	*Withdrawal First*	*Withdrawal Last*	*Remarks*
RF	1718	478	12	1930	Derby	68′×9′3″×12′4¾″	43T	II(Flush)	4-7, 11-18	11/60	9/62	Lot 525 were originally marked on Diagram 1718 and certainly showed identical external features. The main changes seem to have been on lot 616 only. These had slightly longer glass vane ventilators over the windows, Stones ventilators rather than the 'fall back' type over the toilet and 'squared off' interior partition corners. The ex-works livery and toilet/pantry areas also showed differences.
RF	1810	525	6	1930	Derby		45T	II(Flush)	1-3, 8-10	7/59	7/62	
		616	6	1932	Wolverton		45T		19-24	10/60	9/62	
RF	1857	689	4	1933	Wolverton	68′×9′3″×12′4⅞″	45T	III(Shallow ventilator)	25-28	4/62	12/62	Full livery when new.
RF	1900	732	4	1933	Wolverton	68′×9′3″×12′4⅞″	46T	III	29-32	3/62	12/62	Lot 732 came out with simple livery and were some of the earliest coaches to do so. They were plated 1934. Car 41 had a coal fired stove. Lots 914/1046 may have had pressure heating/ventilation equipment in common with the contemporary RCs and RTs.
		865	4	1935	Wolverton		46T		33-36	11/62	12/64	
		914	4	1936	Wolverton		47T		37-40	12/62	3/66	
		1046	4	1937	Wolverton		47T		41-44	7/63	4/64	
RF	2120	Ex-1046	1	1947	Derby	68′×9′3″×12′4⅞″	47T	III	43	—	3/62	The post-war rebuild with loose seating and one single seating area.
RT	1861	685	10	1933	Derby	68′×9′3″×12′4⅞″	45T	III(Shallow ventilator)	101-110	4/53	13/62	The prototype LMS standard RT. Full livery when new.
RT	1901	733	10	1933	Derby	68′×9′3″×12′4⅞″	45T	III	111-120	4/58	13/63	The only real difference was that D1923 had rounded interior partition corners. All were 24 smoking plus 6 non-smoking whereas D1861 was 18 + 12. Lot 903 and 1034 had pressure heating/ventilation.
RT	1923	852	10	1935	Derby	68′×9′3″×12′4⅞″	45T	III	121-130	13/62	13/62	
		903	4	1936	Derby		45T		135-138	13/62	13/62	
		1034	10	1937	Derby		45T		139-148	7/63	7/64	
RC	1743	28	6	1925	Wolverton	68′×9′1½″×12′4¾″	43T	see remarks	222-227	All to D2180-RKB (see Table 7b below)		The LNWR styled cars and 'neutral' in use (1st *or* 3rd). The width of 9′1½″ (Plated 9′2″) was the same as the contemporary SLFs to D1739–see Table 1a. Plated 1924.
RC	1811	617	12	1932	Derby	68′×9′3″×12′4¾″	44T	II(Flush)	228-239	8/59	12/62	'Neutral' cars.
RC	1938	905	10	1936	Wolverton	68′×9′3″×12′4⅞″	46T	III	240-249	12/56	13/63	All cars fitted pressure heating and ventilation equipment.
		1045	3	1937	Wolverton		46T		250-252	13/63	13/63	
RB	1848	646	1	1932	Derby	57′×9′2¼″×12′4¾″	29T	II(Flush)	100		2/61	Prototype car, plated 31T by 1942.
RB	1948	902	4	1936	Derby	57′×9′3″×12′4¾″	32T	III	131-134	13/62	2/63	
RK	1697	65	8	1924	Derby	50′×9′3″×12′4¾″	29T	I(Flush sided)	30000-30007	6/55	11/59	*Lot 153:* Only 19 renumbered in 1932/3, Lot 627 being the replacement for the vehicle lost in the Leighton Buzzard crash. 30034 later 'rebuilt' to D1912. Several converted to Cafeterias in 1953–see Table 2b (below).
		100	10	1925	Derby		30T		30008-30017	7/56	2/61	
		153	20	1925	Derby		30T		30018-30036	1/56	7/61	
		234	20	1926	Derby		30T		30037-30056	1/56	12/62	
		382	15	1928	Derby		29T		30057-30071	9/59	12/62	
		627	1	1932	Derby		30T		30072		13/62	
RK	1855	670	2	1933	Derby	60′×9′3″×12′4⅞″	45T	III(but see remarks)	30073-30074	1/56	2/56	The diesel electric cars. 30073 had shallow ventilators and full livery while 30074 had deep ventilators and simple livery not being finished until 1934. 30073 to America in 1933 and cars were probably built for this purpose. Stored out of use 1942-56 and never repainted by BR.
RK	1912	779	1	1934	Wolverton	50′×9′3″×12′4⅝″	33T	III	30075	—	13/62	*Lot 956:* Later examples plated 1937. Six of these cars modified for the 1937 'Coronation Scot' train (30084-30089) and on conversion tared 34T.
		956	20	1936	Glos. C&W		33T		30076-30095	7/56	13/65	
		1039	5	1937	Derby		35T		30096-30100	13/62	13/65	
		1081	6	1938	Derby		35T		30101-30106	7/56	12/63	
		1128	1	1938	Derby		32T		30034	—	1/56	*Lot 1128:* 'Rebuild' of accident victim.

TABLE 2b: SUMMARY TABLE OF LMS STANDARD COACHES SUBSEQUENTLY CONVERTED TO CAFETERIA/BUFFET CARS

Type	*Diag*	*Original Veh. Type*	*Qty*	*Date/Place Converted*	*Original Running Numbers*	*Running Numbers on Conversion*	*Withdrawals First*	*Withdrawals Last*	*Remarks*
RKB	2180	RC-D1743	6	1954 Wolverton	222-227	222-227	12/61	13/62	Rebuilds of the pioneer LMS built RCs.
RKB	2182	RT-D1861	1	1954 Wolverton	105	105	—	13/62	Rebuild of early Period III RT. Designed to run with RFO No. 7555–see Table 4a.
RB	2197	RT-D1901	1	1955 Eastleigh	117	253	not known		Rebuild of standard Period III RT retaining kitchen and 18 seats. Unlike D2182, this conversion involved a re-numbering and was designated 'Cafeteria Car'.
RB	2184	RK-D1697	6	1953 Eastleigh	30001/3/6/7/17/8	30001/3/6/7/17/8	13/62	4/65	Rebuilds of Period I RKs. Designated 'Party Cars'.
RB	2195	SLT-D1709	7	1955 Eastleigh	503/4/12/26/59/70/4	254-7/65/8/9	12/64	11/65	Rebuilds of ex-ambulance train coaches which had originally been third class sleeping cars. D2195 designated 'Party Car' and D2196/8 designated 'Cafeteria Cars'.
RB	2196	SLT-D1709	6	1955 Eastleigh	539/45/58/61/7/75	259/60/4/6/7/70	3/62	11/65	
RB	2198	SLT-D1709	4	1955 Eastleigh	536/48/50/3	258/61-3	3/62	7/63	

D1848(RB)

New No.	Old No.
100	40

D1743(RC)*

1st New No.	Old No.	Final 'New' No.
200	10578	222
1	10579	223
2	10580	224
3	10642	225
4	10643	226
5	10644	227

D1811(RC)

206	1866	228
7	2078	229
8	2082	230
9	2083	231
210	3898	232
11	3899	233
12	10436	234
13	10437	235
14	10438	236
215	10439	237
16	10440	238
17	10441	239

D1697(RK)

New No.	Old No.	New No.	Old No.	New No.	Old No.
30000	239	30024	302	30049	3316
30001	248	30025	306	30050	3317
30002	312	30026	307	30051	3318
30003	364	30027	3294	30052	3319
30004	3285	30028	3295	30053	3320
30005	3286	30029	3296	30054	3321
30006	3287	30030	3297	30055	3322
30007	3288	30031	3298	30056	3323
30008	54	30032	3299	30057	3324
30009	238	30033	3300	30058	3325
30010	284	30034	3301	30059	3326
30011	298	30035	3302	30060	3327
30012	308	30036	3303	30061	3328
30013	3289	30037	3304	30062	3329
30014	3290	30038	3305	30063	3330
30015	3291	30039	3306	30064	3331
30016	3292	30040	3307	30065	3332
30017	3293	30041	3308	30066	3333
30018	47	30042	3309	30067	3334
30019	106	30043	3310	30068	3335
30020	236	30044	3311	30069	3336
30021	245	30046	3313	30070	3337
30022	251	30047	3314	30071	3338
30023	262	30048	3315	30072	315

*The first 18 LMS Standard Composite Dining Cars were originally intended to carry Nos 200–217 under the new scheme. For reasons unknown to the authors, these numbers (including 218–221) were then given to former Pullman cars (running in Scotland) which were purchased by the LMS in the mid-1930s, causing the LMS built cars to be given the 222–239 series. It is not known whether any of them actually carried their originally allocated 1933 series numbers during the brief intervening period.

D1718(RF)

New No.	Old No.
1	2557
2	2558
3	2591
4	2592
5	2755
6	3128
7	3129
8	10413
9	10414
10	10415
11	10432
12	10433

D1810(RF)

New No.	Old No.
13	10434
14	10435
15	15333
16	15334
17	15335
18	18586
19	1864
20	1865
1	2074
2	2075
3	2076
4	2077

Plates 55-66. These two interiors of different examples of D1718 indicate that the LMS did not furnish all examples of the same type in identical manner, another example of the similarity of approach to that of Pullman which we have already noted. Given that the floral design was in No. 2592 (later No. 4) and the striped pattern was in No. 3129 (later No. 7), it seems probable that the twelve examples of Lot 478 may have included six each of the two styles.

INTRODUCTION TO THE TYPE BY TYPE SURVEY

The next section covers all the vehicle diagrams in conventional LMS sequence (first, third, composite) and, as with sleeping cars, we are often able to provide the original diagram. Once again, where diagrams are not very clear, we have occasionally thought it helpful to supplement these with more detailed dimensioned drawings. Extra pictures and other information are placed as close as possible to the diagrams to which they refer.

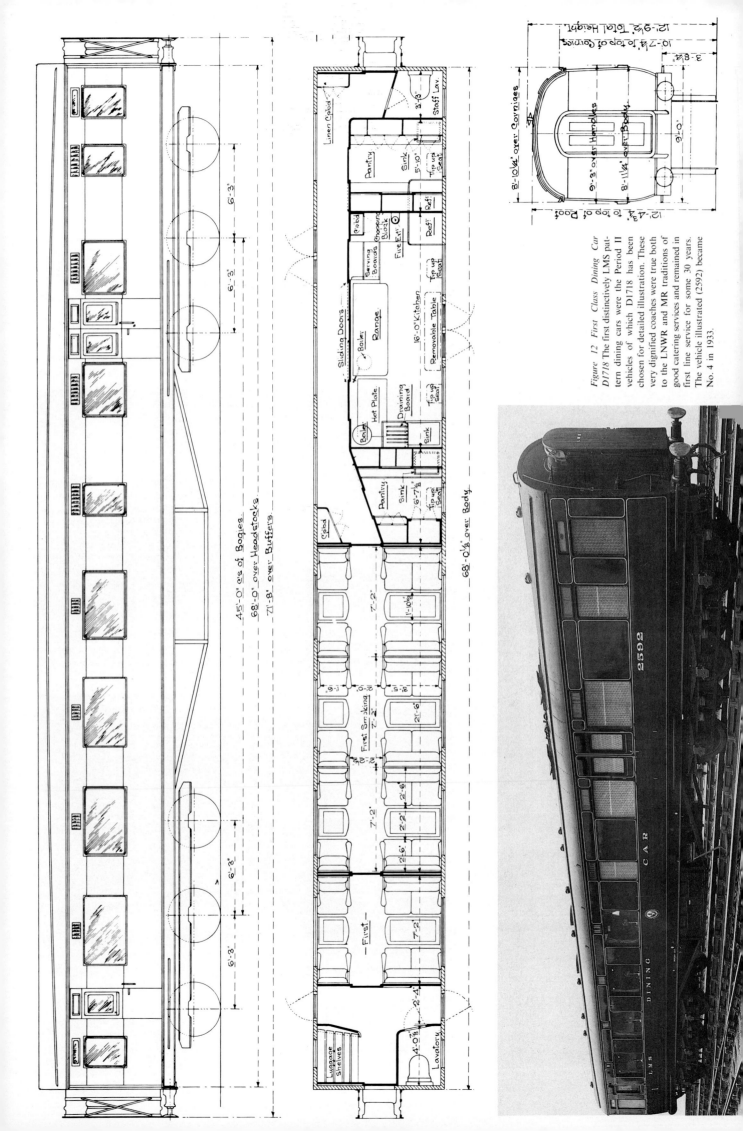

Figure 12 First Class Dining Car
D1718 The first distinctively LMS pattern dining cars were the Period II
vehicles of which D1718 has been
chosen for detailed illustration. These
very dignified coaches were true both
to the LNWR and MR traditions of
good catering services and remained in
first line service for some 30 years.
The vehicle illustrated (2592) became
No. 4 in 1933.

12'-9¾' Total Height.
10'-7¾' to top of cornice.
3'-8¼'
8'-10¼' over Cornices
9'-3' over Handholes
8'-11¼' over Body
9'-0'
12'-4¾' to top of Roof

6'-3'
6'-3'
6'-3'
6'-3'
6'-3'
45'-0' c's of Bogies
68'-0' over Headstocks
71'-8' over Buffers

Linen Cbd
Pantry
Sink
3'-3'
Staff Lav.
Tip up Seat
5'-10½'
Ref.
Cbd
Serving Boards
Chopping Block
Fire Ext.
Ref.
Sliding Doors
Boiler
Range
16'-0' Kitchen
Tip up Seat
Removable Table
Hot Plate.
Draining Board
Boiler
Sink
Tip up Seat
Cbd
Pantry
Sink
6'-7⅛'
Tip up Seat

7'-2'
1'-10½'
First Smoking
7'-2'
21'-6'
2'-2'
2'-6'
7'-2'
2'-2'
2'-6'
9'-1'
9'-0'
—First—
7'-2'
4'-0⅛'
2'-4'
Luggage Shelves
Lavatory
68'-0⅛' over Body

LMS
2592
DINING CAR

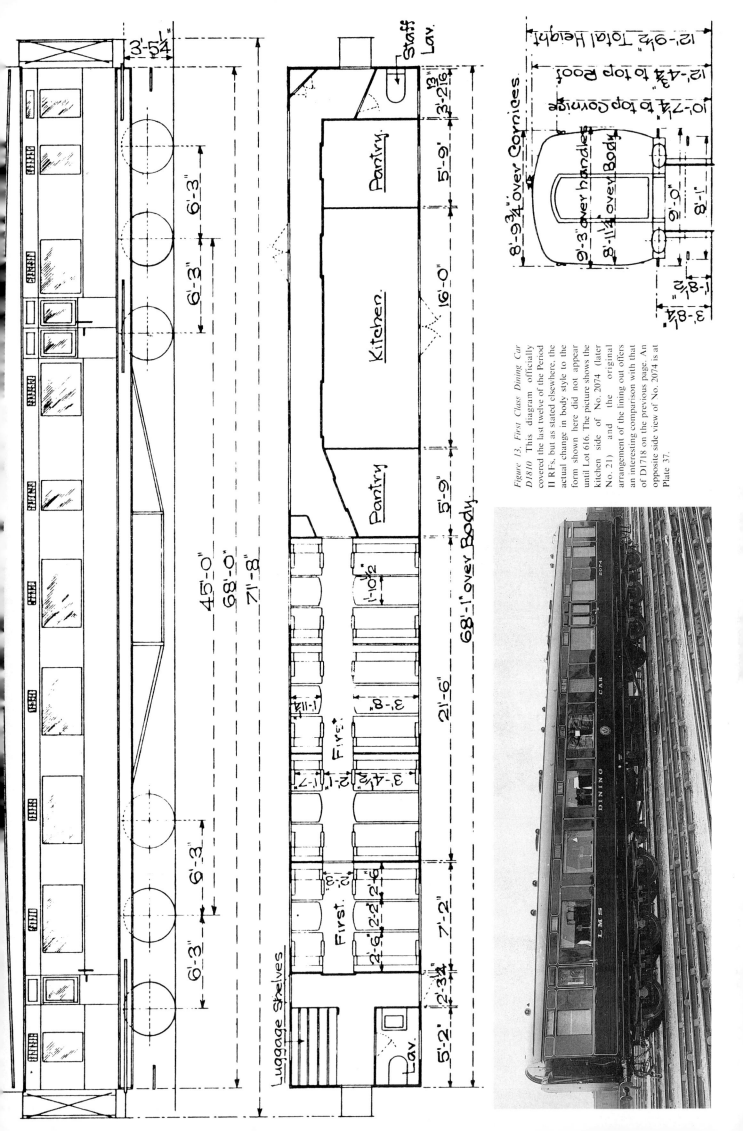

3'-5¼"

6'-3"

6'-3"

6'-9"

45'-0"

68'-0"

71'-8"

6'-3"

6'-3"

5'-2" 2'-3¼"

Luggage Shelves

Lav.

First.

2'-6" 2'-2" 2'-6"

7'-2"

First

3'-4½" 2'-1"

1'-11·1

3'-8"

21'-6"

1'-10½

Pantry

5'-9"

Kitchen

16'-0"

Pantry

5'-9" 3'-2½ 1'-3"

Staff Lav.

68'-1" over Body

12'-9½" Total Height

12'-4¾" to top Roof

10'-7¼" to top cornice

8'-9¾" over Cornices

9'-3" over handles

8'-11¼" over Body

1'-8"

9'-0"

1'-8½"

3'-8¼"

Figure 13, First Class Dining Car D1810 This diagram officially covered the last twelve of the Period II RFs, but as stated elsewhere, the actual change in body style to the form shown here did not appear until Lot 616. The picture shows the kitchen side of No. 2074 (later No. 21) and the original arrangement of the lining out offers an interesting comparison with that of D1718 on the previous page. An opposite side view of No. 2074 is at Plate 37.

Plates 57-58. These two official views are of especial interest in showing the first carriage of D1810, Lot 616 (No. 1864, later No. 19) at the beginning and towards the end of its active career. Close examination reveals that although little of structural significance has changed, the new BR livery has profoundly affected the overall appearance. No. M19 was photographed in 1949, apparently to demonstrate the new BR red and cream livery on older stock. In later years, the BR running number moved back to the traditional right hand end.

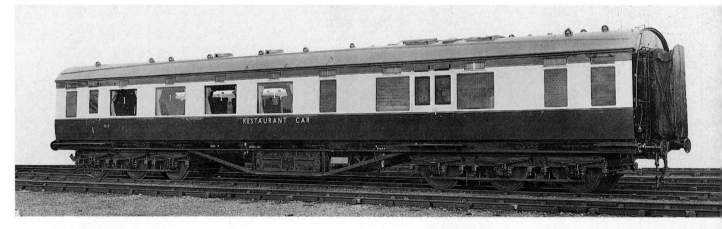

Plates 59-60. Two more interior views of the period II LMS RFs show the Butler's pantry of old No. 2592 (D1718) and a 'set' table from an unidentified example of Lot 616 (D1810) which shows yet another pattern of interior trim.

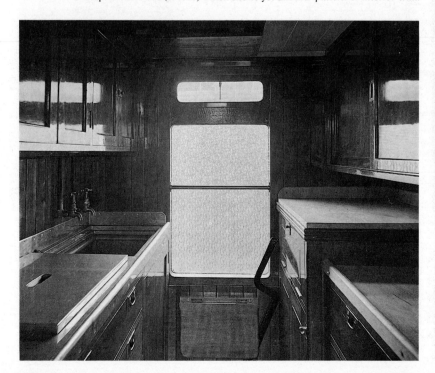

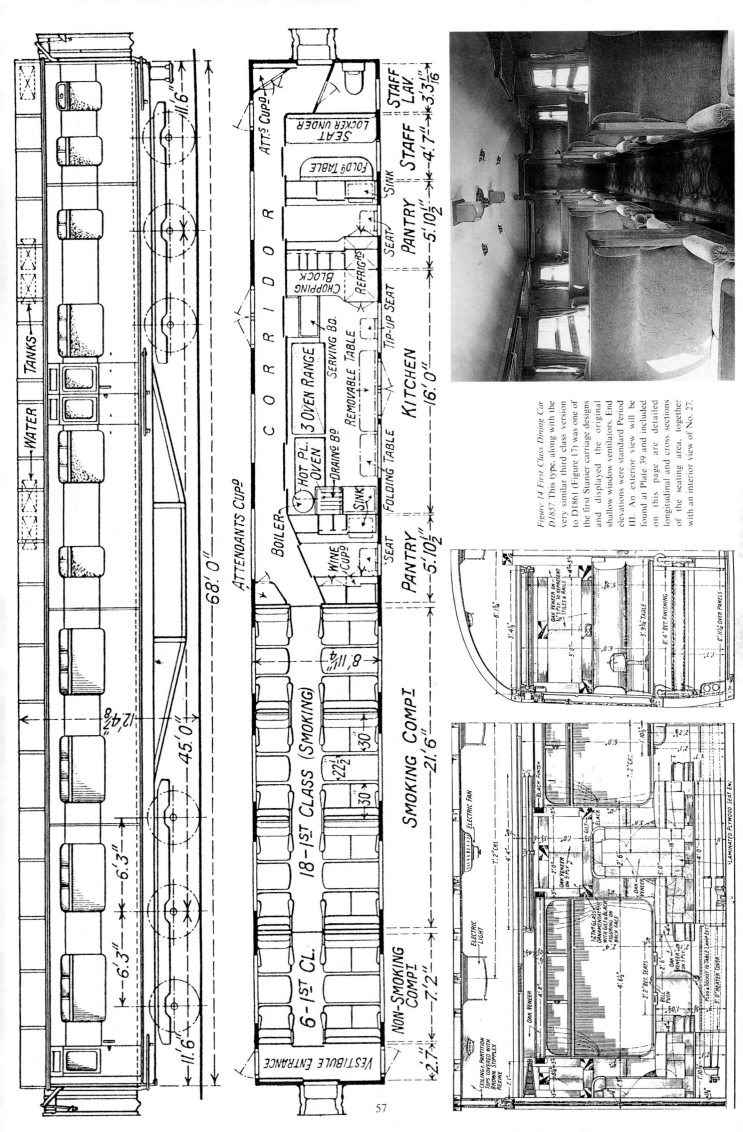

Figure 14 First Class Dining Car D1857 This type, along with the very similar third class version to D1861 (Figure 17) was one of the first Stanier carriage designs and displayed the original shallow window ventilators. End elevations were standard Period III. An exterior view will be found at Plate 39 and included on this page are detailed longitudinal and cross sections of the seating area, together with an interior view of No. 27.

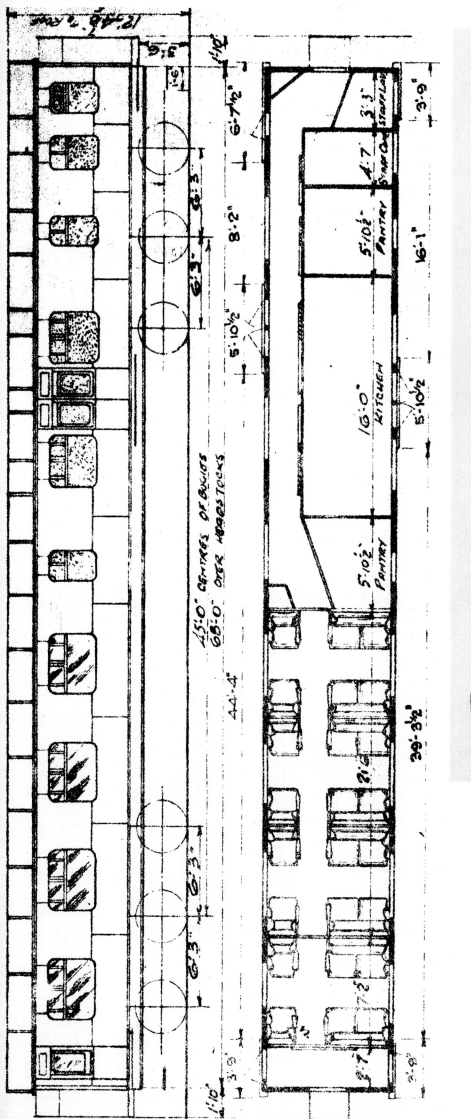

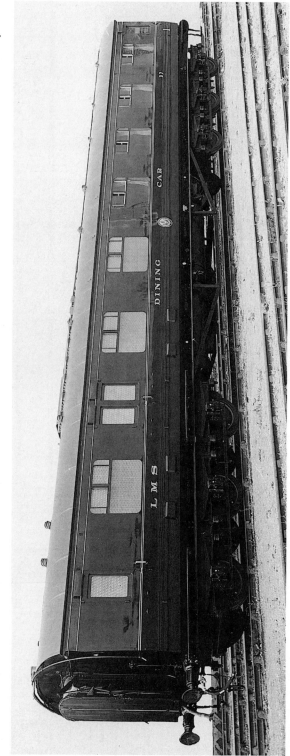

Figure 15 First Class Dining Car D1900 After D1857, all Period III RFs were built with deep window ventilators and simple livery to D1900, for which only the appended rather crude diagram can be offered. However, general dimensions were as for D1857 and detail features were broadly as for the third class D1901, of which detailed drawings are provided at Figure 18. The exterior views show Nos. 29 (the first example), 37 and 42 from Lots 732, 914 and 1046 respectively. The air scoops seen below the waist at the corridor side of the kitchen end of No. 37 (they were also on the same side of No. 42) offer evidence of the pressure heating/ventilation equipment on these two lots–see note to Table 2a. Note, (vide the opposite side view of No. 42), that they did not appear on both sides of the coaches.

Figure 15 First Class Dining car D1900 – continued

Plate 61. The kitchen of D1900 No. 42–not noticeably changed in its general arrangement from the Period II version shown at Plate 35.

Plates 62-64. These three interiors, taken together with that given with Figure 14, show that as with their Period II predecessors, most series of Period III RFs displayed different interior trims–would that we knew the colours! The vehicles featured are Nos 29 (plain luggage rack ends), 37 (striped upholstery with monogrammed luggage rack ends) and 42 (corner seat with wall fan)

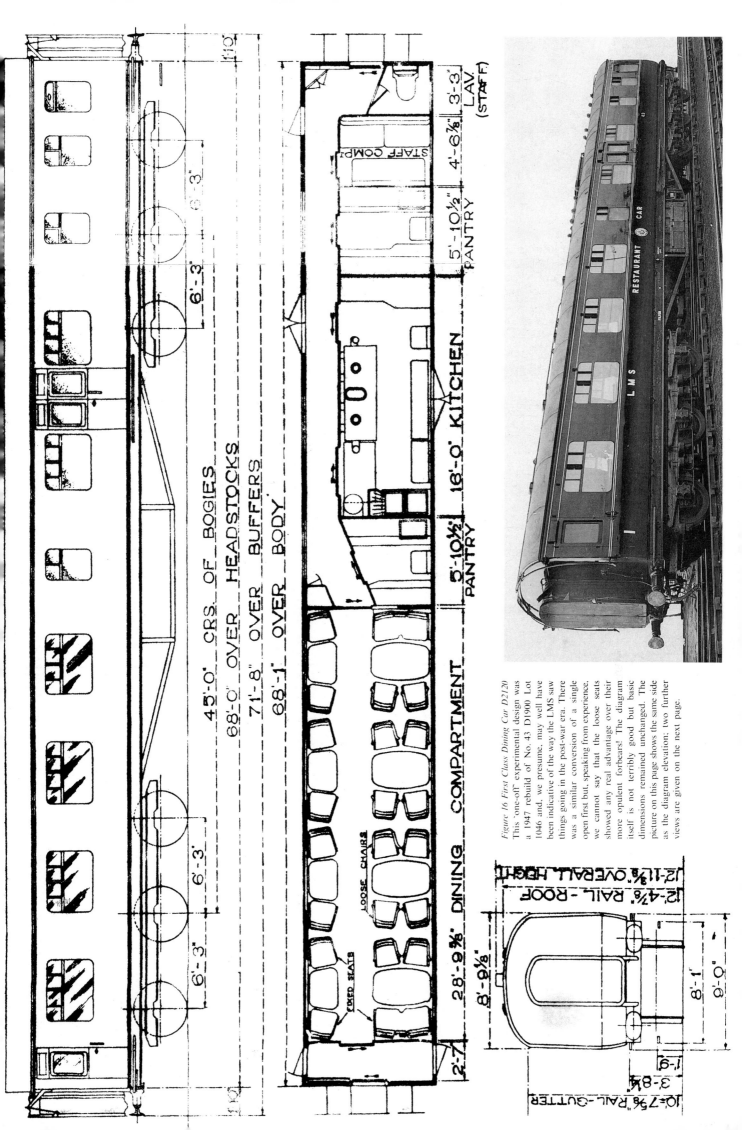

Figure 16 First Class Dining Car D2120)
This 'one-off' experimental design was a 1947 rebuild of No. 43 D1900 Lot 1046 and, we presume, may well have been indicative of the way the LMS saw things going in the post-war era. There was a similar conversion of a single open first but, speaking from experience, we cannot say that the loose seats showed any real advantage over their more opulent forbears! The diagram itself is not terribly good but basic dimensions remained unchanged. The picture on this page shows the same side as the diagram elevation; two further views are given on the next page.

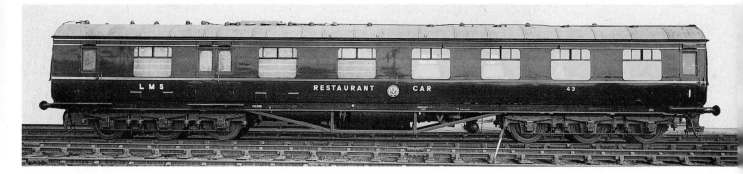

Plates 65-66. The broadside view of the corridor side of No. 43 shows how the original sliding window ventilators at the passenger end were replaced by the post war version with shorter moving portions. These views also give a good impression of what would have been the post-war standard LMS carriage insignia but for Nationalisation. They broadly follow the 1946 style for the locomotive fleet but, as with the locomotives, relatively few examples were to carry it. However, and for the first time officially, the base colour was named as 'maroon' and the lining as 'straw' (not crimson lake and chrome yellow); those who recall the few fully repainted LMS coaches from this short lived period (whether or not the new post-war insignia were carried), will recollect that the maroon was indeed a much darker shade than the old LMS colour and the lining much paler in hue. The close-up view was taken at Euston when No. 43 and the refurbished open first No. 7555 (seen beyond No. 43) were exhibited there.

Plates 67-68. A pair of obviously posed close-up views of the refurbished interior of No. 43–see also Plate 42 for a more general impression.

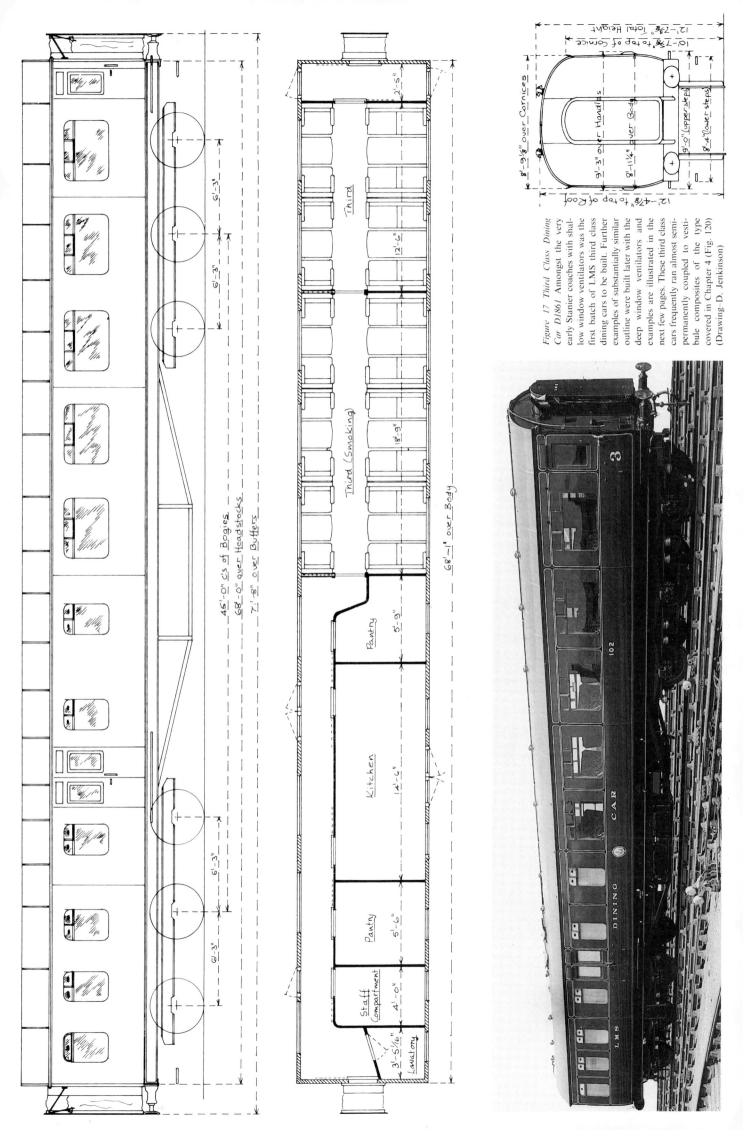

Figure 17 Third Class Dining Car D1861 Amongst the very early Stanier coaches with shallow window ventilators was the first batch of LMS third class dining cars to be built. Further examples of substantially similar outline were built later with the deep window ventilators and examples are illustrated in the next few pages. These third class cars frequently ran almost semi-permanently coupled to vestibule composites of the type covered in Chapter 4 (Fig. 120) (Drawing–D. Jenkinson)

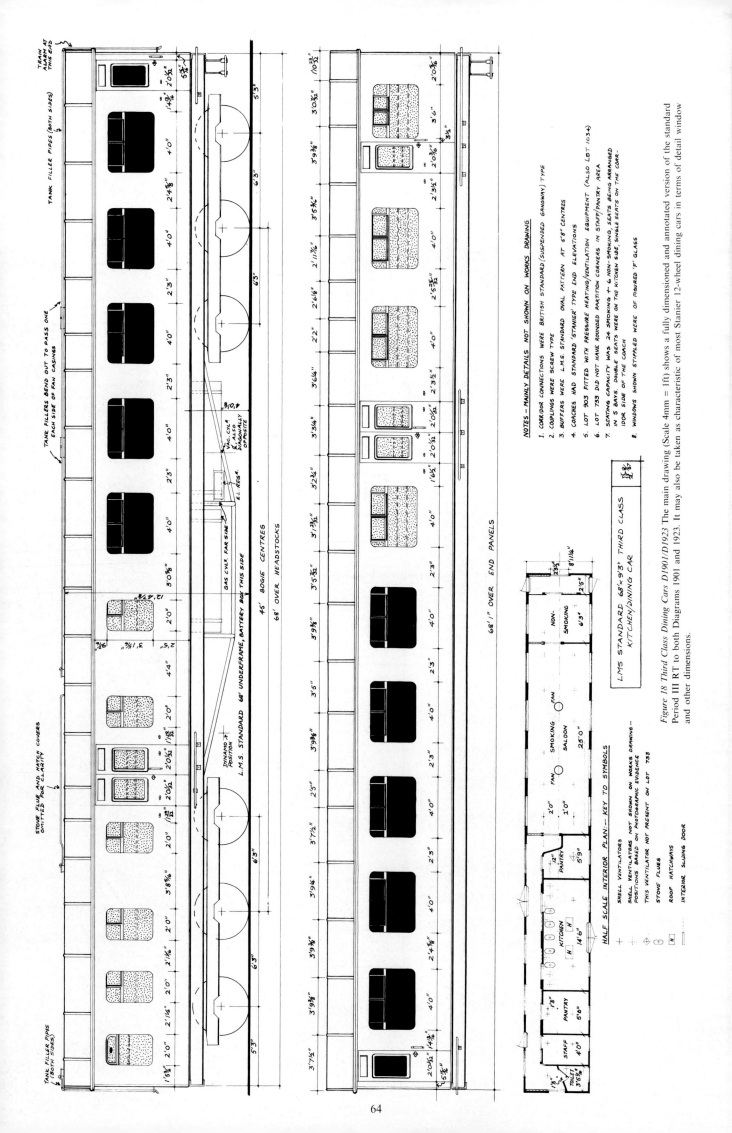

TRAIN ALARM AT THIS END

TANK FILLER PIPES (BOTH SIDES)

TANK FILLER PIPES (BOTH SIDES)

TANK FILLERS BEND OUT TO PASS ONE EACH SIDE OF FAN CASINGS

STOVE FLUE AND HATCH COVERS OMITTED FOR CLARITY

VAC. CYL. & ALSO DIAGONALLY OPPOSITE

E.L. REGR.

GAS CYLR. FAR SIDE

DYNAMO POSITION

L.M.S. STANDARD 68' UNDERFRAME, BATTERY BOX THIS SIDE

45' BOGIE CENTRES

68' OVER HEADSTOCKS

68' 1" OVER END PANELS

HALF SCALE INTERIOR PLAN:— KEY TO SYMBOLS

SHELL VENTILATORS NOT SHOWN ON WORKS DRAWING —
POSITIONS BASED ON PHOTOGRAPHIC EVIDENCE

THIS VENTILATOR NOT PRESENT ON LOT 733

STOVE FLUES

ROOF HATCHWAYS

INTERIOR SLIDING DOOR

STAFF 4'0"
PANTRY 5'6"
KITCHEN 14'6"
PANTRY 5'9"
SMOKING SALOON 25'0"
NON-SMOKING 6'3"

FAN
FAN

LMS STANDARD 68'x9'3" THIRD CLASS
KITCHEN/DINING CAR

NOTES — MAINLY DETAILS NOT SHOWN ON WORKS DRAWING

1. CORRIDOR CONNECTIONS WERE BRITISH STANDARD (SUSPENDED GANGWAY) TYPE
2. COUPLINGS WERE SCREW TYPE
3. BUFFERS WERE L.M.S. STANDARD OVAL PATTERN AT 6'8" CENTRES
4. COACHES HAD STANDARD 'STANIER' TYPE END ELEVATIONS
5. LOT 903 FITTED WITH PRESSURE HEATING/VENTILATION EQUIPMENT (ALSO LOT 1034)
6. LOT 733 DID NOT HAVE ROUNDED PARTITION CORNERS IN STAFF/PANTRY AREA
7. SEATING CAPACITY WAS 24 SMOKING + 6 NON-SMOKING, SEATS BEING ARRANGED IN 5 BAYS. DOUBLE SEATS WERE ON THE KITCHEN SIDE, SINGLE SEATS ON THE CORRIDOR SIDE OF THE COACH
8. WINDOWS SHOWN STIPPLED WERE OF FIGURED 'F' GLASS

Figure 18 Third Class Dining Cars D1901/D1923 The main drawing (Scale 4mm = 1ft) shows a fully dimensioned and annotated version of the standard Period III RT to both Diagrams 1901 and 1923. It may also be taken as characteristic of most Stanier 12-wheel dining cars in terms of detail window and other dimensions.

64

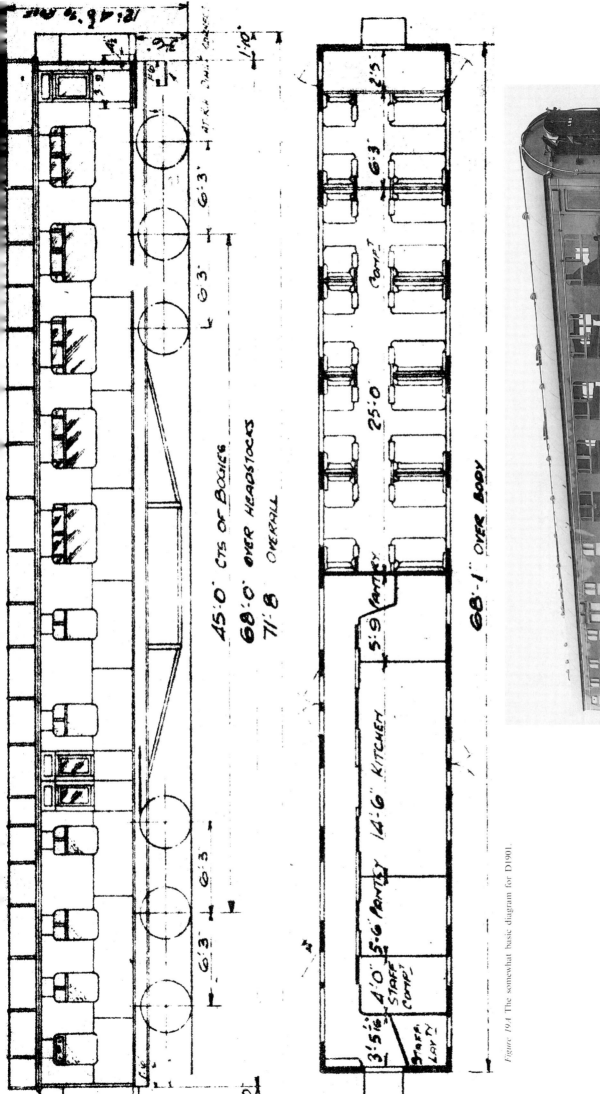

Figure 19.1 The somewhat basic diagram for D1901.

45'-0" CTS OF BOGIES
68'-0" OVER HEADSTOCKS
71'-8" OVERALL

6'-3"
6'-3"
6'-3"
6'-3"
6'-3"

1'-0"

6'-3"
6'-3"

68'-1" OVER BODY

25'-0"

6'-3"

14'-6" KITCHEN
5'-6" PANTRY
4'-0" STAFF COMPT
3'-5" STAFF LAV'Y
5'-9" PANTRY

Plates 69-70. The picture right and overleaf appeared in Volume 1 but are the only known official exterior views of the type. They show the kitchen side of D1901 (No. 118) and the corridor side of D1923 (No. 142). Note the pressure ventilation scoops fitted to the left of the double doors on No. 142, a feature of both Lots 903 and 1034 see note to Table 2a. They only appeared on the corridor side.

Plate 70

45'·0" CENTRES OF BOGIE

68'·0" OVER HEADSTOCKS

71'·8" OVER BUFFERS

68'·1" OVER BODY

PANTRY

KITCHEN

STAFF
COMPT

PANTRY

6'·3"   6'·3"   9'·0"   5'·8"   10'·6"   5'·0"

6'·3"   6'·3"

LMS   DINING CAR   142   3

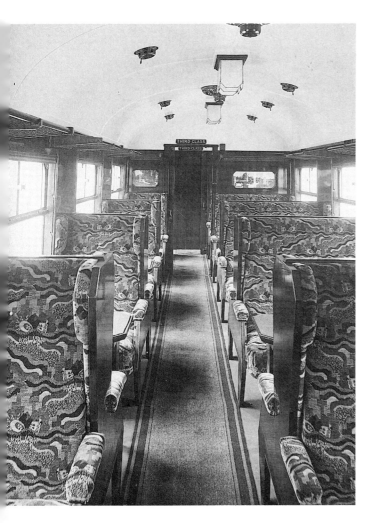 

Plates 71-72. These two interior comparisons of D1901 No. 118 (looking away from the kitchen end) and D1923 No. 124 (looking towards the kitchen end) show that just as with the first class versions, Period III third class dining cars were given different types of interior trim. As is almost always the case with this sort of detail, the interior colour scheme was not recorded.

Plates 73-74. Comparative views of the kitchens of the same two third class cars (Nos 118–with the reflections on the sink–and 124) show that though broadly similar, they were not wholly identical.

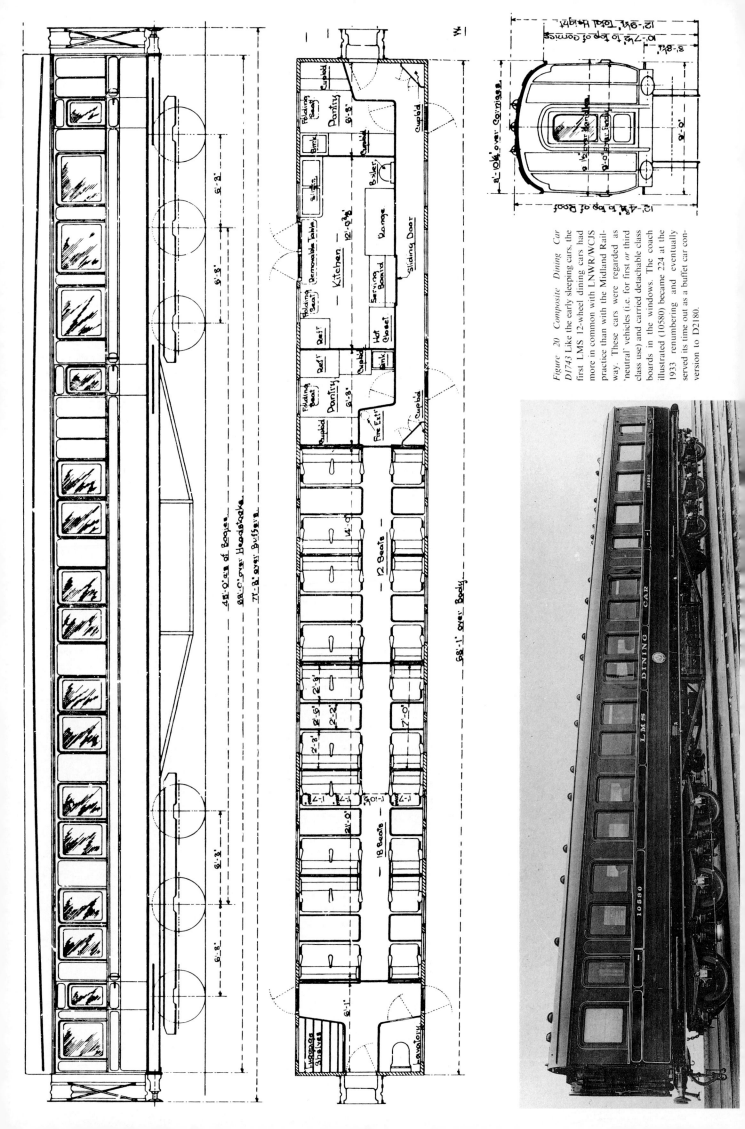

Figure 20 Composite Dining Car D1743 Like the early sleeping cars, the first LMS 12-wheel dining cars had more in common with LNWR/WCJS practice than with the Midland Railway. These cars were regarded as 'neutral' vehicles (i.e. for first or third class use) and carried detachable class boards in the windows. The coach illustrated (10580) became 224 at the 1933 renumbering and eventually served its time out as a buffet car conversion to D2180.

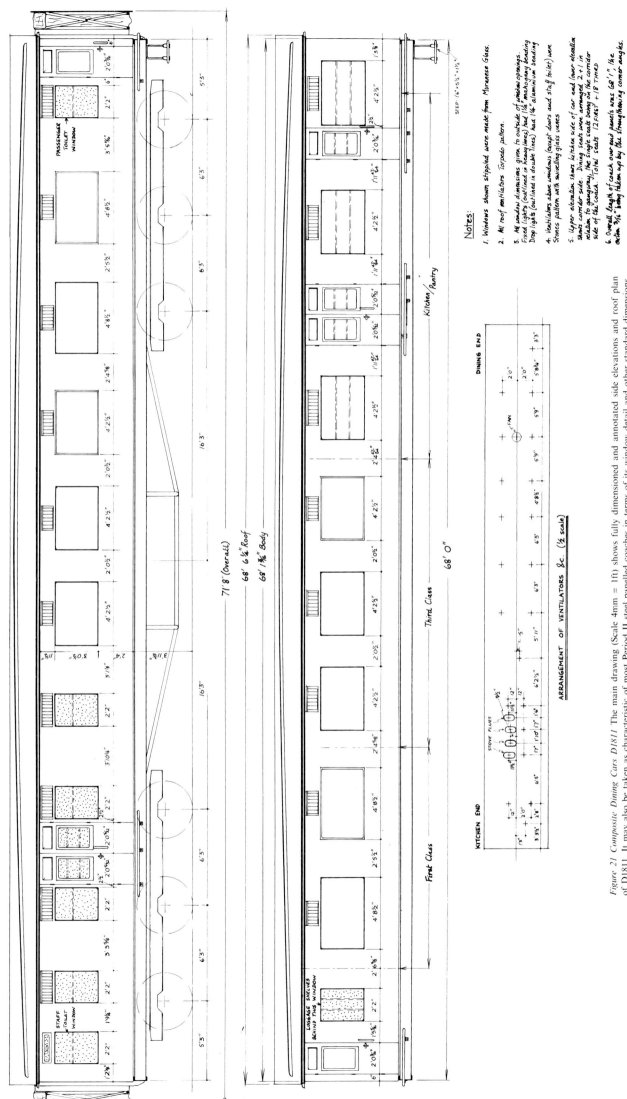

Notes:

1. Windows shown stippled were made from *Muranese Glass.*

2. All roof ventilators Torpedo pattern.

3. All window dimensions given to outside of window openings. Fixed lights (outlined in heavy lines) had 1½" mahogany beading. Drop lights (outlined in double lines) had 1¼" aluminium beading.

4. Ventilators above windows (except doors and staff (toilet)) were Stones pattern with swivelling glass vanes.

5. Upper elevation shows kitchen side of car and *lower elevation* shows corridor side. Dining seats were arranged 2 + 1 in relation to gangway, the single seats being on the corridor side of the coach. Total seats 12 *First* + 18 *Third*.

6. Overall length of coach over end panels was 68' 1", the extra ⅜" being taken up by the strengthening corner angles.

ARRANGEMENT OF VENTILATORS &c. (½ scale)

Figure 21 Composite Dining Cars D1811 The main drawing (Scale 4mm = 1ft) shows fully dimensioned and annotated side elevations and roof plan of D1811. It may also be taken as characteristic of most Period II steel panelled coaches in terms of its window detail and other standard dimensions. We also append the official diagram overleaf, one of the first to be issued under the new utilitarian scheme! The only known official view of this type is at Plate 38, and no interior views appear to have survived.

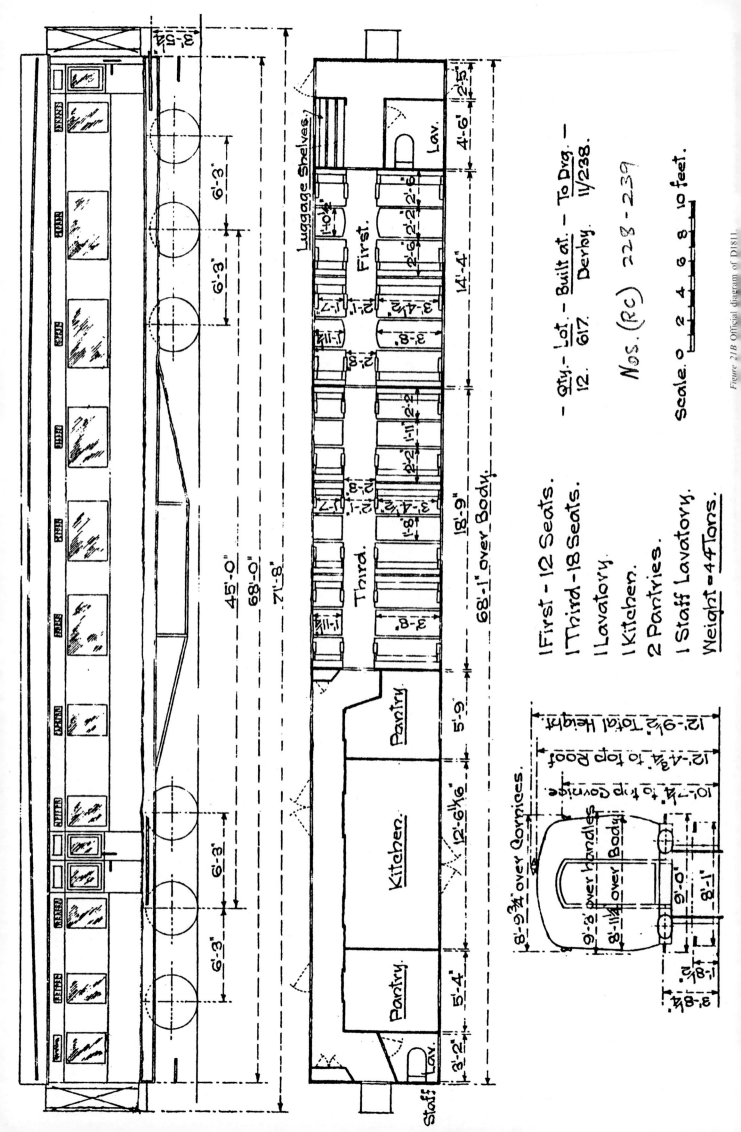

Figure 21B Official diagram of D181L.

Plates 75-76. By way of introduction to D1938, these two views show the first class interior of Period III composite dining car No. 241 and the kitchen of No. 250. The third class section of No. 241 had the same upholstery as third class car No. 124 (Plate 72) but with monogrammed luggage rack ends.

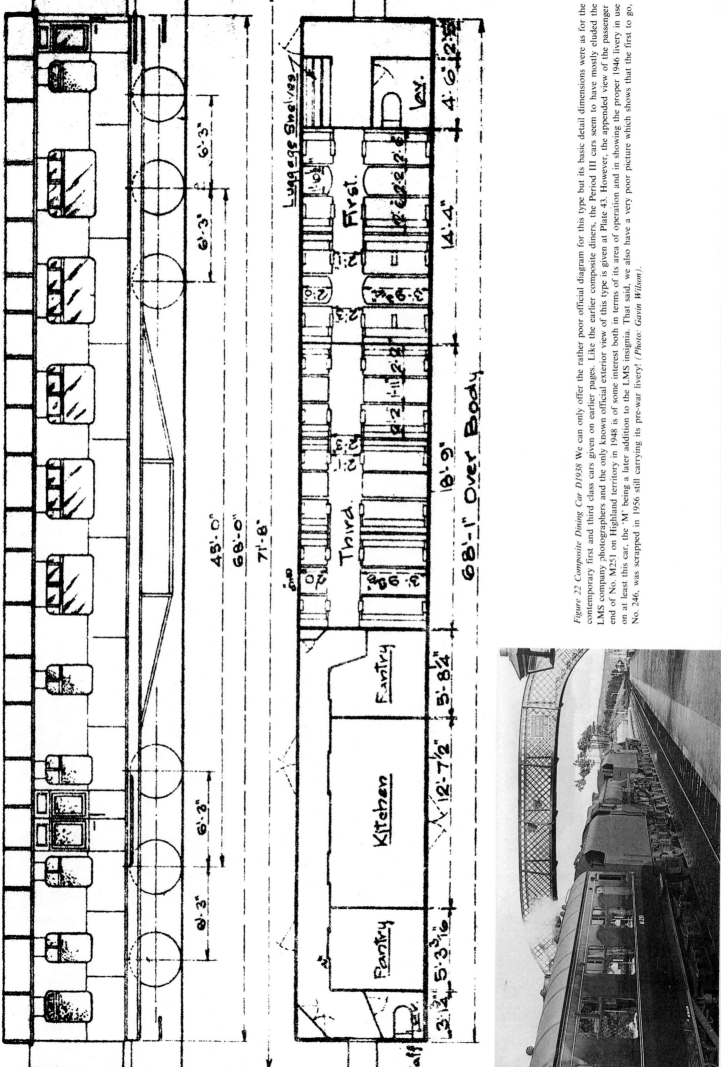

Figure 22 Composite Dining Car D1938 We can only offer the rather poor official diagram for this type but its basic detail dimensions were as for the contemporary first and third class cars given on earlier pages. Like the earlier composite diners, the Period III cars seem to have mostly eluded the LMS company photographers and the only known official exterior view of this type is given at Plate 43. However, the appended view of the passenger end of No. M251 on Highland territory in 1948 is of some interest both in terms of its area of operation and in showing the proper 1946 livery of the passenger on at least this car, the 'M' being a later addition to the LMS insignia. That said, we also have a very poor picture which shows that the first to go, No. 246, was scrapped in 1956 still carrying its pre-war livery! *(Photo: Gavin Wilson).*

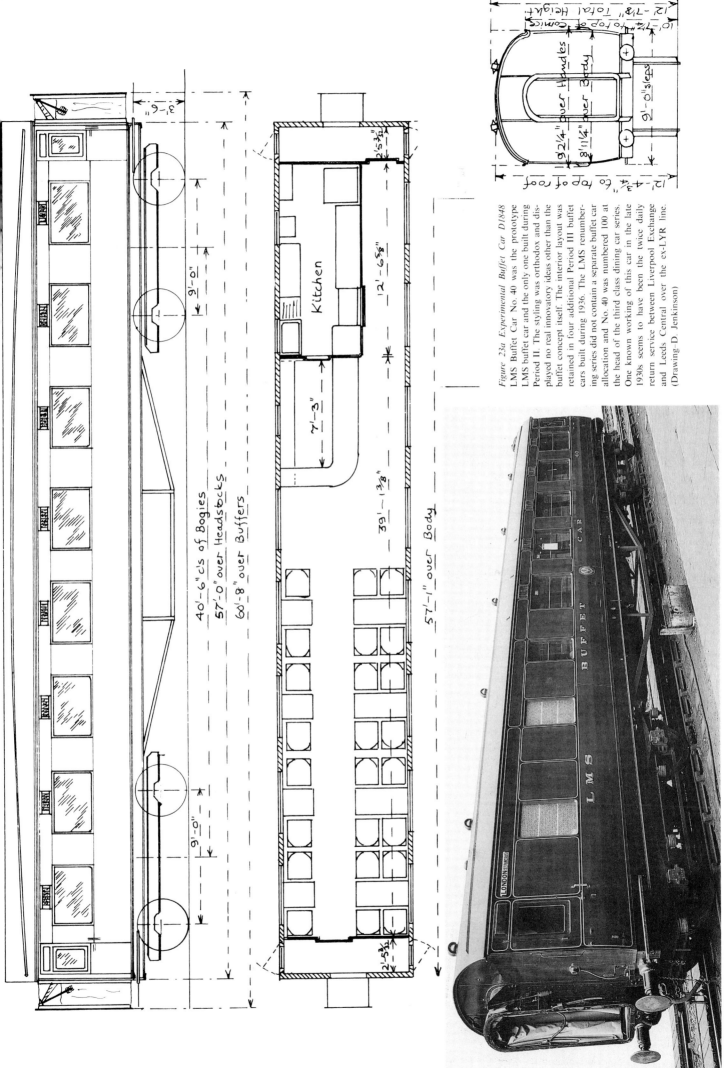

Figure 23a Experimental Buffet Car D1848
LMS Buffet Car No. 40 was the prototype LMS buffet car and the only one built during Period II. The styling was orthodox and displayed no real innovatory ideas other than the buffet concept itself. The interior layout was retained in four additional Period III buffet cars built during 1936. The LMS renumbering series did not contain a separate buffet car allocation and No. 40 was numbered 100 at the head of the third class dining car series. One known working of this car in the late 1930s seems to have been the twice daily return service between Liverpool Exchange and Leeds Central over the ex-LYR line. (Drawing–D. Jenkinson)

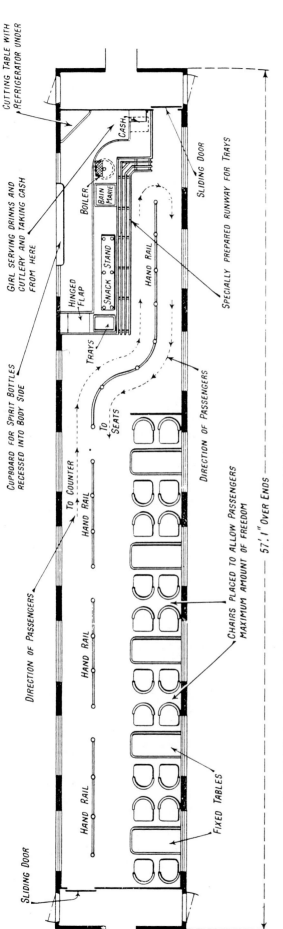

Figure 23b This plan shows the original floor layout of D1848 and the detailed labelling gives some indication of the contemporary LMS thinking as regards this vehicle.

Within the plan (Figure 23b):

SLIDING DOOR

DIRECTION OF PASSENGERS

HAND RAIL

HAND RAIL

HAND RAIL

FIXED TABLES

CHAIRS PLACED TO ALLOW PASSENGERS MAXIMUM AMOUNT OF FREEDOM

57.1" OVER ENDS

DIRECTION OF PASSENGERS

TO COUNTER

TO SEATS

HAND RAIL

TRAYS

SNACK STAND

HINGED FLAP

BAIN MARIE

BOILER

CASH

SLIDING DOOR

SPECIALLY PREPARED RUNWAY FOR TRAYS

CUPBOARD FOR SPIRIT BOTTLES RECESSED INTO BODY SIDE

GIRL SERVING DRINKS AND CUTLERY AND TAKING CASH FROM HERE

CUTTING TABLE WITH REFRIGERATOR UNDER

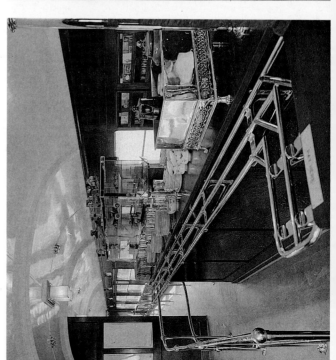

Plates 77-79. These self-explanatory interior views of D1848 show how the traditional wall finishes combined with the 'modern' furniture and much chrome plate to give a curiously ambivalent stylistic effect. The first two pictures show the car interior as originally conceived and the final view shows how the interior was later modified to set the layout for the subsequent D1948 cars. As usual, the colour scheme is not known.

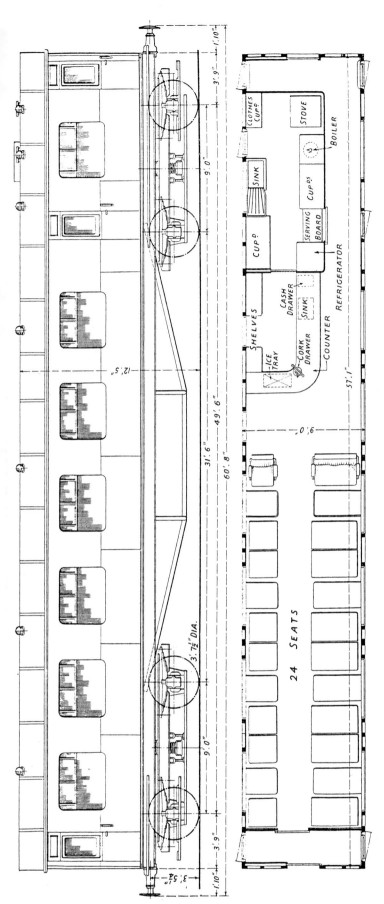

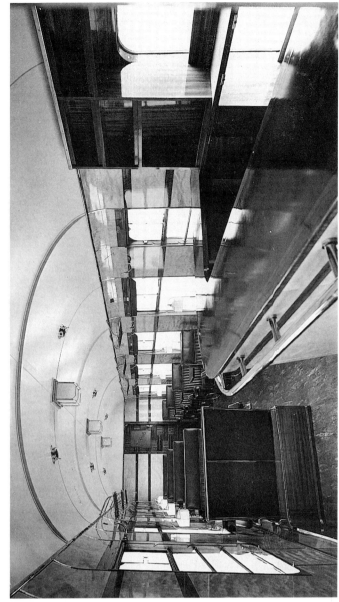

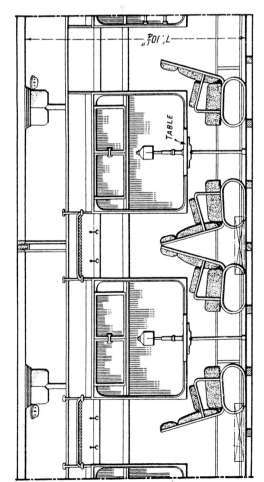

Figure 24 Buffet Car D1948 These drawings show elevation and plan of D1948 (end elevations were standard) together with a cross-section of the seating. The latter had tubular frames with Dunlopillo leather covered cushions, backs and other detail. The 'Odeon like' interior is well shown in the general view from the bar end. Other pictures of this type are at Plates 44 and 45.

SHELVES
ICE TRAY
CORK DRAWER
CUP'D.
CASH DRAWER
SINK
COUNTER
CLOTHES CUP'D.
SINK
SERVING BOARD
CUP'DS
STOVE
BOILER
REFRIGERATOR

24 SEATS

TABLE

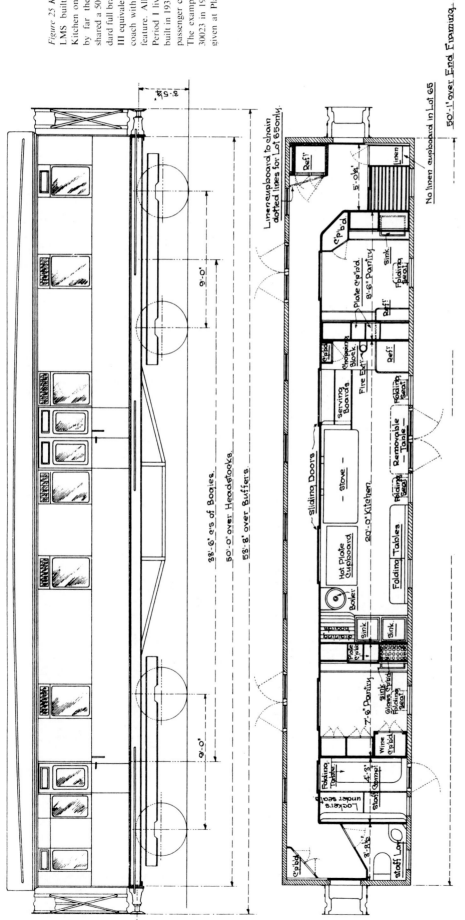

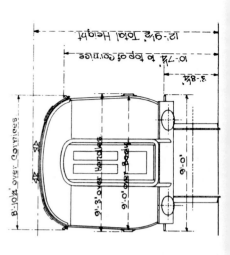

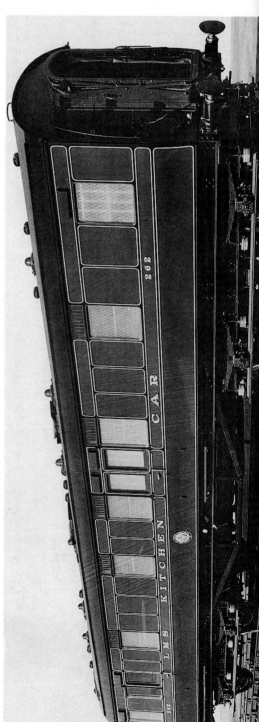

Figure 25 Kitchen Only Car D1697 The LMS built a very large number of Kitchen only cars and this design was by far the most numerous type. It shared a 50ft length with the LMS standard full brake and along with its Period III equivalent, was the only LMS design coach with gas lighting as a standard feature. All were given the fully lined Period I livery (except possibly 30072, built in 1932) to match the fully beaded passenger carrying coaches of the day. The example illustrated (262) became 30023 in 1933. A corridor side view is given at Plate 46.

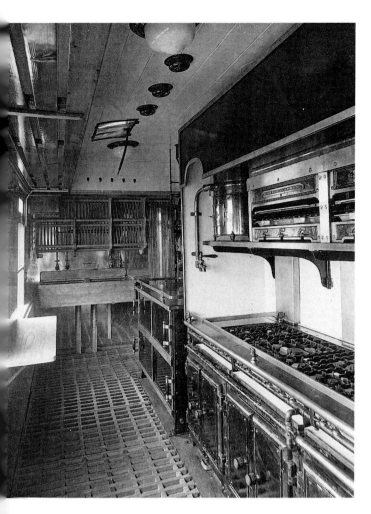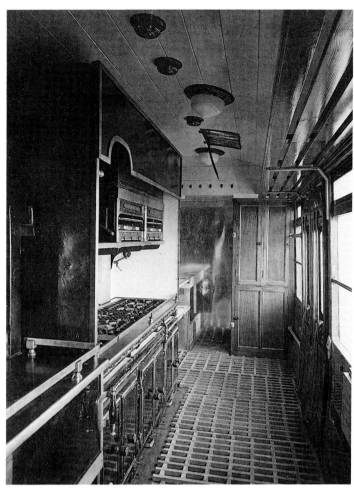

Plates 80-81. Within D1697, the kitchen itself was between 4ft and 7ft 6in longer than that found in any of the 12-wheel cars, thus allowing for more meals to be prepared. The layout, however, followed the familiar LMS form as seen here in the shape of both ends of the kitchen of No. 248 (later No. 30001).

Plate 82. When the diesel electric cars to D1855 were introduced, the LMS kept to its traditional kitchen layout, but the massive array of gas burners gave way to smooth topped hotplates and rather tidier plumbing in consequence. This is the interior of No. 30073 when new in March 1993.

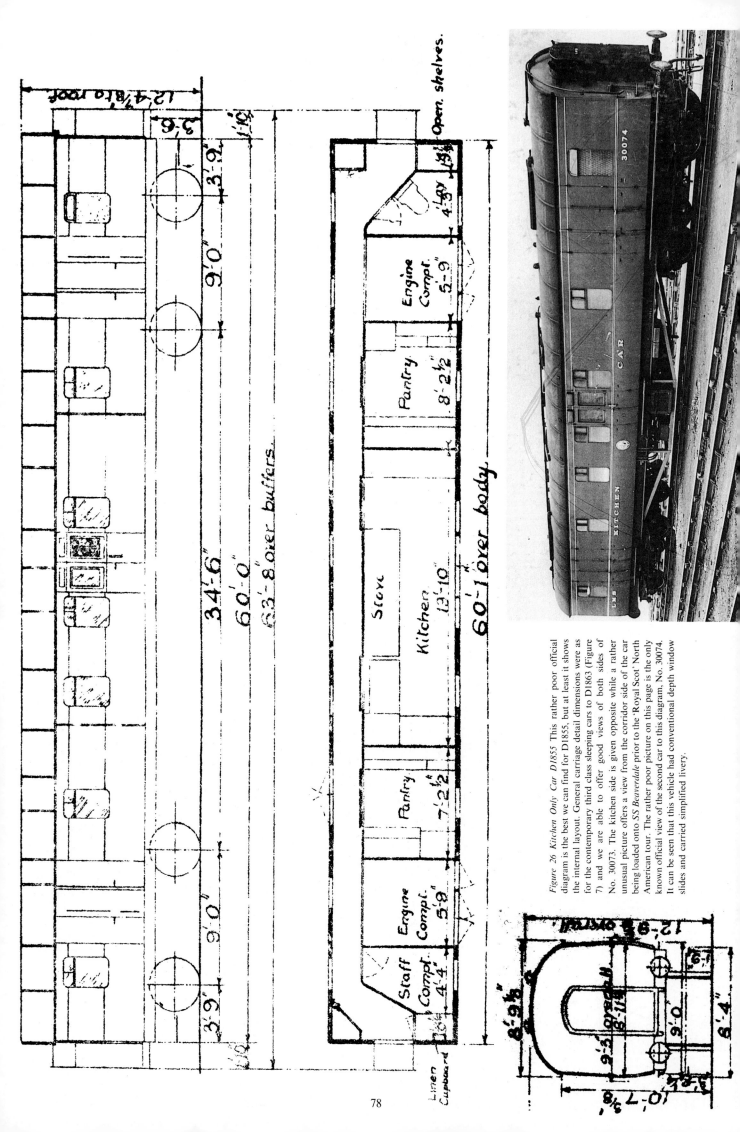

Figure 26 Kitchen Only Car D1855 This rather poor official diagram is the best we can find for D1855, but at least it shows the internal layout. General carriage detail dimensions were as for the contemporary third class sleeping cars to D1863 (Figure 7) and we are able to offer good views of both sides of No. 30073. The kitchen side is given opposite while a rather unusual picture offers a view from the corridor side of the car being loaded onto *SS Beaverdale* prior to the 'Royal Scot' North American tour. The rather poor picture on this page is the only known official view of the second car to this diagram, No. 30074. It can be seen that this vehicle had conventional depth window slides and carried simplified livery.

Plate 83. No. 30075, a one-off to Lot 779, was the first 50ft Stanier kitchen car, undoubtedly why this ex-works view was taken at Wolverton in 1934.

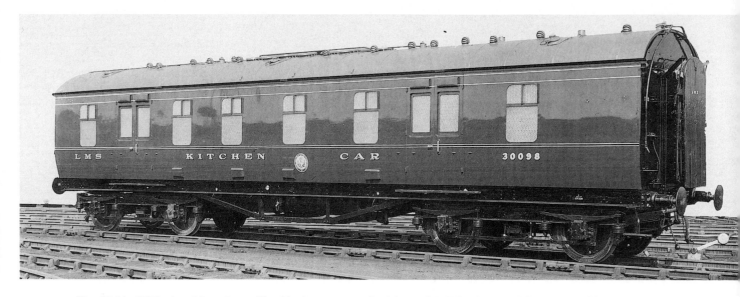

Plate 84. No. 30098, viewed from the corridor side, shows an example of the small 1937 batch to Lot 1039. Note, as with the contemporary dining cars, the presence of air inlet scoops on the lower body panels.

Plate 85. This is No. M30087M in BR red and cream livery at Birmingham New Street in March 1955. This was one of the largest single batch of D1912 cars (Lot 956) and also one of the six which were modified in 1937 for the original "Coronation Scot" sets–see also Plate 49. The example shown here has now received reinforcement strips over some of the panel joins. *(J. E. Cull)*

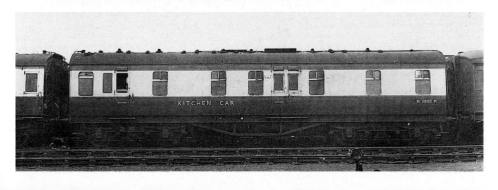

Plate 86. No. M30103M was one of Lot 1081, built in 1938. The date and location of this view are not known but we suspect much the same time as the previous example (c.1955). This example, like most, retained its flush exterior panelling until withdrawal. *(The late Gavin Wilson collection)*

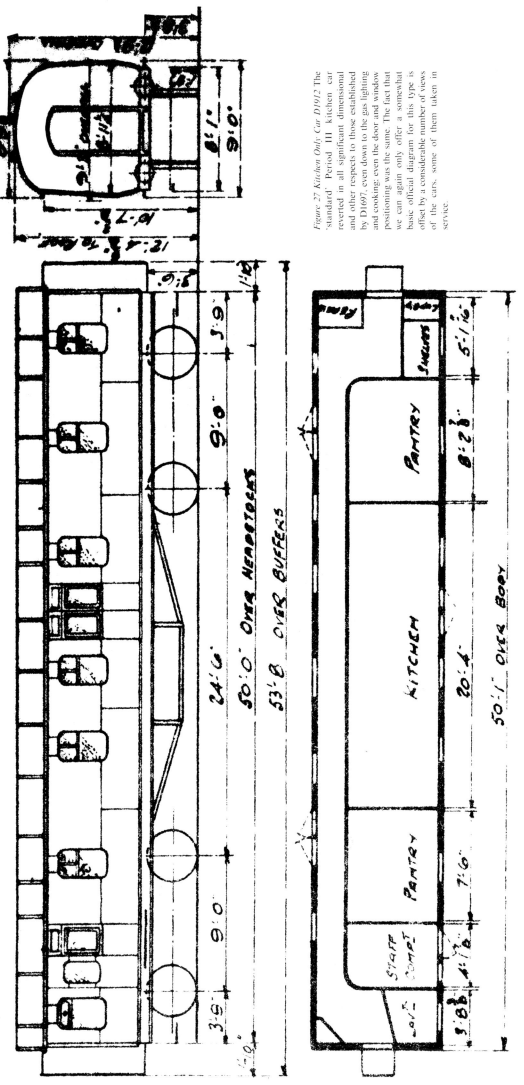

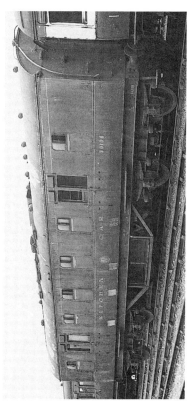

Figure 27 Kitchen Only Car D1912 The 'standard' Period III kitchen car reverted in all significant dimensional and other respects to those established by D1697, even down to the gas lighting and cooking; even the door and window positioning was the same. The fact that we can again only offer a somewhat basic official diagram for this type is offset by a considerable number of views of the cars, some of them taken in service.

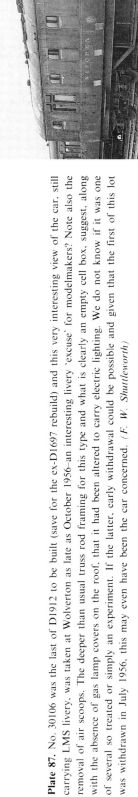

Plate 87. No. 30106 was the last of D1912 to be built (save for the ex-D1697 rebuild) and this very interesting view of the car, still carrying LMS livery, was taken at Wolverton as late as October 1956–an interesting livery 'excuse' for modelmakers? Note also the removal of air scoops. The deeper than usual truss rod framing for this type and what is clearly an empty cell box, suggest, along with the absence of gas lamp covers on the roof, that it had been altered to carry electric lighting. We do not know if it was one of several so treated or simply an experiment. If the latter, early withdrawal could be possible and given that the first of this lot was withdrawn in July 1956, this may even have been the car concerned. *(F. W. Shuttleworth)*

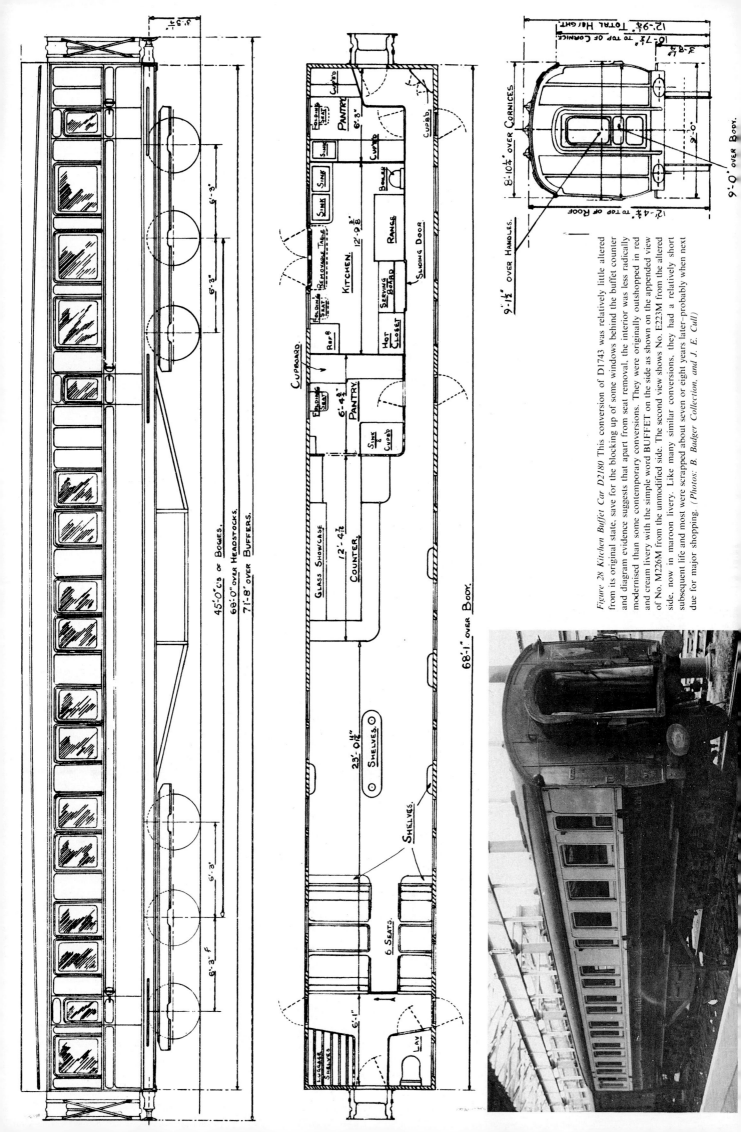

6'-3"

45'-0" C'S OF BOGIES.
60'-0" OVER HEADSTOCKS.
71'-8" OVER BUFFERS.

6'-3"   6'-3"   6'-3"

CUPBD
PANTRY 6'-3"
SINK
SINK
FOLDING SEAT
REMOVABLE TABLE
FOLDING SEAT
CUPBD
CUPBD
BOILER
Ref'r
KITCHEN. 12'-9⅛"
SERVING BOARD
RANGE
HOT CLOSET
SLIDING DOOR.
CUPBOARD.
FOLDING SEAT
6'-4½" PANTRY.
SINK & CUPBD
GLASS SHOWCASE
12'-4⅛"
COUNTER.
23'-1⅛"
SHELVES.
SHELVES.
6 SEATS.
6'-1"
LUGGAGE SHELVES.
LAV.

68'-1" OVER BODY.

12'-9½" TOTAL HEIGHT.
10'-7½" TO TOP OF CORNICE.
3'-8½"
8'-10¾" OVER CORNICES.
2'-0"
12'-4¾" TO TOP OF ROOF.
9'-0" OVER BODY.
9'-1½" OVER HANDLES.

Figure 28 Kitchen Buffet Car D2180 This conversion of D1743 was relatively little altered from its original state, save for the blocking up of some windows behind the buffet counter and diagram evidence suggests that apart from seat removal, the interior was less radically modernised than some contemporary conversions. They were originally outshopped in red and cream livery with the simple word BUFFET on the side as shown on the appended view of No. M226M from the unmodified side. The second view shows No. E223M from the altered side, now in maroon livery. Like many similar conversions, they had a relatively short subsequent life and most were scrapped about seven or eight years later–probably when next due for major shopping. (*Photos: B. Badger Collection, and J. E. Cull*)

Figure 28 – continued

Plates 88-89. These two views of the exterior and interior of No. M105M (Figure 29 overleaf) are taken from the opposite direction to that above.

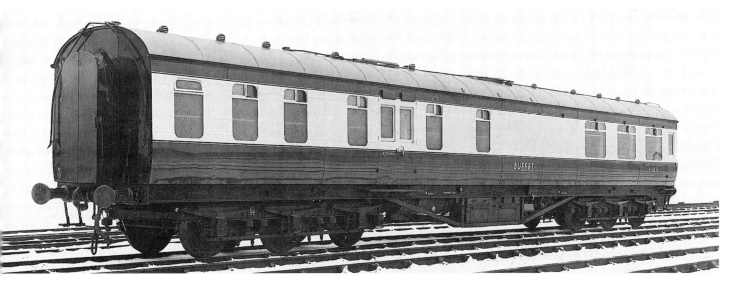

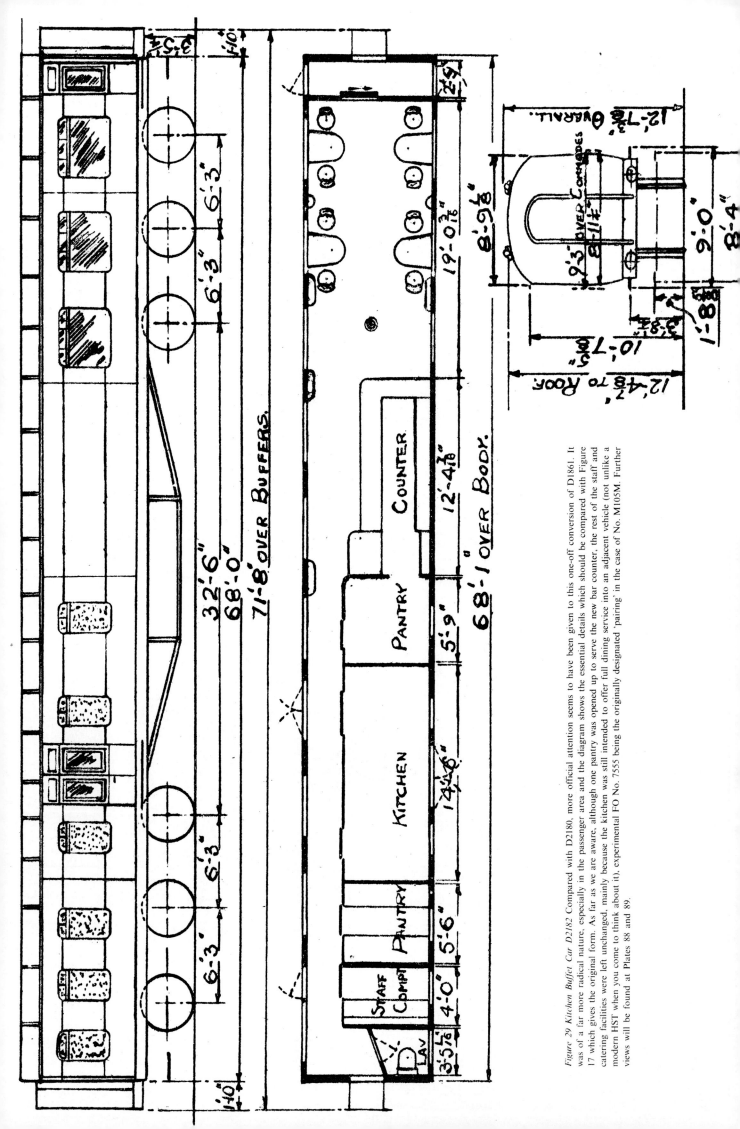

Figure 29 Kitchen Buffet Car D2182 Compared with D2180, more official attention seems to have been given to this one-off conversion of D1861. It was of a far more radical nature, especially in the passenger area and the diagram shows the essential details which should be compared with Figure 17 which gives the original form. As far as we are aware, although one pantry was opened up to serve the new bar counter, the rest of the staff and catering facilities were left unchanged, mainly because the kitchen was still intended to offer full dining service into an adjacent vehicle (not unlike a modern HST when you come to think about it), experimental FO No. 7555 being the originally designated 'pairing' in the case of No. M105M. Further views will be found at Plates 88 and 89.

The following labels appear on the plan view:

STAFF COMP'T · PANTRY · KITCHEN · PANTRY · COUNTER

Dimensions shown: 3'-5½", 4'-0", 5'-6", 14'-4⅝", 5'-9", 12'-4⅝", 19'-0⅝", 2'-9"

68'-1 OVER BODY.

Side elevation dimensions: 1'-0", 6'-3", 6'-3", 6'-3", 32'-6", 68'-0", 71'-8 OVER BUFFERS, 6'-3", 6'-3", 3'-5¾", 1'-0"

End view dimensions: 12'-7⅞" OVERALL, 9'-3" OVER CORNICES, 8'-11¼", 9'-0", 8'-4", 8'-9½", 12'-4⅞" TO ROOF, 10'-7½", 3'-8¾", 1'-8¾"

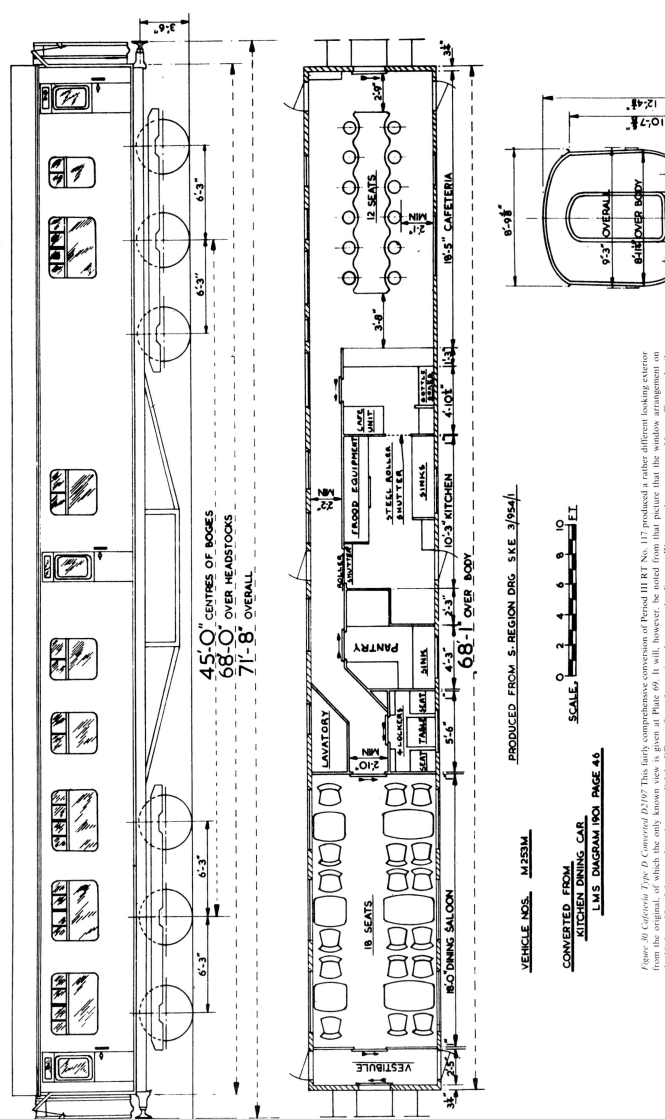

3'-6"

6'-3"

6'-3"

45'-0" CENTRES OF BOGES

68'-0" OVER HEADSTOCKS

71'-8" OVERALL

6'-3"

6'-3"

3¾"

2'-5⅝"

12 SEATS

2'-1" MIN

18'-5" CAFETERIA

3'-8"

11'-3"

BOTTLE RACK

CAFE UNIT

FROOD EQUIPMENT

2'-2" MIN

STEEL ROLLER SHUTTER

SINKS

4'-10½"

10'-3" KITCHEN

ROLLER SHUTTER

2'-3"

PANTRY

SINK

4'-3"

68'-1" OVER BODY

LAVATORY

4 LOCKERS

SEAT TANK HEAT

5'-6"

2'-10" MIN

18 SEATS

18'-0" DINING SALOON

VESTIBULE

1"

2'-5"

3¾"

3¾"

12'-4½"

10'-7"

3'-8⅛"

9'-3" OVERALL

8'-9¾"

8'-11⅛" OVER BODY

9'-0"

PRODUCED FROM S. REGION DRG. SKE 3/954/1

SCALE, 0 2 4 6 8 10 FT

VEHICLE NOS. M253M

CONVERTED FROM
KITCHEN DINING CAR
L M S DIAGRAM 1901 PAGE 46

Figure 30 Cafeteria Type D Converted D2197 This fairly comprehensive conversion of Period III RT No. 117 produced a rather different looking exterior from the original, of which the only known view is given at Plate 69. It will, however, be noted from that picture that the window arrangement on the kitchen side of the actual carriage was slightly different from the version shown on the diagram. We regret that we are unable to offer any details of the opposite side elevation.

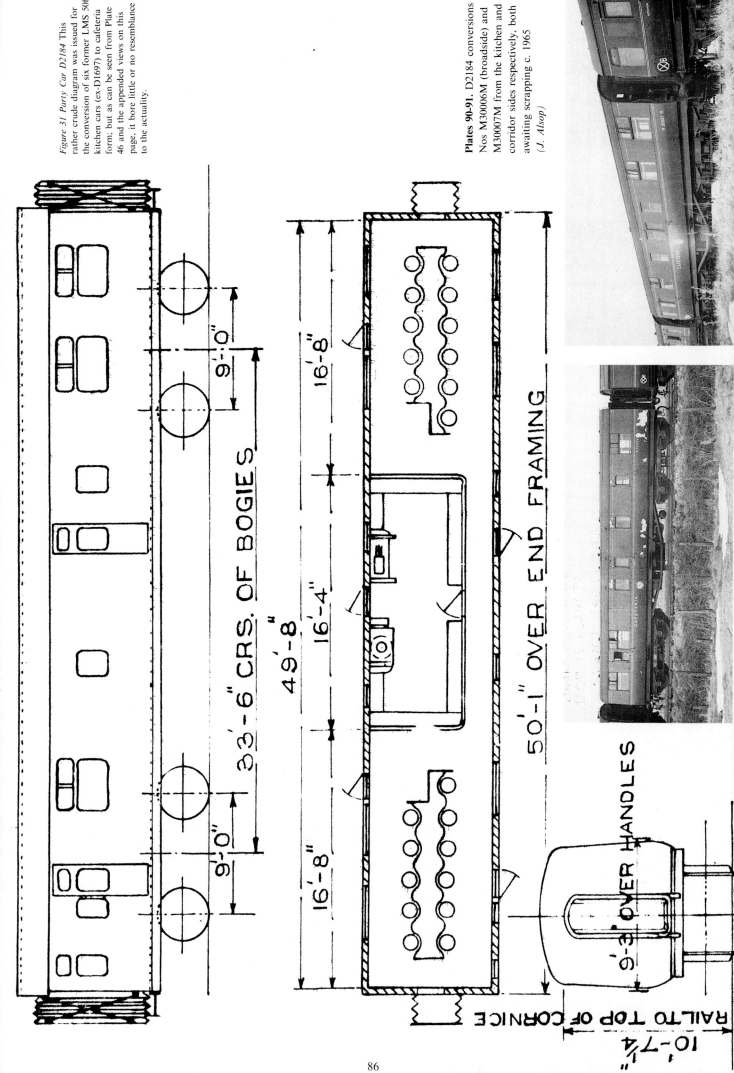

Figure 31 Party Car D2184 This rather crude diagram was issued for the conversion of six former LMS 50ft kitchen cars (ex-D1697) to cafeteria form; but as can be seen from Plate 46 and the appended views on this page, it bore little or no resemblance to the actuality.

Plates 90-91. D2184 conversions Nos M30006M (broadside) and M30007M from the kitchen and corridor sides respectively, both awaiting scrapping c. 1965
(J. Alsop)

9'-0"

9'-0"

33'-6" CRS. OF BOGIES

49'-8"

16'-8"

16'-4"

16'-8"

16'-8"

50'-1" OVER END FRAMING

9'-3" OVER HANDLES

10'-7¼"

RAIL TO TOP OF CORNICE

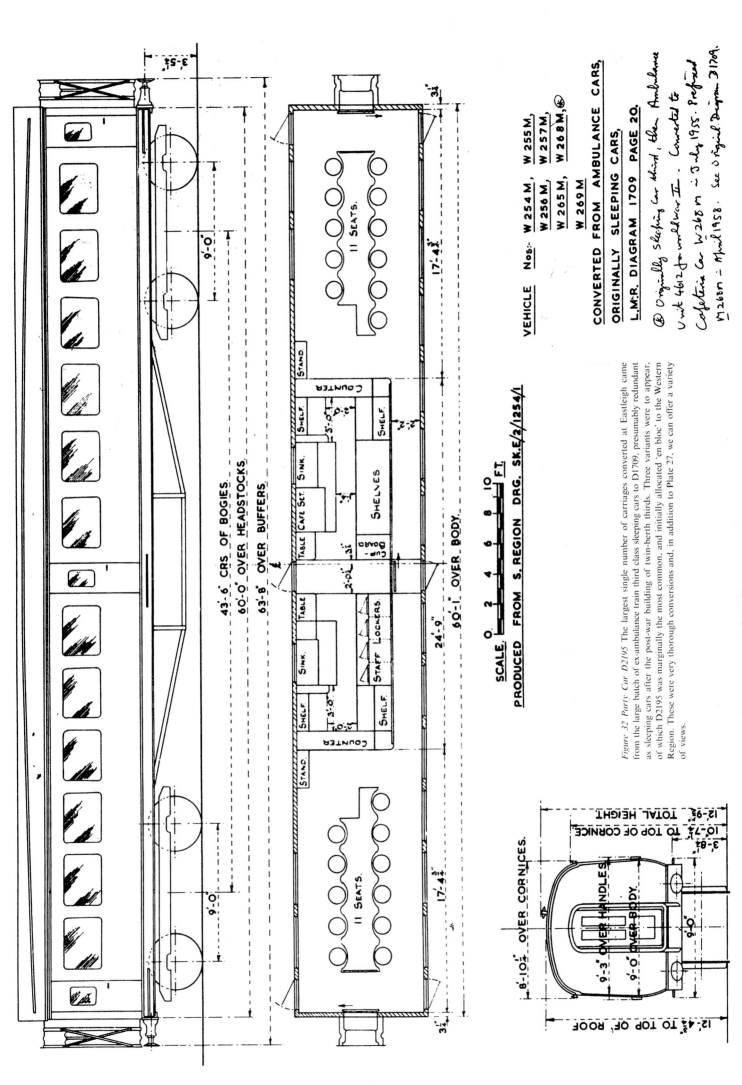

3'-5½"

9'-0"

43'-6" CRS OF BOGIES.

60'-0" OVER HEADSTOCKS.

63'-8" OVER BUFFERS.

9'-0"

17'-4¾"

3¼"

3¼"

11 SEATS.

STAND

COUNTER

SHELF.

SHELF.

2'-0"

SHELVES

CAFE SET.

SINK.

TABLE

DRAWERS

2'-0½"

TABLE

SINK

STAFF LOCKERS.

SHELF

3'-0"

SHELF.

COUNTER

STAND.

24'-9"

60'-1" OVER BODY.

17'-4¾"

11 SEATS.

3¼"

SCALE. 0 2 4 6 8 10 FT.

PRODUCED FROM S. REGION DRG. SK.E/2/1254/1

12'-9⅝" TOTAL HEIGHT.

10'-7¾" TO TOP OF CORNICE.

3'-8½"

9'-3" OVER HANDLES.

9'-0" OVER BODY.

9'-0"

8'-10½" OVER CORNICES.

12'-4½" TO TOP OF ROOF.

VEHICLE Nos:- W254M, W255M,
W256M, W257M,
W265M, W268M, ⊛
W269M

CONVERTED FROM AMBULANCE CARS,
ORIGINALLY SLEEPING CARS,
L.M.R. DIAGRAM 1709 PAGE 20.

⊛ Originally sleeping car third, the Ambulance
Unit 4612 formed Ambulance II. Converted to
Cafeteria Car W268M ~ 3 July 1955. Prefixed
M268M ~ April 1958. See Original Diagram D1709.

Figure 32 Party Car D2195 The largest single number of carriages converted at Eastleigh came from the large batch of ex-ambulance train third class sleeping cars to D1709, presumably redundant as sleeping cars after the post-war building of twin-berth thirds. Three variants were to appear, of which D2195 was marginally the most common, and initially allocated 'en bloc' to the Western Region. These were very thorough conversions and, in addition to Plate 27, we can offer a variety of views.

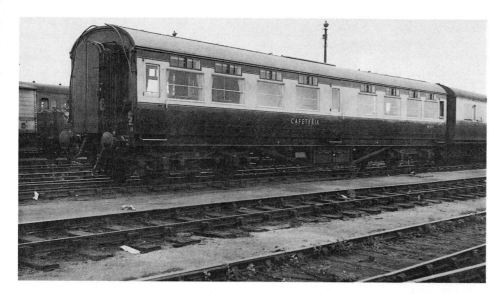

Plates 92-93. Opposite side views of the first and last examples of D2195, Nos W254M (corridor side) and W269M at Tyseley on 23rd June 1955, very soon after entering service. (*Both J. E. Cull*)

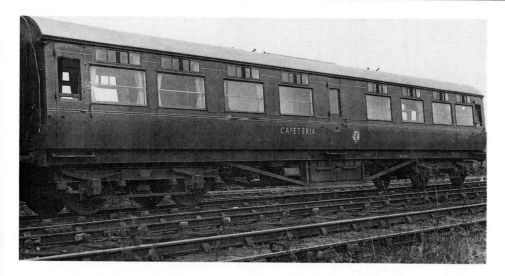

Plates 94-95. Later in their lives, some (possibly all) examples of D2195 were transferred to the LM Region. These views show two of them in BR maroon livery. The full elevation shows No. M255M at an unknown location while the close up view shows No. M268M at Wolverton in February 1965. (*Authors' Collection*)

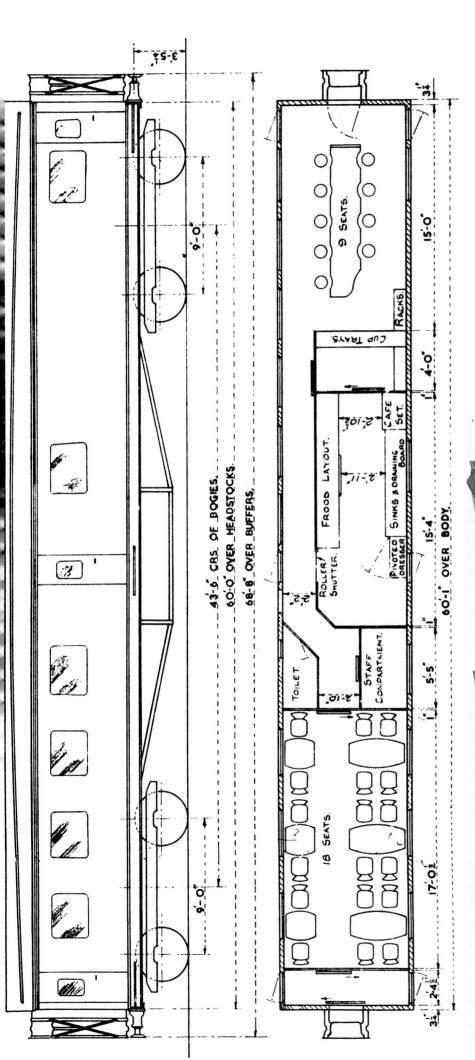

Plate 96. This view of D2196 shows the kitchen side elevation of No. M267M in maroon livery and awaiting scrap in 1962. (J. Alsop)

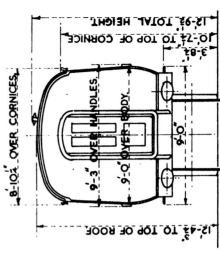

Figure 33 Cafeteria Car Type D Converted D2196 The second and third conversions from D1709 were classified 'Cafeteria' as well as being branded thus, and the difference between these and the 'Party' cars lay in the fact that the 'proper' cafeterias had tables and chairs at one end. Their initial allocation was to the LM Region and they are believed to have remained there throughout.

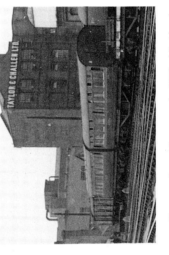

Plate 97. This enlargement from a more general view is included solely because it shows the corridor side of D2196 (nearer to the camera) sufficiently clearly to indicate the rather different window arrangement on this side of the vehicle. The picture was taken on 15th September 1962 at Birmingham Snow Hill and shows No. M270M. Beyond it is No. W7853S, a cafeteria conversion of a former Southern Railway carriage. (J. E. Cull)

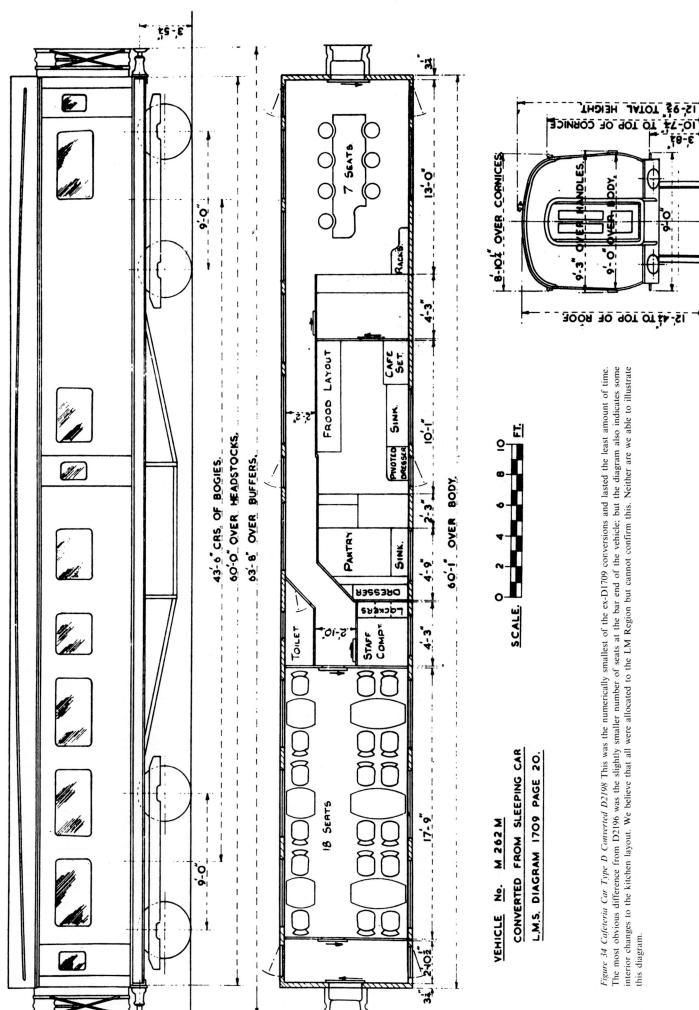

VEHICLE No. M 262 M

CONVERTED FROM SLEEPING CAR

L.M.S. DIAGRAM 1709 PAGE 20.

SCALE.

0 2 4 6 8 10
FT.

Figure 34 Cafeteria Car Type D Converted D2198 This was the numerically smallest of the ex-D1709 conversions and lasted the least amount of time. The most obvious difference from D2196 was the slightly smaller number of seats at the bar end of the vehicle; but the diagram also indicates some interior changes to the kitchen layout. We believe that all were allocated to the LM Region but cannot confirm this. Neither are we able to illustrate this diagram.

Chapter 3 – Side Corridor Coaches

Period I designs; Period II designs; Period III designs; Summary Tables; Survey by Diagrams

WHEN one considers the grand total of coaches built to LMS designs, it is a little surprising to find that only in the side corridor type of vehicle were all possible design and style phases represented, from the early all-door versions of the 1923-30 period to the post-nationalisation composites.

PERIOD I DESIGNS

For the first four years or so after grouping, the Period I LMS side corridor coach was characterised by a full complement of outside doors to the compartments and most vehicles were mounted on the 57ft standard underframe. However, during the first year or two, a few small batches of non-standard coaches emerged from Wolverton some of which might almost be considered as the last of the LNWR coach designs, with, of course, the notable exception of the 12 wheel sleepers and diners.

The first of these non-standard batches was a strange little group of three FKs to D1698. These were six-compartment coaches and plated 54ft x 9ft 4in, although not really exhibiting any marked external differences from an orthodox Period I coach; if anything, they were more MR than LNWR in appearance, in spite of the 9ft 4in overall width. Of more characteristic LNWR style were five TKs to D1710 and eight BTKs to D1712. The former were 52ft 6in x 9ft 4in and converted from ambulance coaches while the latter were 57ft x 9ft 4in and converted from ambulance train Kitchen/ Mess cars. All had toplights over the corridor windows and LNWR style end panelling. The original vehicles dated from the pre-1914 period and the brakes were opposite handed to the LMS standard style. Several other similar conversions of LNWR stock also took place but were not included in the LMS Diagram Book.

Apart from these three diagrams, the remainder of the Period I coaches were to LMS standard design and will be considered by classes.

First Class Coaches

The all-first was never a common LMS corridor coach and only 48 were built during Period I, including the above mentioned vehicles to D1698. Of the 48 coaches, no fewer than 25 were brake ended.

Chronologically, the earliest standard design was D1747 which was an all-door full first with six compartments and a centre coupé with three seats. It was a little behind the times and, with D1698, represented the only Period I full firsts with a full set of outside compartment doors.

The remaining coaches were ten full firsts to D1748 and 25 matching brake firsts to D1654. These were more spacious vehicles than their predecessors, having larger compartments. They had no outside compartment doors but the end entrance vestibules necessitated by the lack of outside doors, together with the extra compartment size, led to a reduction in passenger seating accommodation. The coaches had 5½ and 4½ compartments respectively and the 5½ compartment layout in the full firsts set the pattern until after the second world war.

Externally, the coaches were typical Period I designs but the compartments now had the Midland style twin-window arrangement which had, hitherto, been confined to open stock. The windows differed from those of the contemporary open stock in that both were surmounted by Stones pattern ventilators in the eaves panel. The left hand window was now a frameless droplight and not a heavy wood framed version. The double doors on the brake compartment of D1654 had one door opening inwards (for the guard and one opening outwards.)

Plate 98 Period I FK No. Sc1017M in BR crimson/cream livery, August 1956. This coach was to D1748 and on the compartment side, the vehicle exhibited the 'twin window' style–see Figure 37. Note that by the time this picture was taken, much of the wood panelling had been replaced by steel and the lower waist beading removed. *(J. E. Cull)*

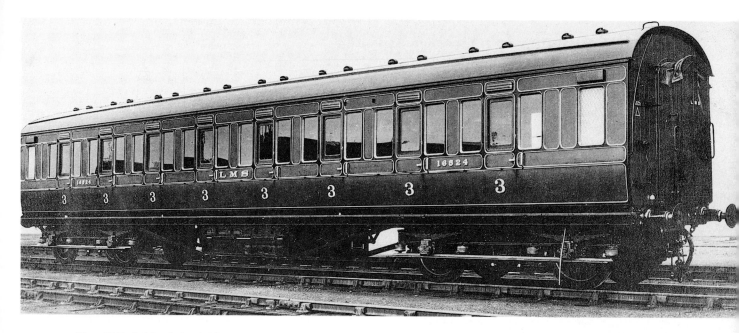

Plate 99 Period I 'all door' TK No. LMS 16524, later 1323, the earliest standard LMS corridor third type (D1695) whose ancestry is only too obvious–see Volume I. This example still retained hooded ventilators over the toilets rather than the hinged 'fall-back' type of later batches.

Third Class Coaches

Apart from the odd LNWR coaches already mentioned, the all-door Period I corridor third did not vary from grouping until 1928. It was built to two diagrams (D1756, D1695); the only difference between them being the slightly greater height and the MR pattern locks and handles on the 50 coaches to D1756 which gave them a width of 9ft 1½in. Almost 300 coaches of the style were built and, unlike the firsts and composites, the twin-window style was never adopted. D1695 is also shown as 9ft 1½in wide but most seem to have been standard 9ft 3in coaches.

The brake thirds were almost equally consistent in styling apart from the eight LNWR coaches to D1712. There were again two diagrams (D1758, D1696), both all-door types, of which D1758 seems to have been slightly experimental. Although built with standard LMS fittings and 9ft 3in wide, it was a four-compartment coach, intermediate between the MR three-compartment and the later LMS standard five-compartment layout. Only 14 were built before the five compartment D1696 version came into being. This design continued building until as late as 1930, long after the Period II single window styles had appeared in other coaches. It seems that the improvement of corridor thirds was probably accorded a low priority in early LMS days.

Composite Coaches

The corridor composite and brake composite type of coach received considerable attention by the LMS in early years and several attempts were made to achieve an ideal combination within the coach. Many of the type were built, the coaches obviously being in great demand for through working as well as for normal services and designs changes were continuous throughout the whole LMS period.

Plate 100 Ambulance train kitchen and mess car No. 5414, photographed in September 1939. This vehicle was converted from a Period I corridor composite to D1694. Very little alteration to the original panelling was caused by this conversion. The red cross on the side is painted on the side panelling which, in the original form, marked the corridor door between the first class (far end) and third class (near end) of the vehicle. The full thirds (e.g. Plate 99), had an almost identical corridor side arrangement with a window in place of the blank panel.

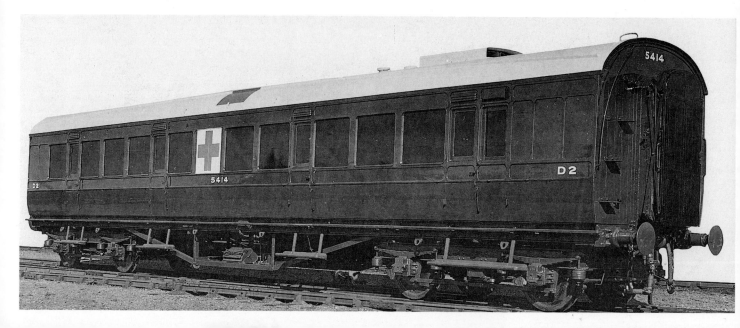

Plate 101 Period I (two window) 60ft CK to D1716 No. 9383, later 3748. These coaches were very similar to the FKs and BFKs of a year or two earlier, but had only one Stones ventilator over the window pairs. The corridor side of these coaches had seven large (4ft 6in) windows opposite the compartments arranged in very similar fashion to the 60ft third class sleeping cars—see Plate 28.

The first design was to D1694, an orthodox, seven compartment all-door coach built in quantity. It had four third and three first class compartments. During 1925, two variants were tried. D1751 had three third and four first class compartments while in D1752 the first were split first coupé/first/first/first coupé at the expense of some lavatory space. This latter scheme was identical to the final MR design but neither it nor the D1751 version seemed to find favour and the original D1694 coaches continued to be built until 1929.

The brake composites saw similar variations to the full composites. The first standard design was D1754 which was an all-door six compartment coach (two firsts plus four thirds), D1755 had an identical layout but with the firsts moved to the guard's end of the coach; while D1755A was a later rebuild of some of D1755 with three a side seating in the thirds, which improvement took place along with the general modernisation of many older brake composites in the 1930s—see below.

During 1928/9, the LMS must have received adverse comments about the standard of accommodation provided in its composite coaches and there were introduced some far reaching changes. From the point of view of the passenger, the first class compartments in the composites did not compare favourably with the larger compartments of the twin-window style adopted in 1927 in the corridor firsts and brake firsts. The external compartment door was probably another objection. Thus, at the end of 1929, D1716 and D1704 were introduced which brought the two-window style to the composites and brake composites.

The coaches emerged after a whole series of projected designs had been studied and rejected. These exhibited varying interior arrangements and lengths. The problem seems to have stemmed from the desire to get larger sized first class compartments, together with the necessary thirds (and luggage space, too, in the case of the brake ends) onto a standard 57ft underframe. At first layouts involving half compartments were suggested but this did not meet with approval. The LMS chiefs were not keen on reducing the size of compartment to the old value either so the final solution was to build the coaches on the 60ft underframe first introduced on the third class sleepers in 1928.

Both composite designs were late Period I vehicles and, in consequence, were transitional to the single window style. The corridor sides had single 4ft 6in windows (like the contemporary SLTs) rather than the older 3ft 0in wide corridor side windows of the twin-window firsts and brake firsts. Another point of difference was that the composites had a single nine-element Stones pattern ventilator centrally over the window pairs rather than two separate ventilators as on the first class coaches of 1927.

The perpetuation of the twin-window feature was interesting as by this time, large single windows and ever Period II styling were beginning to be established in other vehicles. However, amongst the rejected designs for composite coaches were some schemes which were drawn out with single windows on the compartment side too. These would have been high waisted and very similar in appearance to the 1928 'Royal Scot' stock (see page 201). The LMS had, therefore, clearly opted for the single-window style at this time and the only reason which can be offered for the appearance of the composites with the by-now obsolete twin-window arrangement was that they were urgently needed. As it had taken some time to settle the design of the coaches it may well have been that the quickest way to get them in service was to use existing patterns and jigs. There must have been some urgency about it because barely a year was to pass before the Period II versions appeared to D1791 and D1720. On the other hand, it may have been nothing more than a convenient excuse to use up spare parts in view of the forthcoming general change in styling.

An amusing sidelight to D1704 (brake composites) was the provision of a corridor door between the first and third class sections. Apparently, and probably again because of the urgency to get them in service, the first batch of coaches was built without a connecting door. The vehicles must have gone on to the North Wales route for the Marquess of Anglesey complained about the third class passengers being able to gain easy access to the first class end of the coach and this,

93

Plate 102 Rebuilt Period I BCK No. Sc6691M to D1704A seen at Colwyn Bay in BR livery. This picture clearly shows the retention by the rebuilt vehicle of the original roof.

apparently, was frowned upon. The LMS quickly rectified matters! The complaint stemmed from the fact that the D1704 coaches were originally built without a lavatory at the third class end. This was later rectified by using a portion of the, already small, brake compartment when coaches were rebuilt to D1704A (see below).

The brake composites were later given three-a-side third class seating and, still later, given Stanier style external body side panels. They retained the wood/canvas roof and the matchboard ends. This conversion coincided with the outbreak of the second world war and was held in abeyance for some time with only some of the coaches modified until policy had been settled. The decision was made to complete the rebuilding and all were eventually converted. Although the LMS was doing its best to improve coaches, two major refurbishments in about 10 years is distinctly unusual and the same sort of thing was to happen to the succeeding Period II design to D1720.

Several Period I corridor coaches were converted for ambulance use during the second world war and subsequently to full brakes. Their history in the latter guise is in Volume III.

PERIOD II DESIGNS

As has been seen above, Period I style coaches continued building well after the introduction of the low waisted body styling. In consequence, only a relatively small quantity of Period II corridor vehicles were built but they represented major improvements in design and amenity.

First Class Coaches

Unlike the thirds and composites, Period II styling was immediately adopted for first class coaches and the vehicles to D1717 were, in fact, in November 1929, the first of all the Period II designs to make an appearance. They were four compartment luxury style brake coaches with only four seats in each compartment. Everybody thus had corner seats! All compartments were differently finished and the coaches had very palatial toilets—almost miniature powder rooms. They were used on the prestige trains of the day and there is some reason to believe that they were the Period II equivalent of the Period I lounge brakes (see page 180) which were not too popular. The coaches were wood-panelled and beaded but one of them was written off in the Leighton Buzzard smash and replaced by a steel panelled version (Lot 625) in 1932.

The only other first class side corridor coaches built during this phase were again brake firsts and built to D1845. These were 4½ compartment coaches of all steel construction without conventional underframe trussing. They were built partially by outside contractors and had no raised beading. Three were rebuilt to D1962 with two-a-side seating for the 'Royal Scot'.

Third Class Coaches

The late building of the all-door Period I coaches meant that Period II styling was later to appear in corridor third class coaches and, in the event, only two designs were built.

The corridor third to D1872 was a very handsome design and set completely new standards. On a 60ft underframe it had but seven compartments which were 6ft 6in between partitions–an increase of 6in over the previous size and a dimension hitherto only used in the late Period I 60ft composites. It seated four on each side of the compartment but only 10 coaches were built–possibly because it was rather an extravagant design. No reason can be adduced why the LMS departed from the 57ft length for this batch of coaches but as it was the period when the company was actively experimenting with new ideas, the coaches were probably something of an experimental design. They were, allegedly, very comfortable vehicles to ride in and remained the sole examples of 60ft corridor thirds until the end of LMS designs. They may have been built to 60ft length to match the 60ft opens (see page 181). In fact the LMS almost became a '60ft line' at this period.

The brake third version to D1730 was a much more numerous design. Externally it was of all-steel construction and matched the D1845 BFKs–page 95. Although it perpetuated the 57ft length and five compartment layout of the Period I brake third, it had the 6ft 6in compartment dimension of the 60ft corridor thirds. This made the guard's compartment rather small.

Composite Coaches

The evolution of the Period I composite coach has been commented upon already and the Period II versions were very similar in layout to the final twin-window Period I designs.

The full composite to D1791, was a steel-panelled Period II design and saw the perpetuation of the 60ft length which, henceforward, remained standard for LMS corridor composites. The extra length provided space for the larger third class compartments and to increase the size of the toilet compartments. Clearly, the third class passenger was, at last, getting his share of new ideas. One of the coaches was rebuilt in 1937 to Period III D1969 following a fire.

The brake ended version to D1720 was the first Period II composite to appear and differed from its Period I predecessor in having the lavatory separating the two classes of accommodation. It was a wood-panelled and beaded design and, like D1704, the coaches were later modified to three-a-side third class seating and, ultimately, Stanier pattern side panelling and windows. They were very similar to the D1704 rebuilds but the centre lavatory was a distinguishing feature.

PERIOD III DESIGNS

Period III corridor coaches went through all the variations of Stanier coach design but, considering the vast number built, the variations of layout were surprisingly few.

First Class Coaches

The standard LMS Period III corridor first was a 57ft, $5\frac{1}{2}$ compartment vehicle with 7ft 6in compartments. The various diagrams denote such differences as four or six seats in each compartment and the alteration in position of the non-smoking areas but there was, in fact, no basic change in layout until after nationalisation. These coaches included three vehicles for the 1937 'Coronation Scot' train for which a separate diagram was raised. The coaches were built new for this service and had luxury two-a-side seating.

After nationalisation, there was a slight change of design in D2121. The compartment dimension was reduced to 7ft 2in and this enabled six compartments to be achieved on the 57ft underframe. Two extra doors were also added on the corridor side of the coach (D2121). Finally, the 'porthole' type of window appeared in D2162 of 1950 but with no other significant changes.

Brake firsts were equally consistent. Until the war, a $4\frac{1}{2}$ compartment layout was standardised—again with a separate diagram raised for the 1937 'Coronation Scot' stock. These latter coaches were, in fact, apart from an odd coach built in 1934, the first Stanier pattern brake firsts to be built. After nationalisation, a five-compartment brake first was introduced with 'Porthole' toilet windows and on a 60ft underframe (D2168). This represented the only change in basic design of the Period III brake first.

Plate 103 Period III FK No. 1047 as built to D1909. All the pre-war FKs were of this general style, including those built for the 1937 Coronation Scot sets. The absence of the LMS crest on this coach was somewhat unusual for a *first* class coach, as was the 'all smoking' accommodation.

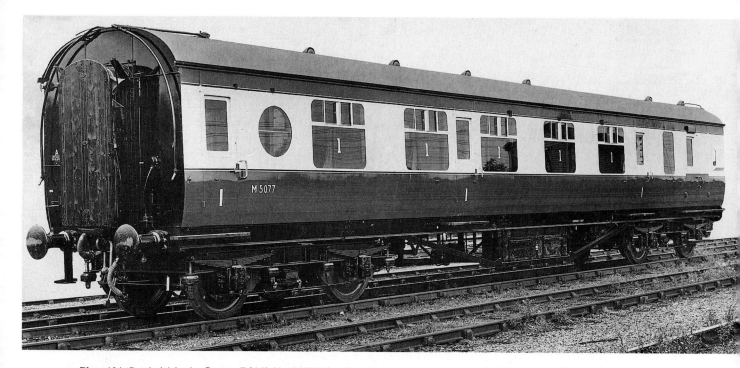

Plate 104 'Porthole' brake first to D2168 No. M5077 in BR crimson/cream livery as built. These were 60ft coaches the only LMS pattern BFKs to be built to this length. Note the extra corridor door, the window opposite the toilet and five main windows. They were five-compartment coaches.

Third Class Coaches

Over 1400 Period III corridor thirds were built between 1933 and 1950 yet to only two basic layouts. The pre-war version had two doors on the corridor side while the post-war variety had four corridor doors. All were seven compartment, 57ft coaches. Of the two major types, the post-war variant was, ultimately, the more numerous—although not until after nationalisation. As late as 1968, many of the post-nationalisation coaches still survived. A reduction in compartment size from 6ft 6in to 6ft 3in was made in the first Stanier corridor thirds and this remained standard, although not adopted in the brake thirds until after the war.

Turning now to detail variations, the pre-war coaches were built to two diagrams, the earlier one being the shallow-window ventilator version. The post-war coaches were also built to two diagrams of which the later version was the porthole variety.

There was also a little batch of three luxury corridor thirds built after the war at Derby. These were the 1939 'Coronation Scot' style coaches, considered in more detail in Volume III.

Period III brake thirds were even more numerous and showed slightly more design changes than did the full thirds. All of them exhibited one basic change from most pervious LMS coaches of the type in having a standardised four-compartment layout. Mention was made on page 95 of the rather small guard's compartment in the five compartment Period II brake thirds and this may have been one reason for the dropping of one compartment from the layout.

Unusually, there were two shallow ventilator BTK diagrams issued in 1933. The earlier coaches (D1851), had one single and one double door to the guard's van while the later version (D1852) had two pairs of double doors. They were amongst the few Stanier coaches to be built before the 1932/3 renumbering. A few were converted to push-pull operation by BR (Table 3a). D1905 was the standard deep-window ventilator version and was multiplied extensively until 1936 when lighter versions (D1963/D1971) made their appearance.

In 1937, a change was made by moving the toilet to the end of the coach rather than adjacent to the guard's van. This placed the compartments more between the bogies than hitherto and this design straddled the war years. It was superseded after nationalisation by D2123 and D2161 both of which had the reduced size of compartment (6ft 3in instead of 6ft 6in) and an extra corridor side door. D2161 was the porthole version and none were built until after the LMS ceased to exist. Several of the latter survived long enough to see overhauled service in the BR blue/grey livery.

Plate 105 Pioneer Period III TK to D1860 No. 1536. This set the style for all subsequent LMS corridor thirds–a seven compartment layout with extreme end doors on a 57ft chassis. This view is from the corridor side, the compartment side being identical (except for sliding window ventilator style) to the standard Period III version.

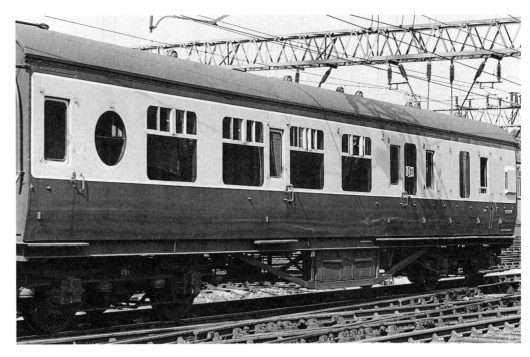

Plate 106 The final Period III design of BTK No. M27001M (D2161), the variation with extra corridor side door and 'porthole' windows. None was built until after 1947. The coach is shown in BR blue/grey livery and, as far as is known, these BTKs were the only variety of LMS pattern *day* coach to be thus treated. Note the BR type of roof vents and shorter sliding window ventilators.

Composite Coaches

It was again the composite coach which underwent most changes in Period III and it is not without significance that the first ever Stanier gangwayed coaches to be built were brake composites to D1850, some of which appeared in December 1932. For the most part, the significant developments were confined to the brake ended designs and the full composites retained the 60ft, seven compartment layout to the end. They only witnessed detail modifications, principally the reduction of third class compartment size from 6ft 6in to 6ft 3in with D1925 of 1935.

At the same time, Period III brake composites, although built to several designs, were not very numerous mainly because of the large scale rebuilding to Period III styling of the D1704 and D1720 coaches.

The genuine Stanier pattern brake composites still indicated that the LMS could not make up its mind what to do. Clearly the four third plus two first class arrangement of the Period I/II coaches must have given too small a brake compartment and the first Stanier examples had 3½ thirds plus 1½ firsts, still on a 60ft underframe.

This development was rather wasteful of space and seems to have flown in the face of the views current at the time the final Period I coaches were being designed—it was thus only multiplied to the tune of 22 coaches— mostly shallow ventilator types. The standard Period III version evolved from this design and saw yet another increase in length, this time to 62ft (D1932). This with a reduction to 6ft 3in third class compartments gave room for two first plus 3½ thirds and was built in some numbers, eventually becoming the numerically largest type of LMS brake composite. There were two diagrams for the coaches of almost identical style but the later one (D2010) had slightly different toilets and removable compartment tables. They were the longest side corridor LMS design coaches and the only 62ft coaches built by the company. No examples were built after the war.

Plate 107 LMS No. 3868 from the compartment side. This coach to D1898 was typical of the pre-war Stanier CKs and was in all essentials a Period III version of Figure 75. It is one of the earlier examples in full livery but after the change to deep window ventilators.

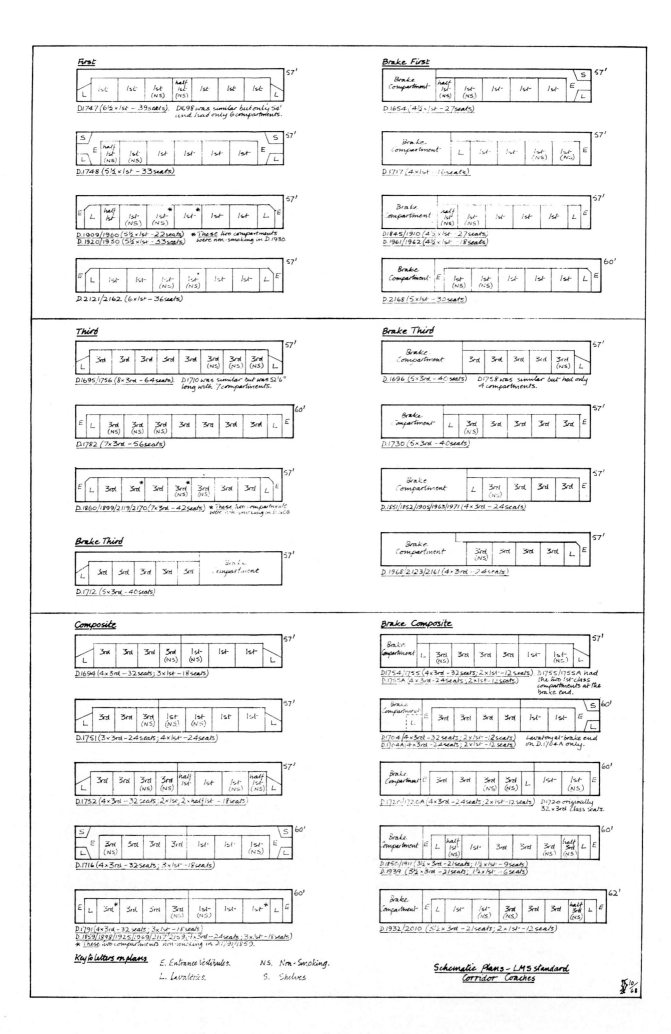

First

D.1747 (6½ × 1st – 39 seats). D.1698 was similar but only 54' and had only 6 compartments.

D.1748 (5½ × 1st – 33 seats)

D.1909/1960 (5½ × 1st – 22 seats)   * These two compartments were non-smoking in D.1930.
D.1920/1930 (5½ × 1st – 33 seats)

D.2121/2162 (6 × 1st – 36 seats)

Brake First

D.1654 (4½ × 1st – 27 seats)

D.1717 (4 × 1st – 16 seats)

D.1845/1910 (4½ × 1st – 27 seats)
D.1961/1962 (4½ × 1st – 18 seats)

D.2168 (5 × 1st – 30 seats)

Third

D.1695/1756 (8 × 3rd – 64 seats). D.1710 was similar but was 52'6" long with 7 compartments.

D.1782 (7 × 3rd – 56 seats)

D.1860/1899/2119/2170 (7 × 3rd – 42 seats)   * These two compartments were non-smoking in D.1860

Brake Third

D.1712 (5 × 3rd – 40 seats)

Brake Third

D.1696 (5 × 3rd – 40 seats)   D.1758 was similar but had only 4 compartments.

D.1730 (5 × 3rd – 40 seats)

D.1851/1852/1905/1963/1971 (4 × 3rd – 24 seats)

D.1968/2123/2161 (4 × 3rd – 24 seats)

Composite

D.1694 (4 × 3rd – 32 seats; 3 × 1st – 18 seats)

D.1751 (3 × 3rd – 24 seats; 4 × 1st – 24 seats)

D.1752 (4 × 3rd – 32 seats; 2 × 1st, 2 × half 1st – 18 seats)

D.1716 (4 × 3rd – 32 seats; 3 × 1st – 18 seats)

D.1791 (4 × 3rd – 32 seats; 3 × 1st – 18 seats)
D.1859/1898/1925/1969/2117/2159 (7 × 3rd – 24 seats; 3 × 1st – 18 seats)
* These two compartments non-smoking in D.1791/1859.

Brake Composite

D.1754/1755 (4 × 3rd – 32 seats; 2 × 1st – 12 seats). D.1755/1755A had the two 1st-class compartments at the brake end.
D.1755A (4 × 3rd – 24 seats; 2 × 1st – 12 seats)

D.1704 (4 × 3rd – 32 seats; 2 × 1st – 12 seats)   Lavatory at brake end on D.1704A only.
D.1704A (4 × 3rd – 24 seats; 2 × 1st – 12 seats)

D.1720/1720A (4 × 3rd – 24 seats; 2 × 1st – 12 seats)   D.1720 originally 32 × 3rd class seats.

D.1850/1911 (3½ × 3rd – 21 seats; 1½ × 1st – 9 seats)
D.1939 (3½ × 3rd – 21 seats; 1½ × 1st – 6 seats)

D.1932/2010 (5½ × 3rd – 21 seats; 2 × 1st – 12 seats)

Key to letters on plans

E. Entrance Vestibules.   N.S. Non-Smoking.
L. Lavatories.   S. Shelves

Schematic Plans – LMS standard Corridor Coaches

LMS standard corridor stock – sketch plans (Drawn by D. Jenkinson)

98

Note: This table should be read in conjunction with the list of standard dimensions and details on page 9.

Type	Diag	Lot	Qty	Date	Built	Dimensions (L×W×H)	Weight	Period	Running Numbers	First	Last	Remarks
FK	1698	29	3	1924	Wolverton	54'×9'1½"×12'4¾"	28T	I (All door)	1000-1002	7/56	1/61	Diagram shows 9'1½" width but coaches were plated 9'4" and 29T. Probably Derby issued the drawings assuming MR pattern fittings but Wolverton used up LNWR style handles &c.
FK	1747	246	10	1926	Wolverton	57'×9'3"×12'4¾"	29T	I (All door)	1003-1012	5/59	10/61	
FK	1748	325	10	1927	Wolverton	57'×9'3"×12'4¾"	29T	I (Two window style)	1013-1022	2/59	10/61	Compartment size increased from 7'3" to 7'6".
FK	1920	775	1	1934	Derby	57'×9'3"×12'4⅝"	31T	III	1038	—	10/63	The prototype Period III FK.
FK	1909	793	12	1934	Derby	57'×9'3"×12'4⅝"	31T	III	1039-1050	9/62	1/65	As for D1920 but with two a side seating.
FK	1930	904	11	1936	Wolverton	57'×9'3"×12'4⅝"	32T	III	1051-1061	7/64	3/65	Luxury finish but three a side seating. Identical to D1920 except for the arrangement of non-smoking compartments.
		1041	7	1937	Wolverton		32T		1062-1068	7/64	11/65	
		1092	7	1938	Wolverton		31T		1072-1083	1/64	1/65	
FK	1960	1062	3	1937	Wolverton	57'×9'3"×12'4⅝"	33T	III	1069-1071	12/63	12/64	The 1937 'Coronation Scot' coaches with two a side seating and heavier than the D1930 equivalent. Probably diverted from Lot 1041.
FK	2121	1439	30	1948	Wolverton	57'×9'3"×12'4⅝"	31T	III	1084-1113	10/64	9/65	The post-war version with compartments reduced from 7'6" to 7'2". All given post war LMS livery but with 'M' prefix and no 'LMS' on coach side. Fitted with final style of sliding ventilators.
FK	2162	1585	15	1950	Wolverton	57'×9'3"×12'4⅝"	30T	III (Port-hole)	1114-1128	12/64	12/65	As for D2121 but with post-war torpedo ventilators. Finished in BR crimson/cream when new and somewhat accident prone: 1123/5₄ (Weedon 21/9/51); 1124 (Harrow 8/10/52).
BFK	1654	326	25	1927	Derby	57'×9'3"×12'4¾"	27T	I (Two window style)	5011-5035	6/59	11/64	Brake version of D1748. 5034 to Royal train (11/35). 5035 had LNER type bogies supplied in 1931!
BFK	1717	477	6	1929	Derby	57'×9'3"×12'4¾"	29T	II (beaded)	5005-5009	13/59	12/62	The pioneer Period II coaches. Only five of Lot 477 were renumbered and Lot 625 was a replacement for the missing one (old 15458) written off after the Leighton Buzzard accident. 5006 was fitted with very long wheelbase bogies. When new, the coaches had small scroll type figures.
		625	1	1932	Derby		29T	II (flush)	5010	—	11/61	
BFK	1845	582	15	1931	see remarks	57'×9'3"×12'4¾"	32T	II (Flush)	5036-5050	6/61	10/63	Bogies and interiors built at Wolverton, the remainder by Birmingham C&W. They were 'all steel' coaches with deeper than normal eaves panelling and no conventional underframe. D1962 was a later conversion to two a side seating.
BFK	1962	Part 582	3		see remarks	57'×9'3"×12'4¾"	32T	II (Flush)	5036-5038	11/61	12/61	
BFK	1910	776	1	1934	Derby	57'×9'3"×12'4⅝"	31T	III	5051	—	10/64	The standard Period III BFK.
		1093	8	1938	Wolverton		31T		5055-5062	6/64	3/65	
BFK	1961	1063	3	1937	Wolverton	57'×9'3"×12'4⅝"	32T	III	5052-5054	4/64	12/64	The 'Coronation Scot' version of D1910 with two a side seating and heavier tare weight.
BFK	2168	1504	15	1949	Wolverton	60'×9'3"×12'4⅝"	30T	III (Port-hole)	5063-5077	11/64	5/65	The post-war version with five 7'2" compartments on a longer underframe. All finished in BR crimson/cream livery when new and fitted with the final style of sliding ventilators.
TK	1756	7	25	1924	Derby	57'×9'1½"×12'5½"	27T	I (All door)	1212-1236	6/53	2/61	Coaches with MR style fittings. Lot 7 plated 1923 and both lots carried MR type works plates.
		8	25	1924	Derby		27T		1237-1261	11/51	4/60	
TK	1710	87	5	1924	Wolverton	52'6"×9'4"×12'5½"	28T	see remarks	1207-1211	4/51	12/56	The LNWR type coaches with corridor toplights and LNWR panelled ends. Converted from WWI ambulance vehicles.
TK	1695	9	18	1924	Derby	57'×9'1½"×12'4¾"	28T	I (all door)	1262-1279	11/58	8/62	Although shown as 9'1½" wide, this was the 9'3" wide standard Period I TK, otherwise identical to D1756. Only Lots 9/71 had MR pattern commode handles. Over 60 coaches (mostly Lot 388) saw active service in the war and only about half returned to traffic, the others being lost in France. 1301/17/33/62 had gangways removed (1948) for CLC service. Lots 147/158 plated 1925, Lot 388 plated 29T.
		71	17	1924	Derby		28T	door	1280-1296	5/58	9/61	
		95	45	1925	Derby		28T		1297-1341	7/58	13/62	
		147	40	1926	Derby		28T		1342-1381	11/58	10/63	
		158	40	1926	Derby		28T		1382-1421	3/59	13/62	
		388	75	1928	Wolverton		28T		1422-1496	3/59	2/64	
TK	1782	551	10	1930	Derby	60'×9'3"×12'4¾"	30T	II (beaded)	1497-1506	5/59	5/62	The palatial 60' coaches with compartments increased in size from 6'0" to 6'6".
TK	1860	695	30	1933	Wolverton	57'×9'3"×12'4¾"	31T	III (Shallow) ventilator)	1507-1536	8/62	12/64	The first Period III TK and had full livery when new. Also the first LMS TKs with three a side seating from new. The compartment size was reduced to 6'3" on these and subsequent coaches.
TK	1899	730	35	1933	Derby	57'×9'3"×12'4¾"	31T	III	1537-1571	3/62	3/65	The standard Period III TK and the most numerous single type of coach built by the LMS although eventually outnumbered by D2119 (below). Lots 730/731 were outshopped in fully lined livery.
		731	34	1934	Derby		31T		1572-1605	13/61	4/66	
		795	35	1934	Derby		31T		1606-1640	10/62	6/65	
		796	25	1934	Derby		31T		1641-1665	2/62	12/65	
		797	20	1934	Derby		31T		1666-1685	12/62	11/65	
		798	25	1934	Derby		31T		1686-1710	11/61	3/66	
		799	30	1934	Derby		31T		1711-1740	7/62	6/65	
		800	20	1934	Wolverton		32T		1741-1760	8/62	9/65	
		801	35	1934	Wolverton		32T		1761-1795	1/62	6/65	
		802	35	1934	Wolverton		32T		1796-1830	12/61	10/64	
		803	30	1934	Wolverton		32T		1831-1860	5/62	11/64	

TABLE 3a: LMS SIDE CORRIDOR STOCK (continued)

Type	Diag	Lot	Qty	Date	Built	Dimensions (L×W×H)	Weight	Period	Running Numbers	First	Last	Remarks
TK	1899	846	65	1935	Derby		31T		1861-1925	5/62	10/65	
		896	25	1936/7	Derby		31T		1926-1950	6/63	4/65	
		897	50	1936	Derby		31T		1951-2000	9/62	11/65	
		998	40	1937	Wolverton	57'×9'3"×12'4¾"	32T		2001-2040	5/63	12/65	
		1089	44	1938	Wolverton		32T		2041-2084	9/62	8/65	
		1090	45	1938	Wolverton		32T		2085-2129	2/61	8/65	
		1191	18	1939	Wolverton		31T		2130-2147	13/63	7/65	
TK	2119	1405	50	1946	Derby		31T	III	2151-2200	13/63	3/67	The post-war version with two extra doors on the corridor side. Some date discrepancies on works plates: Lot 1407 plated 1946. Lot 1447 plated 1947. Lot 1483 plated variously 1948/1949 and possibly some 1950. The change to the final style of sliding ventilator probably came somewhere in Lot 1436.
		1406	50	1946	Derby		31T		2201-2250	13/63	5/68	
		1407	100	1946-7	Derby		31T		2251-2350	3/64	Many still extant (1968)	
		1436	116	1946-7	Met-Cammell	57'×9'3"×12'4⅝"	31T		2351-2466	13/63		
		1447	50	1947-8	Derby		31T		2467-2516	11/65		
		1483	200	1948-50	Met-Cammell		31T		12750-12949	13/63		
		1484	135	1949-50	B'ham C&W		30T		12950-13084	7/64		

Ex-works livery:
Lots 1405-1436: LMS post war livery
Lots 1436-1483: LMS livery but no LMS markings
Lot 1484: BR Crimson/Cream
2221/35/50 were converted to Tea Cars (Jan. 1950) for the Irish Mail service, three compartments being used as a serving area. 2235 was destroyed at Penmaenmawr on 27/8/50 so in April 1953, 2211 was altered to a Tea Car as a replacement.

Type	Diag	Lot	Qty	Date	Built	Dimensions (L×W×H)	Weight	Period	Running Numbers	First	Last	Remarks
TK	2170	1621	100	1950	Met-Cammell	57'×9'2½"×12'4⅝"	30T	III (Port-hole)	13085-13184	5/64	Many still extant (1968)	All given Crimson/Cream livery and believed to have had torpedo ventilators (post-war type).

Note: One further TK diagram issued (D2019) for the 1939 'Coronation Scot' coaches. These are included in Volume III.

Type	Diag	Lot	Qty	Date	Built	Dimensions (L×W×H)	Weight	Period	Running Numbers	First	Last	Remarks
BTK	1712	91	8	1924	Wolverton	57'×9'4"×12'5½"	28T	see remarks	5200-5201	1/51	6/51	The LNWR style coaches converted from Kitchen/Mess cars. Some seem to have been plated 27T. 5200/1 had only three compartments and it is odd that they should be on the same diagram. These brakes were opposite handed to the MR and LMS standard layout.
									5216-5221	3/52	4/56	
BTK	1758	11	14	1925	Derby	57'×9'3"×12'4¾"	27T	I (All door)	5202-5215	11/58	13/62	These were the four compartment brakes and the building date is confirmed despite the early lot number.
BTK	1696	125	40	1926	Derby		27T	I (All door)	5222-5261	5/59	7/62	The standard five compartment version. Lot 412 were the last LMS corridor coaches with compartment doors. Over 80 saw active service during the war and many were lost overseas. The majority that returned were converted to full brakes to D2129/D2130—see Volume III.
		148	60	1926	Derby	57'×9'3"×12'4¾"	27T		5262-5321	8/57	13/62	
		412	25	1929-30	Derby		28T		5322-5346	5/59	12/62	
BTK	1730	507	5	1930	Met-Cammell		32T	II (Flush)	5347-5351	11/61	7/63	Lots 508/542 had Metro-Cammell bodies and underframes, the rest being built at Derby. Lot 578 were built at Wolverton, again on Metro-Cammell frames. The diagram shows all to have been 32T but apparently most were 30T. The coaches had a slightly deeper than normal eaves panel because of the 'all steel' construction and had no conventional underframe. There were slight livery variations when new viz:
		508	5	1930	see remarks		32T		5352-5356	5/59	11/62	
		542	40	1930-1		57'×9'3"×12'4⅝"	32T		5357-5396	6/59	2/64	
		578	50	1931-2			32T		5397-5446	13/58	5/64	

Lot 508: Lined edge of windows, no crest and small scroll figures.
Lot 542: Lined edge of windows, rather more 'panelling' at brake end, no crest and stretched scroll figures.
Lot 578: Lined between the windows and no vertical dividers in the eaves panel. Stretched scroll figures and crest carried on side. These coaches had larger Stones ventilators over the windows than the previous lots.
Lot 507 was probably like Lot 508.
All lots had 6'6" compartments.

Type	Diag	Lot	Qty	Date	Built	Dimensions (L×W×H)	Weight	Period	Running Numbers	First	Last	Remarks
BTK	1851	659	20	1933	Derby		30T	III (Shallow ventilator)	5447-5466	11/61	9/65	The first Period III design and a change to four compartments and three a side seating. Lot 659 plated 1932. Full livery from new. Torpedo vents. 5476/91/96 converted to Push-Pull (1954-5) and renumbered 3497-9 in order
		Part 692	34	1933	Derby	57'×9'3"×12'4⅝"	30T		5467-5500	11/61	13/64	
BTK	1852	Part 692	16	1933	Derby	57'×9'3"×12'4¾"	30T	III (Shallow ventilator)	5501-5516	3/61	5/64	As for D1851 but two pairs of double doors at brake end. Again Torpedo vents and full livery.
BTK	1905	737	25	1934	Derby		30T	III	5517-5541	6/62	3/66	* Also 5617-5618 The standard Period III coach of which Lot 737 had full livery. Later Modifications: 5517-24 had Guard's lookout and top commode handles removed for working on the 'Sunny South Express'. 5792/5812/5814 were modernised with air conditioning in 1937 for the 'Coronation Scot' train—all tared 32T after conversion.
		738	27	1934	Derby		30T		5542-5566*	5/62	5/65	
		739	25	1934	Wolverton		30T		5567-5591	9/62	11/65	
		740	25	1934	Wolverton		30T		5592-5616	1/62	4/66	
		794	25	1934	Wolverton		30T		5619-5643	10/62	12/64	
		858	65	1935	Wolverton	57'×9'3"×12'4⅝"	31T		5644-5708	8/62	1/66	
		859	60	1935	Wolverton		31T		5709-5768	6/63	9/66	
		898	50	1936	Derby		30T		5769-5818	7/63	7/65	
		899	25	1936	Derby		30T		5819-5843	11/63	11/65	
		910	44	1936	Wolverton		31T		5869-5912	4/63	12/66	
		911	44	1936	Wolverton		31T		5913-5956	5/63	7/65	

Type	Diag	Lot	Qty	Date	Built	Dimensions (L×W×H)	Weight	Period	Running Numbers	Withdrawals First	Last	Remarks
BTK	1963	950	24	1936-7	Derby	57'×9'3"×12'4¼"	29T	III	5845-5868	6/63	1/65	From the numbers these may have been cancelled from Lot 899. All 25 were a little lower than D1905 but only D1971 was classified 'lightweight'. The frame of 5844 was probably a 'try-out' for the centrally trussed frame used on the articulated stock and by BR at a later date—see also p.152 although the articulated stock was first into service.
BTK	1971	976	1	1937	Derby	57'×9'3"×12'2 9/16"	26T	III	5844	—	6/62	
BTK	1968	1035	64	1937	Derby		30T	III	5957-6020	12/63	3/66	* 20 were 'fully fabricated' and 36 were 'non-fabricated'; 26298 upwards plated 31T. Number 26190 was never used on these coaches. These were the later standard coaches with lavatories at the end of the vehicle. Lots 1408 upwards came out with post-war maroon livery, small scroll numbers and flat topped '3's'.
		1082	45	1938	Derby		30T	III	26100-26144	12/63	11/65	
		1083	45	1938	Derby		30T	III	26145-26189	12/63	6/65	
		1175	74	1939	Derby	57'×9'3"×12'4¼	30T	III	26191-26264	12/63	10/67	
		1192	56*	1939	Wolverton		30T	III	26265-26320	12/63	10/67	
		1408	50	1945	Derby		30T	III	26321-26370	7/64	11/67	
		1409	75	1945-6	Derby		30T	III	26371-26445	2/64		
		1410	100	1946	Derby		30T	III	26446-26545	11/65	12/67	
BTK	2123	1448	120	1948-9	Derby	57'×9'3"×12'4¼'	31T	III	26546-26665	13/63	many extant (1968)	Extra door on corridor side, compartments reduced from 6'6" to 6'3" and probably with first-style of window ventilator. All had LMS post-war livery but no LMS marks.
BTK	2161	1501	90	1950	Derby		30T	III	26666-26755	3/64	1/68	The final variety and all built after nationalisation. Believed all BR Crimson/cream when new and with post-war (BR type) torpedo ventilators.
		1505	125	1949-50	W'ton		30T (P'hole)	III	26756-26880	13/63	many extant (1968) still extant (1968)	
		1506	125	1950	Wolverton		30T	III	26881-27005	11/65		
		1575	40	1950-1	Derby	57'×9'3"×12'4⅝"	30T	III	27006-27045	12/65		
		1587	9	1950	Derby		30T	III	6030-6038	12/64	10/67	
		1597	50	1950	Wolverton		30T	III	27046-27095	11/65		
CK	1694	30	41	1924	Wolverton		29T	I (All door)	3505-3545	4/57	11/61	The standard Period I CK, perpetuated after other versions had been tried out. 3531 recorded on LNWR bogies at some time. Several modified to 9'1½"for use in M&CR section narrow set of coaches, including 3535/3659/60/85/8/94/3701. 39 coaches to wartime ambulances. Survivors rebuilt as full brakes (see Volume III).
		72	15	1925	Wolverton		29T	door	3546-3560	3/57	10/61	
		120	25	1925	Wolverton		28T		3561-3585	3/57	4/61	
		157	35	1925	Derby	57'×9'3"×12'4¾"	28T		3586-3620	5/57	3/62	
		207	35	1926	Derby		28T		3621-3655	1/58	13/62	
		319	50	1927-8	W'ton		28T		3656-3705	5/59	10/62	
CK	1751	101	5	1925	Wolverton	57'×9 3"×12'4¾"	29T	I (All door)	3500-3504	1/58	3/62	The 4×1st + 3×3rd version with slightly smaller toilets to compensate.
CK	1752	139	25	1925	Wolverton	57'×9'3"×12 5½"	28T	I (All door)	3706-3730	4/57	7/62	The version with 2×1st + 2×½1st + 4×3rd. Even smaller toilets than D1751.
CK	1716	450	50	1930	Wolverton	60'×9'3"×12'4¾"	30T	I (2-window)	3731-3780	5/59	10/63	Early coaches plated 1929, but all built 1930.
CK	1791	531	48	1931	Wolverton	60'×9'3" ×12'4¾"	32T	II (Flush)	3781-3828	8/59	7/64	Early coaches plated 1930. 3818 later rebuilt to D1969 after a fire—see below.
CK	1859	694	35	1933	Wolverton	60'×9'3"×12'4¾"	33T	III (Shallow ventilator)	3829-3863	2/62	4/65	Full livery when new, torpedo ventilators.
CK	1898	728	35	1934	Wolverton	60'×9'3"×12'4⅝"	32T	III	3864-3898	6/62	11/64	Lot 728 had full livery and were mostly plated 1933 but Lot 729 may have had simple style since most coaches carried 1934 works plates. Lot 728 had torpedo vents.
		729	35	1934	Wolverton		32T		3899-3933	5/62	2/66	
CK	1925	856	20	1935-6	Derby		32T	III	3934-3953	4/63	2/65	The standard version and almost identical in layout to D1859/D1898. Lot 856 all plated 1935. The thirds were reduced from 6'6" to 6'3" and the extra space given to the lavatories. *Official date—coach (4027) was actually broken up in 1965!
		862	70	1935	Wolverton	60'×9'3"×12'4⅝"	33T		3954-4023	10/62	7/65	
		912	45	1936	Wolverton		32T		4024-4068	11/63	8/67*	
		913	45	1936	Wolverton		32T		4069-4113	4/63	1/65	
CK	1969	1042	69	1937	Wolverton		32T	III	4114-4182	9/62	12/65	This version was identical to D1925 except that the interior layout of the toilet was changed to have the WC adjacent to the vestibule wall of the toilet rather than on the wall adjacent to the passenger compartments. Lot 1100 plated 1938. Coaches 4327-9 were the only locomotive hauled passenger carrying coaches built in 1940 and the last until 1945.
		Part 531	1	1937	Wolverton		32T		3818	—	4/64	
		1099	33	1938-9	W'ton		33T		4183-4215	13/63	9/65	
		1100	40	1939	Wolverton	60'×9'3"×12'4⅝"	33T		4216-4255	5/63	11/65	
		1189	44	1939	Wolverton		32T		4256-4299	12/63	12/66	
		1190	30	1939-40	W'ton		32T		4300-4329	13/63	11/65	
CK	2117	1403	50	1946-7	W'ton		31T	III	4330-4379	9/61	4/67	The post-war version with two extra doors on the corridor side. All given post-war LMS livery, Lot 1446 with 1946 insignia. Lots 1440/6 probably had last style of window ventilator.
		1404	75	1946-7	W'ton		31T		4380-4454	3/64	some extant (1968)	
		1440	100	1947-8	W'ton	60'×9 3"×12'4⅝"	31T		4800-4899	13/63	12/67	
		1446	60	1947	Derby		31T		4455-4514	7/64	11/67	
CK	2159	1499	75	1949	Derby		30T	III	24500-24574	12/63	many still extant (1968)	The 'all steel' design with the modified profile. Most had post-war (BRstyle) torpedo vents but there were exceptions. LMS livery on Lot 1499, BR on remainder.
		1500	75	1949-50	Derby	60'0¾"×9'3"×12'4½"	30T (P'hole)		24575-24649	13/63		
		1586	90	1950	Derby		30T		24650-24739	13/63		

Type	Diag	Lot	Qty	Date	Built	Dimensions (L×W×H)	Weight	Period	Running Numbers	Withdrawals First	Last	Remarks
BCK	1754	31	29	1924	Wolverton	57'×9'3" 12'4¾"	29T	I (All door)	6600-6628	8/56	8/63	Brake version of D1694.
BCK	1755	208	30	1926	Wolverton	57'×9'3"×12'4¾"	29T	I (All door)	6629-6658	3/59	6/62	As for D1754 but firsts at brake end adjacent to guard's van. Lot 320 later rebuilt to D1755A with three a side in the thirds.
		320	25	1927	Wolverton		29T		6659-6683	5/59	5/63	
BCK	1704	454	50	1929-30	W'ton	60'×9'3"×12'4¾"	30T	I (2-window)	6684-6733	2/59	5/64	Later to D1704A—three a side 3rds with Period III side panels (c. 1940). An extra toilet was fitted at brake end between guard's compartment and entrance.
BCK	1720	490	25	1930	Wolverton	60'×9'3"×12'4¾"	30T	II (Beaded)	6734-6758	5/59	7/64	Later to D1720A with three a side thirds and later still (c. 1940) given Period III side panels as per D1704. Before rebuilding, 6741/5/51/65/7/71/7/9 had lookouts and top commode handles removed for working on the 'Sunny South Express'.
		550	25	1930	Wolverton		30T		6759-6783	5/59	2/64	
BCK	1850	658	20	1932-3	W'ton	60'×9'3"×12'4¾"	33T	III (Shallow ventilator)	6784-6803	6/60	9/64	The first Period III gangwayed design, many being plated 1932. Coaches had full livery when new, stretched scroll pre-'33 numbers and torpedo ventilators.
BCK	1939	Part 658	2	1933	Wolverton	60'×9'3"×12'4¾"	33T	III (Shallow ventilator)	6784-6785	—	11/63	Converted to have luxury first class with two a side seating.
BCK	1911	777	2	1934	Wolverton	60'×9'3"×12'4¾"	32T	III	6804-6805	8/62	6/64	Deep ventilator version of D1850 and with rounded interior partition corners.
BCK	1932	861	35	1935	Wolverton	62'×9'3"×12'4⅝"	35T	III	6806-6840	11/63	10/65	The standard version with 62' underframe and two first class compartments.
		908	16	1936	Wolverton		35T		6841-6856	12/63	4/65	
BCK	2010	1098	20	1938	Wolverton	62'×9'3"×12'4⅝"	35T	III	6857-6876	13/63	8/65	As for D1932 but layout of toilet was changed and the vehicles had removable tables. 6876 was altered to a secretary vehicle in 1957, reverting to normal in 1958. Many of the 62' underframes were converted to car flats.

TABLE 3b: SUMMARY OF THE 1933 RENUMBERING OF LMS CORRIDOR COACHES

The side corridor group is the first instance in this volume where the pre-1933 numbers loom large. They were, of course, mostly applicable to Period I and II stock only, but one batch of Period III coaches (BCK–D1850) came out in 1932–3 and received old series numbers in the 'stretched' scroll numerals for a short period prior to the change. The contemporary BTKs to D1851 and D1852 were also allocated old series numbers but we have no hard evidence that any of them ever carried them; a few may have done but we think not many. We have listed the old numbers by generic type and diagram number, in the same sequence as Table 3a.

First Class Corridor Coaches

D1698

New No.	Old No.
1000	15359
1001	16443
1002	16502

D1747

New No.	Old No.
1003	15301
1404	15332
1005	15397
1006	15349
1007	15452
1008	15454
1009	15460
1010	15498
1011	15504
1012	15505

D1748

New No.	Old No.
1013	3499
1014	3541
1015	16145
1016	16221
1017	16390
1018	16565
1019	16880
1020	16897
1021	16898
1022	17587

First Class Corridor Brakes

D1741

New No.	Old No.	
5000	15349	Lounge
5001	15413	"
5002	15438	"
5003	15455	"
5004	15493	"

D1717

New No.	Old No.
5005	15470
5006	15506
5007	15533
5008	15556
5009	15581
5010	15458

D1654

New No.	Old No.
5011	18493
5012	18494
5013	18496
5014	18501
5015	18503
5016	18504
5017	18505
5018	18506
5019	18507
5020	18513

D1654 cont.

New No.	Old No.
5021	18514
5022	18515
5023	18516
5024	18518
5025	18519
5026	18520
5027	18540
5028	18541
5029	18544
5030	18559
5031	18560
5032	18561
5033	18562
5034	18563
5035	18564

D1845

New No.	Old No.
5036	2554
5037	2555
5038	3742
5039	10241
5040	10272
5041	10274
5042	15550
5043	17503
5044	17510
5045	17512
5046	17528
5047	17534
5048	17537
5049	17584
5050	17596

Third Class Corridor Coaches

New No.	Old No.
1200	5224
1201	5225
1202	5226
1203	5227
1204	5228
1205	5229
1206	5230

D1710

New No.	Old No.
1207	5231
1208	5232
1209	5233
1210	5234
1211	5235

D1756

New No.	Old No.
1212	389
1213	906
1214	924
1215	957
1216	1199
1217	1251
1218	2684
1219	2685
1220	2689
1221	2690
1222	2694
1223	2696
1224	2699
1225	2700
1226	2701
1227	2703
1228	2710

D1756 Cont.

New No.	Old No.
1229	2711
1230	2712
1231	2713
1232	6234
1233	6236
1234	6237
1235	6238
1236	6240
1237	6241
1238	6242
1239	6243
1240	6244
1241	6245
1242	6246
1243	6290
1244	6291
1245	6293
1246	6294
1247	6295
1248	6395
1249	6396
1250	6397
1251	6398
1252	6399
1253	6400
1254	6401
1255	6402
1256	6403
1257	6405
1258	6410
1259	6418
1260	6419
1261	6420

D1695

New No.	Old No.
1262	16183
1263	16263
1264	16267
1265	16306
1266	16320
1267	16336
1268	16627
1269	16649
1270	16728
1271	16730
1272	16782
1273	16795
1274	16820
1275	16821
1276	16822
1277	16825
1278	16859
1279	16869
1280	25
1281	39
1282	71
1283	267
1284	341
1285	392
1286	491
1287	839
1288	920
1289	972
1290	1017
1291	1135
1292	1149
1293	1304
1294	1329
1295	1371
1296	1702
1297	15781
1298	16099
1299	16106
1300	16118
1301	16121
1302	16137
1303	16146
1304	16159
1305	16177
1306	16237
1307	16243
1308	16271
1309	16296
1310	16307
1311	16321
1312	16322
1313	16332
1314	16333
1315	16413
1316	16415
1317	16467
1318	16470
1319	16478
1320	16491
1321	16500
1322	16515
1323	16524
1324	16525
1325	16570

D1695 Cont.

New No.	Old No.
1326	16633
1327	16636
1328	16659
1329	16715
1330	16758
1331	16766
1332	16771
1333	16826
1334	16854
1335	16912
1336	17008
1337	17029
1338	17041
1339	17053
1340	17338
1341	19128
1342	15325
1343	15386
1344	15400
1345	15621
1346	15645
1347	15699
1348	15785
1349	15806
1350	15810
1351	15866
1352	15873
1353	15921
1354	16000
1355	16076
1356	16095
1357	16161
1358	16289
1359	16290
1360	16304
1361	16335
1362	16417
1363	16519
1364	16583
1365	16693
1366	16702
1367	16731
1368	16737
1369	16738
1370	16743
1371	16776
1372	16804
1373	16807
1374	16808
1375	16823
1376	16837
1377	16840
1378	16916
1379	17011
1380	17040
1381	17177
1382	15327
1383	15342
1384	15358
1385	15366
1386	15387
1387	15440
1388	15453
1389	15669
1390	15677
1391	15805
1392	16082
1393	16150
1394	16162
1395	16324
1396	16337
1397	16341
1398	16350
1399	16383
1400	16386
1401	16446
1402	16472
1403	16504
1404	16794
1405	16796
1406	16798
1407	16799
1408	16816
1409	16819
1410	16829
1411	16834
1412	16862
1413	16894
1414	16900
1415	16902
1416	16903
1417	16956
1418	17213
1419	17332
1420	17353
1421	19099
1422	14250
1423	14251
1424	14252
1425	14253
1426	14254
1427	14255

D1695 Cont.

New No.	Old No.
1428	14256
1429	14257
1430	14258
1431	14259
1432	14260
1433	14261
1434	14262
1435	14263
1436	14264
1437	14265
1438	14266
1439	14267
1440	14268
1441	14269
1442	14271
1443	14273
1444	14274
1445	14275
1446	14276
1447	14277
1448	14278
1449	14279
1450	14280
1451	14281
1452	14282
1453	14283
1454	14284
1455	14285
1456	14286
1457	14287
1458	14288
1459	14289
1460	14291
1461	14292
1462	14293
1463	14294
1464	14295
1465	14296
1466	14297
1467	14298
1468	14299
1469	14300
1470	14301
1471	14302
1472	14303
1473	14304
1474	14306
1475	14307
1476	14308
1477	14309
1478	14310
1479	14311
1480	14312
1481	14313
1482	14314
1483	14316
1484	14317
1485	14318
1486	14319
1487	14322
1488	14323
1489	14324
1490	14325
1491	14326
1492	14327
1493	14328
1494	14329
1495	14330
1496	14331

D1782

New No.	Old No.
1497	3026
1498	3027
1499	3028
1500	3029
1501	3030
1502	3031
1503	3032
1504	3033
1505	3034
1506	3035

Third Class Corridor Brakes

D1712

New No.	Old No.
5200	6761
5201	6764

D1758

New No.	Old No.
5202	7585
5203	7596
5204	7597
5205	7598
5206	7601
5207	7602
5208	7603
5209	7604
5210	7605
5211	7668
5212	16334
5213	16475
5214	16485
5215	17019

D1712

New No.	Old No.
5216	6739
5217	6762
5218	6763
5219	6765
5220	6766
5221	6767

D1696

New No.	Old No.
5222	15319
5223	15320
5224	15344
5225	15345
5226	15363
5227	15364
5228	15365
5229	15367
5230	15398
5231	15427
5232	15436
5233	15481
5234	15488
5235	15589
5236	15612
5237	15613
5238	15616
5239	15628
5240	15629
5241	15640
5242	15642
5243	15643
5244	15667
5245	15673
5246	15727
5247	15739
5248	15745
5249	15748
5251	15782
5252	15786
5253	15791
5254	15721
5255	15850
5256	15863
5257	15864
5258	15881
5259	16621
5260	16707
5261	17129
5262	15381
5263	15409
5264	15434
5265	15457
5266	15482
5267	15499
5268	15519
5269	15663
5270	15670
5271	15678
5272	15874
5273	15876
5274	15887
5275	15890
5276	15894
5277	15908
5278	15912
5279	16083
5280	16087
5281	16100
5282	16107

D1696 Cont.

New No.	Old No.
5283	16178
5284	16186
5285	16250
5286	16269
5287	16283
5288	16292
5289	16298
5290	16349
5291	16400
5292	16421
5293	16488
5294	16492
5295	16493
5296	16499
5297	16507
5298	16554
5299	16561
5300	16580
5301	16610
5302	16611
5303	16635
5304	16666
5305	16733
5306	16735
5307	16797
5308	16806
5309	16845
5310	16851
5311	16875
5312	16919
5313	16924
5315	17017
5316	17032
5317	17185
5318	17225
5319	17335
5320	17335
5321	17389
5322	200
5323	201
5324	817
5325	828
5326	862
5327	865
5328	877
5329	1358
5330	1360
5331	1826
5332	1851
5333	1856
5334	6196
5335	6197
5336	6198
5337	6221
5338	7772
5339	11751
5340	11797
5341	11923
5342	11959
5343	14006
5344	16432
5345	16933
5346	17122

D1730

New No.	Old No.
5347	6219
5348	6220
5349	7683
5350	7776
5351	7819
5352	6018
5353	6081
5354	6179
5355	6187
5356	6191
5357	5342
5358	5345
5359	5354
5360	5563
5361	5564
5362	5566
5363	5567
5364	5569
5365	5572
5366	5576
5367	5580
5368	5584
5369	5585
5370	5588
5371	5589
5873	5593
5374	5600
5375	5602
5376	5603
5377	5604
5378	5605
5379	5606
5380	5607
5381	5608

D1730 Cont.

New No.	Old No.
5382	5609
5383	5610
5384	5611
5385	5613
5386	5632
5387	5633
5388	5634
5389	5635
5390	5636
5391	5637
5392	5640
5393	5667
5394	5673
5395	5674
5396	5675
5397	2257
5398	5070
5399	5162
5400	5163
5401	5164
5402	5165
5403	5166
5404	5167
5405	5168
5406	5169
5407	5170
5408	5171
5409	5172
5410	5173
5411	5174
5412	5175
5413	5176
5414	5177
5415	5178
5416	5179
5417	5180
5418	5181
5419	5182
5420	5183
5421	5184
5422	5185
5423	5186
5424	5187
5425	5188
5426	5189
5427	5190
5428	5191
5429	5192
5430	5193
5431	5194
5432	5195
5434	6870
5435	6871
5436	6873
5437	6874
5438	6875
5439	6876
5440	6877
5441	6878
5442	6879
5444	10497
5445	10498
5446	10499

D1851

New No.	Old No.
5447	6093
5448	6094
5449	6095
5450	6100
5451	6125
5452	6135
5453	6173
5454	6176
5455	6177
5456	6189
5457	6192
5458	6204
5459	6205
5460	6214
5461	6223
5462	6229
5463	6230
5464	6231
5465	6248
5466	6261
5467	5854
5468	6025
5469	6027
5470	6040
5471	6052
5472	6070
5473	6080
5474	6082
5475	6089
5476	6301
5477	6302
5478	6303
5479	6311
5480	6313

D1851 Cont.

New No.	Old No.
5481	6314
5482	6315
5483	6337
5484	6340
5485	6343
5486	6344
5487	6345
5488	6355
5489	6358
5490	6360
5491	6364
5492	6365
5493	6377
5494	6379
5495	6428
5496	7019
5497	7119
5498	7120
5499	7366
5500	7589

D1852

New No.	Old No.
5501	7609
5502	7610
5503	7627
5504	7694
5505	7800
5506	7852
5507	7860
5508	14029
5509	14720
5510	14761
5511	14766
5512	14779
5513	14780
5514	14789
5515	14794
5516	15266

Composite Corridor Coaches

New No.	Old No.
3500	11576
3501	11577
3502	11578
3503	11579
3504	11580

D1694

New No.	Old No.
3505	8712
3506	8713
3507	8714
3508	8751
3509	8752
3510	8753
3511	8754
3512	8755
3513	8759
3514	8760
3515	8761
3516	8762
3517	8703
3518	8764
3519	8765
3520	8766
3521	8767
3522	8768
3523	9221
3524	9222
3525	9225
3526	9232
3527	9233
3528	9262
3529	9291
3530	9295
3531	9296
3532	9297
3533	9298
3534	9299
3535	16517
3536	16560
3537	16699
3538	16701
3539	16760
3540	16879
3541	17015
3542	17028
3543	17035
3544	17350
3545	17388
3546	8747

D1694 cont.

New No.	Old No.
3547	9234
3548	9252
3549	9266
3550	9278
3551	9301
3552	9306
3553	9308
3554	9309
3555	9310
3556	9313
3557	9317
3558	9319
3559	9361
3560	9895
3561	8715
3562	9226
3563	9227
3564	9228
3565	9229
3566	9230
3567	9235
3568	9236
3569	9237
3570	9238
3571	9239
3572	9240
3573	9241
3574	9242
3575	9250
3576	9251
3577	9253
3578	9254
3579	9255
3580	9269
3581	9271
3582	9274
3583	9275
3584	9280
3585	9282
3586	693
3587	1537
3588	1620
3589	1701
3590	1909
3591	3486
3592	3971
3593	3987
3594	3994
3595	15331
3596	15377
3597	15384
3598	15389
3599	15417
3600	15450
3601	15471
3602	15715
3603	15777
3604	15783
3605	15800
3606	16144
3607	16151
3608	16163
3609	16197
3610	16319
3611	18991
3612	18992
3613	18994
3614	18995
3615	18997
3616	18998
3617	18999
3618	19002
3619	19003
3620	19004
3621	15383
3622	15419
3623	15437
3624	15599
3625	15614
3626	15626
3627	15789
3628	15793
3629	15797
3630	15798
3631	15865
3632	15885
3633	16089
3634	16113
3635	16126
3636	16157
3637	16170
3638	16203
3639	16282
3640	16364
3641	16439
3642	16461
3643	16523
3644	16544
3645	16546
3646	16667
3647	16754
3648	16763

D1694 Cont.

New No.	Old No.
3649	16896
3650	16901
3651	16989
3652	16992
3653	17012
3654	17174
3655	19125
3656	2932
3657	3456
3658	3479
3659	3481
3660	3488
3661	3502
3662	3507
3663	3508
3664	3522
3665	3523
3666	3528
3667	3531
3668	3549
3669	3559
3670	3571
3671	3575
3672	3680
3673	3682
3674	3685
3675	3690
3676	3693
3677	3699
3678	3702
3679	3706
3680	3707
3681	4044
3682	15159
3683	15180
3684	15181
3685	15183
3686	15184
3687	15186
3688	15253
3689	15292
3690	15314
3691	15315
3692	15468
3693	15534
3694	15609
3695	15631
3696	15635
3697	15679
3698	15870
3699	15888
3700	15922
3701	15988
3702	15997
3703	19017
3704	19035
3705	19133

D1752

New No.	Old No.
3706	9284
3707	9289
3708	9292
3709	9293
3710	9294
3711	9305
3712	9316
3713	9322
3714	9323
3715	9325
3716	9326
3717	9328
3718	9329
3719	9332
3720	9333
3721	9334
3722	9335
3723	9337
3724	9338
3725	9342
3726	9343
3727	9920
3728	9937
3729	9938
3730	9939

D1716

New No.	Old No.
3731	2602
3732	2603
3733	2604
3734	2605
3735	2606
3736	9270
3737	9285
3738	9286
3739	9287
3740	9288
3741	9302
3742	9312
3743	9315
3744	9369
3745	9374
3746	9379
3747	9382
3748	9383
3749	9384
3750	9387
3751	9389
3752	9390
3753	9391
3754	9393
3755	9395
3756	9396
3757	9397
3758	9399
3759	9400
3760	9401
3761	9404
3762	9405
3763	9406
3764	9407
3765	9408
3766	9409
3767	9410
3768	9411
3769	9412
3770	9413
3771	9414
3772	9417
3773	10706
3774	10709
3775	10712
3776	10714
3777	15396
3778	15399
3779	15401
3780	15461

D1791

New No.	Old No.
3781	3478
3782	8571
3783	8586
3784	8590
3785	8605
3786	9353
3787	9428
3788	9832
3789	11010
3790	11034
3791	11035
3792	11037
3793	11038
3794	11039
3795	11040
3796	11042
3797	11043
3798	11045
3799	11046
3800	11047
3801	11049
3802	11050
3803	11051
3804	11100
3805	11173
3806	11349
3807	11393
3808	11600
3809	11619
3810	14993
3811	15036
3812	15472
3813	15473
3814	15491

D1791 Cont.

New No.	Old No.
3815	15496
3816	15500
3817	15501
3818	15503
3819	15507
3820	15509
3821	15752
3822	15753
3823	15754
3824	15758
3825	15814
3826	15938
3827	15977
3828	15995

Composite Corridor Brakes

D1754

New No.	Old No.
6600	15654
6601	15889
6602	16308
6603	16312
6604	16352
6605	16513
6606	16520
6607	16639
6608	16805
6609	16827
6610	16846
6611	16847
6612	16852
6613	17352
6614	9880
6615	9881
6616	9882
6617	9883
6618	9884
6619	9885
6620	9886
6621	9887
6622	9888
6623	9889
6624	9890
6625	9891
6626	9892
6627	9893
6628	9894

D1755

Old No.	New No.
6629	15411
6630	15432
6631	15516
6632	15521
6633	15546
6634	15598
6635	15602
6636	15780
6637	15788
6638	15851
6639	15868
6640	15915
6641	15924
6642	15994
6643	16105
6644	16112
6645	16120
6646	16222
6647	16242
6648	16368
6649	16404
6650	16411
6651	16429
6652	16431
6653	16435
6654	16512
6655	16892
6656	16969
6657	17227
6658	17331

D1755 Cont.

New No.	Old No.
6659	17620
6660	17633
6661	17634
6662	17636
6663	17656
6664	17657
6665	17660
6666	17716
6667	17728
6668	17731
6669	17737
6670	17741
6671	17743
6672	17969
6673	17970
6674	17973
6675	17977
6676	18014
6677	18015
6678	18017
6679	18023
6680	18026
6681	18029
6682	18042
6683	18209

D1704

Old No.	New No.
6684	2862
6685	3341
6686	3347
6687	3354
6688	3579
6689	3580
6690	3583
6691	3584
6692	9827
6693	9833
6694	9834
6695	9835
6696	9837
6697	9839
6698	9840
6699	9842
6700	9843
6701	9844
6702	9846
6703	9847
6704	9848
6705	9849
6706	9850
6707	9851
6708	9852
6709	9853
6710	9854
6711	9855
6712	9856
6713	9857
6714	9858
6715	9859
6716	9860
6717	9861
6718	9862
6719	9863
6720	9864
6721	9865
6722	9866
6723	9867

D1704

New No.	Old No.
6724	15639
6725	15655
6726	15680
6727	15836
6728	15856
6729	15857
6730	15858
6731	15859
6732	15878
6733	9868

D1720

New No.	Old No.
6734	3010
6735	3091
6736	3177
6737	3199
6738	3348
6739	3383
6740	3396
6741	3455
6742	3530
6743	3588
6744	3590
6745	3652
6746	3684
6747	8613
6748	8688
6749	9423
6750	9432
6751	9440
6752	9451
6753	9481
6754	9483
6755	9484
6756	9486
6757	9488
6758	9493
6759	11019
6760	11032
6761	11048
6762	11069
6763	11070
6764	11071
6765	11072
6766	11092
6767	11156
6768	11157
6769	11158
6770	11159
6771	11160
6772	11161
6773	11162
6774	11163
6775	11164
6776	11238
6777	15662
6778	15683
6779	15685
6780	15686
6781	15687
6782	18523
6783	18524

D1850

New No.	Old No.
6784	9318
6785	9434
6786	9452
6787	9453
6788	9458
6789	9470
6790	9476
6791	9482
6792	9485
6793	9487
6794	9490
6795	9491
6796	9497
6797	9589
6798	9702
6799	9773
6800	9808
6801	9869
6802	10112
6803	10193

INTRODUCTION TO THE TYPE BY TYPE SURVEY

The next section covers all the LMS side-corridor diagrams in the same sequence as Table 3b. As usual, especially where original diagrams are not very clear, we have thought it helpful to include some more detailed dimensioned drawings. All extra pictures and other information are placed as close as possible to the diagrams to which relevant.

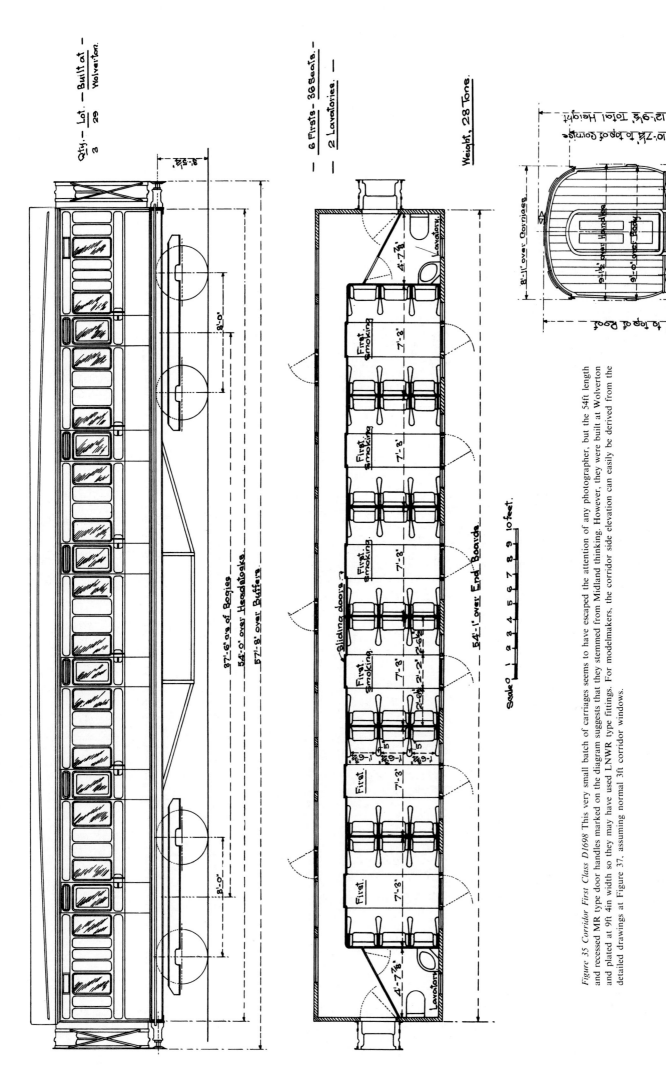

Figure 35 Corridor First Class D1698 This very small batch of carriages seems to have escaped the attention of any photographer, but the 54ft length and recessed **MR** type door handles marked on the diagram suggests that they stemmed from Midland thinking. However, they were built at Wolverton and plated at 9ft 4in width so they may have used LNWR type fittings. For modelmakers, the corridor side elevation can easily be derived from the detailed drawings at Figure 37, assuming normal 3ft corridor windows.

Qty. – Lot. – Built at Wolverton.
3   29

6 Firsts – 36 Seats.
2 Lavatories.

Weight, 28 Tons.

8'-5⅝"

8'-0"

8'-0"

37'-6" c/s of Bogies.
54'-0" over Headstocks.
57'-8' over Buffers.

First. 7'-3'

First. 7'-3'

First Smoking. 7'-3'

First Smoking. 7'-3'

First Smoking. 7'-3'

First Smoking. 7'-3'

Sliding doors.

Lavatory.

Lavatory.

4'-7⅞"

4'-7⅞"

2'-6½" 2'-2" 2'-6½"

54'-1" over End Boards.

Scale 0 1 2 3 4 5 6 7 8 9 10 feet.

12'-9⅜" Total Height.
10'-7⅜" to top of Carriage.
3'-8⅜"
8'-11" over Cornices.

12'-4⅜" to Top of Roof.
9'-11½" over Handles.
9'-0" over Body.
9'-4"

3'-8⅝"

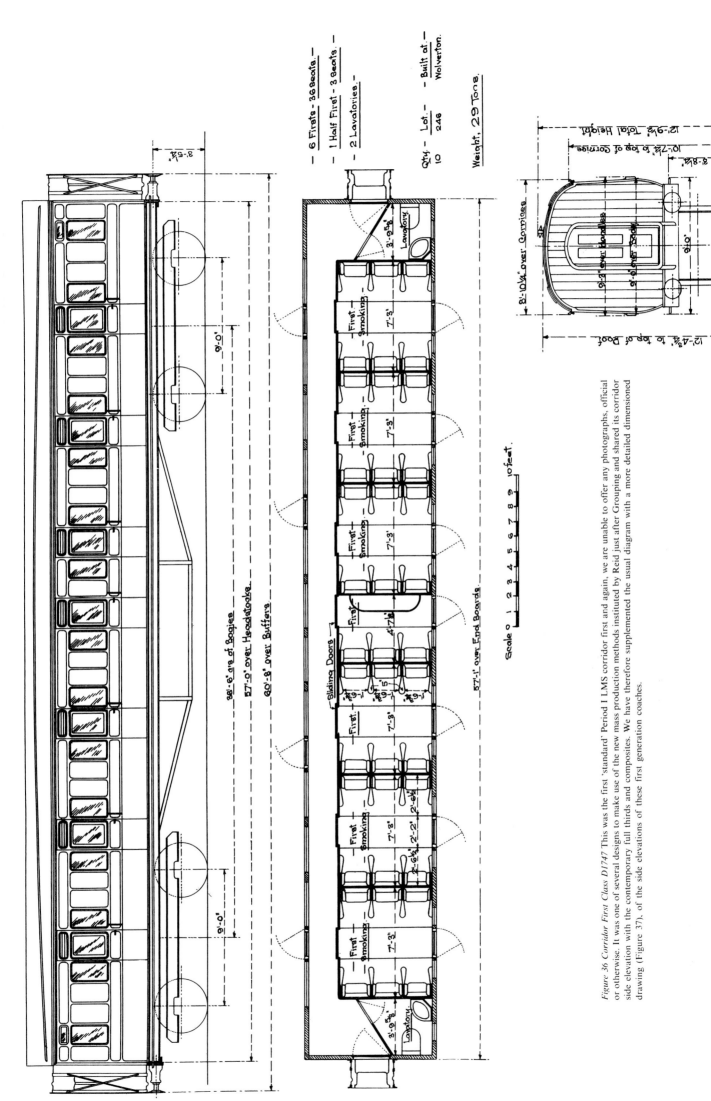

Figure 36 Corridor First Class D1747 This was the first 'standard' Period I LMS corridor first and again, we are unable to offer any photographs, official or otherwise. It was one of several designs to make use of the new mass production methods instituted by Reid just after Grouping and shared its corridor side elevation with the contemporary full thirds and composites. We have therefore supplemented the usual diagram with a more detailed dimensioned drawing (Figure 37), of the side elevations of these first generation coaches.

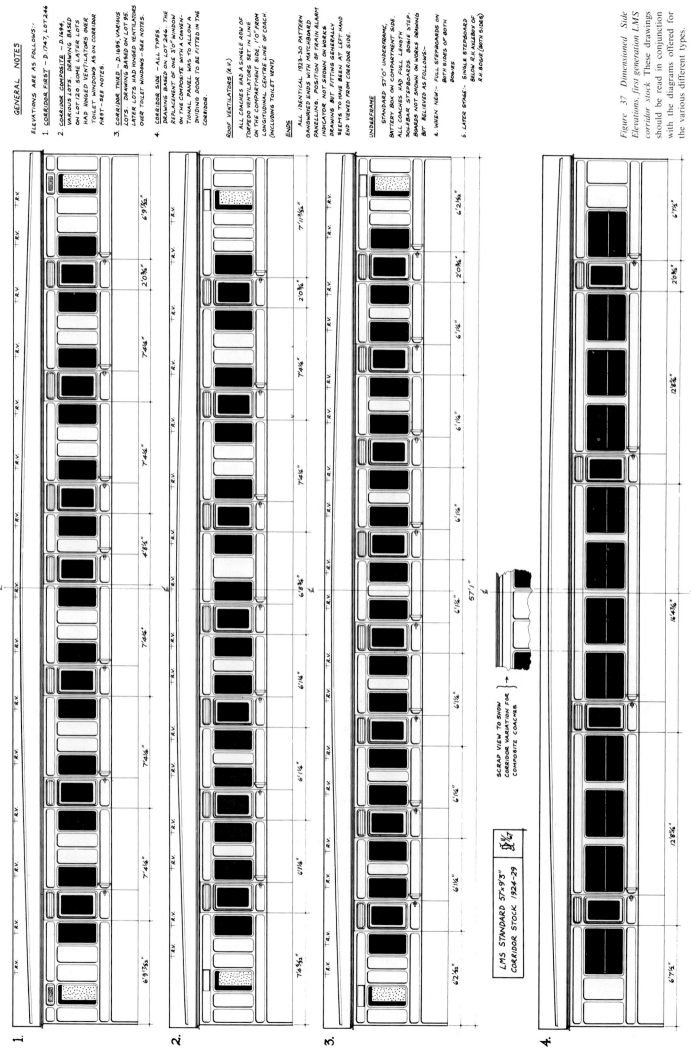

GENERAL NOTES

ELEVATIONS ARE AS FOLLOWS:-

1. CORRIDOR FIRST – D.1747, LOT 244

2. CORRIDOR COMPOSITE – D.1694. VARIOUS LOTS. DRAWING BASED ON LOT 120. SOME LATER LOTS HAD HINGED VENTILATORS OVER TOILET WINDOWS AS ON CORRIDOR FIRST – SEE NOTES.

3. CORRIDOR THIRD – D.1695, VARIOUS LOTS. DRAWING BASED ON LOT 95. LATER LOTS HAD HINGED VENTILATORS OVER TOILET WINDOWS – SEE NOTES.

4. CORRIDOR SIDE – ALL TYPES. DRAWING BASED ON LOT 244. THE REPLACEMENT OF ONE 3'0" WINDOW ON THE COMPOSITE WITH A CONVENTIONAL PANEL WAS TO ALLOW A DIVIDING DOOR TO BE FITTED IN THE CORRIDOR.

ROOF VENTILATORS (R.V.)

ALL COACHES HAD A SINGLE ROW OF TORPEDO VENTILATORS SET IN LINE ON THE COMPARTMENT SIDE, 1'0" FROM LONGITUDINAL CENTRE LINE OF COACH. (INCLUDING TOILET VENT.)

ENDS

ALL IDENTICAL 1923-30 PATTERN GANGWAYED ENDS WITH MATCHBOARD PANELLING. POSITION OF TRAIN ALARM INDICATOR NOT SHOWN ON WORKS DRAWINGS BUT FITTING GENERALLY SEEMS TO HAVE BEEN AT LEFT HAND END VIEWED FROM CORRIDOR SIDE.

UNDERFRAME

STANDARD 57'0" UNDERFRAME. BATTERY BOX ON COMPARTMENT SIDE. ALL COACHES HAD FULL LENGTH SOLEBAR STEPBOARDS. BOGIE STEPBOARDS NOT SHOWN ON WORKS DRAWINGS BUT BELIEVED AS FOLLOWS:-

4. WHEN NEW:- FULL STEPBOARDS ON BOTH SIDES OF BOTH BOGIES.

6. LATER STAGE:- SINGLE STEPBOARD BELOW R.H. AXLEBOX OF R.H. BOGIE (BOTH SIDES)

SCRAP VIEW TO SHOW CORRIDOR VARIATION FOR COMPOSITE COACHES

LMS STANDARD 57'×9'3" CORRIDOR STOCK 1924-29

Figure 37 Dimensioned Side Elevations, first generation LMS corridor stock. These drawings should be read in conjunction with the diagrams offered for the various different types.

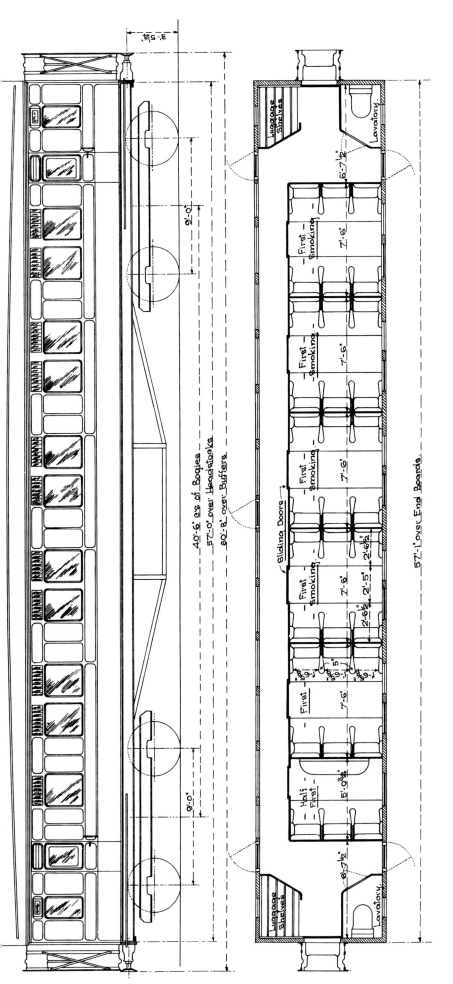

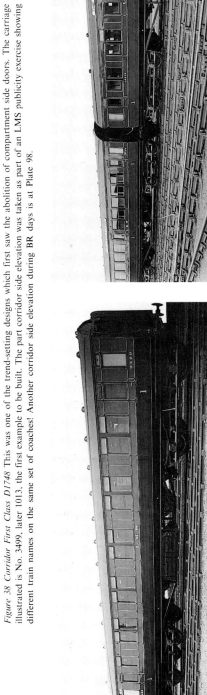

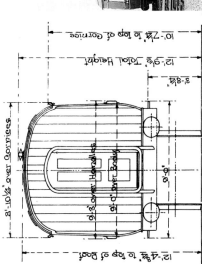

Figure 38 Corridor First Class D1748 This was one of the trend-setting designs which first saw the abolition of compartment side doors. The carriage illustrated is No. 3499, later 1013, the first example to be built. The part corridor side elevation was taken as part of an LMS publicity exercise showing different train names on the same set of coaches! Another corridor side elevation during BR days is at Plate 98.

Scale 0 1 2 3 4 5 6 7 8 9 10 feet

109

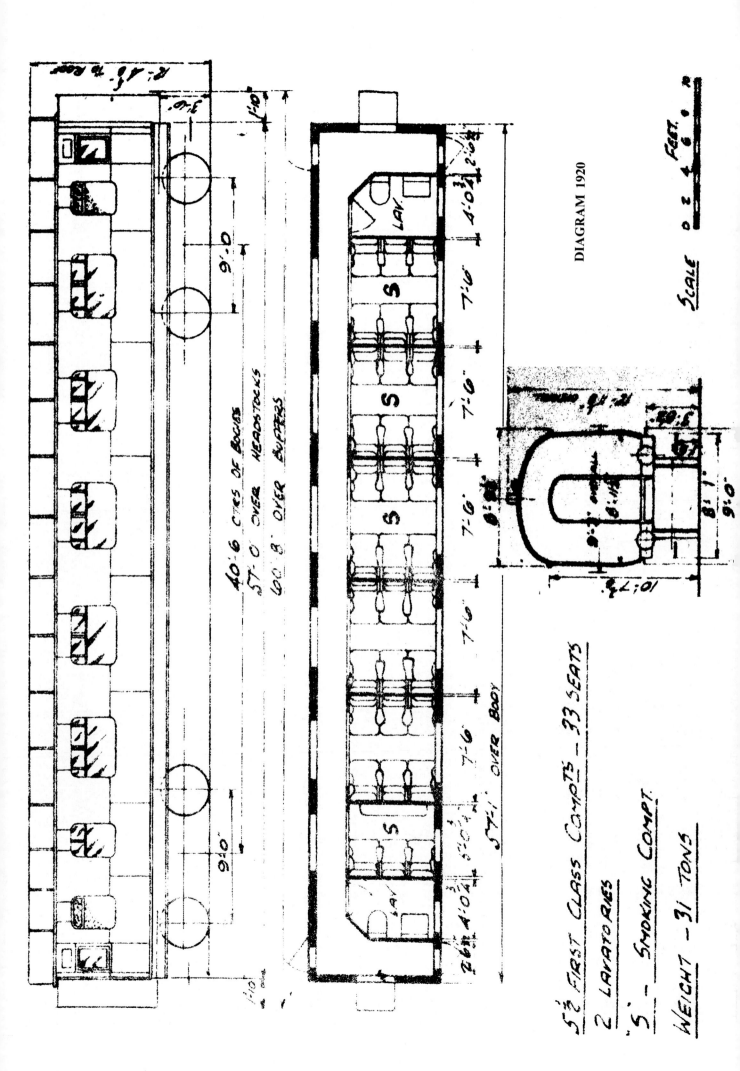

57' FIRST CLASS COMPTS – 33 SEATS

2 LAVATORIES

S – SMOKING COMPT.

WEIGHT – 31 TONS

DIAGRAM 1920

SCALE

FEET.

Figure 39 Corridor First Class D1920/D1909/D1930/D1960 It will be convenient to have these four diagrams on facing pages since there was only one essential design. A detailed dimension drawing of the side elevations will be found on the next page, followed by a selection of views, while on this page we give the basic diagrams to reduced scale simply to point out the similarities. The diagrams differed solely in terms of smoking/non-smoking distribution and the number of seats offered. It should be noted that D1960 was issued for the 1937 'Coronation Scot' vehicles which, unlike most coaches for these sets, were built new rather than rebuilt from older stock.

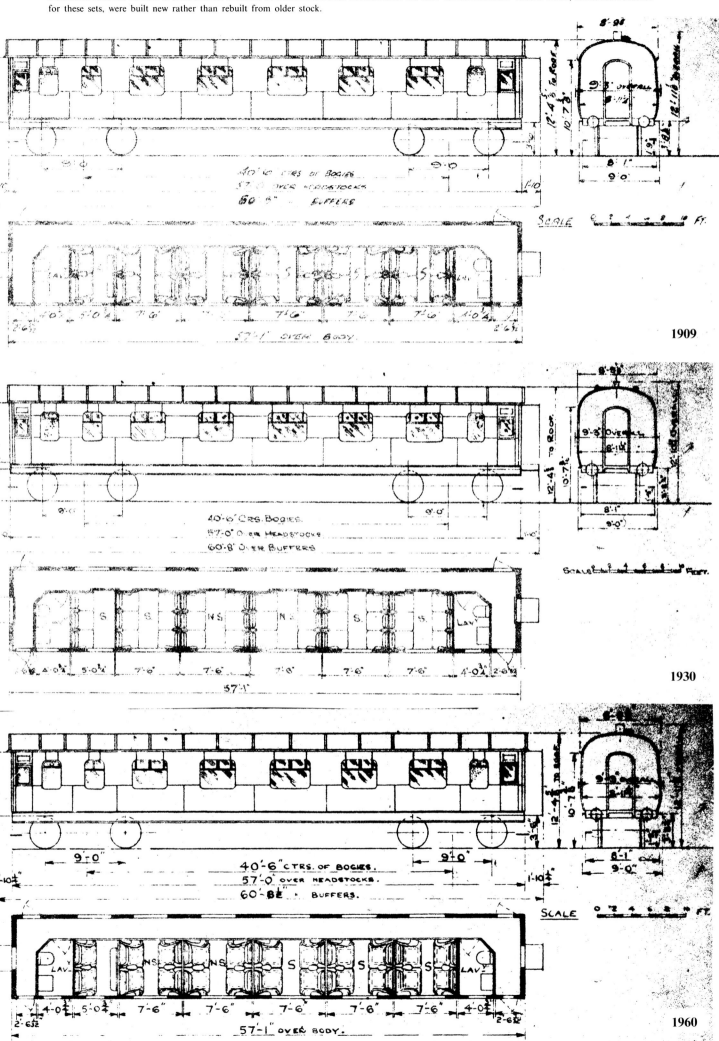

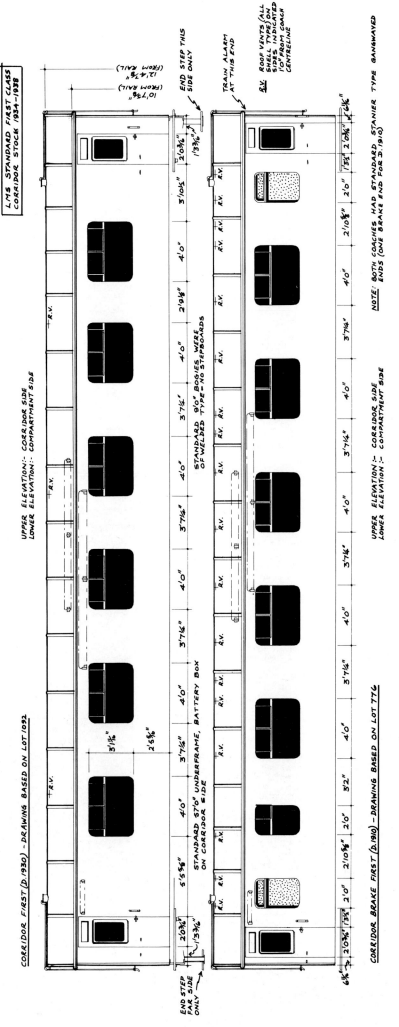

LMS STANDARD FIRST CLASS
CORRIDOR STOCK 1934-1938

CORRIDOR FIRST (D.1930) - DRAWING BASED ON LOT 1092

UPPER ELEVATION :- CORRIDOR SIDE
LOWER ELEVATION :- COMPARTMENT SIDE

END STEP THIS
SIDE ONLY

10'7⅜"
(FROM RAIL)

12'4⅞"
(FROM RAIL)

R.V.

TRAIN ALARM
AT THIS END

R.V. ROOF VENTS (ALL
SHELL TYPE) ON
SIDES INDICATED
1'0" FROM COACH
CENTRELINE

END STEP
FAR SIDE
ONLY

STANDARD 57'6" UNDERFRAME, BATTERY BOX
ON CORRIDOR SIDE

STANDARD 9'0" BOGIES WERE
OF WELDED TYPE - NO STEPBOARDS

CORRIDOR BRAKE FIRST (D.1910) - DRAWING BASED ON LOT 776

UPPER ELEVATION :- CORRIDOR SIDE
LOWER ELEVATION :- COMPARTMENT SIDE

NOTE: BOTH COACHES HAD STANDARD STANIER TYPE GANGWAYED
ENDS (ONE BRAKE END FOR D.1910)

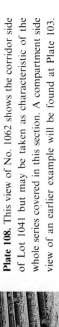

Figure 40 Dimensioned side elevations. Period III Corridor Firsts, 1934–8 This drawing, based on D1930, Lot 1092, should be taken in conjunction with the diagrams offered on the previous page.

Plate 108. This view of No. 1062 shows the corridor side of Lot 1041 but may be taken as characteristic of the whole series covered in this section. A compartment side view of an earlier example will be found at Plate 103.

Plate 109. This view, taken c.1957 at an unknown location, shows the last example to be built of D1960 No. M1071M in BR red/cream livery. The air duct along the roof gives away its 'Coronation Scot' origins, but one wonders how many passengers appreciated the fact! (*The late Gavin Wilson collection*)

Plates 110-111. The LMS prided itself on its interior finishes and these two examples seem to lack little in the way of comfort and luxury. The first view (note the smaller window and courtesy footstool) shows the luxury two per side coupè compartment of No. 1047 from Lot 793, built in 1934, (the trim is stated to be in greywood), while the second interior shows a normal six-seat compartment inside No. 1072, built in 1938.

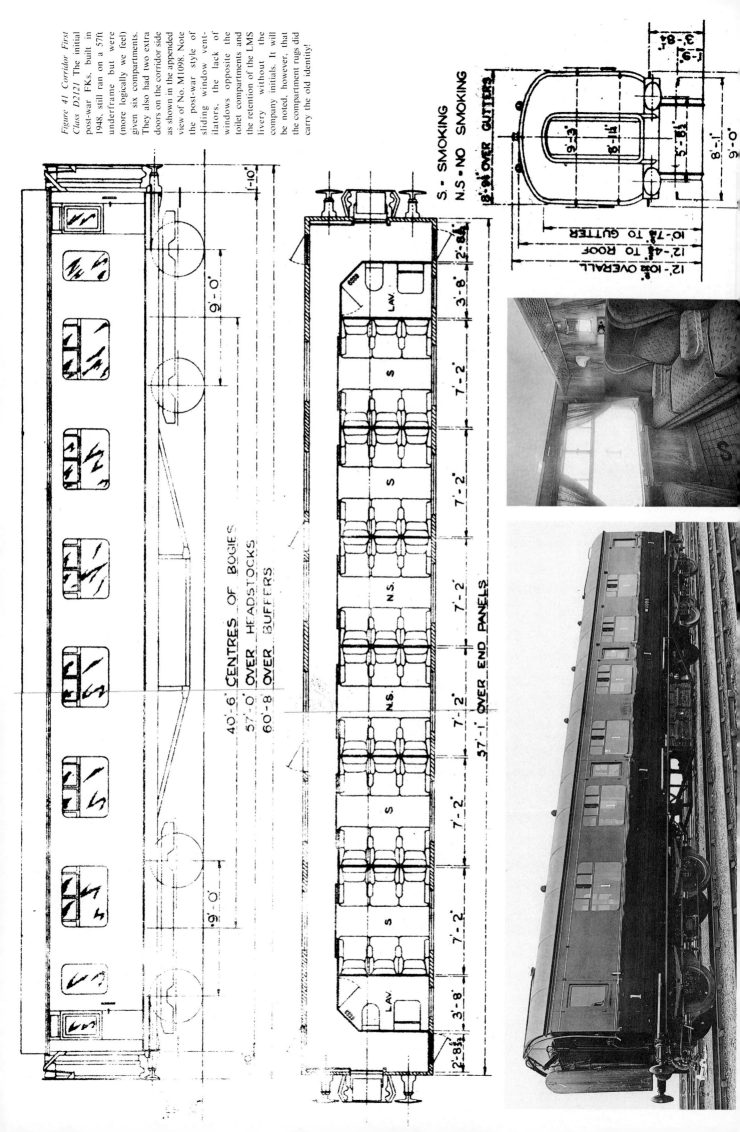

Figure 41 Corridor First Class D2121 The initial post-war FKs, built in 1948, still ran on a 57ft underframe but were (more logically we feel) given six compartments. They also had two extra doors on the corridor side as shown in the appended view of No. M1098. Note the post-war style of sliding window ventilators, the lack of windows opposite the toilet compartments and the retention of the LMS livery without the company initials. It will be noted, however, that the compartment rugs did carry the old identity!

S – SMOKING
N.S – NO SMOKING

3'-8¼'
9'-1½'
8'-9' OVER GUTTER
9'-3'
8'-1¼'
5'-8½'
8'-1'
9'-0'
10'-7⅜' TO GUTTER
12'-4⅜' TO ROOF
12'-10⅞' OVERALL

1'-10'
9'-0'
9'-0'

40'-6' CENTRES OF BOGIES
57'-0' OVER HEADSTOCKS
60'-8' OVER BUFFERS

LAV.
FOOD
S
7'-2'
3'-8'
2'-8½'
S
7'-2'
S
7'-2'
N.S.
7'-2'
N.S.
7'-2'
S
7'-2'
S
7'-2'
LAV.
2'-8½'
3'-8'
57'-1' OVER END PANELS

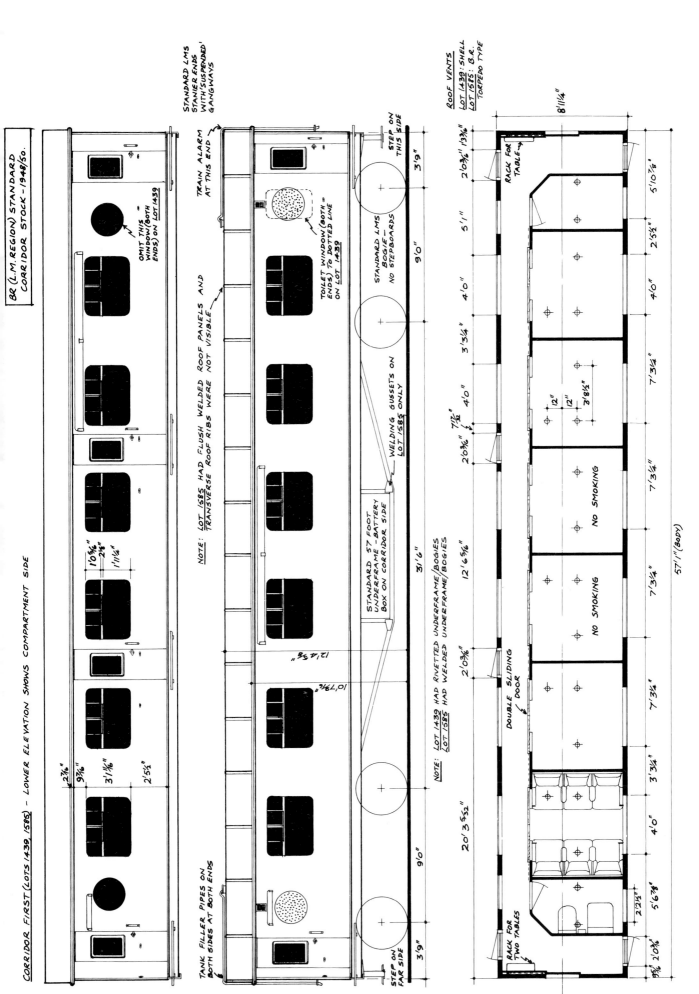

Figure 42 Dimensioned side elevations. Period III Corridor Firsts: 1948–50 These drawings should be read in conjunction with Figures 41 and 43 and are designed to cover both post-war variants

BR (L.M. REGION) STANDARD CORRIDOR STOCK - 1948/50.

STANDARD LMS STANIER ENDS WITH 'SUSPENDED' GANGWAYS

CORRIDOR FIRST (LOTS 1439, 1585) - LOWER ELEVATION SHOWS COMPARTMENT SIDE

OMIT THIS WINDOW (BOTH ENDS) ON LOT 1439

TRAIN ALARM AT THIS END

TOILET WINDOW (BOTH ENDS) TO DOTTED LINE ON LOT 1439

STEP ON THIS SIDE

NOTE: LOT 1585 HAD FLUSH WELDED ROOF PANELS AND TRANSVERSE ROOF RIBS WERE NOT VISIBLE

TANK FILLER PIPES ON BOTH SIDES AT BOTH ENDS

STANDARD LMS BOGIE — NO STEPBOARDS

WELDING GUSSETS ON LOT 1585 ONLY

STANDARD 57 FOOT UNDERFRAME - BATTERY BOX ON CORRIDOR SIDE

STEP ON FAR SIDE

NOTE: LOT 1439 HAD RIVETTED UNDERFRAME/BOGIES LOT 1585 HAD WELDED UNDERFRAME/BOGIES

ROOF VENTS LOT 1439: SHELL LOT 1585: B.R. TORPEDO TYPE

RACK FOR TABLE

NO SMOKING   NO SMOKING

DOUBLE SLIDING DOOR

RACK FOR TWO TABLES

57'1" (BODY)

115

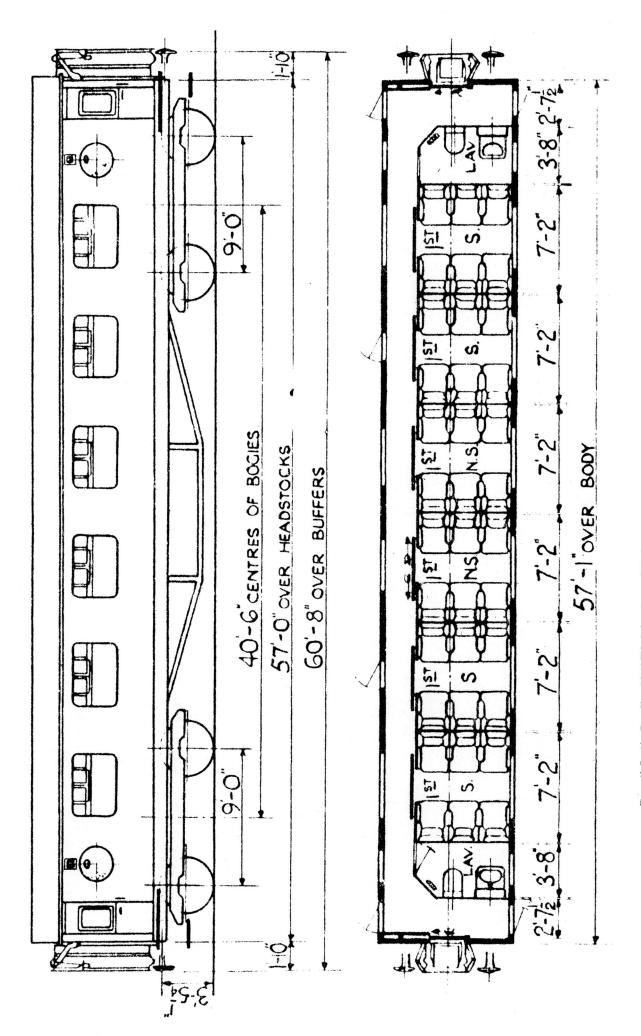

Figure 43 Corridor First Class D2162 This design, the so-called 'porthole' variant, appeared in 1950 and carried BR livery from new. They were dimensionally much as D2121 but did have matching circular windows on the corridor side opposite the toilets. The pictures show both sides of No. M1122.

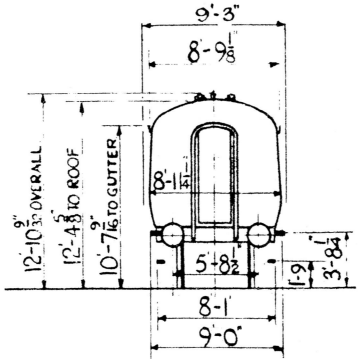

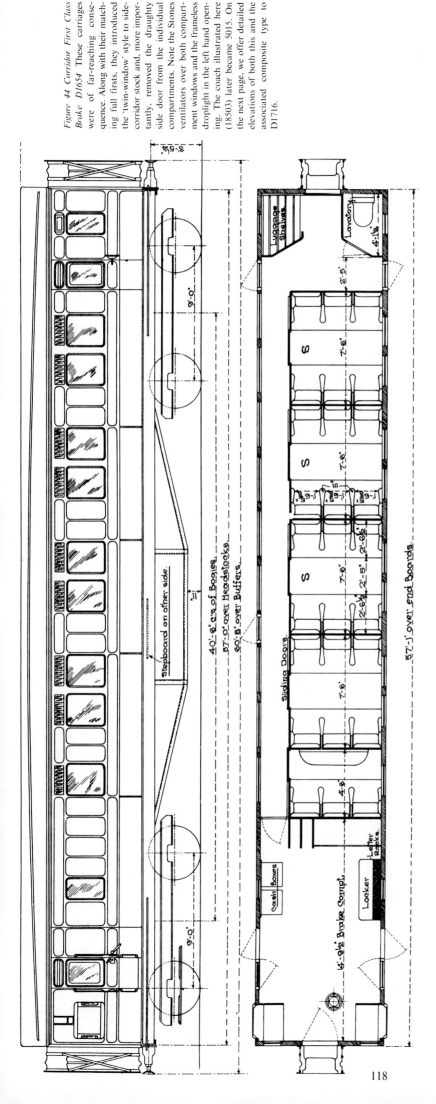

Figure 44 Corridor First Class Brake D1654 These carriages were of far-reaching consequence. Along with their matching full firsts, they introduced the 'twin-window' style to side-corridor stock and, more importantly, removed the draughty side door from the individual compartments. Note the Stones ventilators over both compartment windows and the frameless droplight in the left hand opening. The coach illustrated here (18503) later became 5015. On the next page, we offer detailed elevations of both this and the associated composite type to D1716.

Luggage Shelves.

Lavatory.

4'-1¼"

2'-5"

S

7'-6"

S

7'-6"

1'-9" road 5"

1'-9" road 5"

1'-9" road 5"

2'-6½" 2'-5" 2'-6½"

S

7'-6"

Sliding Doors.

S

7'-6"

4'-6"

Letter Racks.

Locker

Cash Boxes

4'-9½" Brake Compt.

57'-1" over end Boards.

40'-6" c'rs of Bogies.

57'-0" over Headstocks.

60'-8" over Buffers.

Stepboard on other side.

9'-0"

3'-5¾"

9'-0"

9'-0"

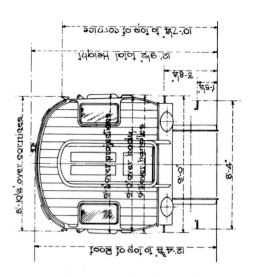

8'-10¼" over cornice.

9'-6" over projections.

9'-0" over body.

9'-6" over handles.

10'-7½" to top of cornice.

12'-9½" total Height.

3'-8¾"

1'-5½"

9'-0"

8'-4"

12'-4¾" to top of Roof.

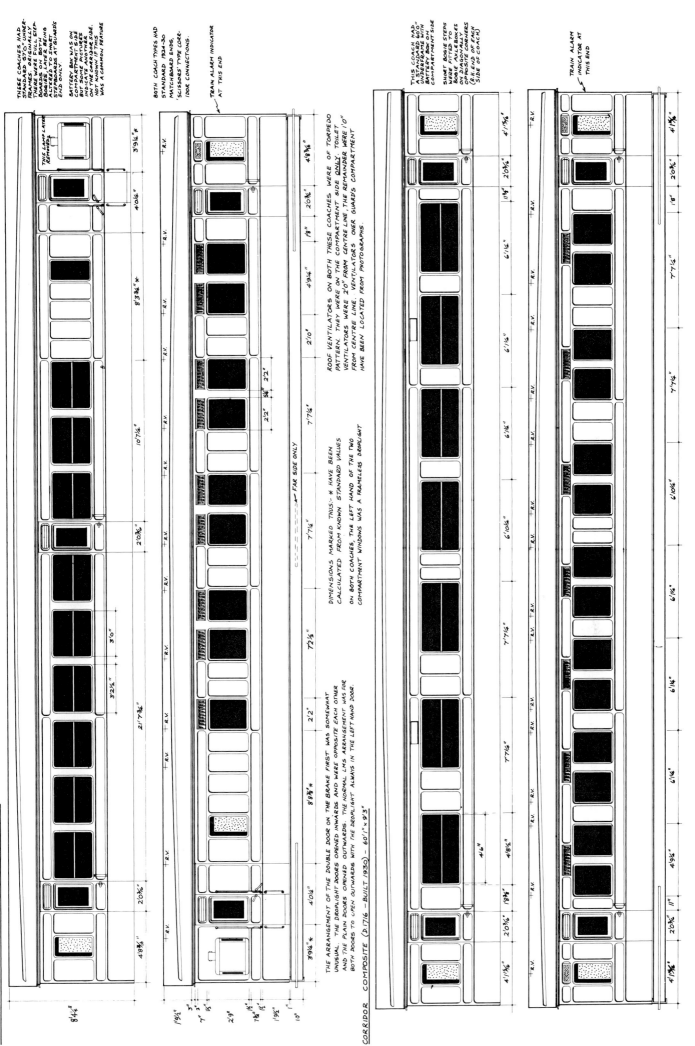

THESE COACHES HAD STANDARD 57'0" UNDERFRAMES. ORIGINALLY THERE WERE FULL STEP-BOARDS ON BOTH BOGIES, LATER BEING ALTERED TO SHORT STEPBOARDS AT GUARDS END ONLY.

BATTERY BOX WAS ON COMPARTMENT SIDE BUT SOME PICTURES INDICATE ANOTHER ON THE CORRIDOR SIDE. NOT KNOWN IF THIS WAS A COMMON FEATURE.

THIS LAMP LATER REMOVED.

BOTH COACH TYPES HAD STANDARD 1924-30 MATCHBOARD ENDS, 'SCISSORS' TYPE CORRIDOR CONNECTIONS.

TRAIN ALARM INDICATOR AT THIS END

8'4½" 4'8⅜" * 2'0⅝" 3'2½" 3'0" 2'11'7¾" 107'½" 8'3¾" * 4'0¼" 3'9¼" *

◁———————————— FAR SIDE ONLY

1'9½" 3" 7" 1½" 2'9" 7¼" 1¼" 1½" 10" 3'9¼" * 4'0¼" 8'8¾" * 2'2" 72'5½" 7'1½" 5¼" 2'2" 2'2" 2'0¾" 1'8" 4'9⅜"

THE ARRANGEMENT OF THE DOUBLE DOOR ON THE BRAKE FIRST WAS SOMEWHAT UNUSUAL. THE DROPLIGHT DOORS OPENED INWARDS AND WERE OPPOSITE EACH OTHER AND THE PLAIN DOORS OPENED OUTWARDS. THE NORMAL LMS ARRANGEMENT WAS FOR BOTH DOORS TO OPEN OUTWARDS WITH THE DROPLIGHT ALWAYS IN THE LEFT HAND DOOR.

CORRIDOR COMPOSITE (D1716 - BUILT 1930) - 60'1" × 9'3"

ROOF VENTILATORS ON BOTH THESE COACHES WERE OF TORPEDO PATTERN. THEY WERE ON THE COMPARTMENT SIDE ONLY. TOILET VENTILATORS WERE 2'0" FROM CENTRE LINE, THE REMAINDER WERE 1'0" FROM CENTRE LINE. VENTILATORS OVER GUARDS COMPARTMENT HAVE BEEN LOCATED FROM PHOTOGRAPHS.

DIMENSIONS MARKED THUS:- * HAVE BEEN CALCULATED FROM KNOWN STANDARD VALUES ON BOTH COACHES. THE LEFT HAND OF THE TWO COMPARTMENT WINDOWS WAS A FRAMELESS DROPLIGHT

THIS COACH HAD A STANDARD 60'0" UNDERFRAME WITH BATTERY BOX ON COMPARTMENT SIDE

SHORT BOGIE STEPS WERE FITTED TO BOGIE AXLEBOXES ON DIAGONALLY OPPOSITE CORNERS (R.H. END OF EACH SIDE OF COACH)

4'1⅝" 2'0⅝" 1'1" 7'7½" 6'½" 6'4½" 6'½" 7'7½" 4'8½" 1'8¼" 2'0¾" 1'1½" 4'9⅜"

TRAIN ALARM INDICATOR AT THIS END

4'1⅝" 2'0⅝" 1'8" 7'7½" 6'10½" 6'¼" 6'¼" 6'10½" 7'7½" 4'9¾" 1'8" 2'0¾" 4'1⅝"

Figure 45 Dimensioned side elevations, 'twin window' corridor stock: 1927–30 These carriages, both first class and composite, were very significant in the evolution of the later LMS standard types. These drawings should be taken in conjunction with the diagrams on the previous page (BFK–D1654) and on page 155 (CK–D1716). Additionally, most of the values apply to the contemporary FKs and BCKs to D1748 (page 109) and D1704 (page 168).

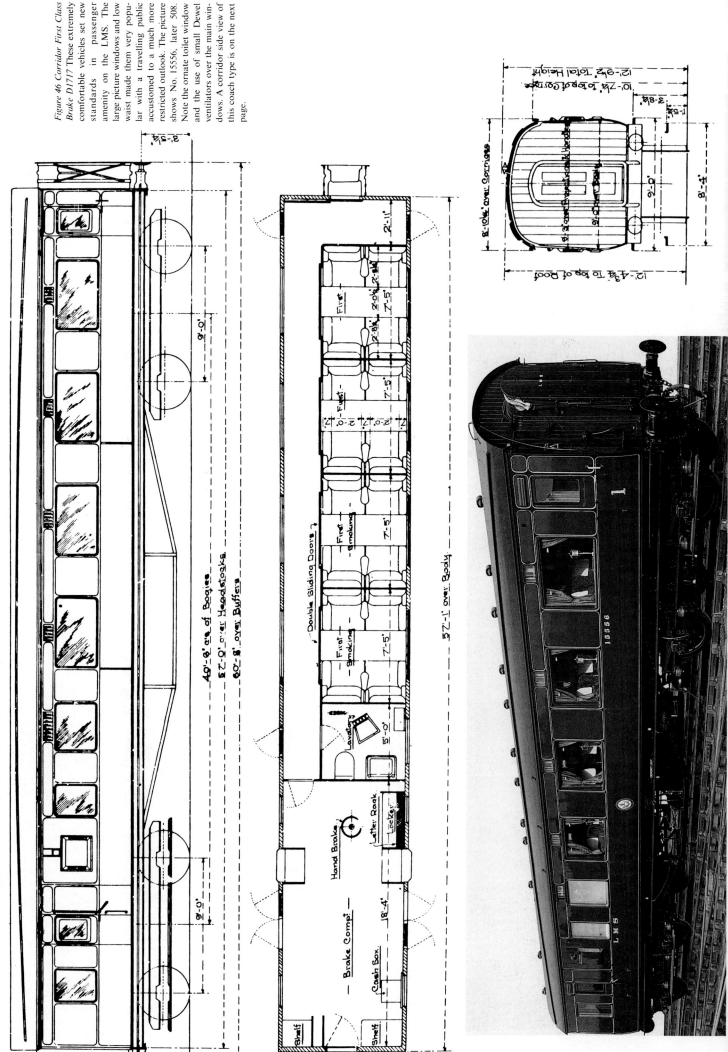

Figure 46 Corridor First Class Brake D1717 These extremely comfortable vehicles set new standards in passenger amenity on the LMS. The large picture windows and low waist made them very popular with a travelling public accustomed to a much more restricted outlook. The picture shows No. 15556, later 508. Note the ornate toilet window and the use of small Dewel ventilators over the main windows. A corridor side view of this coach type is on the next page.

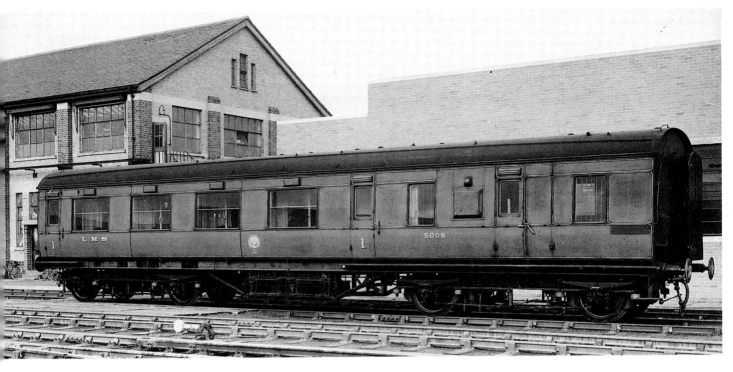

Plate 112. This view has already appeared in Volume I page 12, but we repeat it here for convenience since it is the only known official view of D1717 to show the corridor side of these handsome vehicles. Despite our best endeavours, we are no nearer to knowing why the vehicle was fitted with long wheelbase bogies but we have established that the picture was taken early in 1939 (confirmed by a 1/39 chalk inscription on the cell box) which says much for the quality of the original fully lined livery which cannot have been applied any later than c.1934, probably when the carriage was given its new number in unshaded gold figures (it was No. 15506).

Plate 113. As a preliminary to the 'all steel' Period II BFKs on the next page, this view of No. 2554 (later 5036) of D1845 makes an interesting comparison with No. 5006 (above), taken from much the same angle. Within the coaches, passengers would have been greeted by much the same sort of compartment amenity but there can be little doubt that the external styling was subtly different. No. 2554 was the first of this diagram to be built and later became one of the three to be modified to D1962 with 'luxury' finish.

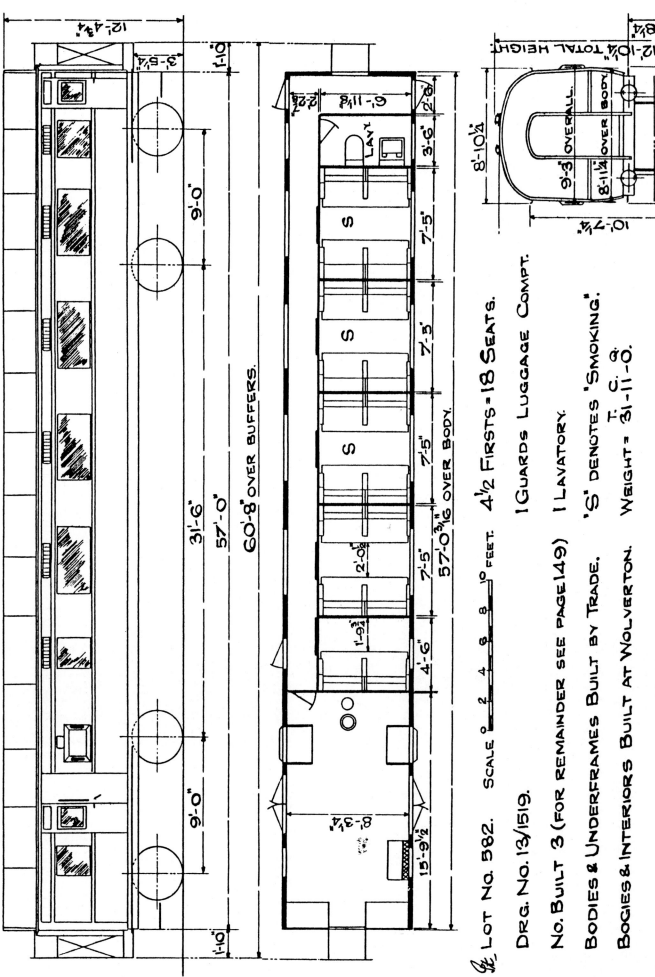

LOT No. 582. SCALE 0 2 4 6 8 10 FEET. 4½ FIRSTS = 18 SEATS.

DRG. No. 13/1519. 1 GUARDS LUGGAGE COMPT.

No. BUILT 3 (FOR REMAINDER SEE PAGE 149) 1 LAVATORY.

BODIES & UNDERFRAMES BUILT BY TRADE. 'S' DENOTES "SMOKING".

BOGIES & INTERIORS BUILT AT WOLVERTON. WEIGHT = 31-11-0.

T. C. O.

Figure 47 First Class Corridor Brake D1845/1962 The only difference between these two diagrams was the later conversion of the first three examples to luxury pattern with two per side seating. This diagram offered is of this conversion (D1962). The picture at the foot of the previous page shows the compartment side view of the first example built (later No. 5036). Note, compared with the corridor side (Plate 113), that the brake-end roof rainstrip is shorter, not having to extend to cover a passenger entrance door. It will also be noted that all 4½ compartments are labelled 'Smoking', in spite of contradictory evidence on both diagrams. Clearly it was a different world!

122

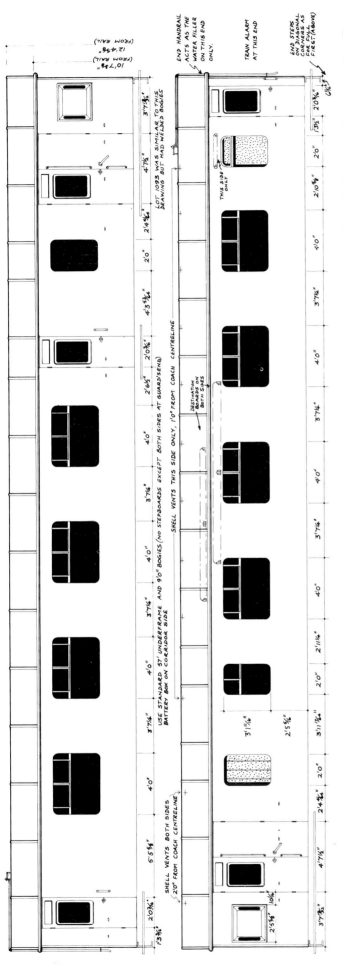

Figure 48 Dimensioned side elevations. First Class Corridor Brakes D1910/D1961 The two pre-war Period III BFKs shared identical dimensions. D1961 being raised in 1937 for the three 'Coronation Scot' carriages which, along with the matching full firsts (page 111) were the only carriages built new for this service. The drawing is based on Lot 776, the first to be built in 1934 and should be used in association with D1961 on the next page. The picture shows the corridor side of No. 5062. Lot 1093.

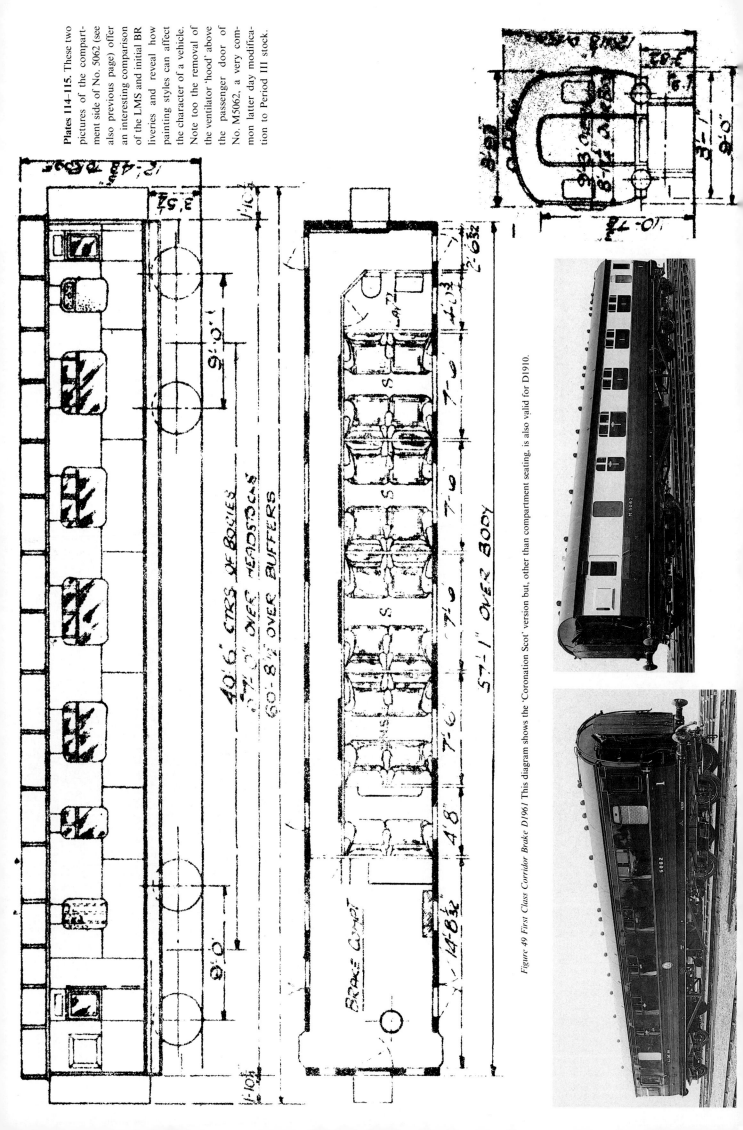

Plates 114–115. These two pictures of the compartment side of No. 5062 (see also previous page) offer an interesting comparison of the LMS and initial BR liveries and reveal how painting styles can affect the character of a vehicle. Note too the removal of the ventilator 'hood' above the passenger door of No. M5062, a very common latter day modification to Period III stock.

40'6" CTRS OF BOGIES
57'0" OVER HEADSTOCKS
60'-8½" OVER BUFFERS
57'-1" OVER BODY

BRAKE COMPT

Figure 49 First Class Corridor Brake D1961 This diagram shows the 'Coronation Scot' version but, other than compartment seating, is also valid for D1910.

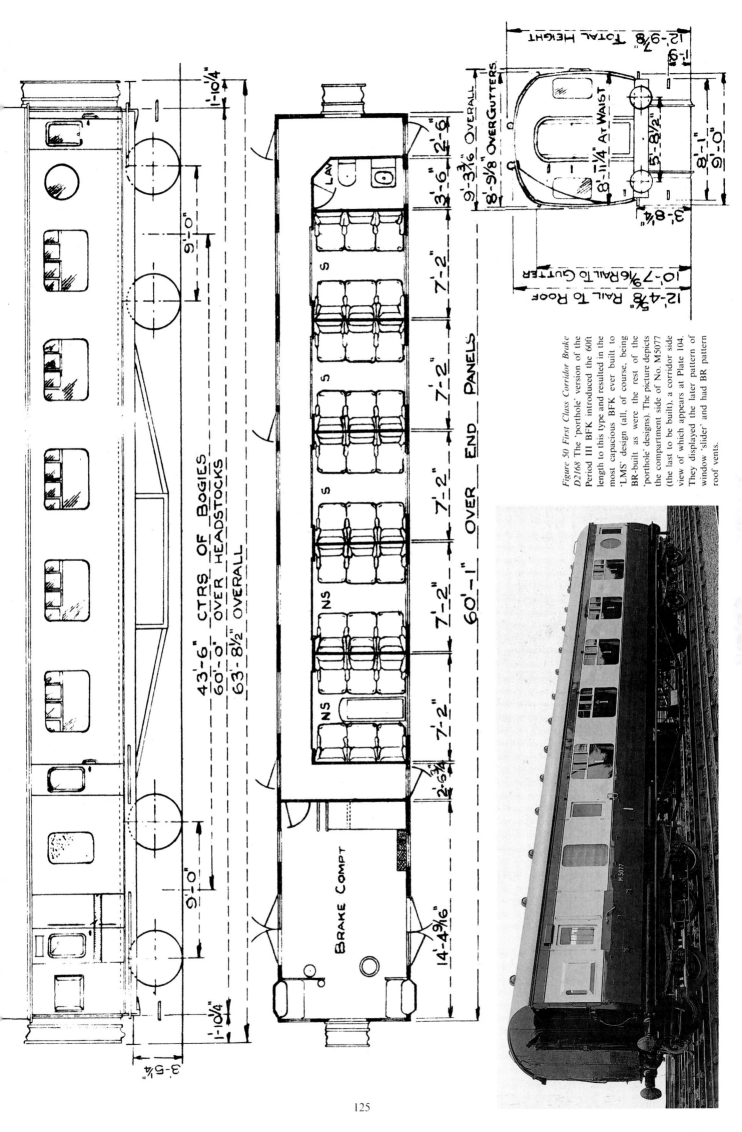

1'-10¼"

9'-0"

43'-6" CTRS OF BOGIES
60'-0" OVER HEADSTOCKS
63'-8½" OVERALL

9'-0"

1'-10¼"

3'-5¾"

2'-6"
3'-6"

LAV

S

7'-2"

S

7'-2"

S

7'-2"

7'-2"

NS

NS

7'-2"

NS

7'-2"

60'-1" OVER END PANELS

2'-3¾"
2'-5¼"

BRAKE COMPT

14'-4⁹⁄₁₆"

12'-9⁷⁄₈" TOTAL HEIGHT

1'-9"

9'-3³⁄₁₆" OVERALL
8'-9⁵⁄₈" OVER GUTTERS

8'-11¼" AT WAIST

5'-8½"

8'-1"
9'-0"

3'-8¾"

10'-7⁹⁄₁₆" RAIL TO GUTTER

12'-4⁵⁄₈" RAIL TO ROOF

Figure 50 First Class Corridor Brake D2168 The 'porthole' version of the Period III BFK introduced the 60ft length to this type and resulted in the most capacious BFK ever built to 'LMS' design (all, of course, being BR-built as were the rest of the 'porthole' designs). The picture depicts the compartment side of No. M5077 (the last to be built), a corridor side view of which appears at Plate 104. They displayed the later pattern of window 'slider' and had BR pattern roof vents.

Plates 116–118. It seems appropriate to conclude the first class section of this chapter with a detailed look at the interior of the last example to be built, BFK No. M5077. The views are self-explanatory and, apart from the changed inscription on the carriage rug, everything is still very much in the company tradition. Bearing in mind that this was not special 'luxury' stock and that we may well be prejudiced(!), we do not think that anything which BR subsequently offered to the first class passenger in the MkI or MkII periods (unless he or she be willing to pay a supplement) showed any significant improvement on this.

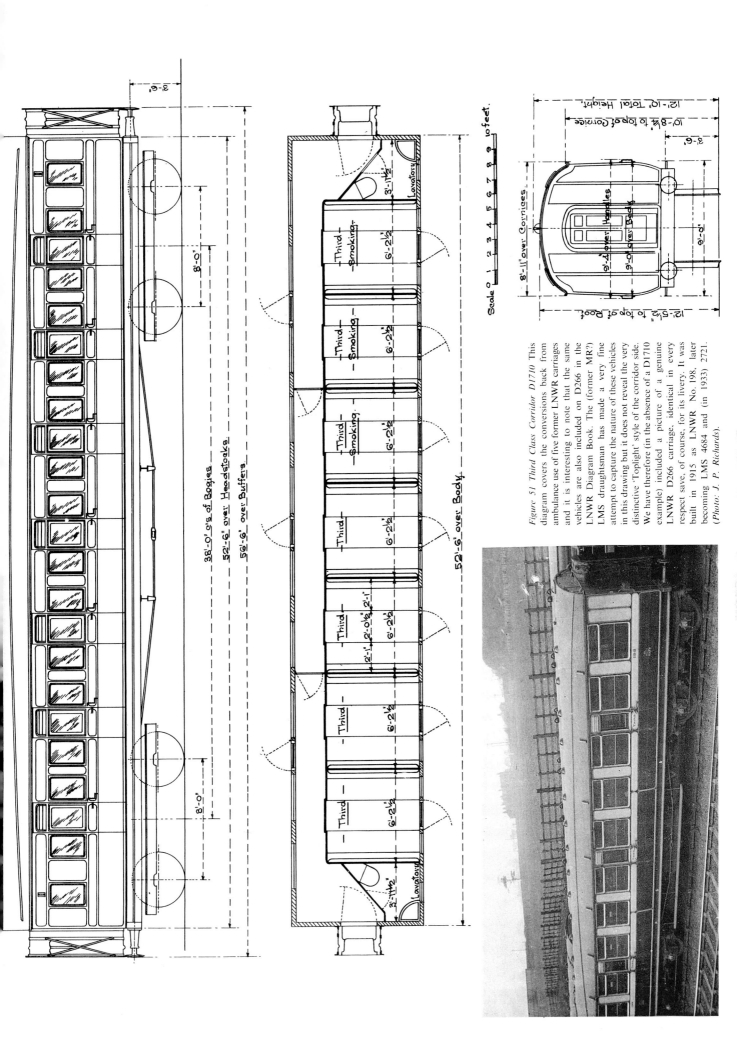

Figure 51 Third Class Corridor D1710 This diagram covers the conversions back from ambulance use of five former LNWR carriages and it is interesting to note that the same vehicles are also included on D266 in the LNWR Diagram Book. The (former MR?) LMS draughtsman has made a very fine attempt to capture the nature of these vehicles in this drawing but it does not reveal the very distinctive 'Toplight' style of the corridor side. We have therefore (in the absence of a D1710 example) included a picture of a genuine LNWR D266 carriage, identical in every respect save, of course, for its livery. It was built in 1915 as LNWR No. 198, later becoming LMS 4684 and (in 1933) 2721. *(Photo: J. P. Richards).*

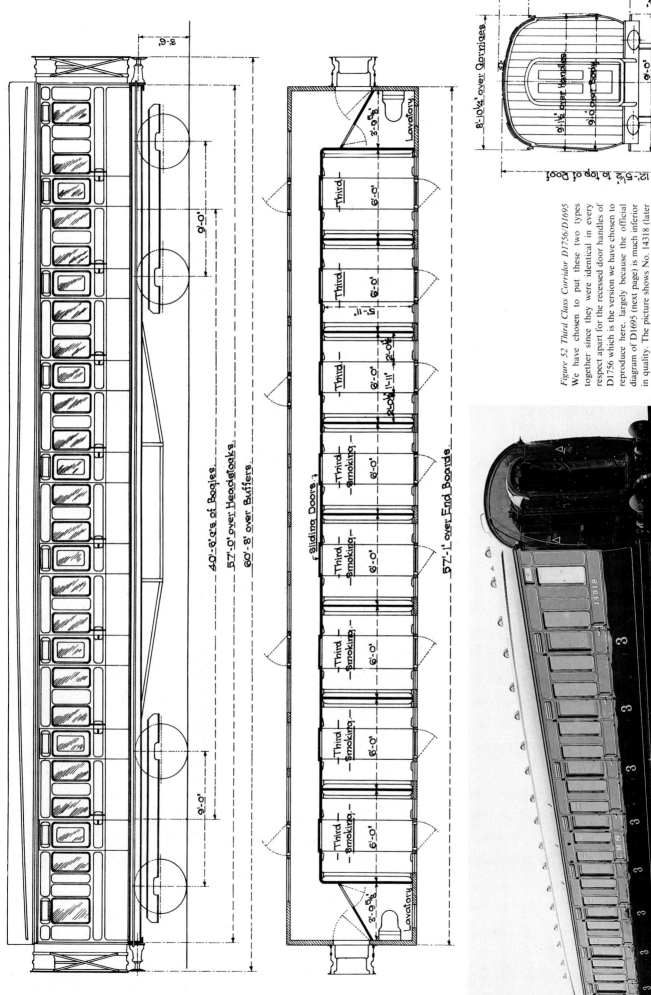

Figure 52 Third Class Corridor D1756/D1695
We have chosen to put these two types together since they were identical in every respect apart for the recessed door handles of D1756 which is the version we have chosen to reproduce here, largely because the official diagram of D1695 (next page) is much inferior in quality. The picture shows No. 14318 (later 1485) of D1695, Lot 388, the last examples to be built of this type. An earlier example is given at Plate 99.

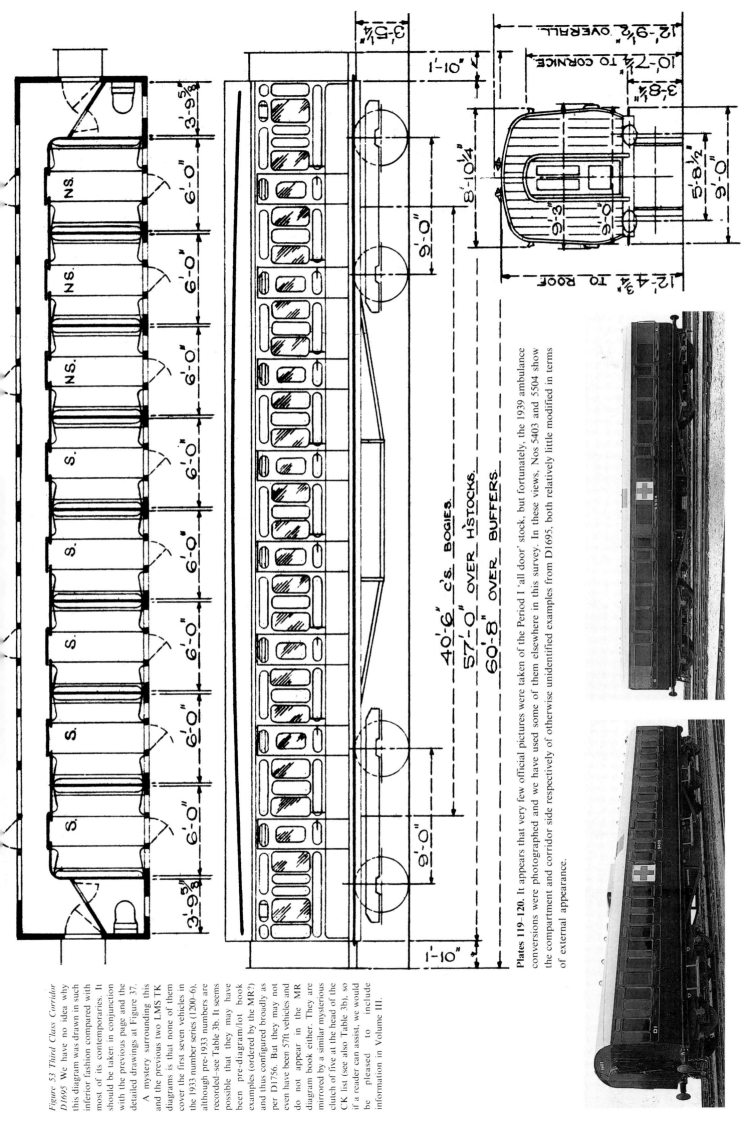

Figure 53 Third Class Corridor D1695 We have no idea why this diagram was drawn in such inferior fashion compared with most of its contemporaries. It should be taken in conjunction with the previous page and the detailed drawings at Figure 37.

A mystery surrounding this and the previous two LMS TK diagrams is that none of them cover the first seven vehicles in the 1933 number series (1200–6), although pre-1933 numbers are recorded—see Table 3b. It seems possible that they may have been pre-diagram/lot book examples (ordered by the MR?) and thus configured broadly as per D1756. But they may not even have been 57ft vehicles and do not appear in the MR diagram book either. They are mirrored by a similar mysterious clutch of five at the head of the CK list (see also Table 3b), so if a reader can assist, we would be pleased to include information in Volume III.

Plates 119–120. It appears that very few official pictures were taken of the Period I 'all door' stock, but fortunately, the 1939 ambulance conversions were photographed and we have used some of them elsewhere in this survey. In these views, Nos 5403 and 5504 show the compartment and corridor side respectively of otherwise unidentified examples from D1695, both relatively little modified in terms of external appearance.

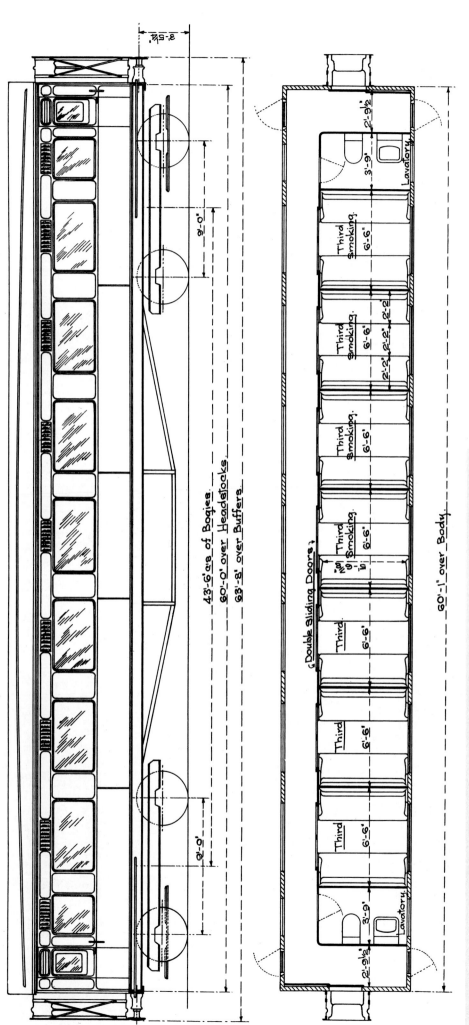

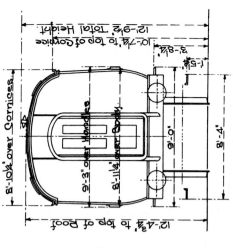

Figure 54 Third Class Corridor D1782 It seems certain that these spacious carriages were designed (along with some of the similarly styled 60ft open stock–see Chapter 4) to be used initially on the re-equipped 'Royal Scot' service of 1930 and there are numerous pictures which indicate that this was indeed their first duty. The appended view shows the corridor side of No. 3031, later 1502, a compartment elevation and interior view being offered on the next page.

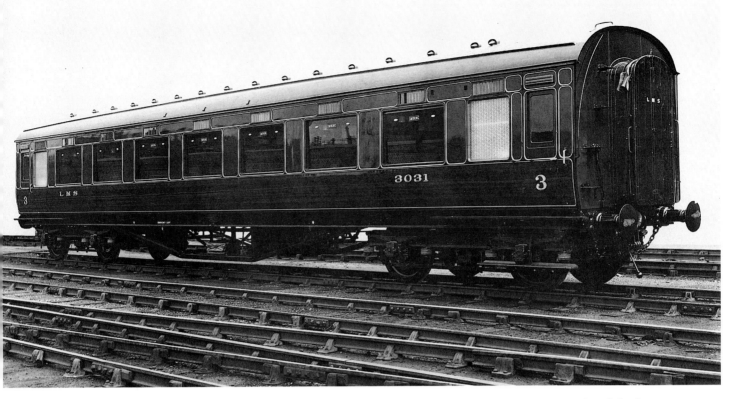

Plate 121. Period II 60ft TK (D1782) No. 3031 later 1502. Only ten were built, the only corridor thirds between the 'all-door' type and the Stanier designs and the only 60ft TKs. Note the absence of the LMS emblem–a not uncommon feature of LMS thirds and brake thirds even with end entrances. The handgrips for lowering the compartment droplights are clear, high on the window.

Plates 122–123. Although D1782 was a very fine design, it was soon overtaken in terms of compartment amenity by the new Period III designs as can be seen in this pair of pictures, taken only three years apart in 1930 and 1933 at a time when the LMS was very fond of simulating exterior scenes by means of 'faking' suitable pictures onto the carriage windows! The interior of the Period II coach is believed to be No. 3031 (already illustrated) and the Period III interior shows an early shallow window ventilator example from BTK No. 5461. D1851 (page 144). It makes a suitable introduction to the Period III survey which follows.

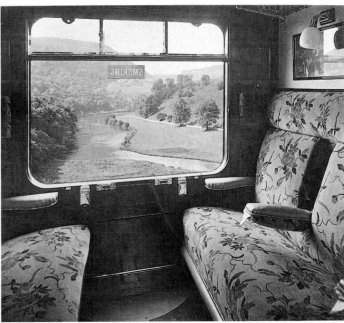

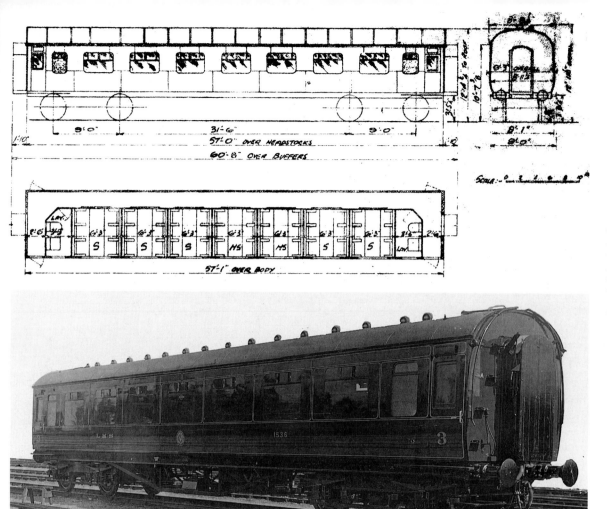

DIAGRAM
1860/1899

Figure 55 Third Class Corridor D1860/D1899 This extremely poor diagram is the best we can offer for the first Period III TK types. It actually shows D1899 but the D1860 version is incapable of any form of reproduction! Fortunately, its basic dimensions were identical, window detail being as for the brake composite to D1850 (page 172) to which reference should be made. We offer a compartment side view of D1860 and a corridor side view of the same coach is at Plate 105. By good fortune, however, we are able to give both detailed drawings and a large selection of pictures of D1899, by far the more important type.

Plate 124. A typical pre-war Stanier corridor third, this particular example being No. 1579 from the batch with full livery (D1899). Note the absence of the LMS crest. The running number was rendered in unshaded block style characters–typical of the early Stanier period.

Plate 125. No. 1906 came from Lot 846 in 1935. The livery is now a simplified style but the carriage still has red ends and unshaded numerals.

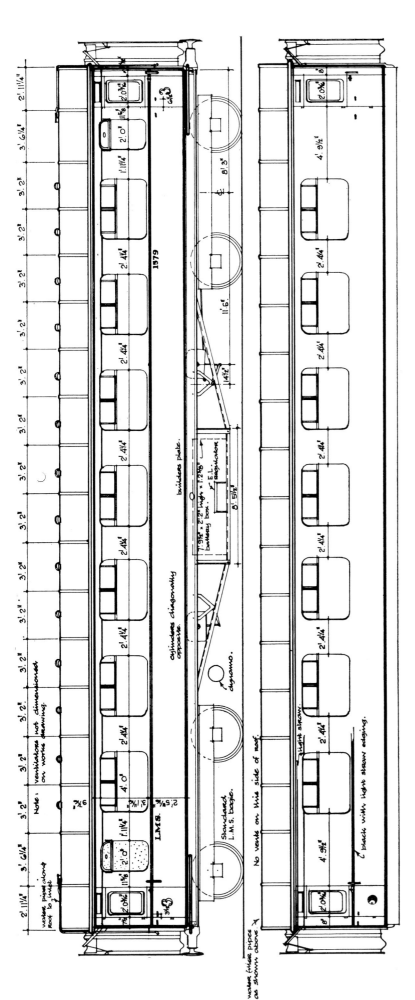

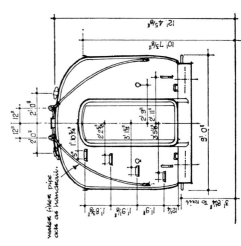

Figure 56 Dimensioned drawings. Third Class Corridor D1899 We are indebted to our good friend Arthur Whitehead for permission to use this drawing, first published way back in 1966. It gives comprehensive dimensions and, together with other detailed drawings of Period III stock elsewhere in this survey, does allow most of the diagram deficiencies to be overcome. The picture shows the corridor side of No. 2040, the last example from Lot 998 of 1937. The numerals are now shaded but the ends are still painted red. We believe that 1937 marked the last examples of red-painted carriage ends for new coaches.

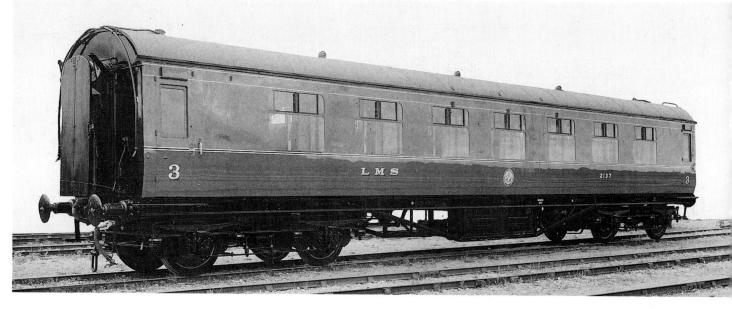

Plate 126. The last of the pre-war examples and of this diagram was Lot 1191 of 1939. This is No. 2137 from the corridor side–shaded numerals and black painted ends.

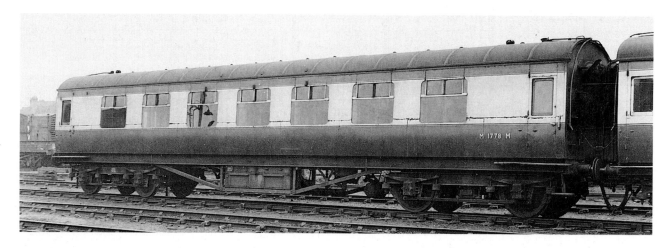

Plates 127–128. Period III carriages were not always renowned for their rust inhibiting quality(!) and these two BR vintage views show what tended to become on all too common sight as coaches approached their shopping date. No. M1778M shows typical wear and tear at the panel joins c.1955 while No. M1852M, seen at Willesden in 1964 has already had many beading strips added to protect these joins. Both carriages have had the door 'bonnets' removed and additionally, M1852M has lost all but its bottom end steps–a standard safety modification undertaken after the 'overhead' wires began to appear in order to prevent too easy access to the roof. (*The late Gavin Wilson collection, Authors' collection*).

Plate 129. A typical third class interior from D1899, No. 1579, see also Plate 124.

Plate 130. *(below)* LMS No. 2151–the post-war development to D2119. This picture shows the later LMS simple livery with flat topped '3s' and a reversion to scroll pattern running numbers. Note the changed design of toilet window omitting the hinged 'fall-back' top section, compared with earlier Period III coaches.

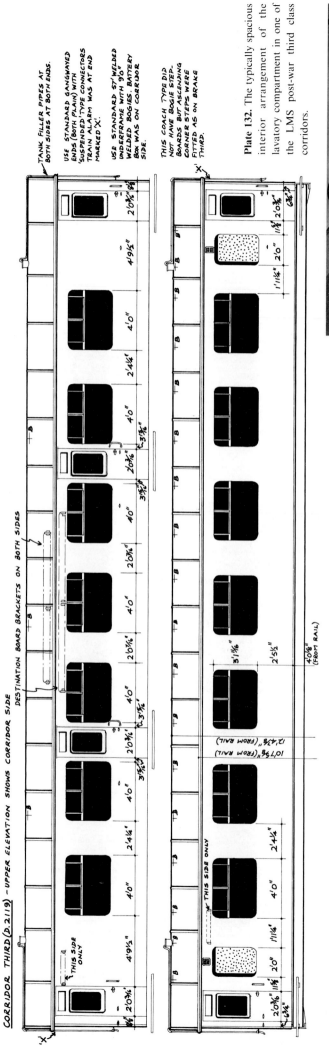

CORRIDOR THIRD (D.2119) — UPPER ELEVATION SHOWS CORRIDOR SIDE

DESTINATION BOARD BRACKETS ON BOTH SIDES

TANK FILLER PIPES AT BOTH SIDES AT BOTH ENDS.

USE STANDARD GANGWAYED ENDS (BOTH PLAIN) WITH 'SUSPENDED' TYPE CONNECTORS TRAIN ALARM WAS AT END MARKED 'X'.

USE STANDARD ST/WELDED UNDERFRAME WITH 9'0" WELDED BOGIES. BATTERY BOX WAS ON CORRIDOR SIDE.

THIS COACH TYPE DID NOT HAVE BOGIE STEP-BOARDS BUT ASCENDING CORNER STEPS WERE FITTED AS ON BRAKE THIRD.

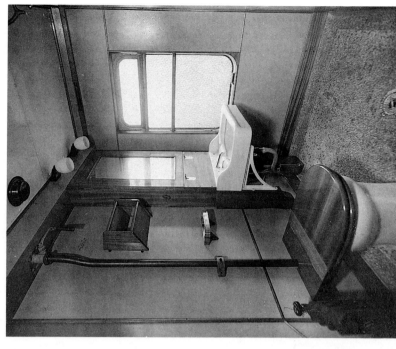

Plate 132. The typically spacious interior arrangement of the lavatory compartment in one of the LMS post-war third class corridors.

Figure 57 Detailed side elevations Third Class Corridor D2119 This type introduced the extra doors on the corridor side which were continued in the BR-built 'porthole' stock with no significant dimensional change either. The roof ventilators (all shell type) are marked 'B' and were set 1ft from the carriage centreline on the sides indicated.

Plate 131. This view of No. 2258 from D2119, Lot 1407 is especially useful in showing the layout of the LMS livery with the extra corridor side doors. Note again the flat-topped '3s' and a reversion to scroll numerals, a feature of most LMS post-war 'new build' coaches. We also believe that many of these vehicles were delivered in the new darker 'maroon' colour adopted in 1946. (S. N. J. White, courtesy G. Toms).

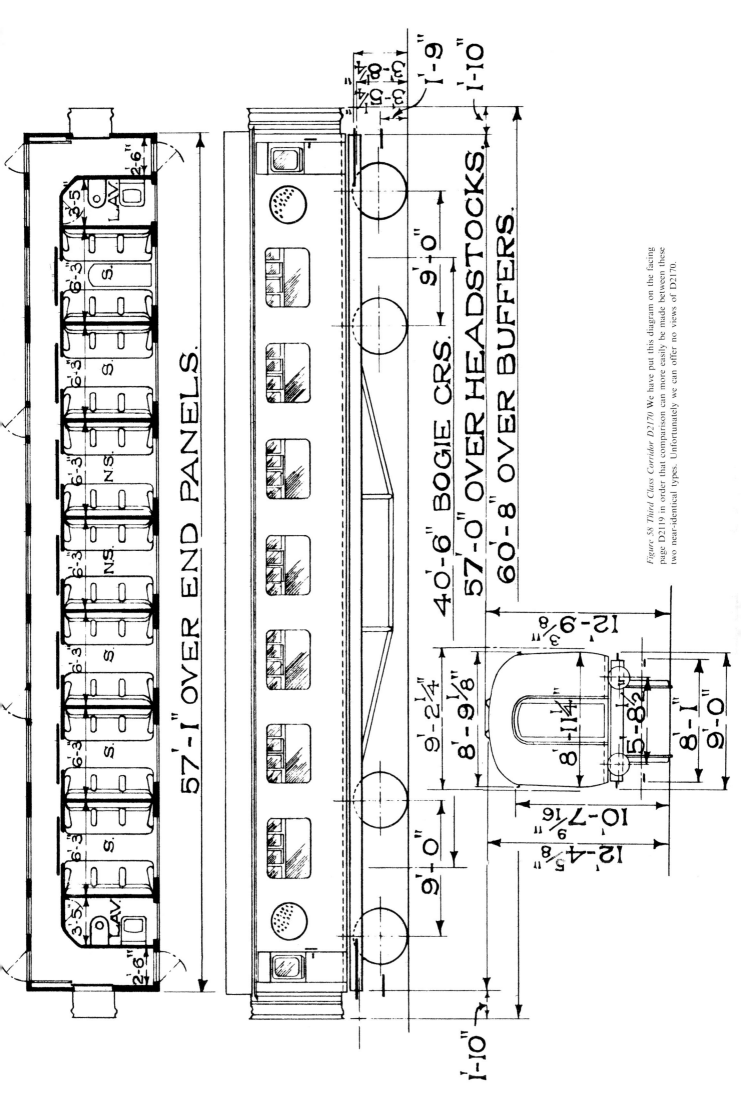

Figure 58 Third Class Corridor D2170 We have put this diagram on the facing page D2119 in order that comparison can more easily be made between these two near-identical types. Unfortunately we can offer no views of D2170.

57'-1" OVER END PANELS.

40'-6" BOGIE CRS.

57'-0" OVER HEADSTOCKS.

60'-8" OVER BUFFERS.

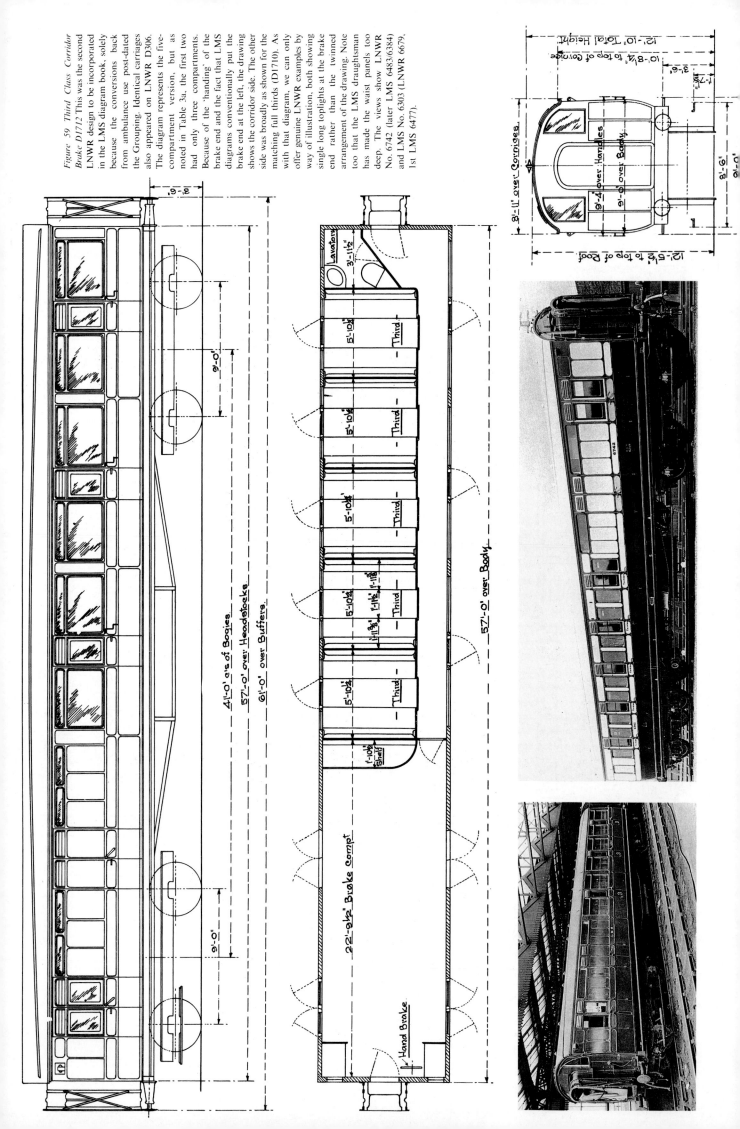

Figure 59 Third Class Corridor Brake D1712 This was the second LNWR design to be incorporated in the LMS diagram book, solely because the conversions back from ambulance use post-dated the Grouping. Identical carriages also appeared on LNWR D306. The diagram represents the five-compartment version, but as noted in Table 3a, the first two had only three compartments. Because of the 'handing' of the brake end and the fact that LMS diagrams conventionally put the brake end at the left, the drawing shows the corridor side. The other side was broadly as shown for the matching full thirds (D1710). As with that diagram, we can only offer genuine LNWR examples by way of illustration, both showing single long toplights at the brake end rather than the twinned arrangement of the drawing. Note too that the LMS draughtsman has made the waist panels too deep. The views show LNWR No. 6742 (later LMS 6483/6384) and LMS No. 6303 (LNWR 6679, 1st LMS 6477).

3'-6"

9'-0"

41'-0" c's of Bogies

57'-0" over Headstocks

61'-0" over Buffers

9'-0"

Lavatory

3'-1½"

5'-10¼"   Third

5'-10¼"   Third

5'-10¼"   Third

5'-10¼"   Third

5'-10¼"   Third

1'11¾" 1'-11½" 1'-11⅛"

1'-10½" Shelf

57'-0" over Body

22'-9½" Brake Compt

Hand Brake

12'-10" Total Height

10'-8¼" to top of Cornice

3'-6"

8'-11" over Cornices

9'-4" over Handles

9'-0" over Body

12'-5½" to top of Roof

8'-9"

10'-0"

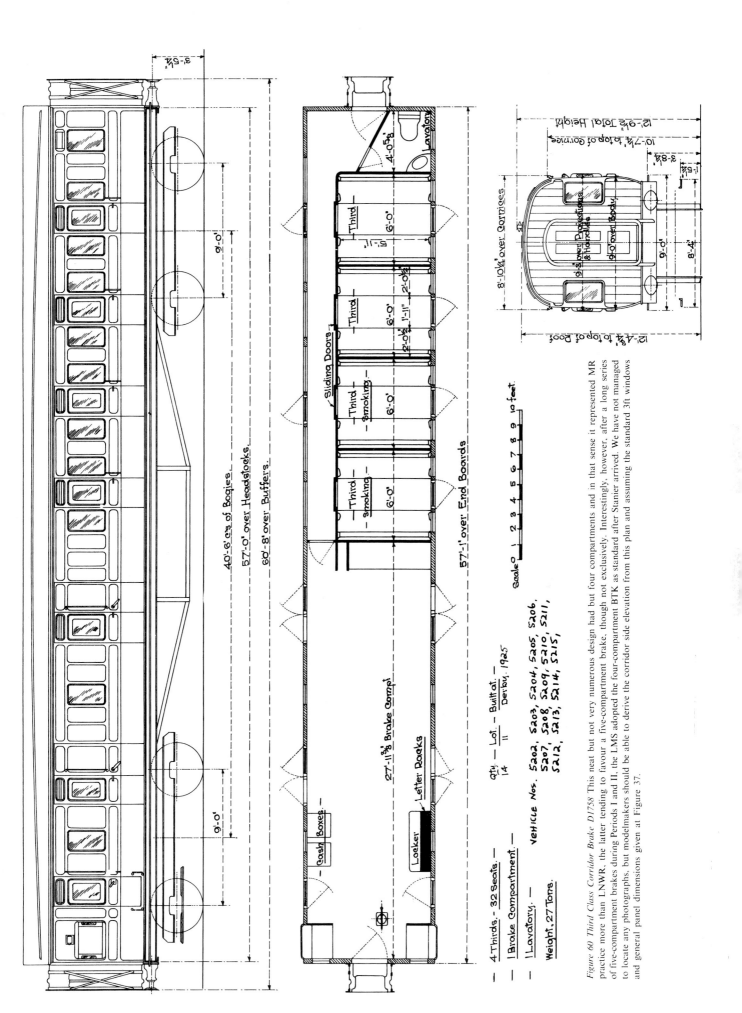

Figure 60 Third Class Corridor Brake D1758 This neat but not very numerous design had but four compartments and in that sense it represented MR practice more than LNWR, the latter tending to favour a five-compartment brake, though not exclusively. Interestingly, however, after a long series of five-compartment brakes during Periods I and II, the LMS adopted the four-compartment BTK as standard after Stanier arrived. We have not managed to locate any photographs, but modelmakers should be able to derive the corridor side elevation from this plan and assuming the standard 3ft windows and general panel dimensions given at Figure 37.

— 4 Thirds. — 32 Seats. —
— 1 Brake Compartment. —
— 1 Lavatory. —
Weight, 27 Tons.

VEHICLE Nos. 5202, 5203, 5204, 5205, 5206, 5207, 5208, 5209, 5210, 5211, 5212, 5213, 5214, 5215,

Qty. — Lot. — Built at. —
14   II   Derby, 1925

Scale 0 1 2 3 4 5 6 7 8 9 10 feet.

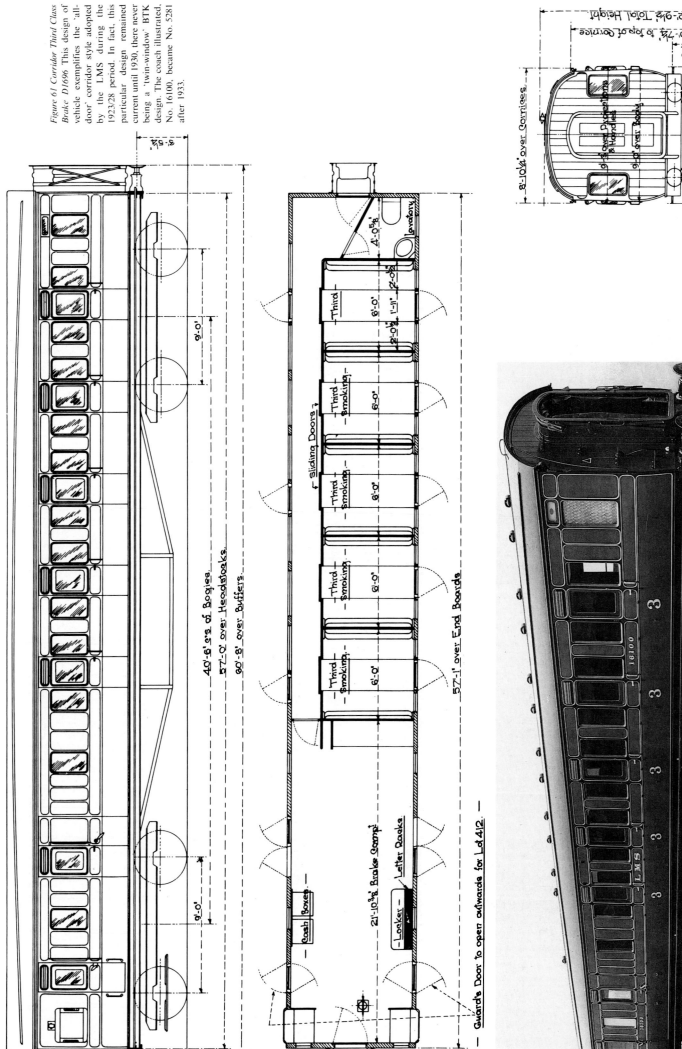

Figure 61 Corridor Third Class Brake D1696 This design of vehicle exemplifies the 'all-door' corridor style adopted by the LMS during the 1923/28 period. In fact, this particular design remained current until 1930, there never being a 'twin-window' BTK design. The coach illustrated, No. 16100, became No. 5281 after 1933.

8'-5½"

9'-0"

40'-6' c's of Bogies.
57'-0" over Headstocks.
60'-8' over Buffers.

9'-0"

Third
6'-0"

Third Smoking
6'-0"

Third Smoking
6'-0"

Third Smoking
6'-0"

Third Smoking
6'-0"

Third Smoking
6'-0"

4'-0⅝"

Lavatory.

2'-0½" 1'-11" 2'-0½"

Sliding Doors

57'-1" over End Boards

21'-10¾" Brake Comp¹

Coach Boxes.

Locker
Letter Racks.

Guard's Door to open outwards for Lot 412.

12'-9⅜" Total Height.

10'-7½" to top of Cornice.

8'-8¾"

8'-4"

9'-0' over Projections & Handles

9'-0" over Corrices

9'-0" over Body

8'-10¼" over Corrices

Plates 133–134. These two pictures offer brake end views of D1696 after conversion for ambulance train use. Relatively little change has taken place in the panelling arrangement but some doorways have been sealed off, especially on the compartment side of No. 816. An interesting detail revealed by No. 5601 is the three vertical panels on either side of the quarterlight between the corridor and double doors (one set covered by the red cross) whereas on the compartment side–see previous page, it was a triple and a double.

Plate 135. Within the 'all steel' third brakes to D1730–see also next two pages–there were some interesting detail variations. This is No. 5354 of Lot 542, one of the main Metro-Cammell/Derby batch with small Dewel ventilators above the windows and lined to simulate real panelling. Superficially, this carriage is identical to that given with the diagram itself on the next page, but the cell box is on the opposite side and roof top ventilators are spaced differently at the van end. It became No. 5359 in 1933, a very rare occasion where old and new numbers were almost alike. Old No. 6179, also Metro-Cammell/Derby (part of Lot 508 and this time identical to 6018 on the next page), became the new 5354: all very confusing!

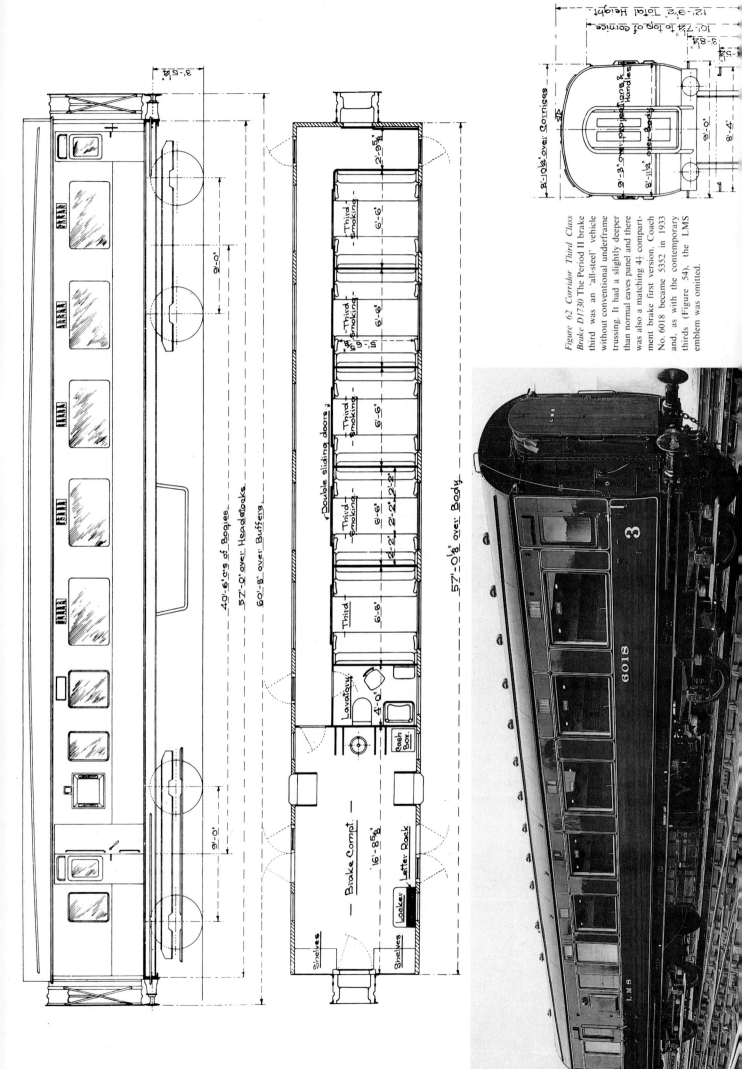

Figure 62 Corridor Third Class Brake D1730 The Period II brake third was an 'all-steel' vehicle without conventional underframe trussing. It had a slightly deeper than normal eaves panel and there was also a matching 4½ compartment brake first version. Coach No. 6018 became 5352 in 1933 and, as with the contemporary thirds (Figure 54), the LMS emblem was omitted.

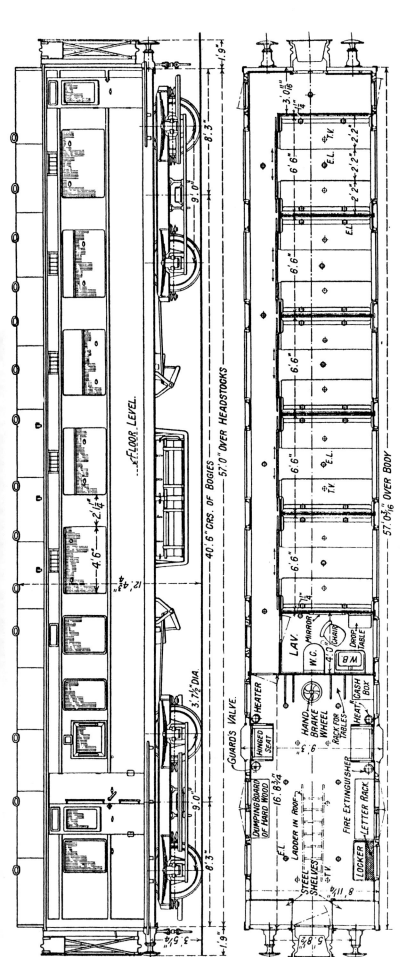

*Figure 63 Third Class Corridor Brake
D1730—alternative form* This drawing of D1730 was
made at about the time the coaches were introduced
and offers a few more variations. There are subtle
dimensional changes in terms of length and height
and although the roof panel sections are indicated,
no roof rainstrips are shown (they were there in
fact). It is believed to represent Lot 578 (the Metro-
Cammell/Wolverton batch) which, as the appended
photograph of No. 5190 (later 5427) shows, were
slightly different. The arrangement of lining out was
changed as was the disposition of insignia–this time
including the LMS emblem. The windows were
surmounted by conventional long pattern Stones
ventilators and the gutter strip was more
pronounced.

The interior view is from coach No. 6018.

143

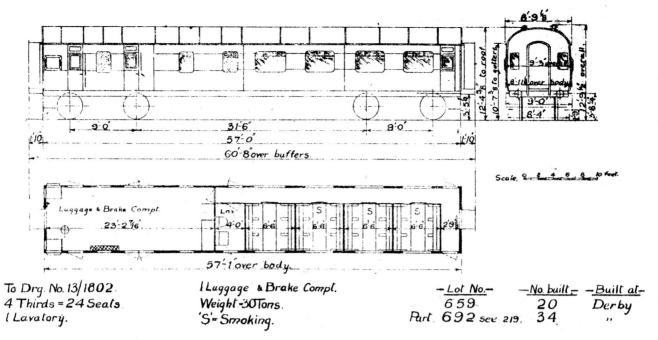

To Drg. No. 13/1802.
4 Thirds = 24 Seats.
1 Lavatory.

1 Luggage & Brake Compt.
Weight-30 Tons.
'S'= Smoking.

—Lot No.—	—No.built—	—Built at—
659	20	Derby
Part 692 see 219.	34	,,

Figure 64 Third Class Corridor Brake D1851 This was an early Period III diagram for which pre-1933 series numbers were allocated, though whether they were ever carried is uncertain–see Table 3b. The illustration shows No. 5461 of the first Lot to be built–note the torpedo ventilators. The lamp above the guard's lookout was soon discontinued on Period III coaches and was also removed from earlier vehicles. More accurate detail of the window sizes will be found at page 172 in relation to the contemporary BCK design to D1850.

Figure 65 Third Class Corridor Brake D1852 This diagram was issued part way through the building of Lot 692 to cover the modification of the van end to take two pairs of double doors.

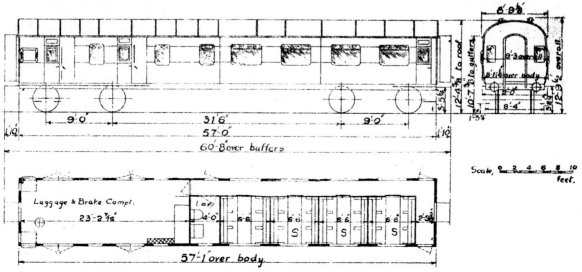

To Drg. No. 13/1802 with altered door.
4 Thirds = 24 Seats.
1 Lavatory.

1 Luggage & Brake Compt.
Weight-30 Tons.
'S'- Smoking.

—Lot No.—	—No. built—	—Built at—
Part 692 see 218.	16	Derby.

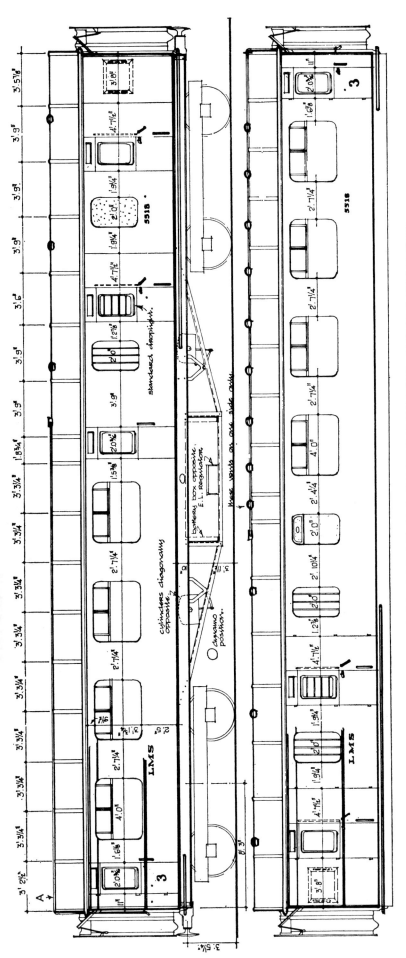

Figure 66 Dimensioned side elevations: Third Class Corridor Brakes D1905/D1963 This detailed set of elevations by Arthur Whitehead is dimensionally correct for both the above diagrams, though actually prepared from D1905, by far the most numerous and significant of the two. There were only fractional differences in height to distinguish them and the 24 examples to D1963 were built before the final examples of D1905 series–see Table 3a. The illustration shows No. 5518 in fully lined livery. It was one of several to D1905 which had the lookouts and top commode handles removed for working the 'Sunny South Express' (see Table 3a).

Plate 136. Compartment interior of D1905 No. 5829.

The plate below refers to figure 67 opposite.

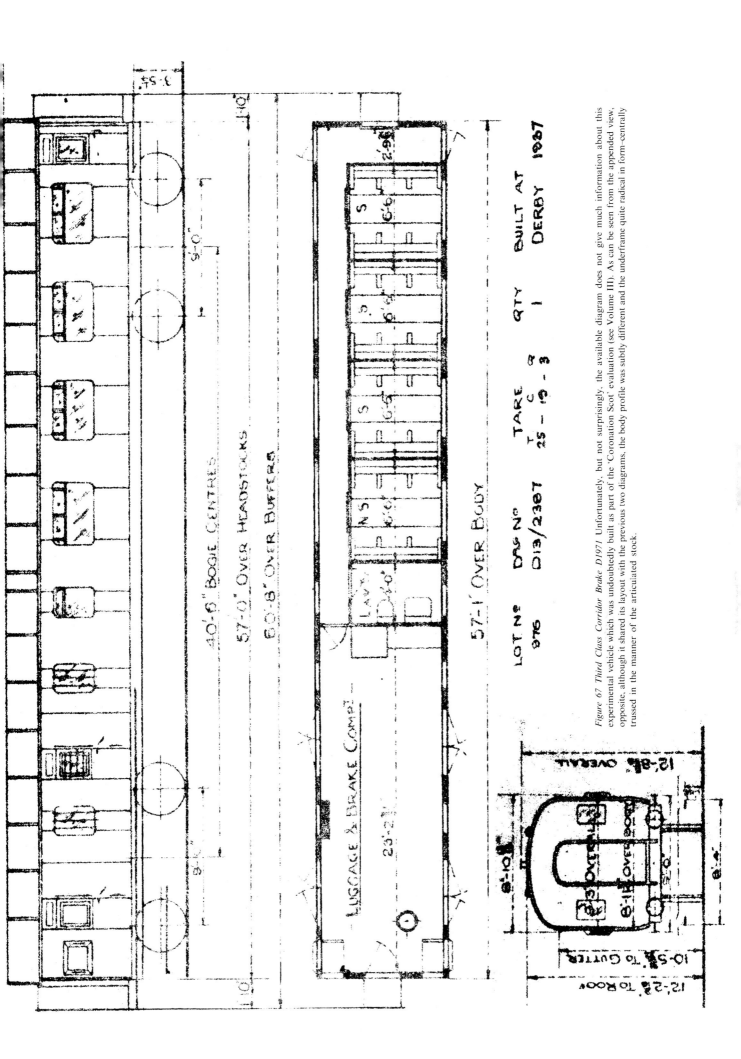

Figure 67 Third Class Corridor Brake D1971 Unfortunately, but not surprisingly, the available diagram does not give much information about this experimental vehicle which was undoubtedly built as part of the 'Coronation Scot' evaluation (see Volume III). As can be seen from the appended view, opposite, although it shared its layout with the previous two diagrams, the body profile was subtly different and the underframe quite radical in form–centrally trussed in the manner of the articulated stock.

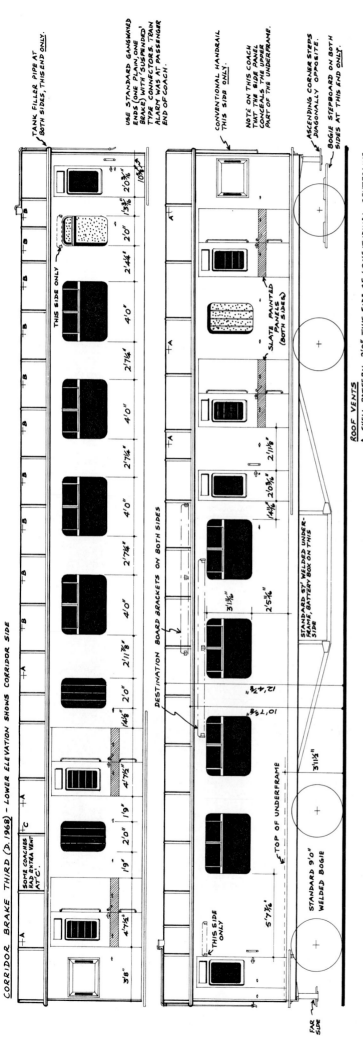

CORRIDOR BRAKE THIRD (D. 1968) – LOWER ELEVATION SHOWS CORRIDOR SIDE

TANK FILLER PIPE AT BOTH SIDES, THIS END ONLY.

USE STANDARD GANGWANED ENDS (ONE PLAIN, ONE BRAKE) WITH 'SUSPENDED' TYPE CONNECTORS. TRAIN ALARM WAS AT PASSENGER END OF COACH.

CONVENTIONAL HANDRAIL THIS SIDE ONLY.

NOTE ON THIS COACH THAT THE SIDE PANEL CONCEALS THE UPPER PART OF THE UNDERFRAME.

ASCENDING CORNER STEPS DIAGONALLY OPPOSITE.

BOGIE STEPBOARD ON BOTH SIDES AT THIS END ONLY.

THIS SIDE ONLY

SOME COACHES HAD EXTRA VENT AT 'C'.

DESTINATION BOARD BRACKETS ON BOTH SIDES

SLATE PAINTED PANELS (BOTH SIDES)

TOP OF UNDERFRAME

THIS SIDE ONLY

STANDARD 9'0" WELDED BOGIE

STANDARD 57' WELDED UNDER-FRAME, BATTERY BOX ON THIS SIDE

FAR SIDE SHOWN

ROOF VENTS
A. SHELL PATTERN   2'0" THIS SIDE OF LONGITUDINAL CENTRELINE
B.   "   "   1'0"   "   "   "   "   "

Figure 68 Dimensioned side elevations. Third Class Corridor Brake DS1968 Diagram 1968, introduced in 1937, marked yet another slight change in the Period III BTK evolution; comparison with Figure 66 will reveal that the repositioned lavatory compartment imparted a somewhat different proportion to the carriages, especially on the corridor side. These were some of the earliest Period III coaches to be given welded underframes as standard (with bodyside panelling concealing the upper edge of the solebars) and their construction spanned the war years. The picture shows No. 6006, one of the first pre-war examples.

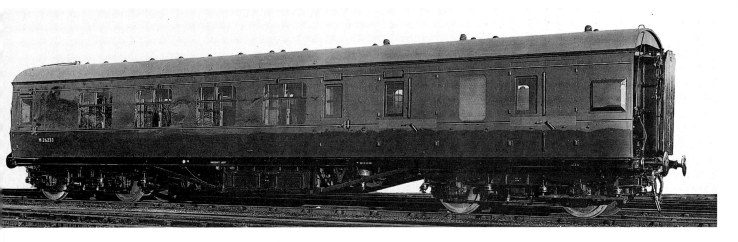

Plate 137. No. M26233 displays the corridor side of D1968. The carriage was built in 1939 but this view was taken when repainted in late 1948. The livery is BR lined crimson–presumably during the livery evaluation period before red and cream was standardised for gangwayed stock, after which lined crimson became confined to non-corridor types.

Plates 138–140. The near ten year building span of D1968 caused the carriages to display some livery variations both in style and positioning of insignia which may have reflected the different works. The three examples here are reasonably typical and are dated (top to bottom) as follows: No. 26191 (Derby 1939); No. 26291 (Wolverton 1939) and No. 26321 (Derby, 1945)–the first new coach to be built by the LMS post-war.

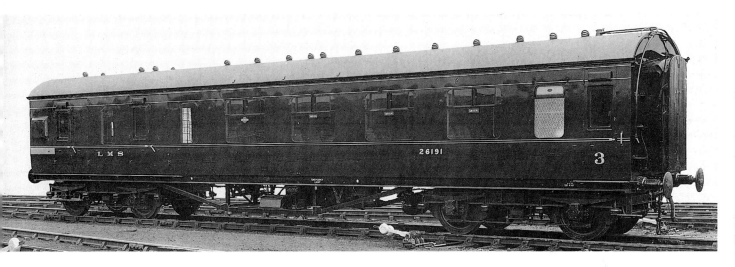

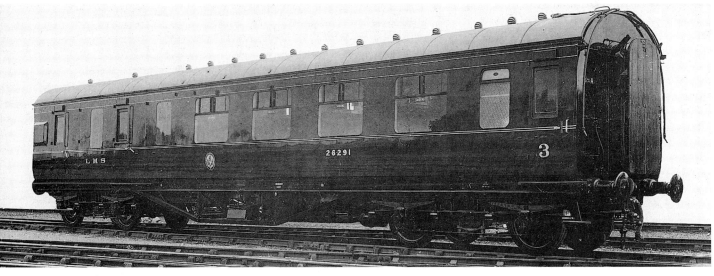

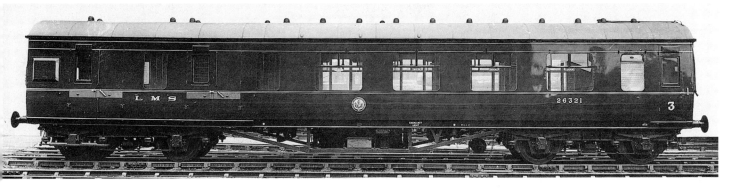

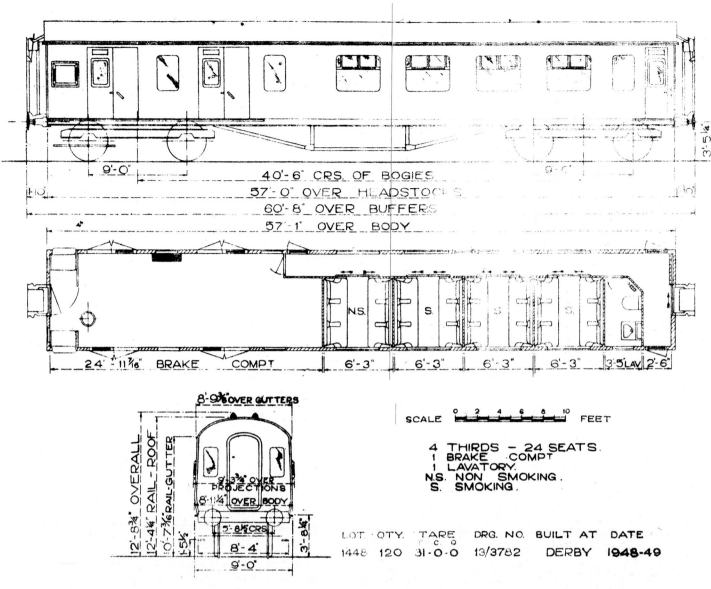

40'-6" CRS. OF BOGIES
57'-0" OVER HEADSTOCKS
60'-8" OVER BUFFERS
57'-1" OVER BODY

9'-0"

3'-5¼"

24'-11⅞" BRAKE COMPT | 6'-3" | 6'-3" | 6'-3" | 6'-3" | 3'-5 LAV | 2'-6"

N.S. | S. | S. | S.

8'-9¾" OVER GUTTERS
8'-3¾" OVER PROJECTIONS
8'-11¼" OVER BODY
12'-8¾" OVERALL
12'-4¼" RAIL — ROOF
10'-7⅜" RAIL-GUTTER
1'-5½"
5'-8½" CRS.
8'-4"
9'-0"
3'-8¼"

SCALE |0 2 4 6 8 10| FEET

4 THIRDS — 24 SEATS.
1 BRAKE COMPT
1 LAVATORY.
N.S. NON SMOKING.
S. SMOKING.

LOT.	QTY.	TARE T.C.Q	DRG. NO.	BUILT AT	DATE
1448	120	31·0·0	13/3782	DERBY	1948-49

Figures 69/70 Third Class Corridor Brakes D2123/D2161 We conclude our review of third class corridors with this pair of diagrams showing the last two BTK types to LMS design, neither of which was built until BR days. The only significant change was the introduction of 'porthole' windows in D2161 and the customary addition of a matching circular corridor window in place of the previous blank panel at this location. Somewhat surprisingly, we are unable to offer views of D2123 (there were considerably fewer of them, of course), but we deduce–vide No. M26668 (below)–that they may well have had the older type of sliding window ventilators.

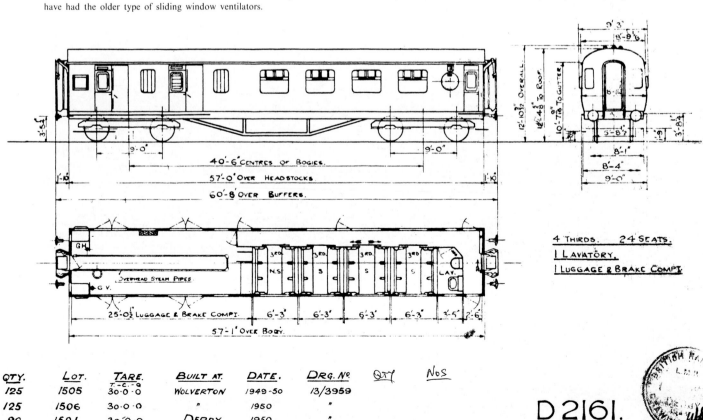

9'-3"
8'-9 ¾"

40'-6" CENTRES OF BOGIES.
57'-0" OVER HEADSTOCKS
60'-8" OVER BUFFERS.

9'-0" | 9'-0"
1'-10" | 1'-10"
3'-5"

12'-10⅜" OVERALL
12'-4⅝" TO ROOF
10'-7⅛" TO GUTTER
8'-11"
8'-1"
8'-4"
9'-0"
5'-8½"
3'-8¼"

GH.
Overhead Steam Pipes
G.V.

3RD | 3RD | 3RD | 3RD
N.S. | S | S | S | LAV.

25'-0½" LUGGAGE & BRAKE COMPT. | 6'-3" | 6'-3" | 6'-3" | 6'-3" | 3'-5" | 2'-6"
57'-1" OVER BODY.

4 THIRDS. 24 SEATS.
1 LAVATORY.
1 LUGGAGE & BRAKE COMPT.

QTY.	LOT.	TARE T-C-Q	BUILT AT	DATE.	DRG. No	QTY	Nos
125	1505	30·0·0	WOLVERTON	1949-50	13/3959		
125	1506	30·0·0	"	1950	"		
90	1501	30·0·0	DERBY.	1950	"		
90	1575	30·0·0	"	1950-51	"		
9	1587	30·0·0	WOLVERTON	1950	"		
50	1597	30·0·0	"	1950	"	50	27046—27095

D 2161.

Plate 141. Compartment side view of D2161 No. M26668 showing the older style window ventilators on this early example from Lot 1501. Note also the BR type roof ventilators, believed to have been normal for this diagram.

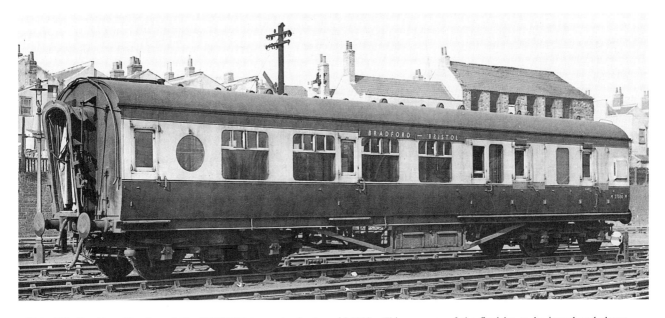

Plate 142. Corridor side view of No. M27050M in service in the mid-1950s. This was one of the final lot to be issued and shows the later style of sliding window ventilators. A later view of this type is at Plate 107.

The plate below refers to Fig. 71 overleaf.

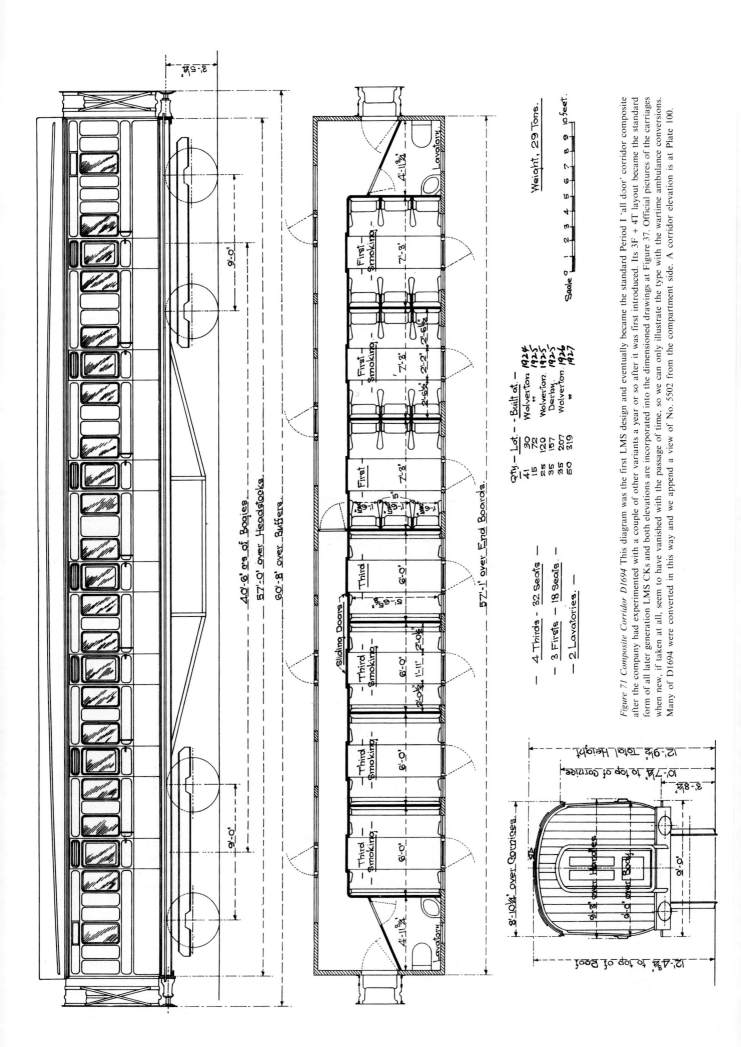

Weight, 29 Tons.

Scale 0 1 2 3 4 5 6 7 8 9 10 feet.

Qty.	Lot.	Built at.
41	30	Wolverton 1924
15	72	" 1925
25	120	Wolverton 1925
35	157	Derby 1925
35	207	Wolverton 1926
50	319	" 1927

— 4 Thirds - 32 Seats —
— 3 Firsts - 18 Seats —
— 2 Lavatories. —

Figure 71 Composite Corridor D1694 This diagram was the first LMS design and eventually became the standard Period I 'all door' corridor composite after the company had experimented with a couple of other variants a year or so after it was first introduced. Its 3F + 4T layout became the standard form of all later generation LMS CKs and both elevations are incorporated into the dimensioned drawings at Figure 37. Official pictures of the carriages when new, if taken at all, seem to have vanished with the passage of time, so we can only illustrate the type with the wartime ambulance conversions. Many of D1694 were converted in this way and we append a view of No. 5502 from the compartment side. A corridor elevation is at Plate 100.

152

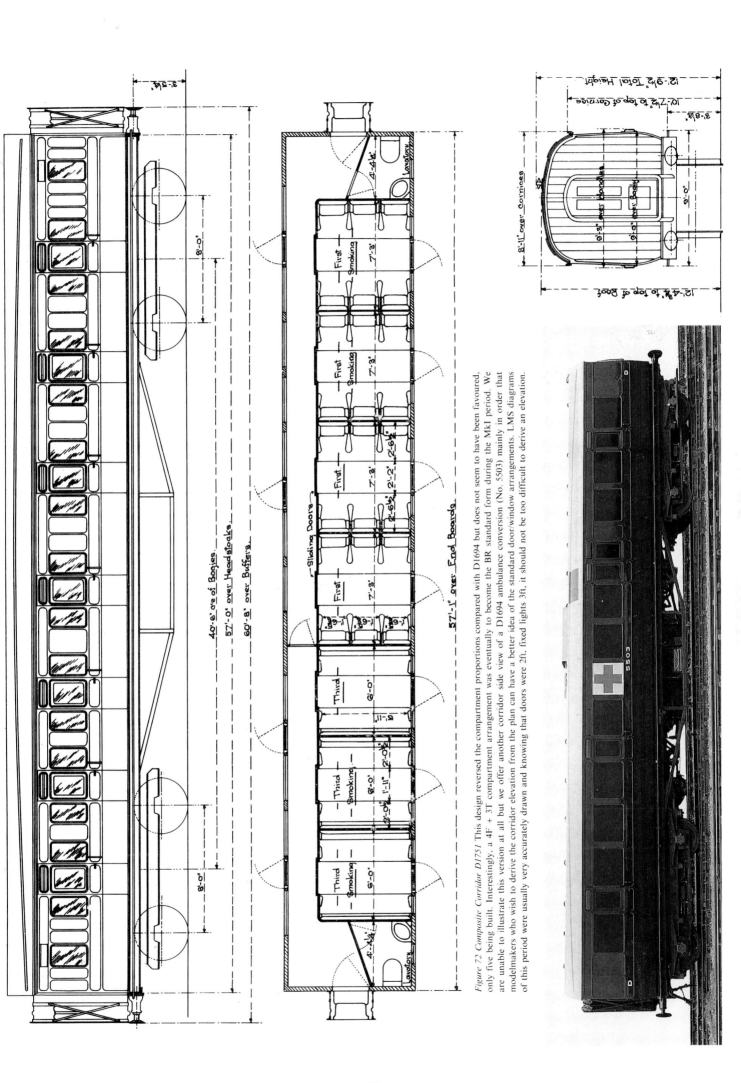

Figure 72 Composite Corridor D1751 This design reversed the compartment proportions compared with D1694 but does not seem to have been favoured, only five being built. Interestingly, a 4F + 3T compartment arrangement was eventually to become the BR standard form during the MkI period. We are unable to illustrate this version at all but we offer another corridor side view of a D1694 ambulance conversion (No. 5503) mainly in order that modelmakers who wish to derive the corridor elevation from the plan can have a better idea of the standard door/window arrangements. LMS diagrams of this period were usually very accurately drawn and knowing that doors were 2ft, fixed lights 3ft, it should not be too difficult to derive an elevation.

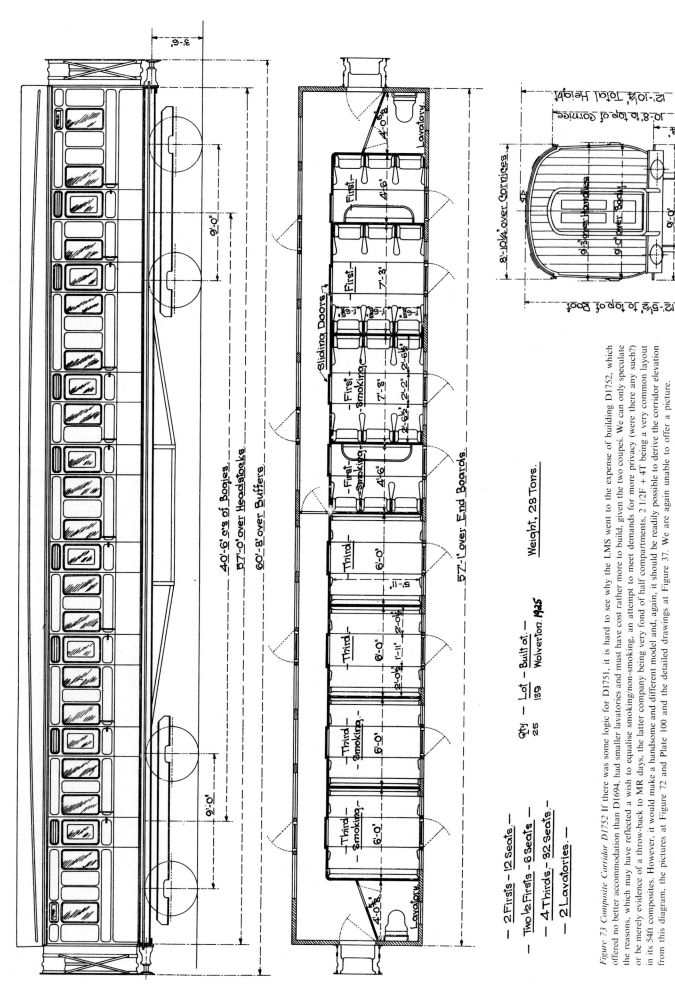

− 2 Firsts − 12 Seats. −
− Two ½ Firsts − 6 Seats −
− 4 Thirds − 32 Seats. −
− 2 Lavatories. −

Qty − Lot − Built at.
25 − 139 − Wolverton. 1925

Weight, 28 Tons.

Figure 73 Composite Corridor D1752 If there was some logic for D1751, it is hard to see why the LMS went to the expense of building D1752, which offered no better accommodation than D1694, had smaller lavatories and must have cost rather more to build, given the two coupes. We can only speculate the reasons, which may have reflected a wish to equalise smoking/non-smoking, an attempt to meet demands for more privacy (were there any such?) or be merely evidence of a throw-back to MR days, the latter company being very fond of half compartments, 2 ½F + 4T being a very common layout in its 54ft composites. However, it would make a handsome and different model and, again, it should be readily possible to derive the corridor elevation from this diagram, the pictures at Figure 72 and Plate 100 and the detailed drawings at Figure 37. We are again unable to offer a picture.

154

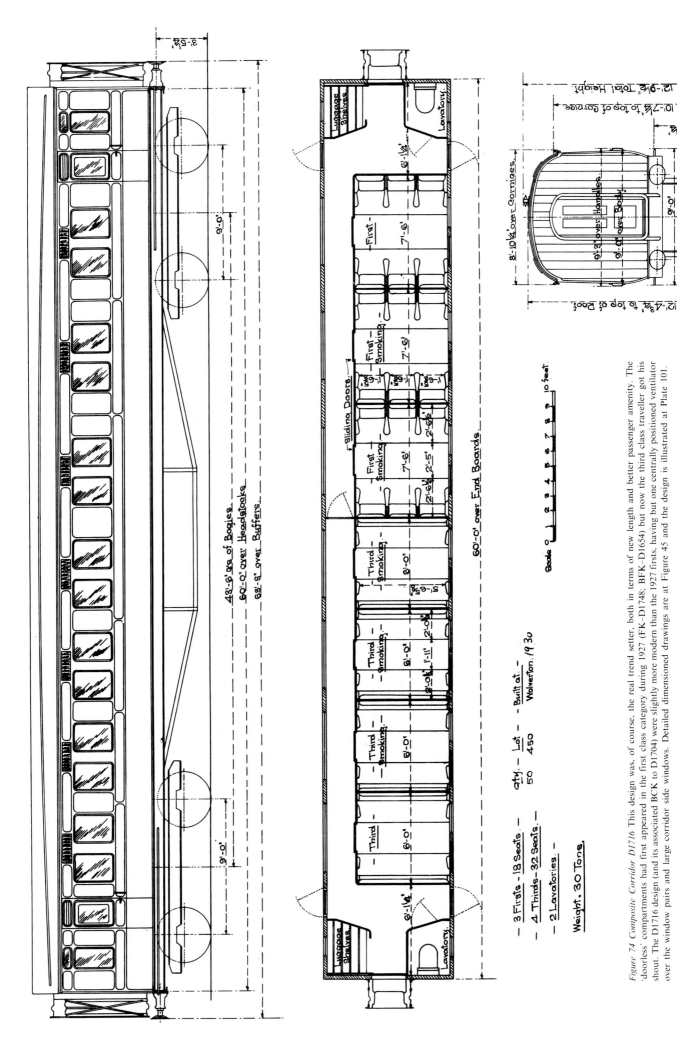

Figure 74 Composite Corridor D1716 This design was, of course, the real trend setter, both in terms of new length and better passenger amenity. The 'doorless' compartments had first appeared in the first class category during 1927 (FK–D1748; BFK–D1654) but now the third class traveller got his shout. The D1716 design (and its associated BCK to D1704) were slightly more modern than the 1927 firsts, having but one centrally positioned ventilator over the window pairs and large corridor side windows. Detailed dimensioned drawings are at Figure 45 and the design is illustrated at Plate 101.

155

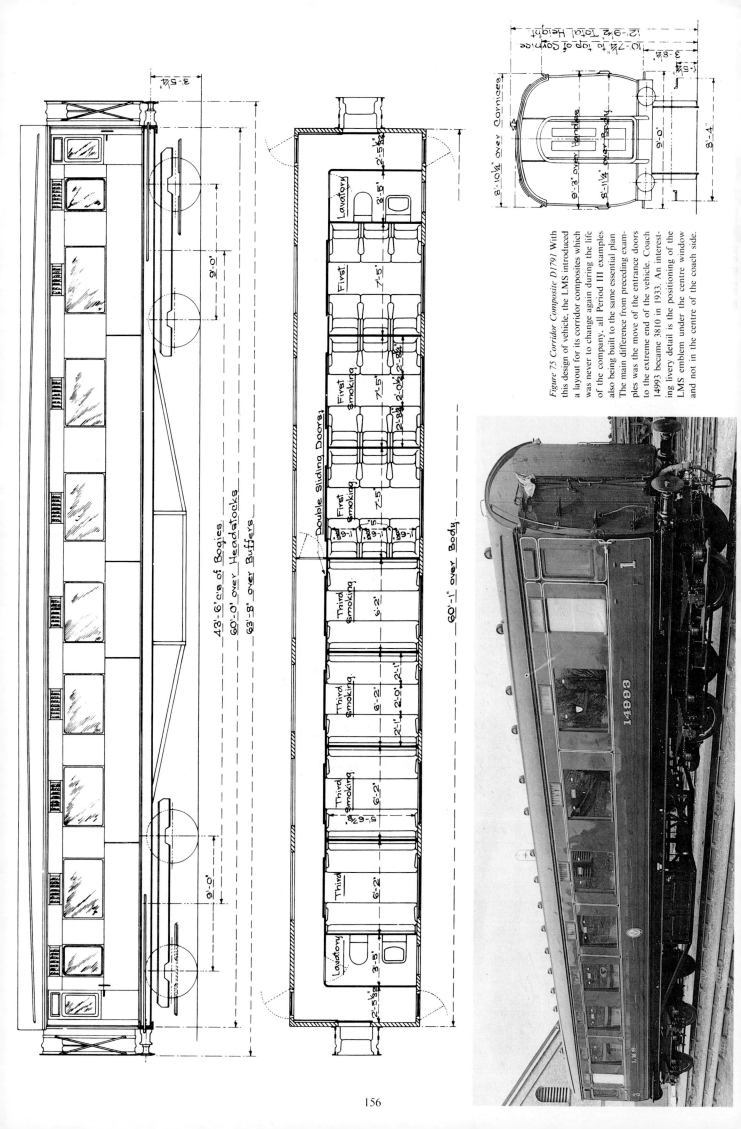

Figure 75 Corridor Composite D1791 With this design of vehicle, the LMS introduced a layout for its corridor composites which was never to change again during the life of the company, all Period III examples also being built to the same essential plan. The main difference from preceding examples was the move of the entrance doors to the extreme end of the vehicle. Coach 14993 became 3810 in 1933. An interesting livery detail is the positioning of the LMS emblem under the centre window and not in the centre of the coach side.

43'-6" c'rs of Bogies
60'-0" over Headstocks
63'-8" over Buffers

60'-1" over Body

Double Sliding Doors

Lavatory First First smoking First smoking Third smoking Third smoking Third smoking Third Lavatory

12'-9½" Total Height
10'-7¼" to top of Cornice
8'-10¾" over Cornices
9'-3" over Handles
9'-0" over Body
8'-11¼" over Body
8'-4"

156

Plates 143–144. D1791 was one of the first steel panelled LMS designs to exhibit a near-flush exterior surface and these views of the opposite sides of two ex-works examples display this to perfection. The corridor side is No. 14993 again, and the compartment elevation features No. 15938, later 3823, the very last to be built. We can only presume that this, or the repositioning of the insignia relative to the windows, was the reason for taking the latter picture. If the running numbers are any guide, most of them came out as per 14993. Another interesting livery detail is the window surround treatment on the corridor side. Fixed light frames were edged in black with the usual lining, but the droplights (technically 'frameless') had red surrounds. This distinction was not maintained on the compartment side, where all windows (including the fixed toilet lights) had red surrounds.

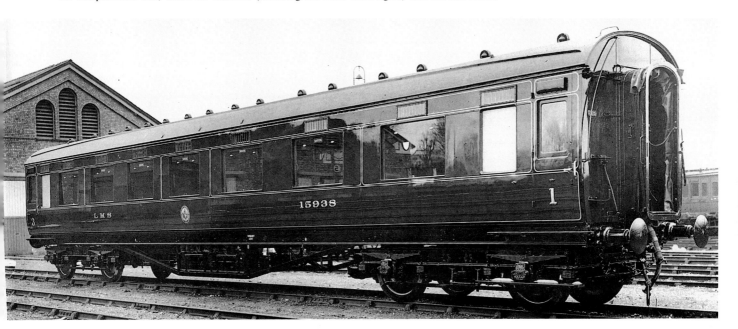

Figure 76 Composite Corridor D1859 Unlike the rest of the pioneer Period III coaches, the corridor composite version with shallow ventilators seems to have escaped the photographers and this typically poor diagram is all that we can offer. However, sufficient information is available elsewhere for the reader who so wishes to interpret the type.

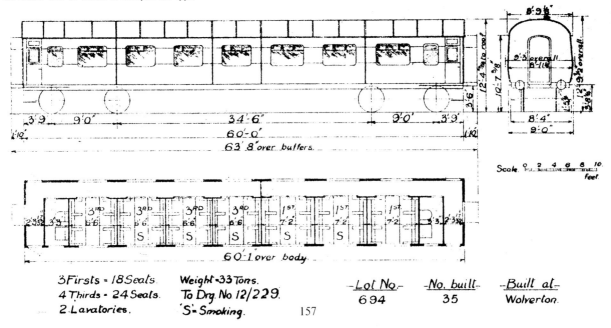

3 Firsts = 18 Seats.
4 Thirds = 24 Seats.
2 Lavatories.

Weight = 33 Tons.
To Drg. No 12/229.
'S'= Smoking.

Lot No. 694

No. built 35

Built at Wolverton.

157

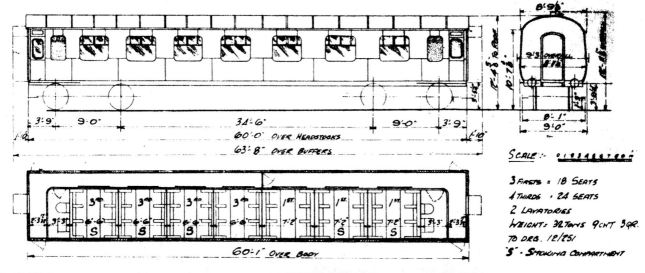

SCALE: 0 1 2 3 4 5 6 7 8 9 10

3 FIRSTS = 18 SEATS
4 THIRDS = 24 SEATS
2 LAVATORIES
WEIGHT: 32 TONS 9 CWT 3 QR.
TO DRG. 12/251
'S' = SMOKING COMPARTMENT

3'-9"   9'-0"   34'-6"   9'-0"   3'-9"
60'-0" OVER HEADSTOCKS
63'-8" OVER BUFFERS
60'-1" OVER BODY

Figure 77 Composite Corridor D1898 This design was identical to D1859, save for the deeper window ventilators, and was the last to incorporate the spacious 6ft 6in third class compartments whose amenable qualities are apparent from the appended interior view. At 7ft 2in the firsts were not quite as big as some which the LMS had sometimes offered but again, they were very agreeable. The interiors are believed to be from No. 3868, whose exterior elevation is given at Plate 107. Once again, we would remind our readers that this was a railway carriage built no less than 60 years before this book was published!

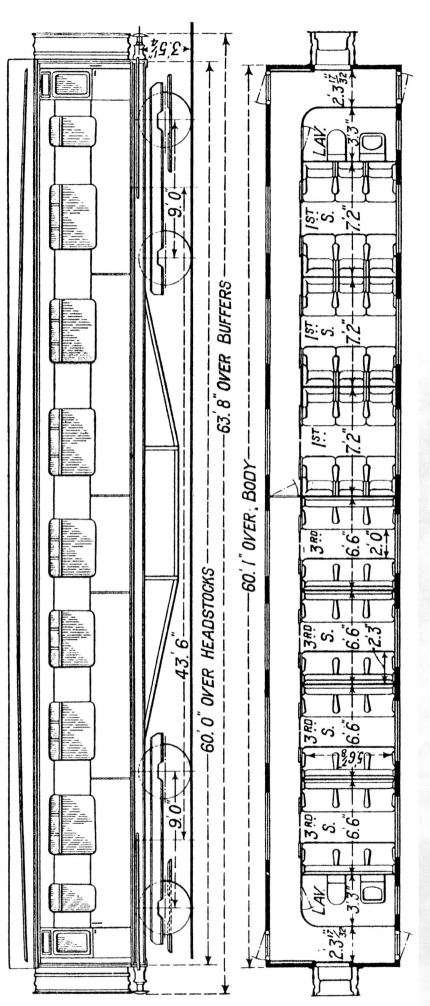

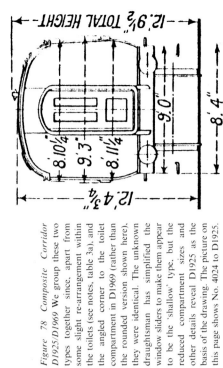

Figure 78 Composite Corridor D1925/D1969 We group these two types together since, apart from some slight re-arrangement within the toilets (see notes, table 3a), and the angled corner to the toilet compartment in D1969 (rather than the rounded version shown here), they were identical. The unknown draughtsman has simplified the window sliders to make them appear to be the 'shallow' type, but the reduced compartment sizes and other details reveal D1925 as the basis of the drawing. The picture on this page shows No. 4024 to D1925.

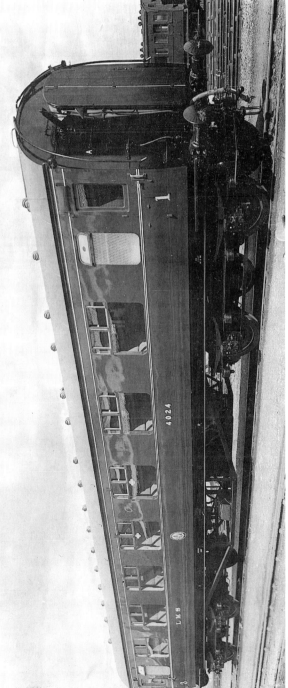

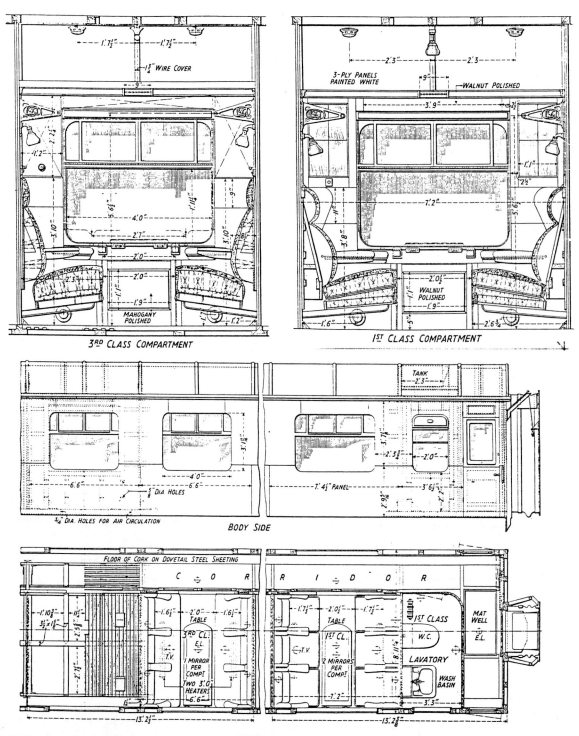

3RD CLASS COMPARTMENT

1ST CLASS COMPARTMENT

BODY SIDE

Figure 79 Dimension and interior details. Composite Corridor D1925/D1969
These detail drawings, which date from the time the carriages were built, give very useful information about Period II stock in general. Close scrutiny of the drawings reveals that the draughtsman seems to have been in two minds about the width of the main windows in first class, the exterior compartment elevation and plan suggesting they were wider than the thirds. In fact, the windows were all the same 4ft width. The appended picture shows No. 4298 of D1969, clearly identical in all significant respects to the D1925 example at Figure 78 save for the welded bogie. The latter was not a determining factor between the diagrams and seems to have appeared indiscriminately with the older pattern on D1969.

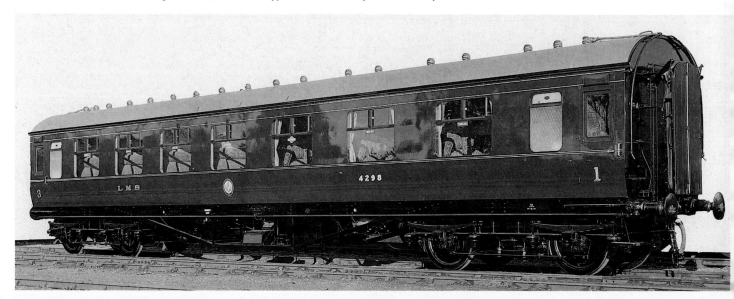

Plates 145–146. These two views of Nos 4121 and 4183, both show the corridor side of D1969. Note that only one has the LMS emblem and that although both are ex-works and new, the later design welded bogie appears on the earlier example to be built.

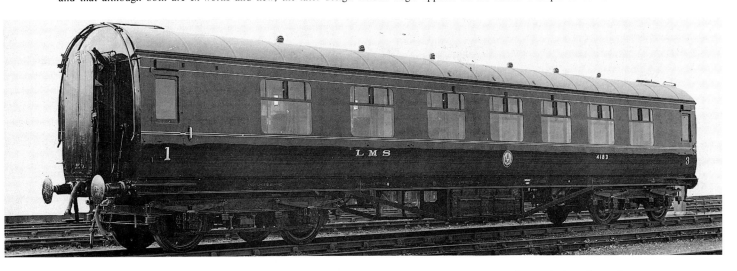

Plates 147–148. First and third class interiors respectively of Nos 4298 and 4121, both to D1969. As usual, the colour schemes are not specified but the third class compartment carries one of the familiar LMS 'Selected Empire Timber' labels: 'Brown Oak England'.

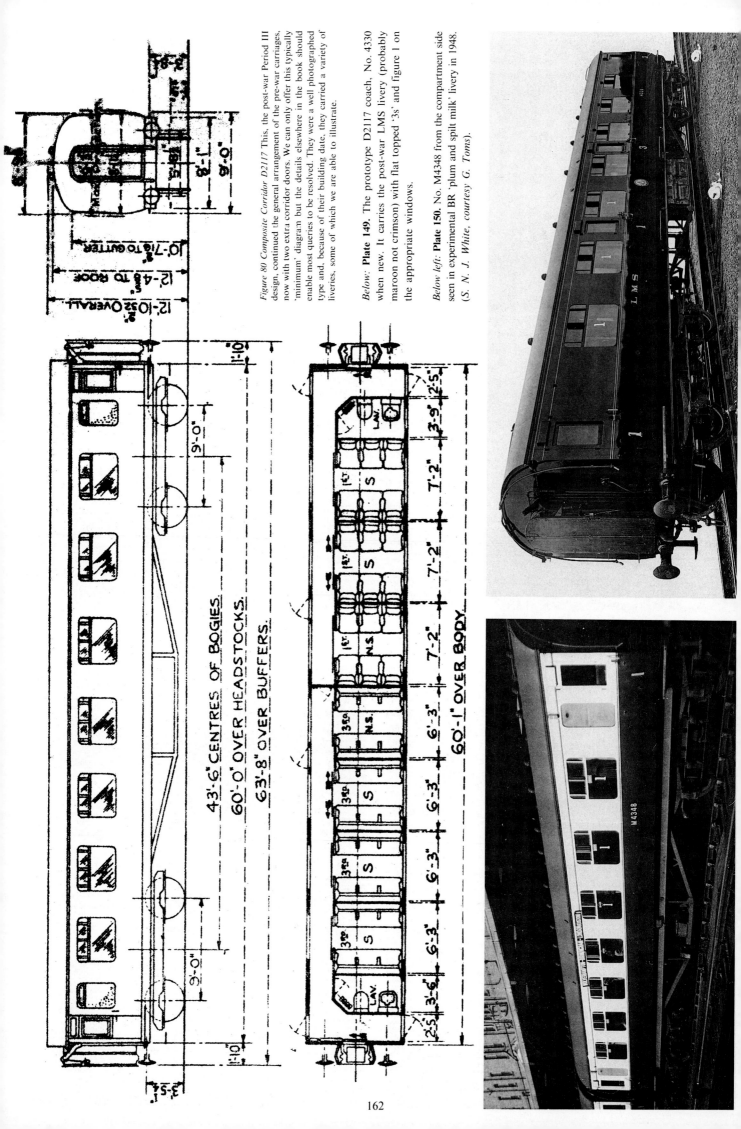

Figure 80 Composite Corridor D2117 This, the post-war Period III design, continued the general arrangement of the pre-war carriages, now with two extra corridor doors. We can only offer this typically 'minimum' diagram but the details elsewhere in the book should enable most queries to be resolved. They were a well photographed type and, because of their building date, they carried a variety of liveries, some of which we are able to illustrate.

Below: **Plate 149.** The prototype D2117 coach, No. 4330 when new. It carries the post-war LMS livery (probably maroon not crimson) with flat topped '3s' and figure 1 on the appropriate windows.

Below left: **Plate 150.** No. M4348 from the compartment side seen in experimental BR 'plum and spilt milk' livery in 1948. (*S. N. J. White, courtesy G. Toms*).

162

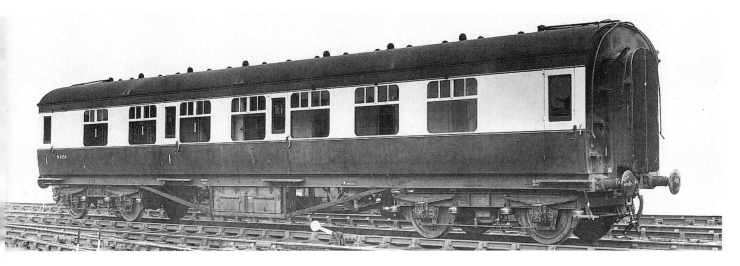

Plate 151. No. M4850 in somewhat grubby BR red/cream, still with LMS type figures on the window.

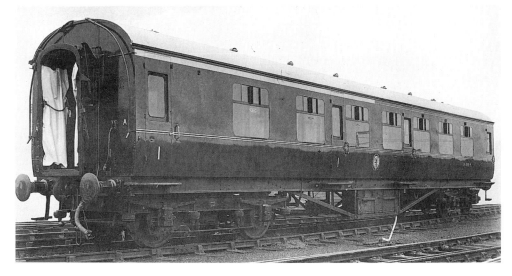

Plate 152. Almost full circle: No. M4878M in the 1956–65 BR maroon livery, a colour deliberately selected to be 'as nearly like the pre-war LMS shade as possible'. Even the BR emblem is reminiscent of the old LMS device, albeit slightly larger. The yellow band above the first class was introduced shortly before this livery gave way to the 1965 blue-grey scheme.

Plates 153–154. These two corridor views show very clearly the change in the cross-profile of the final series of CKs compared with their predecessors. Quite apart from the obvious class distinction revealed by the carpeted floor of the first class section of the slightly older carriage (No. 4330 to D2117), it is also differentiated by having far less turn under below window level than shown in the second view, the interior of No. M24623 to D2159, which we consider on the next page.

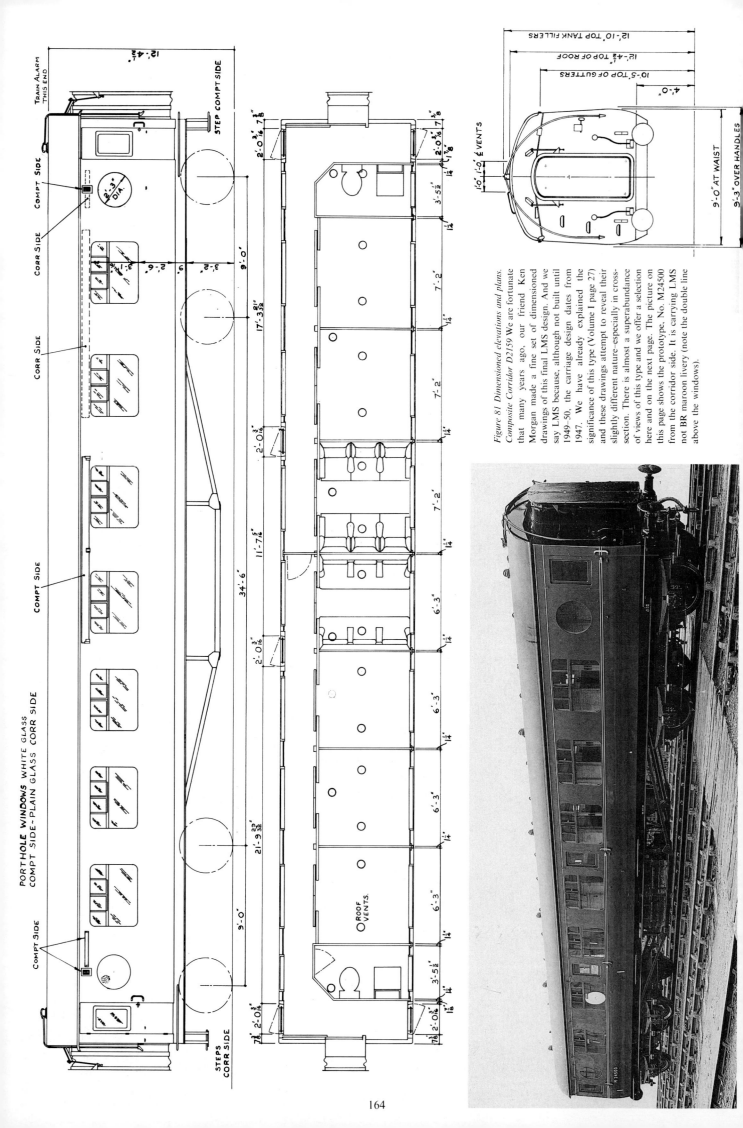

PORTHOLE WINDOWS WHITE GLASS
COMPT SIDE ~ PLAIN GLASS CORR SIDE

Figure 81 Dimensioned elevations and plans.
Composite Corridor D2159 We are fortunate
that many years ago, our friend Ken
Morgan made a fine set of dimensioned
drawings of this final LMS design. And we
say LMS because, although not built until
1949–50, the carriage design dates from
1947. We have already explained the
significance of this type (Volume I page 27)
and these drawings attempt to reveal their
slightly different nature—especially in cross-
section. There is almost a superabundance
of views of this type and we offer a selection
here and on the next page. The picture on
this page shows the prototype, No. M24500
from the corridor side. It is carrying LMS
not BR maroon livery (note the double line
above the windows).

164

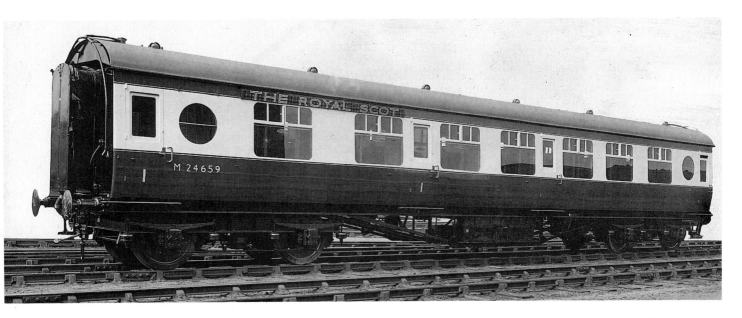

Plate 155. Decorative tartan-backed headboard and the early layout of insignia on the BR red/cream livery on No. M24659, c.1950.

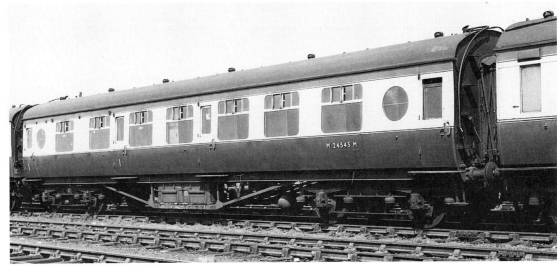

Plates 156–157. Mid-1950s BR red and cream livery with conventional insignia layout on corridor and compartment sides of Nos M24545M and M24561M respectively. (*The late Gavin Wilson collection*)

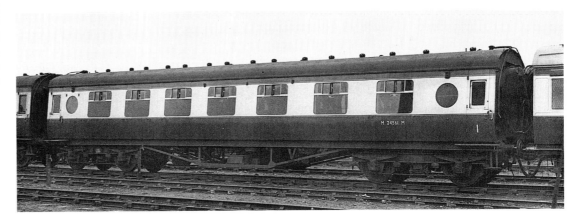

Plate 158. Latter day BR maroon livery (with yellow stripe) on the preserved No. M24617M at Bridgnorth, April 1969. (*J. E. Cull*)

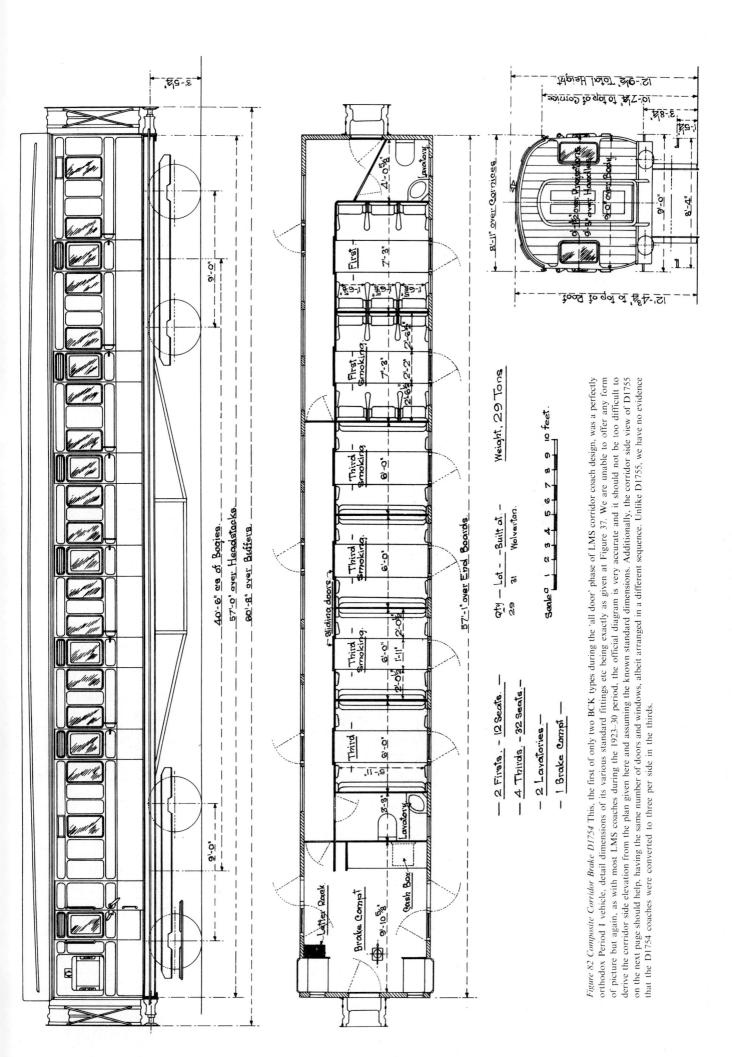

Figure 82 Composite Corridor Brake D1754 This, the first of only two BCK types during the 'all door' phase of LMS corridor coach design, was a perfectly orthodox Period 1 vehicle, detail dimensions of its various standard fittings etc being exactly as given at Figure 37. We are unable to offer any form of picture but again, as with most LMS coaches during the 1923-30 period, the official diagram is very accurate and it should not be too difficult to derive the corridor side elevation from the plan given here and assuming the known standard dimensions. Additionally, the corridor side view of D1755 on the next page should help, having the same number of doors and windows, albeit arranged in a different sequence. Unlike D1755, we have no evidence that the D1754 coaches were converted to three per side in the thirds.

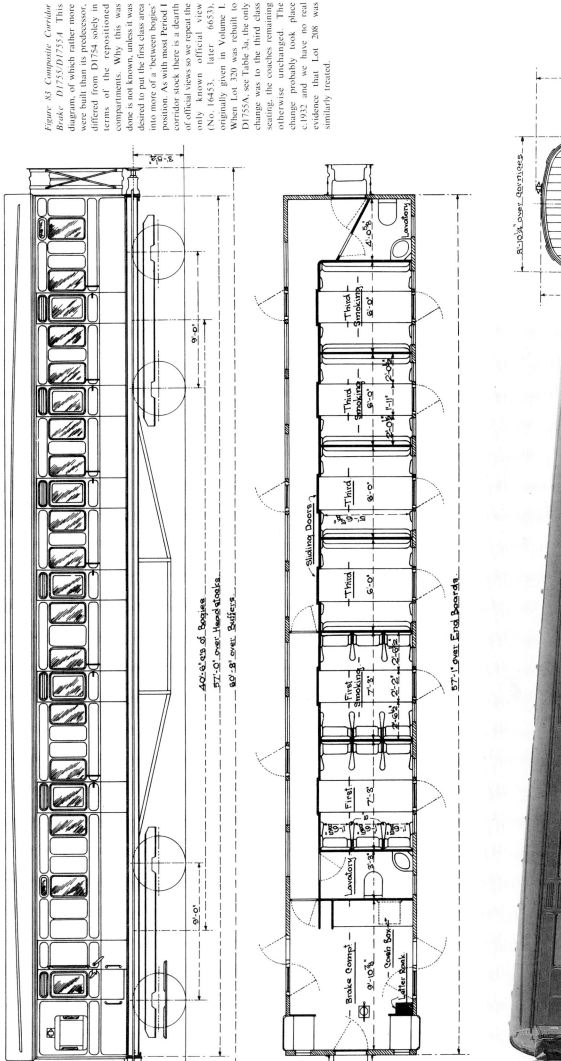
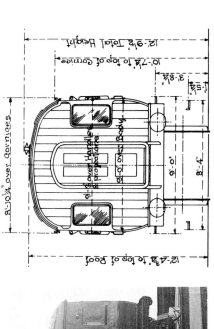

Figure 83 Composite Corridor Brake D1755/D1755A This diagram, of which rather more were built than its predecessor, differed from D1754 solely in terms of the repositioned compartments. Why this was done is not known, unless it was desired to put the first class area into more of a 'between bogies' position. As with most Period I corridor stock there is a dearth of official views so we repeat the only known official view (No. 16453, later 6653), originally given in Volume I. When Lot 320 was rebuilt to D1755A, see Table 3a, the only change was to the third class seating, the coaches remaining otherwise unchanged. The change probably took place c.1932 and we have no real evidence that Lot 208 was similarly treated.

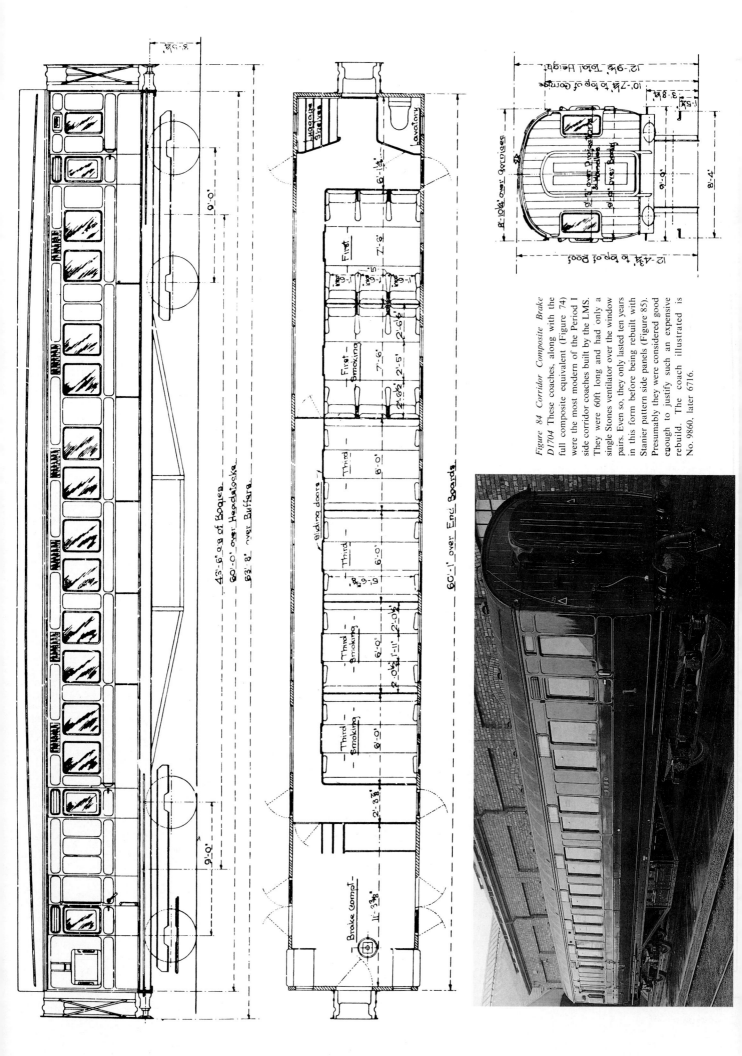

Figure 84 Corridor Composite Brake D1704 These coaches, along with the full composite equivalent (Figure 74) were the most modern of the Period I side corridor coaches built by the LMS. They were 60ft long and had only a single Stones ventilator over the window pairs. Even so, they only lasted ten years in this form before being rebuilt with Stanier pattern side panels (Figure 85). Presumably they were considered good enough to justify such an expensive rebuild. The coach illustrated is No. 9860, later 6716.

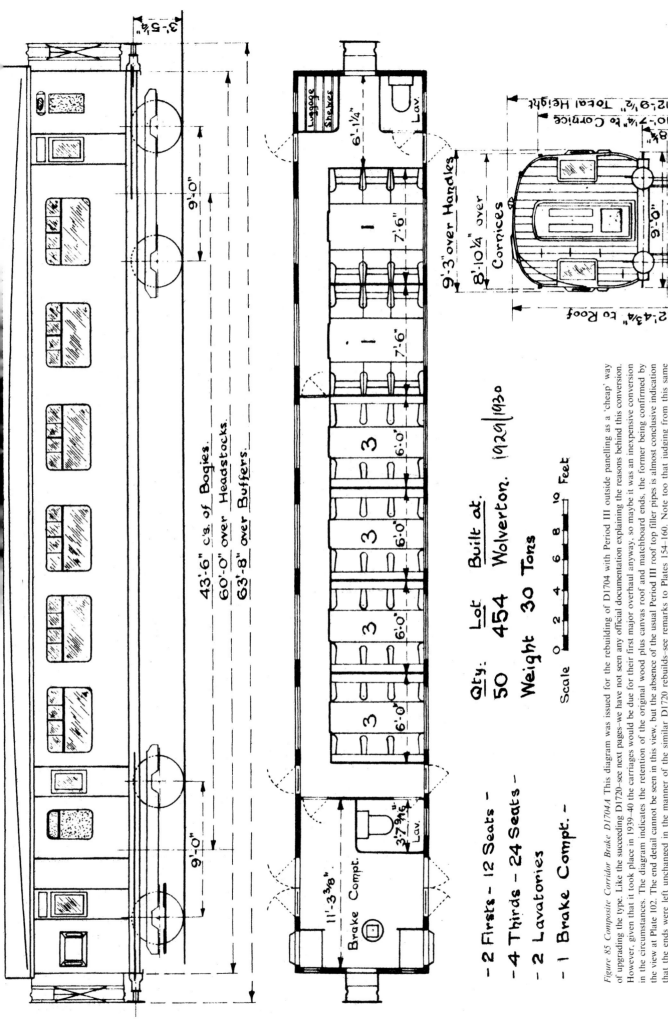

- 2 Firsts – 12 Seats –
- 4 Thirds – 24 Seats –
- 2 Lavatories
- 1 Brake Compt. –

Qty.	Lot	Built at.	
50	454	Wolverton.	1929/1930

Weight 30 Tons

Scale 0 2 4 6 8 10 Feet

3'-5¾"

9'-0"

43'-6" c's. of Bogies.

60'-0" over Headstocks.

63'-8" over Buffers.

9'-0"

6'-1¼"

7'-6"

7'-6"

3 3 3 3

6'-0" 6'-0" 6'-0" 6'-0"

Luggage Shelves

Lav.

3'-7 9/16" Lav.

11'-3⅜"

Brake Compt.

12'-9½" Total Height

10'-7¼" to Cornice

3'-8¾"

1'-5¼"

9'-0"

8'-4"

9'-3" over Handles

8'-10¾" over Cornices

12'-4¾" to Roof

Figure 85 Composite Corridor Brake D1704A This diagram was issued for the rebuilding of D1704 with Period III outside panelling as a 'cheap' way of upgrading the type. Like the succeeding D1720–see next pages–we have not seen any official documentation explaining the reasons behind this conversion. However, given that it took place in 1939–40 the carriages would be due for their first major overhaul anyway, so maybe it was an inexpensive conversion in the circumstances. The diagram indicates the retention of the original wood plus canvas roof and matchboard ends, the former being confirmed by the view at Plate 102. The end detail cannot be seen in this view, but the absence of the usual Period III roof top filler pipes is almost conclusive indication that the ends were left unchanged in the manner of the similar D1720 rebuilds–see remarks to Plates 154–160. Note too that judging from this same picture, the sliding window ventilators were of the later type with smaller centre sections.

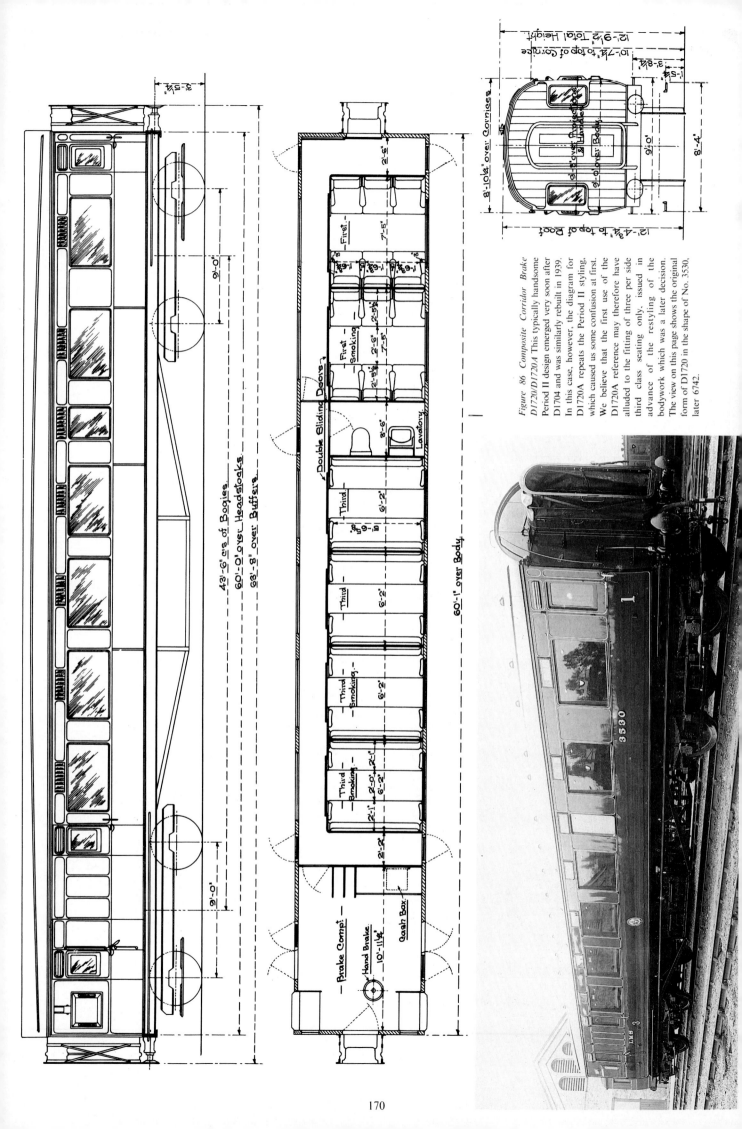

Figure 86 Composite Corridor Brake D1720/D1720A This typically handsome Period II design emerged very soon after D1704 and was similarly rebuilt in 1939. In this case, however, the diagram for D1720A repeats the Period II styling, which caused us some confusion at first. We believe that the first use of the D1720A reference may therefore have alluded to the fitting of three per side third class seating only, issued in advance of the restyling of the bodywork which was a later decision. The view on this page shows the original form of D1720 in the shape of No. 3530, later 6742.

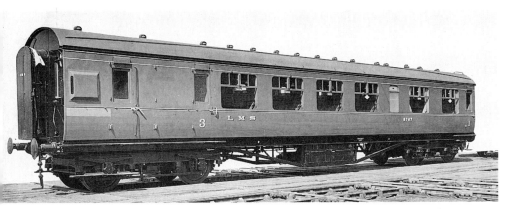

Plates 159-160. For reasons given on the opposite page, we cannot offer a diagram showing the correct external form of D1720A but its basic dimensions were unchanged and the pictures appended should be used in conjunction with the plan of D1720. These views show opposite sides of No. 6767 from which it can be seen that like the D1704 rebuilds, the coaches also retained the original roofs and ends, including scissors gangways, and were given the later pattern sliding window sections.

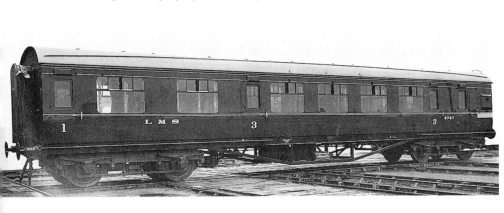

Plate 161-163. These three interior views of D1720A No. 6767 clearly show that the rebuilding was very thorough with little if any signs of the original Period II inside styling. By inference, we presume that D1704A must have been similar.

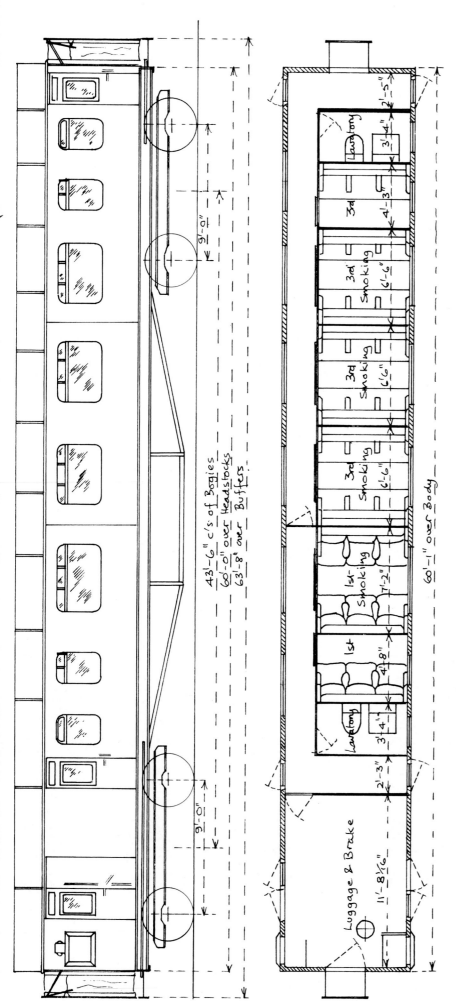

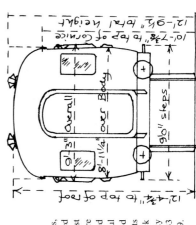

43'-6" c's of Bogies
60'-0" over Headstocks
63'-8" over Buffers

9'-0"

9'-0"

Lavatory 2'-3" 3'-4"

1st 4'-8"

1st Smoking 7'-2"

3rd Smoking 6'-6"

3rd Smoking 6'-6"

3rd Smoking 6'-6"

3rd Smoking 6'-6"

3rd 4'-3"

Lavatory 3'-4" 2'-5"

60'-1" over Body

Luggage & Brake
11'-8½"

10'-7¾" to top of cornice
12'-9½" total height
12'-4¼" to top of roof
9'-3" Overall
8'-11¼" over Body
9'6" steps

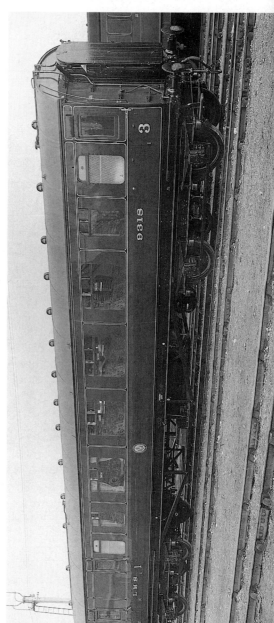

Figure 87 Corridor Composite Brake D1850/1939 This, the pioneer Stanier corridor coach design, introduced a whole new range of features to LMS coaches. Most noticeable was the smooth flush clad exterior, but there were numerous other small details which are described in the main text. The brake composite is a very useful type of vehicle and it is significant that the first Period III design was of this type. This one vehicle exhibits nearly all the features of Stanier pattern corridor stock which were to remain unchanged for almost twenty years. The coach illustrated, 9318, became 6784 in 1933 and was one of the two 'luxury' conversions to D1939. (Drawing-D. Jenkinson)

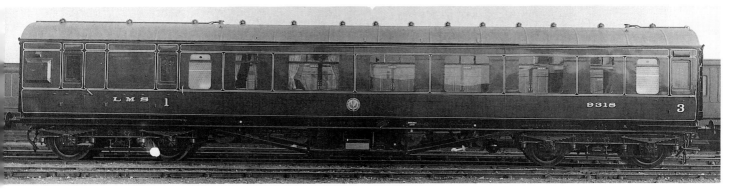

Plates 164-165. The LMS seems to have been rather proud of its very first Period III corridor design and took a number of official pictures. This pair of views gives another compartment side view of No. 9318 together with a corridor side elevation of the same vehicle. These pictures were undoubtedly taken to feature the 'luxury' conversion to D1939 of two vehicles designated for 'Royal Scot' service. Judging from the fact that the vehicle carries its old running number this conversion must have taken place almost immediately after building.

Plate 166. This interesting view, taken at Wolverton in 1933 with a fair number of carriage spares scattered on the ground, shows a still fairly new D1850 coach about to receive its new 1933 series number. The inscription on the third class coupè window indicates that it was No. 9485 about to become No. 6792. Note, compared with the luxury version, that there do not appear to be curtains in the first class compartments, though we suspect they were there. The picture also shows detail of the small destination boards which, at that time, were painted cream with black letters. Note finally, that some of the 'hidden' screw heads fixing the panelling are beginning to be revealed at the right hand end–a not uncommon failing of Period III stock!

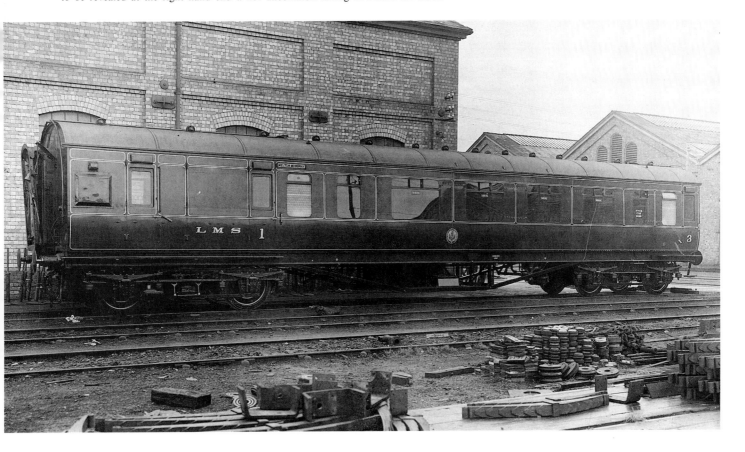

Plates 167-168. First and third class compartment interiors of 'luxury' BCK No. 9318 (later 6784); the coupé views were given at Plates 48/49 of Volume I. The table shown in the first class compartment (and its courtesy lamp) were removable (normally kept in the guard's van) and usually positioned only at the request of passengers. This would enable the compartment to be used for dining, an idea which probably originated on the LNWR, though we cannot state whether these coaches were so utilised. Once again it is worth pointing out that these were ordinary non-supplement carriages and provided as a commonplace by the LMS at that time on its principal trains.

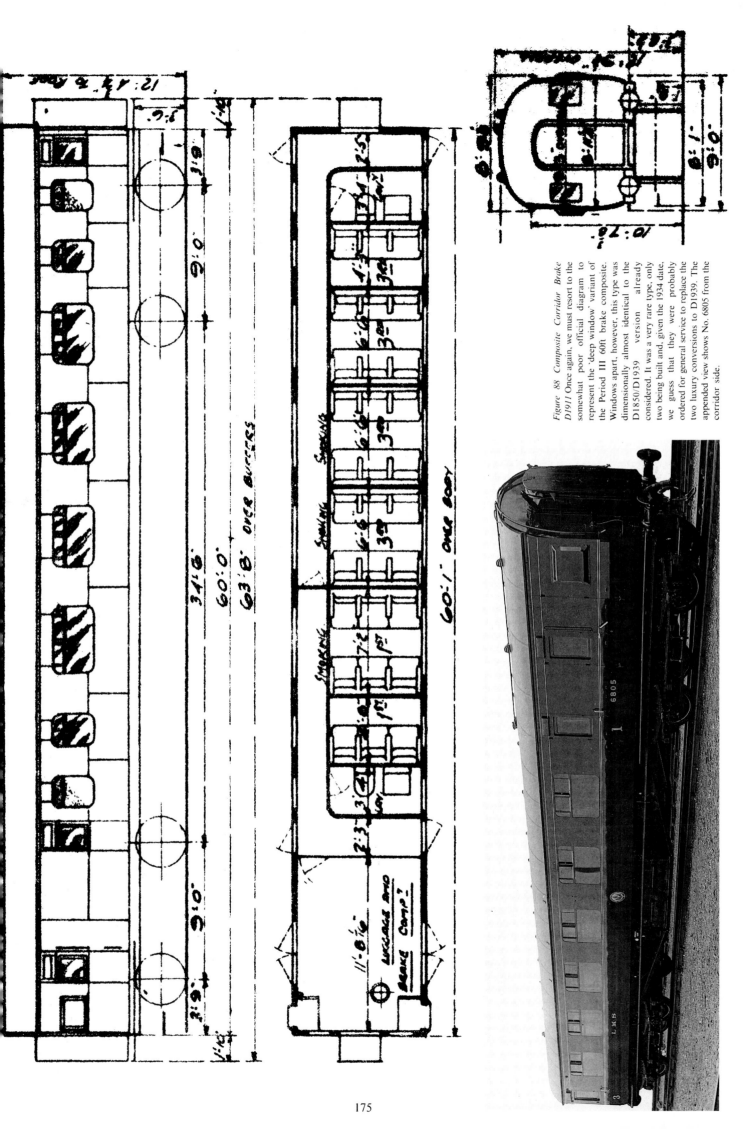

Figure 88 Composite Corridor Brake D1911 Once again, we must resort to the somewhat poor official diagram to represent the 'deep window' variant of the Period III 60ft brake composite. Windows apart, however, this type was dimensionally almost identical to the D1850/D1939 version already considered. It was a very rare type, only two being built and, given the 1934 date, we guess that they were probably ordered for general service to replace the two luxury conversions to D1939. The appended view shows No. 6805 from the corridor side.

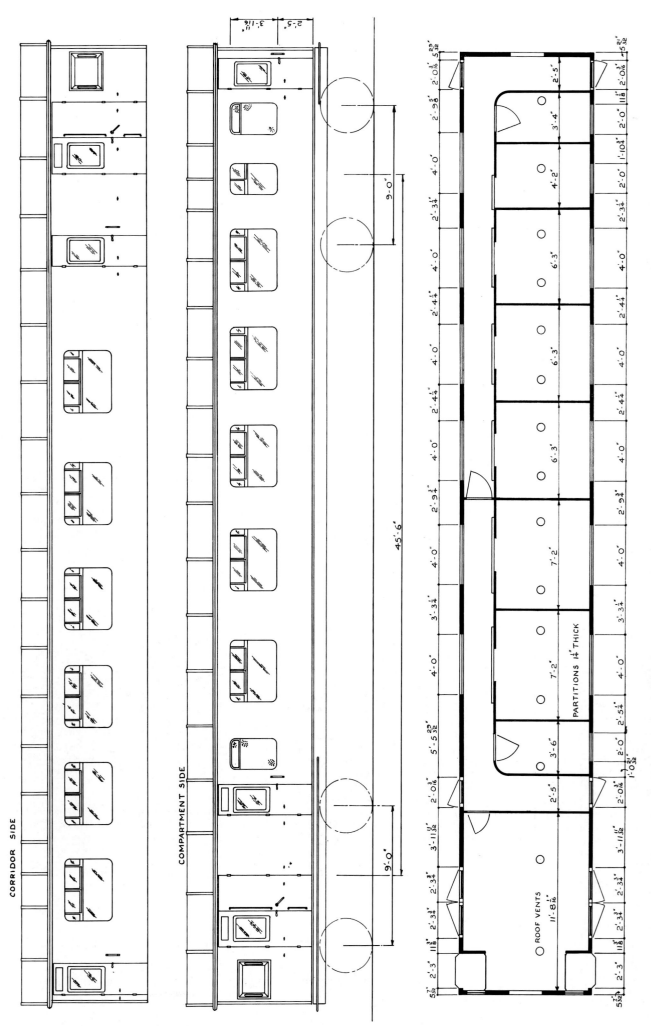

CORRIDOR SIDE

COMPARTMENT SIDE

ROOF VENTS

PARTITIONS 1¼" THICK

Figure 89 Dimensioned elevations and plans. Composite Corridor Brake D1932/D2010 We are pleased to be able to provide, by courtesy of Ken Morgan, a full set of dimensioned side elevations and plans of the last Period III corridor type to be considered in this survey. Quite apart from introducing a unique 62ft length to LMS coaches, these carriages also represented the most numerous form of BCK built to any LMS design. The two diagrams were identical save for the angled corners of the toilet compartment and, not for the first time, we can see no good reason why two separate diagrams were thought necessary. However, we give the diagram for D2010 below. These vehicles were, at 35 tons, the heaviest eight- wheel day coaches built to LMS design.

176

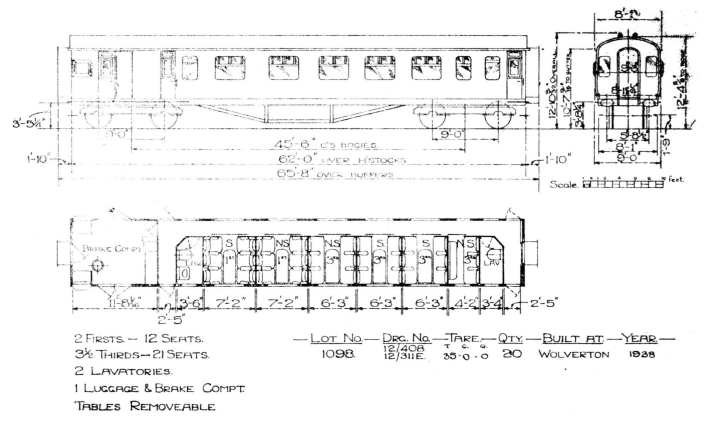

2 FIRSTS. — 12 SEATS.
3½ THIRDS — 21 SEATS.
2 LAVATORIES.
1 LUGGAGE & BRAKE COMPT.
TABLES REMOVEABLE

— LOT NO. —	— DRG. NO. —	— TARE. —	— QTY. —	— BUILT AT. —	— YEAR. —
		T. C. Q.			
1098.	12/408	35·0·0	20	WOLVERTON	1938
	12/311E.				

Figure 90 Composite Corridor Brake D2010 The official diagram for D2010. We are not sure why removable tables are so specified; most Period III carriages could be so adapted.

Plate 169 *(below)* The final Period III BCK designs to D1932 and D2010 were 62ft coaches. The example illustrated here is a D1932 version, No. 6823, ex-shops in 1935. Note the prominent slate painted panel at the brake end.

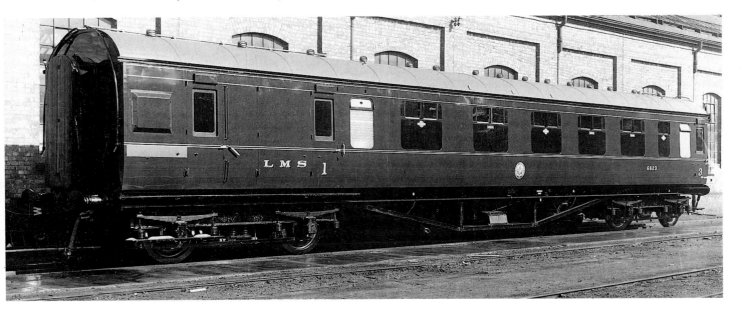

Chapter 4 – Vestibule Coaches

THE gangwayed open coach, or 'vestibule' carriage as the company preferred to call it, was an exceedingly common LMS design and for the first 10 years or more after grouping, this type of vehicle was built in considerably larger numbers than the contemporary side corridor designs. The fashion began to change during the 1930s when the first of the eventual 4000-odd Stanier style side corridor vehicles began to enter service. Even so, Period III open coaches were built to the extent of over 1000 vehicles and, all told, there were put into service over 2750 open coaches to LMS design, mostly before the war. To these must be added the 55 articulated open pairs built for excursion work and considered in Volume III.

This large scale perpetuation of the open coach by the LMS tempts speculation as to why it was such a favoured design since none of the pre-group constituents had favoured the open layout to the extent which the LMS was to do. There was obviously a need for some open stock for dining purposes but this would only account for a small proportion of the total built. No official view has been traced but one possible idea is that the well established Midland Railway tradition of allowing the passengers to travel all the way in the dining cars was beginning, at the time of grouping, to lead to a preference for travelling in open coaches. Certainly, the first LMS standard open coaches were unmodified MR designs. However, according to other sources, the general public were not too enamoured of open coaches on express trains—for example the GWR discontinued building them—so one can hardly really credit that the LMS attracted a different type of passenger than did the other companies! It therefore seems that there may well have been other contributory reasons and the authors are inclined to think that train weight might have been the decisive factor.

There is no doubt that the weight of coach per passenger carried is far less in the case of the open type than in the side corridor coach and, in the light of the MR and early LMS small engine policy, the building of open coaches was probably the easiest way to increase passenger accommodation at minimum cost in extra train weight. Much of the open stock was, of course, used on excursions too where weight is a consideration, but it seems not entirely irrelevant that by 1939/40, when the LMS at last had a reasonable stock of modern express passenger motive power, the building of vestibule coaches all but ceased. There were but a few hundred open coaches built after the war compared with over 2500 side corridor coaches and this imbalance between the two types had never before been witnessed on the LMS. In fact, it was not until this vast post-war building of side corridor coaches took place that the total of all LMS design corridor coaches became appreciably greater than that of LMS designed vestibule vehicles. Since most of this post-war building took place after nationalisation it can safely be stated that as far as the LMS itself was concerned, the vestibule coach was almost as important as the side corridor vehicle. It is interesting to reflect that in the last few years, British Railways have built only open vehicles for second class passengers and most of the important inter-city expresses are now without side-corridor second class accommodation. It must be remembered too that open coaches give slightly more room to seat four-a-side (two-plus-two) than a four-a-side corridor coach. Since latter-day LMS corridor coaches and BR side corridor vehicles allocated to the LMR had three-a-side seating, open vehicles are clearly more economic—whatever the views of passengers.

In the analysis which follows, vestibule dining vehicles will be considered along with their general service equivalents since, for the most part, they were little different in style. The main difference was in the seating arrangements. All dining coaches, first or third, had pairs of seats at one side of the gangway and single seats at the other. The general service open firsts were of similar layout but the third class vehicles had two-and-two seating giving a 33 per cent increase in passenger carrying capacity over the two and one arrangement. They also often tended to be a little more cramped in terms of knee room than did the dining coaches.

PERIOD I DESIGNS

With the exception of a few specialised designs which appeared in 1928, all Period I vestibule stock was derived from the MR twin-window style (see Plate 170). In fact, some of the first LMS coaches were actually built to MR diagrams, albeit in 1923. These were the composites Nos 9700–4 and the thirds Nos 7600–29. Even the first LMS diagrams proper still exhibited MR pattern countersunk locks and handles. There can be no real doubt that whatever the precise reason for the proliferation of open stock after grouping, it was Midland in origin!

Externally, all three classes of coach were very much alike. The firsts had six bays seating 36, the thirds had seven bays seating 56, together with a 42 seat dining version, while the composites had two first class plus 4½ third class bays seating 12 and 35 respectively. The third class end of this version had one seat missing to allow for the offset connecting door between the saloons. All varieties were wood panelled and beaded in orthodox Period I style and all had 57ft underframes.

The first class coaches were all to D1742 (Figure 91) and some, at least, must initially have been utilised for dining purposes. There is little to note about them except to remark that one was converted into a club saloon (later numbered 818) before the 1932/3 renumbering.

The thirds were a little more variable, there being four LMS diagrams plus the aforementioned coaches (7600–29) which are listed on page 175 of the MR Diagram Book. The initial LMS diagram (D1353) was basically the same as the MR version and had the 9ft 1½in width. It was followed by the standard D1692 version with 9ft 3in width while D1699 was the 42 seat dining version. Finally there was a matching five-bay brake ended version to D1693.

Plate 170 Period I coach No. 3465, later 9701. This was one of the five COs actually listed in the MR diagram book. Note the MR style locks and handles. The LMS standard version to D1744 was identical except for the door handles and odd minor details.

The composites, of which there were only 20, were built to D1744 except for the first five (9700–4) which were built in 1923 and appear on page 174 of the MR Diagram book. Apart from the door handles and locks there was no external difference.

During the building of these coaches at Wolverton and Derby, an all-steel version of the full third and brake third designs was built by outside contractors. It is generally understood that these batches were ordered partly to assist the steel industry at the time. The full thirds to D1745 were the steel equivalents of D1692 and the brake ends to D1746 were the equivalents of D1693 which they actually preceded into service. All the steel coaches had flush exteriors but were given fully lined out livery with an imitation waist panel. The batches originating from the different makers exhibited detail variations and livery modifications and these are itemised in the summary tables. Internally they were arranged in identical manner to the LMS built wooden bodied versions.

Towards the end of Period I, in 1928, three designs of coach were introduced which were of more than usual interest in that they paved the way for the single window styles of Period II. There were but 35 coaches all told but they had a pleasing appearance and have been much described and illustrated in other works than this. The most numerous and the most conventional of the three was D1706 which was a seven bay, 42 seat dining coach with high waist and single windows; 25 were built and they were classified as neutral–i.e. for first and/or third class use. In many ways the style was a more up to date version of the D1699 two-window diners and in 1932/3 the coaches were renumbered with the vestibule third diners. It is somewhat doubtful if they were much used as first class dining coaches since shortly after they were built, the more spacious Period II open first made its appearance.

Plate 171 56-seat 'all-steel' open third No. 6206, later 7971 of the batch built by Cammel-Laird to Lot 184. Note the 'squared-off' window corners, simplified full livery and outward facing solebar channel.

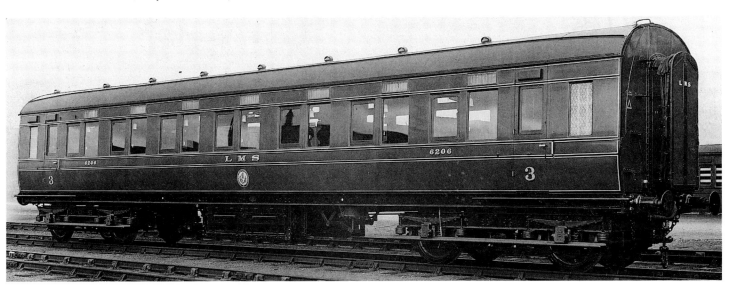

Plates 172-173 The first class corridor/vestibule coaches (or semi-open firsts) to D1707 were one of the three varieties of coach to introduce the large single window style to the passenger seating areas of LMS coaches. These views show the compartment side of No. 15933 (later 1027) and the corridor side of 15412 (later 1023). The centrally positioned door on the corridor side rather spoiled the symmetry of the insignia layout.

The other two 1928 designs were more experimental and do not readily fit into the general classification of LMS coaching stock adopted in this survey. Only five of each kind were built. One was a semi-open first, or corridor/vestibule car to quote the diagram book. It had three compartments which seated a total of 12 passengers only, so each passenger had a corner seat. All compartments were finished differently in high quality Empire timber and the corridor led to a central toilet-cum-powder room containing a separate chair and fitted with a most ornate patterned, full width glass window! Beyond the toilet was a conventional, three-bay, 18 seat dining saloon. Although numbered with the corridor firsts, these coaches are listed in the dining car section of the LMS diagram book and almost always ran next to a kitchen car or kitchen/diner. It therefore seems more logical to consider them with other Period I dining coaches.

The other experimental 1928 design was a first class lounge brake to D1741. These were renumbered in 1932/3 at the head of the corridor brake first list but this may have been because there were no other LMS open first brakes to justify a separate number series. They were, in fact, fully open coaches and had accommodation for 10 passengers in deep leather armchairs and settees. They were lavishly equipped with occasional tables, carefully decorated with selected wood veneers and fully carpeted and the single window styling was again adopted. Unfortunately, although very luxurious, they do not seem to have been very popular and saw little more than 10 years in active passenger service, being out of use during the war. The high waist coupled with the low armchairs may have somewhat impeded the view from the window. At all events, unlike the semi-opens, they were not repeated in Period II and seem to have been replaced by the luxury brake first of D1717–page 120.

It seems odd in some ways that the lounge idea was not repeated a year or two later since its concept would appear to have been more suited to the low-waisted coach style and in this form it might have been more successful.

These two experimental designs, together with the matching open dining coach, have often been referred to as 'Royal Scot' stock and indeed, they were first used on that train. However, at no time did the LMS ever build a special set of coaches for the Royal Scot train and these 1928 designs were also included in some of the other prestige trains of the day. They were extremely good coaches and although few in number, were indicative of the way the LMS design teams were moving.

Lounge brake No 5004 was refitted for the Royal Train in November 1935 and seems to have lost its lower waist panel beading at about the same time. No 5003 became the Preston District inspection saloon during 1947-9 but all five lounges were converted to full brakes during 1949-50 and ran for some 16 more years as 31872–6 in the same order of numbering. The semi-opens lasted until the mid 1950s and four of these were later converted for departmental use as riding/tool vans, the fifth becoming a cycle van for attaching to excursion trains. How were the mighty fallen!

Many Period I open coaches were converted to wartime ambulances, returning in many cases as full brakes. Their history in the latter guise is given in Volume III.

Plate 174 The dining saloon of semi-RFO No. 15933 (Plate 172). The seat design was very similar to the standard Period I/II pattern but the Period II semi-RFOs (Figure 98) had seat designs very similar to those of the Period II dining cars.

Plate 175 Interior of Brake First Lounge No. 15493.

PERIOD II DESIGNS

The first Period II open coach was the low-waisted version of the semi-open first just considered. Ten were built of which one was wrecked at Leighton Buzzard in 1931. It was replaced by a steel panelled version (Lot 626). Other than these coaches, which were not really new designs as such, there were only two designs of Period II open coach. One was a 60ft variety with wood panelling and full beading while the other was a 57ft steel panelled design. Together they totalled 426 coaches.

The 60ft design was the first to appear (in 1930) and was built to no fewer than four separate diagrams depending on the seating arrangement and designed utilisation. Externally, all four diagrams were identical.

The first to appear were 25 coaches to D1722. These were 42 seat, seven bay first class coaches, designated dining vehicles. They were immediately followed by 25 third class diners to D1721. There is no difference shown on the diagrams but the firsts may have had softer seating. However, when the firsts were downgraded to third class in 1934 on the advent of the 65ft Stanier open first, the coaches were inserted on D1721 and are shown as such in the diagram book. This is sufficient evidence that there was no real difference between the two versions.

Later in 1930, 75 more coaches of the type were built, all to the same lot number but to two more diagrams. The first 25 were 56 seaters to D1738 and the last 50 reverted to 42 seaters but were given a new diagram D1795. As far as can be seen, the only justification for a new Diagram number for the 42 seat version was the fact that, originally, they were classed as general service rather than dining vestibules and appear in a different place in the Diagram book. They were, however, identical to D1721/2 and on the renumbering in 1932/3 they were placed in the vestibule third dining coach block. One of these 50 was written off at Leighton Buzzard in 1931 and was replaced by a steel panelled version (Lot 628). This was the only coach of the 126 built not to have raised beading. One of the downgraded firsts was later rebuilt with a Stanier body–see page 185.

The 57ft coaches were all to one diagram (D1807) and appeared in 1931/2. They were all 56 seat general service third class coaches and were all steel panelled. In a sense it was this group of coaches which really established steel panelling as an LMS standard practice. The coaches were building when Sir William Stanier took over as CME and the final 100 coaches had suspended type gangways rather than the scissors type. They also exhibited other slight differences to the first 200 and this may have been the first sign of the Stanier influence. One was lost before 1933, so only 299 received 1932/3 numbers.

Internally, the length saved in the 57ft coaches was all taken from the toilet/luggage accommodation and the passenger saloon was the same size as on the 60ft coaches. The 57ft vehicles had 4ft 0in windows whereas the 60ft coaches had 4ft 6in windows.

PERIOD III DESIGNS

Stanier pattern open coaches were not, relatively speaking, as numerous as their matching side corridor designs. As has been explained on page 178, this reversal of the 1923–32 trend only really became marked after the second world war when corridor coach construction far outstripped that of vestibule designs. Nevertheless, well over 1000 Period III open coaches were built, all except for a few first class coaches being completed before the LMS ceased to exist.

The Period III open first was introduced in 1934 on the same type of 65ft underframe as the pioneer fixed berth third class sleepers (page 17). They thus share the distinction of being the longest locomotive hauled LMS eight-wheeled coaches.

Plate 177 Experimental 'lightweight' CO No. 9729 in full livery (D1984). This 'one-off' diagram was the only Period III composite vestibule with deep window ventilators and full livery. The remaining open composites were of identical appearance but with simple livery.

Plate 178 All but one of the LMS vestibule composites had perfectly standard interior fittings and features (either Period I or Period III). This picture shows the exception–No. 9729–which had new design seats, carpets, upholstery pattern and roof lining. The picture is taken from the first class end. As far as is known, no other coaches were thus finished. The general decor is even more typical of the mid-1930s than most LMS coaches of the period.

The cars themselves were spacious and luxurious seven bay 42 seaters and were classified as dining cars. They had table lamps and generally Pullman-like interiors and were the cause of the Period II open first being downgraded to third class. Three were refurbished in 1937 for the 'Coronation Scot' train.

Two batches of these 65ft cars were built (in 1934 and 1939) and they were separated by a general service 60ft design with the same passenger accommodation but no luggage space at the ends. It seems clear that, although not classified as diners, these 60ft cars were frequently used for dining purposes and after the war, one of them (7555), was rebuilt with double glazing and loose seating to match the converted first class kitchen/diner. No. 43 (page 45) although they did not run together in service.

A porthole window version of the 60ft type was built in 1949 and these coaches were the only LMS pattern open coaches to be built after nationalisation. They were given some of the numbers vacated by the downgraded Period II open firsts.

The Period III vestibule composites were even less variable. All were six bay, 36 seat coaches on 57ft underframes seating 18 first and 18 third in a two-and-one arrangement. There was both a shallow and a deep window ventilator version and the first coach of the latter type was a special lightweight one-off to D1984. It employed welded construction and had a non-standard interior decor.

These composites were not classified as dining coaches although they seem to have been mainly used for this purpose. Many were semi-permanently paired with their contemporary matching third class kitchen/diners. This RT + CO arrangement seems to have been more favoured on the LMS than the RF + TO pairing although the latter was common enough.

By far the most common Period III vestibule coaches were general service third class vehicles. In fact, there were no Stanier pattern vestibule thirds *built* as dining coaches although some were later converted—see below. No doubt the already existing Period I and II coaches were more than enough to cover dining needs, there being 165 of the 42 seat variety already in existence.

There were several subtle changes in the interior layout of the Stanier pattern open third and all varieties were built in some numbers. The earliest to D1904 was basically a Period III version of the 57ft Period II design with lavatory and luggage space at both ends of the coach. Nine of these were converted to 42 seaters in 1937 for the 'Coronation Scot' train and were the only 42 seat Stanier pattern open thirds.

D1904 was followed by a 7½ bay, 60 seat variety to D1915. These were very numerous coaches and the extra half bay was achieved by eliminating the luggage space and placing both lavatories at one end. The lack of luggage space indicates that they were probably designed as excursion vehicles although many doubtless, went into general service use.

In 1938 a reversion to 56 seats was made (D1999) but not to the D1904 layout. The luggage shelves at the end were still omitted and the extra space shared equally between the seven seating bays giving more leg room. These were the last general service open coaches and went on building after the war—the only variety of open coach to do so in any quantity.

Plate 179 The final Period III BTO to D2008, No. 27948. This 5½-bay design has an even smaller brake compartment that the earlier six bay design.

First Class

L	12 seat saloon	24 seat saloon		S	57'
E					
S	non-smoking			L	

D.1742. (36 seats)

S	24 seat dining saloon	18 seat dining saloon	L	60'
E				
		non-smoking	E	

D.1722 (42 seats)   *Third class coaches D1721/1795 were identical. Third class D1755 was 56 seat version (centre gangway). D1722 downgraded to 3rd class later.*

S	24 seat dining saloon	36 seat dining saloon	L	65'
E			E	
L	non-smoking		S	

D.1902. (42 seats)

L	24 seat saloon	36 seat saloon		60'
E			E	
L	non-smoking			

D.1917/2116/2118 (42 seats)   *the single 42 seat saloon with loose chairs on D.2118*

Third Class – see also D.1722 above)

S	24 seat dining saloon	18 seat dining saloon	L	57'
E			E	
L		non-smoking	S	

D.1699/1706/1981 (42 seats)   *gangway on opposite side – D.1981*

S	32 seat saloon	24 seat saloon	L	57'
E			E	
L		non-smoking	S	

D.1355/1692/1745/1850/1904 (56 seats)

| | 36 seat saloon | 24 seat saloon | L | 57' |
| L | | non-smoking | L | |

D.1915/1915A (60 seats)

	32 seat saloon	24 seat saloon	L	57'
E			E	
		non-smoking		

D.1999 (56 seats)

S	32 seat saloon	24 seat saloon	L	60'
E			E	
S		non-smoking	L	

D.2021 (56 seats)

First Class Corridor/Vestibule

| E | 1st | 1st | 1st | | 1st dining saloon | | 57' |
| | | | | L | 18 seats | E | |

D.1707/1719 (3 x 1st comps. – 12 seats; 1 x 1st saloon – 18 seats)

First Class Lounge Brake

	Brake Compartment	1st Class Lounge 10 seats	L	57'
			E	
			S	

D.1741 (10 seats)

Composite

S	3rd non-smoking	3rd	1st	L	57'
E				E	
L	12 seats	23 seats	12 seats	S	

D.1744 (12 x 1st; 35 x 3rd seats)

S	3rd	1st	L	57'
E			E	
L	18 seats	18 seats	S	

D.1862/1984/1903 (18 x 1st; 18 x 3rd seats)

Third Class Brake

	Brake Compartment	18 seat saloon	24 seat saloon	L	57'
				E	
		non-smoking		S	

D.1741/1693/1913 (40 seats)

	Brake Compartment	18 seat saloon	36 seat saloon	L	57'
				E	
		non-smoking		L	

D.1916/1946 (18 seats)

	Brake Compartment	12 seat saloon	32 seat saloon	L	57'
				E	
		non-smoking		L	

D.2008 (44 seats)

Key to letters on plans

E. Entrance Vestibules

L. Lavatories

S. Shelves.

Note: All plans on this drawing are to a constant scale

Schematic Plans – LMS standard Vestibule (Open) Coaches

LMS standard vestibule stock—sketch plans (Drawn by D. Jenkinson)

In addition to the full thirds, there were several types of Period III vestibule third brake coaches. None were built in any great quantity. The first design to D1913 was the Period III version of D1693 with five bays and 40 seats. This was followed by a rather more numerous six bay design for excursion use. This latter type was built to two diagrams (D1916/D1946), although there was no apparent difference. Finally, in 1938 there was introduced a 5½ bay, 44 seat design to D2008 which matched the full open 56 seaters of the same year. This last design had an even smaller brake compartment than the preceding six bay type and the extra space caused by the elimination of the half bay was, like its D1999 equivalent given to the passengers in the form of extra leg room.

Finally, there were diagrams issued for an odd 60ft Period III open third and two 1939 pattern 'Coronation Scot' open thirds. The latter are considered in Volume III while the former was a rebuild on the original frames of 60ft Period II coach No. 9034 which had been involved in the Irish Mail accident at Crewe on April 14, 1937. The original 9034 was one of the downgraded open firsts with 42 seats but the Stanier rebuild was a 56 seater. All in all this was quite a lot of fuss to make about one coach when there were so many hundreds of the other types in service. This, and others like it, were probably accountancy rebuilds.

A few LMS open coaches were converted for push-pull use by B.R. Details are given in Table 4a and the conversion involved D1692.

TABLE 4a: SUMMARY TABLE OF LMS STANDARD GANGWAYED VESTIBULE COACHES, INCLUDING VESTIBULE DINING COACHES

Note: This table should be read in conjunction with the list of standard dimensions and details on page 9. However, before tabulating the vestibule stock, some notes on the 1932/3 renumbering as it applied to vestibule coaches are necessary. Vestibule firsts were numbered between 7400–7599, thirds between 7600–9699, composites between 9700–9799 and third brakes from 9800 upwards. In the first and composite blocks, the numbers ran consecutively through the diagrams–oldest coaches coming first–but in the third class block there were complications. The coaches built to MR diagrams came first followed by the vestibule third diners (i.e. those with 2 + 1 seating). Finally came the general service open thirds starting at 7765. However, the downgrading of D1722 (see p.123) came after this renumbering so there was no space for the coaches in the third dining series without a great deal of fresh renumbering. These 42 seaters were, therefore, given the lowest available numbers in the general service series and do not run consecutively with the other coaches of the type. Finally, the all-steel coaches were numbered 'inside' D1692 in date order thus:

7826-7875—D1692 built in 1925
7876-8075—'All steel' built 1925/6
8076-8580—D1692 built 1927 and later

There was no need to split up the first class and composite coaches in this way since all the firsts and most of the composites could have been used for dining if need be.

Type	Diag	Lot	Qty	Date	Built	Dimensions (L×W×H)	Weight	Period	Running Numbers	Withdrawals First	Last	Remarks
FO	1742	80	6	1925	Derby	57'×9'3"×12'4¾"	28T	I (2-window)	7400-7405	3/59	12/61	Many of these were probably used for dining although not classified RFO. One coach from Lot 138 was rebuilt into saloon and renumbered 818 in 1932-3 (Scrap: 6/62).
		138	10	1925	Derby		28T		7406-7414	4/59	11/62	
		155	20	1925	Derby		28T		7415-7434	3/59	13/62	
		293	30	1926/7	Derby		28T		7435-7464	8/57	12/62	
RFO	1722	519	25	1930	Derby	60'×9'3"×12'4¾"	30T	II (Beaded)	7465-7489	Became 9030-54 see remarks		Downgraded to RTO on advent of D1902.
RFO	1902	734	25	1934	Wolverton	65'×9'3"×12'4⅝"	35T	III	7490-7514	10/62	10/64	Lot 734 had full livery when new. 7507-9 modified for use with the 1937 'Coronation Scot' sets and tared 36T on conversion.
		1187	10	1939	Wolverton		35T		7566-7575	13/64	6/65	
FO	1917	845	10	1935	Derby	60'×9'3"×12'4⅝"	32T	III	7515-7524	8/63	12/64	The 60' general service version numbered in the middle of D1902. Many were probably used for dining purposes, although not classed as such. 7555 rebuilt to D2118.
		909	14	1936	Wolverton		32T		7525-7538	5/63	2/63	
		995	27	1937	Wolverton		32T		7539-7565	12/63	4/65	
RFO	2118 ex-995	1	1947	Derby	60'×9'3"×12'4⅝"	32T	III	7555	—	1/65	Altered to have individual chairs for dining purposes. LMS post war livery and 1946 style insignia on conversion. It later ran with RB No. 105–see Table 2b.
FO	2160	1503	20	1949	Wolverton	60'×9'3"×12'4⅝"	31T	III (P'hole)	7465-7484	11/64	6/65	Post-nationalisation version of D1917. All BR crimson/cream when new with last style of sliding ventilators and torpedo ventilators (post-war pattern). The last vestibule coaches of LMS style to be built.
Semi-RFO	1707	379	5	1928	Derby	57'×9'3"×12'4¾"	29T	I (Single-window)	1023-1027	10/56	4/57	The pioneer single window designs with four seats per compartment, all differently furnished. Four went to departmental use and one to a cycle van on withdrawal. Sometimes referred to as 'Royal Scot' stock.
Semi-RFO	1719	488	10	1930	Derby	57'×9'3"×12'4¾"	29T	II (Beaded)	1028-1036	7/55	10/60	The Period II version of D1707. Only nine of Lot 488 were renumbered, one having been lost in the Leighton Buzzard smash of 1931 (old 15318). Lot 626 was the replacement for this car and is thought possible that it was, in fact, a rebuild of the victim using a new body on the old frames.
		626	1	1932	Derby		29T	II (Flush)	1037		8/56	

TABLE 4a: LMS VESTIBULE COACHES *(continued)*

Type	*Diag*	*Lot*	*Qty*	*Date*	*Built*	*Dimensions* (L×W×H)	*Weight*	*Period*	*Running Numbers*	*Withdrawals First*	*Last*	*Remarks*
BFO Lounge	1741	378	5	1928	Derby	57'×9'3"×12'4¾"	27T	I (Single-window)	5000-5004	12/49	13/50	'Royal Scot' stock again and not very popular designs. 5003 to America in 1933 with the Royal Scot train, later becoming Preston District inspection saloon (1947-49). 5004 refitted for Royal Train (11/35) losing the waist panel beading at the time. On withdrawal all were converted to BG and numbered 31872-6 in same order.
TO	—	—	30	1923	Derby	57'×9'1½"×12'5½"	27T	I (2-window)	7600-7629	6/56	1/61	Although built in 1923 and given LMS series numbers in the 1932/3 renumbering, these coaches were listed on p. 175 of the MR Diagram Book.
TO	1353	1	25	1924	Derby	57'×9'1½"×12'5½"	26T	I (2-window)	7765-7789	2/58	8/62	The LMS version of the MR design but still with MR pattern locks/handles. Lot 1 plated 1923.
		16	6	1924	Derby		27T		7790-7795	11/55	7/60	
		94	30	1924	Derby		27T		7796-7825	6/57	11/61	
TO	1692	154	50	1925	Derby	57'×9'3"×12'4¾"	27T	I (2-window)	7826-7875	7/53	3/62	The official 9'3" wide version of D1353. Many of Lot 154 were 28T. Several later Push Pull conversions (c.1938): 8477—3464; 8509—3463; 8520—3462; 8539—3465. This was the most common LMS TO design and 8207 is preserved in the National collection.
		302	100	1927	Derby		27T		8076-8175	5/59	12/63	
		343	80	1927/8	Derby		27T		8176-8255	5/59	9/63	
		355	100	1928	Derby		27T		8256-8355	5/59	13/63	
		375	100	1928	Derby		27T		8356-8455	5/59	1/64	
		431	125	1929	Derby		27T		8456-8580	5/59	12/62	
TO	1745	183	50	1925/6	B'ham C&W		30T	I (2-window 'all steel')	7876-7925	5/59	13/62	Numbered 'inside' D1692 and the 'all steel' version of D1692. Lot 184 had 'square' cornered panelled lining without vertical waist and eaves panel dividers and had a roof rainstrip. Other lots had rainstrip over doors only. All had rivetted steel roofs. Lot 185 had slightly more rounded window corners with radiussed corner between coach sides and coach ends. All versions given full livery with waist 'Panel'. 21 of Lot 185 were converted by BR to Heater Vans during 1958-63.
		184	50	1925/6	Camm/Laird		30T		7926-7975	5/57	13/62	
		185	100	1926	Met. C&W		30T		7976-8075	9/58	9/64	
RTO	1699	156	35	1925	Derby	57'×9'3"×12'4¾"	27T	I (2-window)	7630-7664	5/59	13/61	The 42 seat dining version of D1692.
RTO	1706	411	25	1929	Derby	57'×9'3"×12'4¾"	27T	I (Single-window)	7665-7689	5/59	13/62	Originally classified RUO but probably rarely used for first class passengers. These were the matching coaches to the 1928 Semi-FOs and Lounge brakes. As diners they were rapidly outmoded by the 60' Period II styles and hence, presumably, renumbered in the RTO series.
RTO	1721	491	25	1930	Derby	60'×9'3"×12'4¾"	29T	II (Beaded)	7690-7714	5/59	13/63	Lot 519 downgraded ex-D1722 (RFO). 9034 was later rebuilt to D2021. Lot 519 plated 29T.
		519	25	1930	Derby		30T		9030-9054	5/59	10/63	
TO	1738	part 522	25	1930	Derby	60'×9'3"×12'4¾"	30T	II (Beaded)	8880-8904	6/58	5/63	The 56 seat version of D1721. For some reason they were renumbered after D1807 in 1932/3.
TO	1795	part 522	50	1930	Derby	60'×9'3"×12'4¾"	30T	II (Beaded)	7715-7763	5/59	8/64	The official 'non-dining' 42 seat version of D1721 although numbered in the dining series. There was no difference between the two. Only 49 of Lot 522 were renumbered in 1932/3 and Lot 628 was a replacement of the 50th coach (old 14733) which was involved in the Leighton Buzzard smash of 1931. It went to the USA in 1933 with the 'Royal Scot'.
		628	1	1932	Derby		30T	II (Flush)	7764	—	12/61	
TO	1807	575	140	1931	Derby	57'×9'3"×12'4¾"	29T	II (Flush)	8581-8720	5/60	7/64	Seating area the same as D1721/38/95 but smaller lavatories and luggage spaces. Lots 575/597 had wide Stones ventilators over all main windows but Lots 648/654 had narrow Stones ventilators over drop-lights only (2nd and 5th from left) and hooded metal ventilators over the rest. Lots 648/654 had suspended type gangways. Lots 575/597 had 'panel' lining between the windows. Lots 648/654 had lining at edge of windows. *Push Pull conversions* (all in 1951): 8723—3484; 8748—3485; 8865—3486 One of Lot 654 was lost before renumbering.
		597	60	1931	Wolverton		29T		8721-8780	7/59	2/66	
		648	50	1932	Wolverton		29T		8781-8830	12/59	1/64	
		654	50	1932	Derby		29T		8831-8879	13/60	7/64	
TO	1904	736	25	1933	Derby	57'×9'3"×12'4⅝"	30T	III	8905-8929	11/62	2/65	Period III version of D1807. Lot 736 had full livery when new. Some converted in 1937 to D1981 (below).
		804	50	1934	Met/Camm.		30T		8930-8979	5/62	2/64	
		805	50	1934	B'ham C&W		30T		8980-9029	5/62	12/64	
RTO	1981	804	3	1937	Wolverton	57'×9'3"×12'4⅝"	32T	III	8931/50/61	10/62	10/64	Converted to 42 seat dining versions for the 1937 'Coronation Scot' sets and pressure ventilated on conversion.
		805	6	1937	Wolverton		32T		8993/6/9003 9004/6/29	8/62	10/64	
TO	1915	843	60	1935	Derby	57'×9'3"×12'4¾"	30T	III	9055-9114	8/63	11/65	The 60 seat excursion version of the Period III TO. Lot 954 plated 30T. 5 or 6 sold to Jamaica (1964) as passenger vehicles.
		857	60	1935	Wolverton		31T		9115-9174	11/62	3/65	
		894	56	1936	Derby		30T		9175-9230	6/63	10/65	
		953	100	1936	Met/Camm.		31T		9231-9330	12/62	7/65	
		954	100	1936	B'ham C&W		31T		9331-9430	4/63	2/66	

TABLE 4a: LMS VESTIBULE COACHES *(continued)*

Type	Diag	Lot	Qty	Date	Built	Dimensions (L×W×H)	Weight	Period	Running Numbers	Withdrawals First	Withdrawals Last	Remarks
TO	1915A	996	4	1937	Wolverton	57'×9'3"×12'4⅝"	30T	III	9431-9434	10/64	3/65	As for D1915 but slightly lower total height (12'10¼" as against 12'11¼") and supposedly lighter in weight.
TO	1999	1084	48	1938	Derby	57'×9'3"×12'4⅝"	28T	III	9435-9482	—	9/66	A reversion to 56 seats with more space for the passenger than the previous 56 seat version to D1904. Lot 1084 were plated 29T. Lot 1400 were the first vehicles to be built by the LMS after the 1939-45 war. All post-war batches had small scroll numbers with flat topped '3' and Lot 1438 probably had the last style of window ventilators. All post-war pre-1948 batches were probably maroon not crimson when new. Some of Lot 1438 given experimental BR liveries from new. Lot 1127 was a replacement. Some of these coaches only had sliding vents in 1st/3rd/5th/7th windows and some had second hand chassis.
		1188	34	1939	Wolverton		31T		9483-9516	—	10/65	
		1127	1	1938	Wolverton		29T		8335	—	2/64	
		1400	50	1945	Wolverton		30T		27100-27149	13/63	12/76	
		1401	100	1945/6	W'ton		30T		27150-27249	8/64	a few	
		1402	100	1947	Wolverton		30T		27250-27349	5/64	extant	
		1438	100	1947/8	W'ton		30T		27350-27459	13/63	(1968)	
TO	2021	1126	1	1938	Derby	60'×9'3"×12'4⅝"	30T	III	9034	--	3/65	A 'one-off' rebuild of a D1721 accident victim. A new diagram was needed as the existing 60' underframe was used. The coach was rebuilt as a 56 seater and had removable tables.

Note: One further TO diagram issued (D2153) for the 1939 'Coronation Scot' coaches. These are included in Chapter 13.

Type	Diag	Lot	Qty	Date	Built	Dimensions (L×W×H)	Weight	Period	Running Numbers	Withdrawals First	Withdrawals Last	Remarks
BTO	1746	181	20	1926	Leeds Fge	57'×9'3"×12'4¼"	31T	I (2-window) 'all steel'	9800-9819	5/59	9/62	The 'All steel' brake version of D1745. Coaches were fully lined with pseudo waist 'panel'. Early coaches in Lot 181 were plated 1925 and Lot 182 were plated as 30T. Lot 181 had full length rainstrips and both lots had rivetted steel roof. 9821/8 converted to DMU in 1957!
		182	15	1926	B'ham C&W		31T		9820-9834	3/57	13/62	
BTO	1693	303	35	1927	Wolverton	57'×9'3"×12'4¾"	28T	I (2-window)	9835-9869	5/59	11/63	The conventional wood panelled brake version of D1692. Identical layout to D1746. Early coaches of Lot 328 plated 1927.
		328	20	1928	Wolverton		28T		9870-9889	9/60	3/64	
BTO	1913	806	20	1934	Pickering	57'×9'3"×12'4⅝"	30T	III	9890-9909	5/62	10/65	Period III version of D1693/1746. This batch may have had serif figures when new —see note to D1946 (below).
BTO	1916	844	26	1934	Derby	57'×9'3"×12'4⅝"	30T	III	9910-9935	5/63	3/65	Six bay, 48 seat excursion version with shorter brake compartment. Possibly excursion stock and matches the D1915 full third version (above).
BTO	1946	895	14	1936	Derby	57'×9'3"×12'4⅝"	30T	III	9936-9949	1/64	5/65	Same layout as D1916. Lot 955 appear to have had scroll numbers and this may have been a feature of the coaches built by Pickering & Co.
		955	50	1936	Pickering		31T		9950-9999	11/63	5/65	
		997	6	1937	Wolverton		31T		27900-27905	10/63	11/64	
BTO	2008	1085	5	1938	Derby	57'×9'3¾"×12'4⅝"	29T	III	27906-27910	12/63	10/64	A 5½ bay type with even less brake van space than D1916/D1946. The extra space was given to the passenger—c.f. D1999 (TO). Lot 1174 also plated 29T. All plated 9'3" although shown 9'3¾" on diagram.
		1174	46	1939	Derby		30T		27911-27956	12/63	12/66	
CO	—	—	5	1923	Derby	57'×9'1½"×12'5½"	27T	I (2-window)	9700-9704	1/58	12/60	Although built in 1923, these coaches were listed on page 174 of the MR Diagram Book. They were all but identical to D1744 except that there was a single panel between 1st and 3rd class ends on the outside of the coach.
CO	1744	2	5	1924	Derby	57'×9'1½"×12'5½"	27T	I (2-window)	9705-9709	1/58	9/61	The official LMS version. Diagram shows 9'1½" width but Lot 93 was plated 9'3" and did not have MR type fittings.
		93	10	1925	Derby		28T		9710-9719	7/59	11/61	
CO	1862	697	9	1933	Derby	57'×9'3"×12'4⅝"	32T	III (Shallow ventilator)	9720-9728	7/62	1/64	Full livery when new. These were almost always used for dining purposes having 2+1 seating at both ends of the coach. Diagram shows 10 coaches but only 9 built.
CO	1984	725	1	1934	Derby	57'×9'3"×12'2⅛"	29T	III	9729	—	1/64	Welded construction and lighter weight than D1862. Full livery from new and the coach may have been the last of Lot 697, given a new diagram and lot number because of the experimental construction.
CO	1903	735	10	1934	Derby	57'×9'3"×12'4⅝"	31T	III	9730-9739	7/62	11/64	The standard deep ventilator version and like all Period III COs, appear to have been used as diners. They were 'fluid' in use with detachable class boards inside the coach between the saloons. However, the coaches had '1' and '3' on the outside doors.
		853	10	1935	Derby		30T		9740-9749	11/62	13/64	
		1049	4	1938	Wolverton		31T		9750-9753	9/64	6/65	
		1101	5	1939	Wolverton		31T		9754-9758	8/64	6/65	

TABLE 4b: SUMMARY OF THE 1933 RENUMBERING OF LMS VESTIBULE COACHES

The vestibule group is the second instance in this volume where the pre-1933 numbers form a long list, mainly of course, because of the huge building of third class carriages during Periods I and II. Unlike the side corridor group, however, there were no Period III vestibule Carriages built with 'old series' numbers. We have listed the old numbers by generic type and diagram number, broadly in the same sequence as for Table 4a. However, in the case of third class vestibules where dining/non-dining use slightly confused the pattern (see introductory note to Table 4a) we have, for ease of reference, tabulated the third class coaches in their 1933 *number* sequence. It should also be noted that the LMS chose to number its Period I and II semi-open firsts in the corridor first class series (even though used for dining and perhaps more logically placed within the vestibule series) and that since there were only five open brake firsts (the lounge coaches), they were numbered at the head of the BFK series rather than being given a fresh number block.

First Class – all types

Vestibules

D1742

New No.	Old No.
7400	2739
7401	2740
7402	2742
7403	10247
7404	10248
7405	10249
7406	2966
7407	3521
7408	3532
7409	3543
7410	3552
7411	3557
7412	3629
7413	3715
7414	3716
7415	3517
7416	3524
7417	3550
7418	3669
7419	3670
7420	3672
7421	3673
7422	3674
7423	3686
7424	3713
7425	9367
7426	9370
7427	9371
7428	9372
7429	9373
7430	9375
7431	9376
7432	9377
7433	9378
7434	9380
7435	15324
7436	15326
7437	15422
7438	15429
7439	15431
7440	15433
7441	15492
7442	15495
7443	15542
7444	15623
7445	15648
7446	15682
7447	15665
7448	15746
7449	15787
7450	15811
7451	15822
7452	15847
7453	15861
7454	15882
7455	15891
7456	15913
7457	15923
7458	15980
7459	15989
7460	16086
7461	16125
7462	16140
7463	16147
7464	16201

D1722

New No.	Old No.	3rd Class No.
7465	604	9030
7466	923	9031
7467	940	9032
7468	1112	9033
7469	5812	9034
7470	5813	9035
7471	5815	9036
7472	5820	9037
7473	5823	9038
7474	6113	9039

D1722 cont.

New No.	Old No.	3rd Class No.
7475	6114	9040
7476	6115	9041
7477	6119	9042
7478	6120	9043
7479	6121	9044
7480	6124	9045
7481	6127	9046
7482	6128	0947
7483	6129	9048
7484	6183	9049
7485	6249	9050
7486	6250	9051
7487	6275	9052
7488	6413	9053
7489	6415	9054

Semi-Open

D1707

New No.	Old No.
1023	15412
1024	15485
1025	15604
1026	15807
1027	15933

D1719

1028	2741
1029	2747
1030	10257
1031	10291
1032	15310
1033	15467
1034	15510
1035	15540
1036	15565
1037	15318

Lounge brake

D1741

New No.	Old No.
5000	15349
5001	15413
5002	15438
5003	15455
5004	15493

Third Class
Vestibules

LMS BUILT TO MR LOTS

New No.	Old No.
7600	139
7601	191
7602	390
7603	400
7604	479
7605	849
7606	911
7607	930
7608	944
7609	1057
7610	1072
7611	1078
7612	1126
7613	1201
7614	1255
7615	1266
7616	1282
7617	1776
7618	1781
7619	1783
7620	1784
7621	1785
7622	1788
7623	1789
7624	1798
7625	1800
7626	1801
7627	1803
7628	1804
7629	1805

D1699

New No.	Old No.
7630	7695
7631	7700
7632	7705
7633	7708
7634	7714
7635	7715
7636	7720
7637	7725
7638	7737
7639	7741
7640	7742
7641	7751
7642	7753
7643	7754
7644	7755
7645	7756
7646	7759
7647	7762
7648	7783
7649	7785
7650	7786
7651	7787
7652	7788
7653	7789
7654	7790
7655	7791
7656	7794
7657	7795
7658	7801
7659	7805
7660	7807
7661	7809
7662	7810
7663	7811
7664	7824

D1706

New No.	Old No.
7665	14212
7666	14213
7667	14215
7668	14216
7669	14217
7670	14218
7671	14219
7672	14220
7673	14221
7674	14222
7675	14223
7676	14413
7677	14414
7678	14415
7679	14416
7680	14444
7681	14445
7682	14446
7683	14447
7684	14448
7685	14449
7686	14450

D1706 cont.

New No.	Old No.
7687	14451
7688	14613
7689	14614

D1721

New No.	Old No.
7690	1260
7691	1262
7692	1263
7693	1265
7694	1270
7695	1274
7696	1275
7697	1280
7698	1291
7699	1292
7700	1294
7701	1298
7702	1303
7703	1307
7704	1313
7705	1314
7706	1315
7707	1317
7708	1318
7709	1320
7710	1323
7711	1324
7712	1325
7713	1618
7714	1619

D1795

New No.	Old No.
7715	5928
7716	5929
7717	5930
7718	5934
7719	6041
7720	6049
7721	6050
7722	6053
7723	6057
7724	6062
7725	6072
7726	6073
7727	6074
7728	6075
7729	6076
7730	6077
7731	6078
7732	6079
7733	6083
7734	6084
7735	6086
7736	6088
7737	6090
7738	6091
7739	6096
7740	6099
7741	6101
7742	6102
7743	6103
7744	6104
7745	6106
7746	13889
7747	13891
7748	13892
7749	13908
7750	14007
7751	14013
7752	14020
7753	14028
7754	14031
7755	14033

D1692 cont.

New No.	Old No.
8245	18033
8246	18034
8247	18035
8248	18036
8249	18037
8250	18038
8251	18130
8252	18208
8253	18210
8254	18211
8255	18212
8256	16473
8257	16889
8258	16923
8259	16927
8260	16934
8261	15018
8262	15019
8263	15038
8264	15039
8265	15040
8266	15041
8267	15104
8268	15158
8269	15160
8270	15161
8271	15162
8272	15163
8273	15164
8274	15165
8275	15166
8276	15167
8277	15168
8278	15169
8279	15171
8280	15185
8281	15187
8282	15188
8283	15189
8284	15190
8285	15191
8286	15192
8287	15193
8288	15194
8289	15195
8290	15196
8291	15197
8292	15198
8293	15199
8294	15200
8295	15201
8296	15202
8297	15203
8298	15204
8299	15205
8300	15206
8301	15207
8302	15208
8303	15209
8304	15210
8305	15211
8306	15212
8307	15213
8308	15214
8309	15215
8310	15216
8311	15217
8312	15218
8313	15219
8314	15220
8315	15221
8316	15222
8317	15223
8318	15224
8319	15225
8320	15226
8321	15227
8322	15228
8323	15229
8324	15230
8325	15231
8326	15232
8327	15233
8328	15234
8329	15235
8330	15236
8331	15275
8332	15276
8333	15277
8334	15278
8335	15279
8336	15280
8337	15281
8338	15282
8339	15283
8340	15284
8341	15285
8342	15286
8343	15287
8344	15288
8345	15289
8346	15290

D1692 cont.

New No.	Old No.
8347	15291
8348	15293
8349	15294
8350	15295
8351	15296
8352	15297
8353	15298
8354	15299
8355	15300
8356	151
8357	162
8358	163
8359	179
8360	180
8361	317
8362	329
8363	365
8364	376
8365	379
8336	386
8367	454
8368	465
8369	496
8370	497
8371	504
8372	603
8373	620
8374	662
8375	665
8376	696
8377	735
8378	822
8379	842
8380	900
8381	901
8382	991
8383	1020
8384	1028
8385	1042
8386	1050
8387	1120
8388	1173
8389	1189
8390	1207
8391	1209
8392	1241
8393	1361
8394	1394
8395	1402
8396	1406
8397	1439
8398	1440
8399	1631
8400	1643
8401	1647
8402	1648
8403	1652
8404	1664
8405	1665
8406	1670
8407	1671
8408	1672
8409	1675
8410	1680
8411	1681
8412	1685
8413	1709
8414	1750
8415	1761
8416	1770
8417	1782
8418	1790
8419	1821
8420	1833
8421	2855
8422	2924
8423	3504
8424	3555
8425	3562
8426	3621
8427	3675
8428	14049
8429	14379
8430	15005
8431	15308
8432	15984
8433	15991
8434	16123
8435	16130
8436	16663
8437	16736
8438	16864
8439	16872
8440	16876
8441	16883
8442	16888
8443	16890
8444	16905
8445	16908
8446	16918
8447	16921
8448	16922

D1692 cont.

New No.	Old No.
8449	16925
8450	16931
8451	17160
8452	18743
8453	18807
8454	18810
8455	18851
8456	6
8457	173
8458	996
8459	1281
8460	1610
8461	1656
8462	1697
8463	1704
8464	2311
8465	6174
8466	6218
8467	6224
8468	6225
8469	14711
8470	16116
8471	16141
8472	16142
8473	16165
8474	16173
8475	16211
8476	16248
8477	16260
8478	16264
8479	16268
8480	16278
8481	16284
8482	16297
8483	16345
8484	16376
8485	16379
8486	16418
8487	16436
8488	16449
8489	16460
8490	16542
8491	16584
8492	16740
8493	16868
8494	16899
8495	16909
8496	16928
8497	16935
8498	16938
8499	16941
8500	16942
8501	16944
8502	16946
8503	16947
8504	16950
8505	16953
8506	16979
8507	17069
8508	17071
8509	17077
8510	17106
8511	17139
8512	17164
8513	17166
8514	17206
8515	17214
8516	18071
8517	18784
8518	18804
8519	8
8520	11
8521	30
8522	43
8523	50
8524	52
8525	55
8526	366
8527	378
8528	384
8529	391
8530	393
8531	395
8532	398
8533	401
8534	402
8535	434
8536	436
8537	438
8538	439
8539	440
8540	460
8541	474
8542	490
8543	499
8544	501
8545	502
8546	505
8547	511
8548	513
8549	516
8550	517

D1692 cont.

New No.	Old No.
8551	520
8552	524
8553	525
8554	526
8555	533
8556	538
8557	542
8558	549
8559	563
8560	566
8561	568
8562	570
8563	572
8564	576
8565	580
8566	585
8567	586
8568	595
8569	606
8570	613
8571	622
8572	623
8573	628
8574	630
8575	641
8576	642
8577	643
8578	645
8579	647
8580	652

D1807

New No.	Old No.
8581	76
8582	136
8583	309
8584	794
8585	826
8586	837
8587	850
8588	1224
8589	1302
8590	1405
8591	1437
8592	1850
8593	1957
8594	1989
8595	3741
8596	3893
8597	3894
8598	5573
8599	5662
8600	6164
8601	6239
8602	6286
8603	6380
8604	6394
8605	6417
8606	6423
8607	7118
8608	7303
8609	7614
8610	7618
8611	7620
8612	7655
8613	7660
8614	7713
8615	7760
8616	7833
8617	7942
8618	9403
8619	10635
8620	10696
8621	10699
8622	10700
8623	11746
8624	11768
8625	11800
8626	11826
8627	12003
8628	12008
8629	12020
8630	12076
8631	12096
8632	12099
8633	12244
8634	12218
8635	12348
8636	12510
8637	12625
8638	12641
8639	12691
8640	12725
8641	12965
8642	12988
8643	13010
8644	13013
8645	13037
8646	13158
8647	13225
8648	13254

D1807 cont.

New No.	Old No.
8649	13262
8650	13435
8651	13503
8652	13629
8653	13742
8654	13888
8655	13895
8656	13902
8657	13904
8658	13905
8659	13909
8660	13911
8661	13912
8662	13918
8663	13919
8664	13927
8665	13928
8666	14027
8667	14040
8668	14041
8669	14048
8670	14746
8671	14765
8672	14768
8673	14797
8674	14801
8675	14809
8676	14819
8677	14820
8678	14852
8679	14870
8680	15007
8681	15062
8682	15244
8683	15245
8684	15247
8685	15259
8686	15265
8687	15303
8688	15313
8689	15328
8690	15329
8691	16683
8692	16970
8693	17098
8694	17108
8695	17140
8696	17173
8697	17622
8698	17630
8699	17638
8700	17649
8701	17651
8702	17789
8703	17791
8704	17807
8705	17812
8706	17829
8707	17833
8708	17840
8709	17860
8710	17891
8711	17904
8712	17916
8713	17917
8714	17945
8715	17996
8716	18381
8717	18574
8718	18578
8719	18858
8720	19043
8721	208
8722	242
8723	266
8724	738
8725	853
8726	857
8727	1169
8728	1359
8729	1443
8730	1831
8731	1841
8732	1848
8733	1852
8734	1857
8735	1979
8736	2575
8737	2744
8738	2746
8739	2750
8740	2751
8741	5874
8742	6136
8743	6881
8744	7617
8745	7682
8746	7743
8747	7796
8748	7797
8749	7906
8750	9352

New No.	Old No.	New No.	Old No.	New No.	Old No.	New No.	Old No.	New No.	Old No.
8751	9455	8809	13906	8867	12031	9810	7642	9863	16843
8752	9495	8810	13913	8868	12052	9811	7643	9864	16964
8753	10298	8811	13917	8869	12275	9812	7645	9865	17189
8754	10890	8812	13932	8870	12325	9813	7646	9866	18521
8755	15306	8813	13936	8871	12661	9814	7647	9867	18543
8756	15309	8814	13937	8872	12669	9815	7666	9868	18552
8757	15346	8815	13939	8873	12690	9816	7670	9869	18581
8758	15347	8816	13940	8874	13057	9817	7674	9870	17658
8759	15351	8817	13943	8875	13135	9818	7675	9871	18277
8760	15405	8818	14008	8876	13198	9819	7736	9872	18597
8761	15415	8819	14012	8877	13438	9820	7112	9873	18599
8762	15423	8820	14016	8878	13462	9821	7113	9874	18608
8763	15463	8821	14026	8879	13817	9822	7114	9875	18728
8764	15475	8822	14050	8880	1808	9823	7115	9876	18731
8765	15479	8823	14051	8881	1811	9824	7613	9877	18732
8766	15480	8824	14052	8882	1812	9825	7616	9878	18738
8767	15483	8825	14053	8883	1827	9826	7619	9879	18805
8768	15497	8826	14054	8884	1830	9827	7648	9880	18808
8769	15508	8827	14055	8885	1834	9828	7649	9881	18848
8770	15539	8828	14056	8886	1836	9829	7679	9882	18849
8771	15541	8829	14057	8887	1837	9830	7680	9883	18850
8772	15544	8830	14059	8888	1838	9831	7744	9884	18852
8773	15548	8831	286	8889	5831	9832	7814	9885	18853
8774	15553	8832	1930	8890	5841	9833	7816	9886	18857
8775	15562	8833	3024	8891	5852	9834	7820	9887	19028
8776	15571	8834	3066	8892	5853			9888	19127
8777	15572	8835	3146	8893	5855			9889	19132
8778	15593	8836	6298	8894	5859	**D1693**			
8779	15833	8837	6299	8895	5864				
8780	15844	8838	6300	8896	5867	New No.	Old No.		
8781	15313	8839	6305	8897	5870	9835	638		
8782	13537	8840	6307	8898	5871	9836	969		
8783	13544	8841	6312	8899	5875	9837	2094		
8784	13548	8842	6329	8900	5885	9838	3897		
8785	13577	8843	6349	8901	5899	9839	7731		
8786	13585	8844	6452	8902	5905	9840	10666		
8787	13606	8845	6453	8903	5906	9841	10668		
8788	13616	8846	7650	8904	5927	9842	10876		
8789	13650	8847	7653			9843	11596		
8790	13667	8848	7689			9844	11661		
8791	13668	8849	7841			9845	13988		
8792	13677	8850	7847			9846	14138		
8793	13689	8851	7951			9847	14178		
8794	13691	8852	8341			9848	14183		

Vestibule Brakes

D1746

New No.	Old No.
9800	7595
9801	7600
9802	7629
9803	7633
9804	7634
9805	7635
9806	7637
9807	7639
9808	7640
9809	7641

(D1807 cont. column 2 continued)

New No.	Old No.
8853	9304
8854	9402
8855	10275
8856	10276
8857	10277
8858	10278
8859	10282
8860	10296
8861	11263
8862	11741
8863	11754
8864	11812
8865	11916
8866	11975

(D1693 cont.)

New No.	Old No.
9849	14270
9850	14305
9851	14320
9852	14321
9853	14418
9854	14792
9855	15002
9856	15004
9857	15105
9858	16382
9859	16479
9860	16483
9861	16572
9862	16718

Composite Vestibules

New No.	Old No.
9700	3460
9701	3465
9702	3485
9703	3544
9704	3565

D1744

New No.	Old No.
9705	4625
9706	4626
9707	4627
9708	4628
9709	4629
9710	8719
9711	8722
9712	8723
9713	9223
9714	9224
9715	9246
9716	9248
9717	9260
9718	9264
9719	9265

INTRODUCTION TO THE TYPE BY TYPE SURVEY

The next section covers all the LMS gangwayed vestibule diagrams in the same sequence as Table 4b. Again, especially where original diagrams are not very clear, we have thought it helpful to include some more detailed dimensioned drawings. All extra pictures and other information are placed as close as possible to the diagrams to which relevant.

Plate 180. This posed view shows the non-smoking end of D1742 overleaf No. 15913 (later 7456) of Lot 293, coupled to FK No. 3499 (see page 109 for the other end of the same view). On this occasion, the 'Royal Scot' headboards are featured.

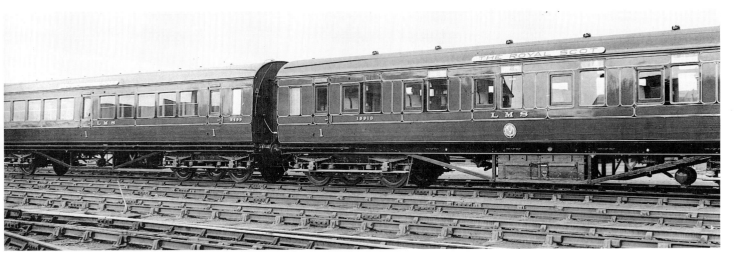

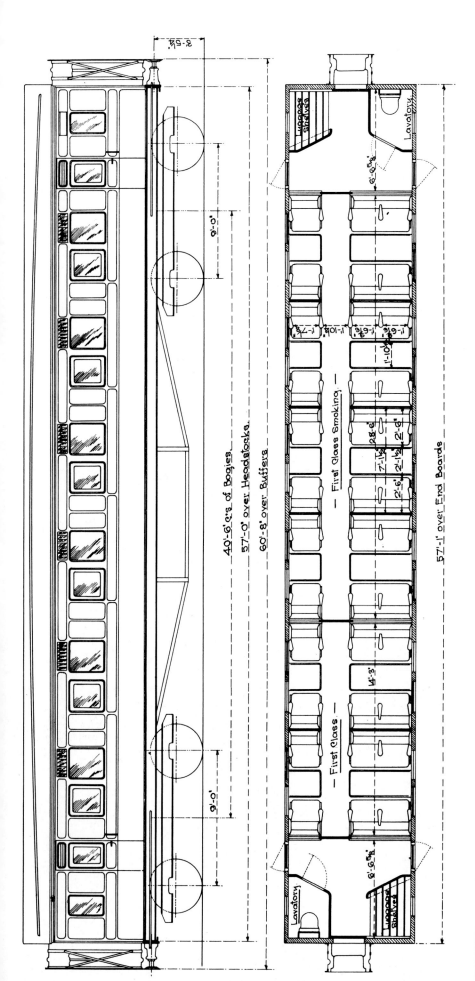

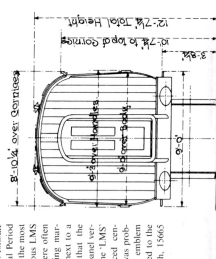

Figure 91 First Class Vestibule D1742 This highly typical Period I open coach design was the most numerous of all the various LMS open first types. They were often used as dining cars, being marshalled for the purpose next to a full kitchen car. Note that the positioning of the waist panel vertical dividers prevented the 'LMS' and emblem being placed centrally, a situation which was probably rectified for the emblem when the LMS was moved to the left hand end. This coach, 15665 later became 7447.

Plate 181. During the building of D1742, the LMS introduced (and photographed) several interior style changes–conceivably as part of an attempt to produce a more modern interior. Some of them are shown in this and the next few views. This first example is believed to be of Lot 80, still displaying Midland pattern luggage rack ends and almost certainly upholstered in the well established 'blue cloth', a popular choice of many railways at the time for the first class.

Plate 182. This elaborately decorated interior treatment comes from No. 3716 (later 7414) of Lot 138. The rear of the original LMS picture is specifically annotated: 'New 1st Class Dining Car' and it may be that this particular lot was so regarded. The trim is probably still in blue cloth but the luggage rack ends now carry the LMS monogram.

Plate 183. This picture shows the interior of No. 15665 (later 7447) of Lot 293. The wall treatment is considerably simplified (as are the seat antimacassars) and the seats themselves are upholstered in a tapestry pattern of unknown hue. The carpet pattern has also changed compared with Plate 181.

Plate 184. This one has us slightly confused, the original print not specifying the vehicle. It is clearly a D1742 carriage, photographed from the smoking end, while the upholstery and carpet patterns are the same as for No. 15665 (above). But the seat ends are much more modern–presumably the reason why the picture was taken. It could be a later example of Lot 293 or, just conceivably, the rebuilt interior of No. 818–see note to diagram in Table 4a.

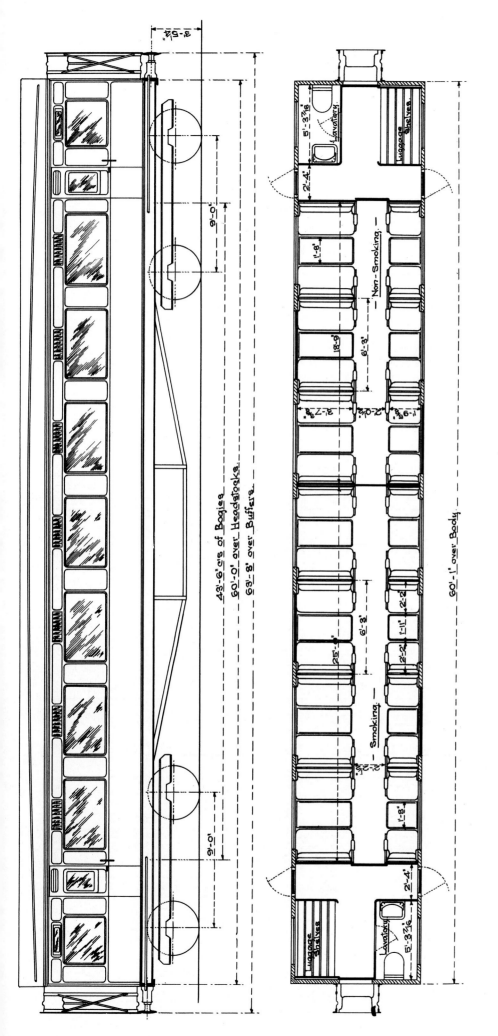

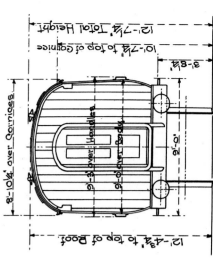

Scale 0 1 2 3 4 5 6 7 8 9 10 feet.

— 2 Compartments - 42 Seats. —
— 2 Lavatories. —

qty.	Lot	Built at.
25	519	Derby.

Figure 92 First Class Vestibule (Dining) D1722 We come now to the first of the very confusing set of four Period II diagrams which all shared the same exterior appearance—see also notes to diagrams in Table 3a. The version here was raised in 1930 for the first class series, all classed as dining vehicles. They were identical to D1721 (third class), the first of these four diagrams to appear (Figure 105) and to which diagram the whole of D1722 was transferred in 1934. In 1933, they were allocated their proper first class numbers (7465–89) but, given the short interval before downgrading to third class, it is not known whether or not every example received its 74xx number before the whole batch was again renumbered 9030–54. Most of the thus vacated 74xx numbers were re-used on Period III D2160.

This design, along with the matching corridor thirds to D1782, the brake composites to D1720 and the 57ft semi-opens to D1719 represented a short lived but particularly handsome link to the steel panelled Period II coaches of 1931/2 and formed an important element in the gradual movement of LMS carriage design away from its pre-group ancestry. We have no views of D1722 itself, but they were in every way identical externally to the third class versions, illustrated at Figures 105-7. A fully dimensioned elevation is also given at Figure 108.

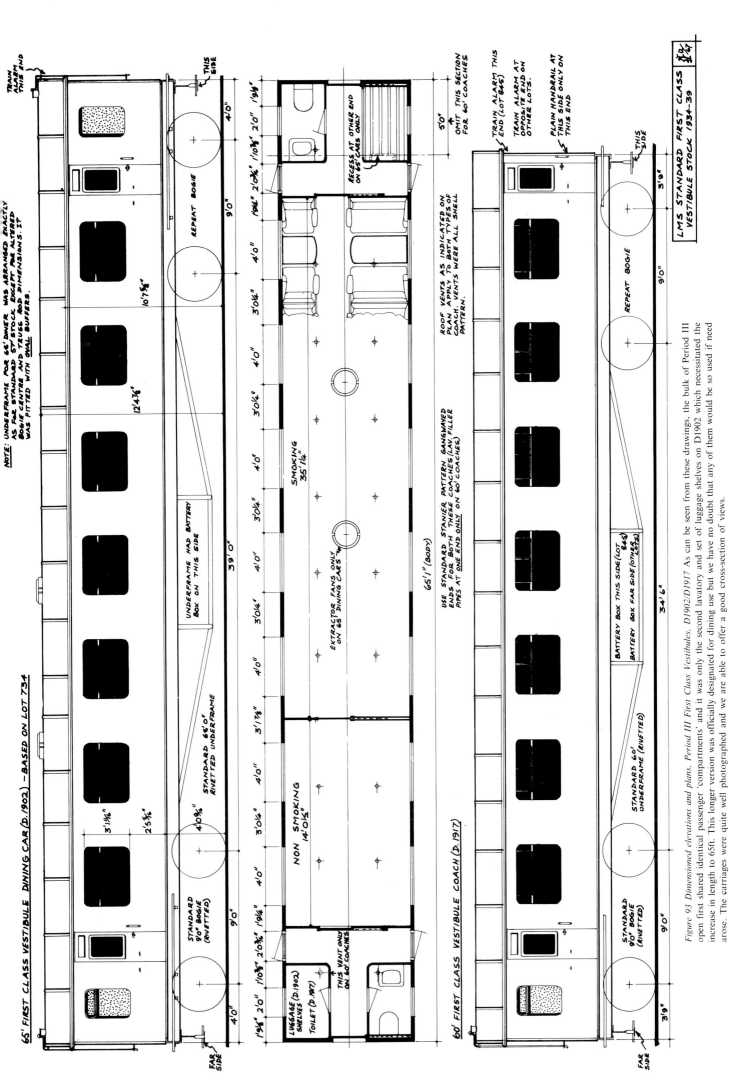

NOTE: UNDERFRAME FOR 65' DINER WAS ARRANGED EXACTLY AS FOR STANDARD 57' STOCK EXCEPT FOR ALTERED BOGIE CENTRE AND TRUSS ROD DIMENSIONS. IT WAS FITTED WITH OVAL BUFFERS.

TRAIN ALARM THIS END

THIS SIDE

4'0"

REPEAT BOGIE

9'0"

10'7⅝"

12'4⅞"

UNDERFRAME HAD BATTERY BOX ON THIS SIDE

39'0"

3'1¹¹⁄₁₆"

2'5⅝"

4'0⅜"

STANDARD 65'0" RIVETTED UNDERFRAME

STANDARD 9'0" BOGIE (RIVETTED)

9'0"

4'0"

65' FIRST CLASS VESTIBULE DINING CAR (D.1902) – BASED ON LOT 734

FAR SIDE

1'9⅜" 2'0" 1'10⅜" 2'0¾⅞" 1'10⅜" 2'0"

RECESS AT OTHER END ON 65' CARS ONLY

5'0"

OMIT THIS SECTION FOR 60' COACHES

3'0⅛" 4'0" 4'0" 3'0⅛"

SMOKING 35'1¼"

EXTRACTOR FANS ONLY ON 65' DINING CARS

65'1" (BODY)

3'0⅛" 4'0" 4'0" 3'0⅛" 3'1⅞"

NON SMOKING 14'0½"

ROOF VENTS AS INDICATED ON PLAN APPLY TO BOTH TYPES OF COACH. VENTS WERE ALL SHELL PATTERN.

USE STANDARD STANIER PATTERN GANGWAYED ENDS FOR BOTH THESE COACHES (LAV. FILLER PIPES AT ONE END ONLY ON 60' COACHES)

60' FIRST CLASS VESTIBULE COACH (D.1917)

1'9⅜" 2'0" 1'10⅜" 2'0¾⅞"

LUGGAGE (D.1902) SHELVES

TOILET (D.1917)

THIS VENT ONLY ON 60' COACHES

TRAIN ALARM THIS END (LOT 845)

TRAIN ALARM AT OPPOSITE END ON OTHER LOTS.

PLAIN HANDRAIL AT THIS SIDE ONLY ON THIS END

THIS SIDE

3'9"

REPEAT BOGIE

9'0"

BATTERY BOX THIS SIDE (LOT 845)

BATTERY BOX FAR SIDE (OTHER LOTS)

34'6"

STANDARD 60' UNDERFRAME (RIVETTED)

STANDARD 9'0" BOGIE (RIVETTED)

9'0"

3'9"

FAR SIDE

LMS STANDARD FIRST CLASS VESTIBULE STOCK 1934–39

Figure 93 Dimensioned elevations and plans. Period III First Class Vestibules, D1902/D1917 As can be seen from these drawings, the bulk of Period III open first shared identical passenger 'compartments' and it was only the second lavatory and set of luggage shelves on D1902 which necessitated the increase in length to 65ft. This longer version was officially designated for dining use but we have no doubt that any of them would be so used if need arose. The carriages were quite well photographed and we are able to offer a good cross-section of views.

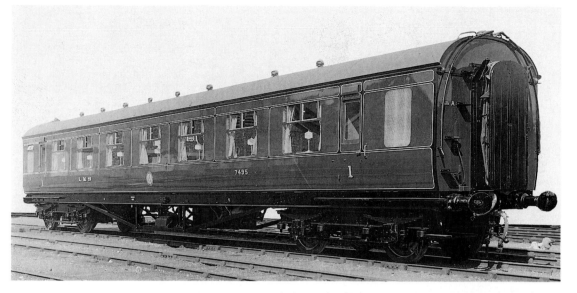

Plate 185. The 65ft Period III RFO to D1902, No. 7495. This coach, from the 1934 batch, was finished in full livery. Note the table lamps in the windows. Three similar coaches were refurbished for the 1937 'Coronation Scot' sets.

Plate 186. No. 7573 was one of the last 65ft open firsts to be built to D1902 and emerged in 1939. Note the changed design of table lamp.

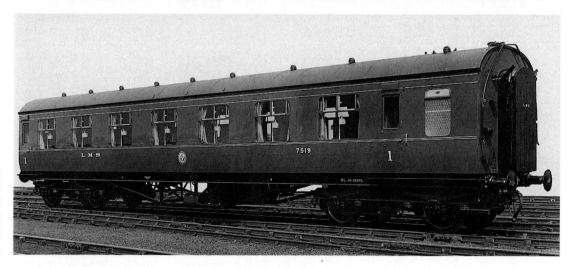

Plates 187-188. These views of Nos 7519 and 7529 show opposite sides of the 60ft D1917 open first from Lots 845 and 909 respectively. Both of them have courtesy table lamps which may have indicated that they were expected to be used for dining purposes.

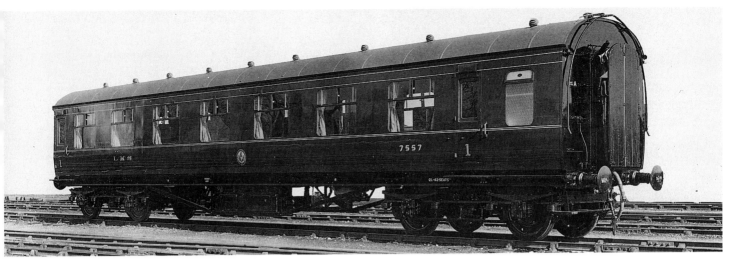

Plate 189. Lot 995 represented the largest single batch of FOs built to D1917 and if this picture of No. 7557 is typical, they did not have table lamps.

Plates 190-191. The larger (smoking) saloon of No. 7519 and close-up detail of opposite end of No. 7557, both to D1917. The decor is nearly identical, but the cloth is slightly more patterned in No. 7519 (it also has the table lamps) and the luggage rack and design has changed in No. 7557.

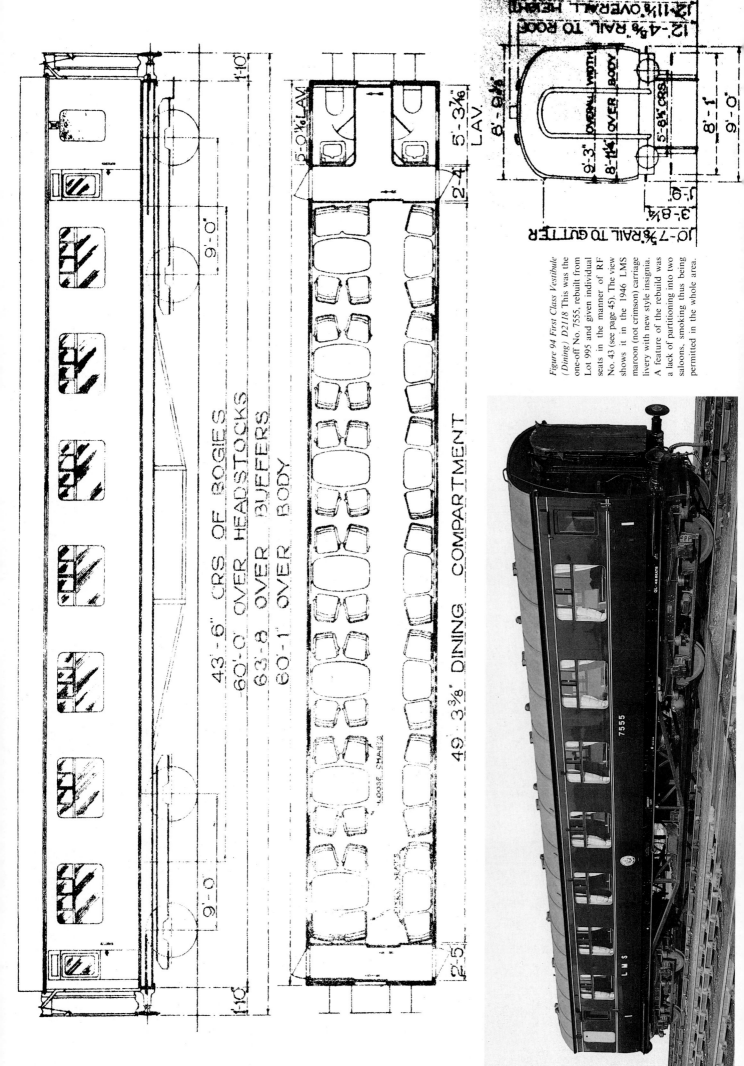

1'-10"

9'-0"

43'-6" CRS OF BOGIES

60'-0" OVER HEADSTOCKS

63'-8" OVER BUFFERS

60'-1" OVER BODY

9'-0"

1'-10"

5'-0½" LAV.

2'-4"

5'-3⅞"
LAV.

LOOSE CHAIRS

2-5"

FIXED SEATS

2'-5"

49'-3⅜" DINING COMPARTMENT

12'-11½" OVERALL HEIGHT

12'-4¾" RAIL TO ROOF

8'-8½"

8'-8½"

9'-3" OVERALL WIDTH

8'-11¼" OVER BODY

5'-8¾" CRS

8'-1"

9'-0"

10'-7⅞" RAIL TO GUTTER

3'-8¾"

3'-9"

Figure 94 First Class Vestibule (Dining) D2118 This was the one-off No. 7555, rebuilt from Lot 995 and given individual seats in the manner of RF No. 43 (see page 45). The view shows it in the 1946 LMS maroon (not crimson) carriage livery with new style insignia. A feature of the rebuild was a lack of partitioning into two saloons, smoking thus being permitted in the whole area.

7555

LMS

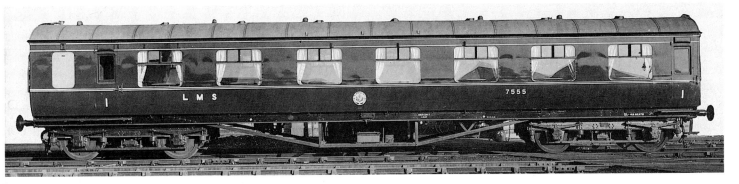

Plate 192. Broadside view of No. 7555, showing LMS insignia placing and later pattern sliding windows.

Plate 193. In November 1951, when running in BR red and cream as M7555, the coach received the form of experimental springing shown here, though we are unable to add details or state the reason.

Plate 194. Almost the full interior length of No. 7555 is shown in this view. The curtain fabric seems to be a 'reversed' version of that in the matching kitchen first diner and the luggage racks/lights seem to anticipate the BR Mk1 period. The four seat tables had loose seats (except at the carriage ends) while the two seat tables had fixed seats and new shaped table tops, both being slightly angled to the wall for ease of access.

Plate 195. Photographs of company dignitaries were always rare, even more so if a new locomotive was not featured, so the LMS must have placed high hopes on the importance of its new experimental open dining cars to have set up this tableau, though to be honest, the group does not seem to be too enthusiastic. The official caption reads: 'Sir Robert Burrows (Chairman LMS) & Mr Evans Bevan (LMS Director) test the comfort of the chairs watched by Mr G. L. Darbyshire (left), LMS Vice President & Mr W. H. Hamlyn (right standing), LMS Chief Architect'. The presence of the last office holder is interesting; where, one wonders, was the CME?

Plate 196 First Class Vestibule D2160 Regrettably, we have been totally unable to find any form of usable diagram for the last of the LMS pattern vestibule firsts so this official view of No. M7481 must suffice. Fortunately, their dimensions were exactly as for the pre-war D1917 and the porthole windows were exactly as shown in earlier detailed drawings of the final Period III stock. Note, however, that they ran on welded underframes and bogies. These were the carriages which took up most of the running numbers vacated by the downgraded D1722 carriages (see page 194) and were also the last LMS pattern open coaches to be built. Note the LMS style '1' on the windows, the shorter type window sliders and non-standard roof vents.

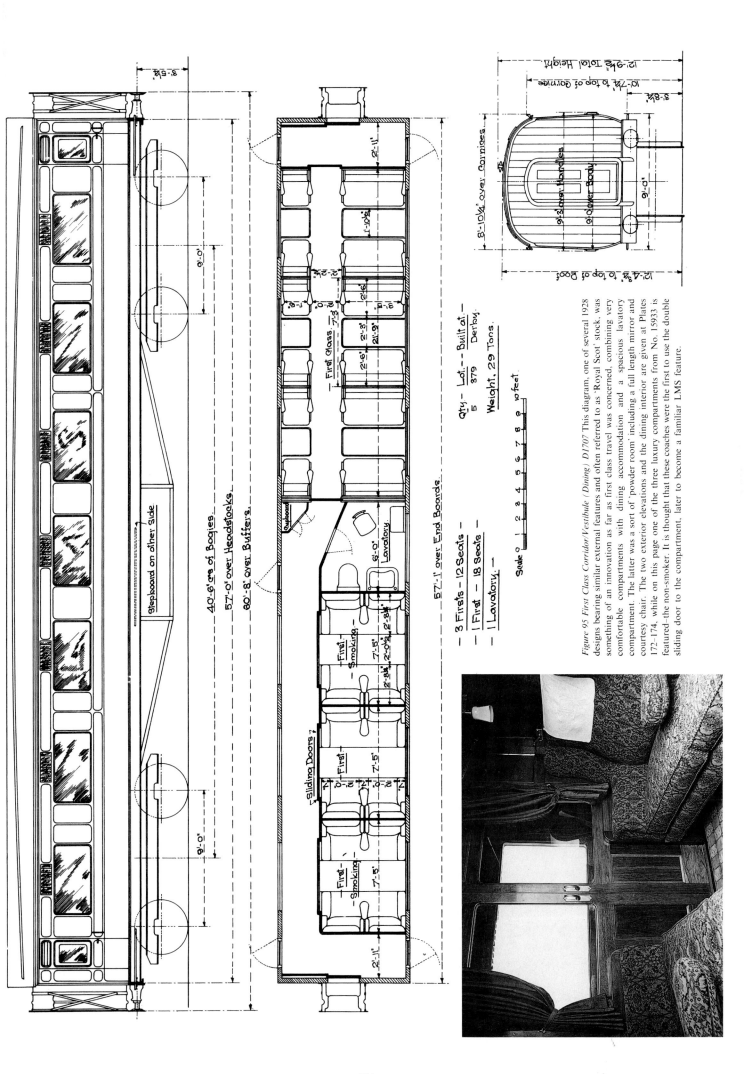

Figure 95 First Class Corridor/Vestibule (Dining) D1707 This diagram, one of several 1928 designs bearing similar external features and often referred to as 'Royal Scot' stock, was something of an innovation as far as first class travel was concerned, combining very comfortable compartments with dining accommodation and a spacious lavatory compartment. The latter was a sort of 'powder room' including a full length mirror and courtesy chair. The two exterior elevations and the dining interior are given at Plates 172–174, while on this page one of the three luxury compartments from No. 15933 is featured–the non-smoker. It is thought that these coaches were the first to use the double sliding door to the compartment, later to become a familiar LMS feature.

3'-5¾"

9'-0"

40'-6" crs of Bogies

57'-0" over Headstocks

60'-8" over Buffers

Stepboard on other Side

9'-0"

2'-11"

1'-0½"

First Class. — 7'-3"

2'-6" 2'-8" 2'-6"
2'-9"

57'-1" over End Boards

Cupboard

6'-0"

Lavatory

First - Smoking

7'-5"

2'-8" 2'-0" 2'-8½"

First -

7'-5"

2'-0" 2'-0" 2'-0"

First - Smoking

7'-5"

Sliding Doors

2'-11"

Qty. - Lot. - Built at. -
5 — 379 — Derby.

Weight, 29 Tons.

— 3 Firsts - 12 Seats -
— 1 First - 18 Seats -
— 1 Lavatory. —

Scale 0 1 2 3 4 5 6 7 8 9 10 feet

3'-8¾"

10'-7¼" to top of Cornice

12'-9¾" Total Height.

12'-4¾" to top of Roof.

9'-3" over Handles.

9'-0" over Body.

9'-0"

8'-10¼" over Cornices.

Plates 197-200. These four views, largely self explanatory, show the two smoking compartments of D1707 (all three compartments were differently trimmed) and two views of the spacious central lavatory compartment.

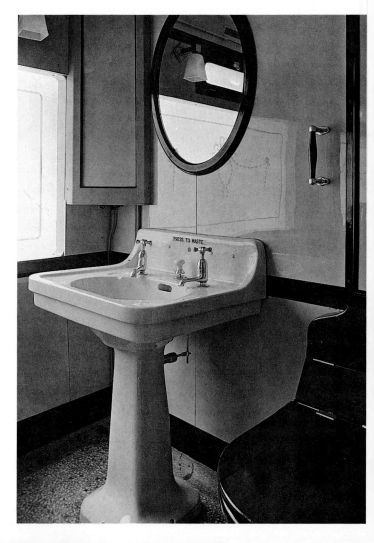

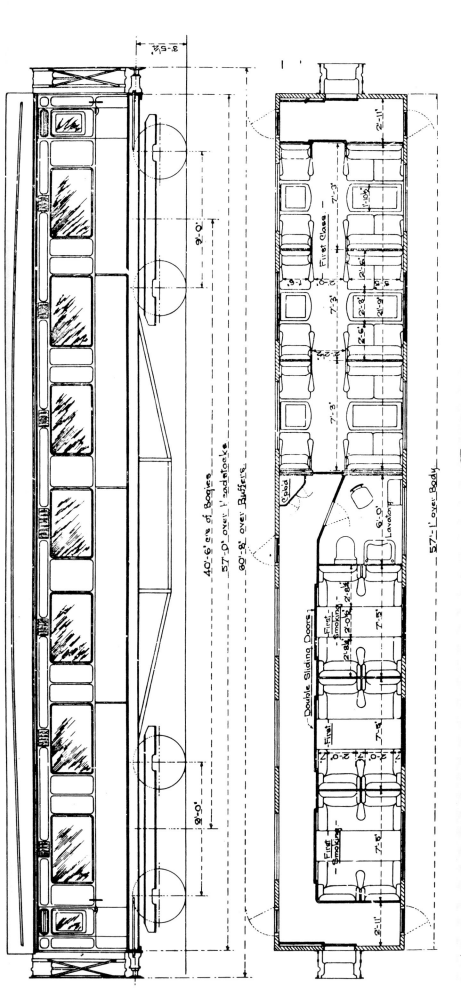

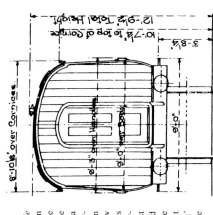

Figure 96 First Class Corridor/Vestibule Coach D1719 The semi-open first design was repeated, unaltered save for the deeper windows, in 1930 and affords the only example of an exact repetition of a Period I design during Period II. Comparison of D1719 with the earlier version described at Figure 97 clearly shows how much the general aspect of LMS coaches was altered by the introduction of the low-waisted style. One of these cars was lost in an accident in 1931 and was replaced by a steel panelled version in 1932—see Table 4a. This steel panelled coach went to North America with the 'Royal Scot' in 1933. The coach illustrated on this page became 1035.

Plate 201. There is some uncertainty whether this compartment interior is from one of the semi-opens to D1719 or a BFK to D1717 (pages 120/201); both types had the luxury two per side seating. The date on the back of the picture is stated to be 1928, which cannot be right either way; for this is undoubtedly a Period II first class compartment–note the lower level of the window sill in relation to the seat arm compared with Figure 96 which shows the Period I equivalent.

Plate 202. This shows the opposite end of the first class lounge in D1741 to that shown at Plate 175. It was an extravagant type for only ten passengers at most, which, along with its alleged unpopularity, may have been the reason why the design was never repeated. The drawing and exterior elevation of this type appear on the next page.

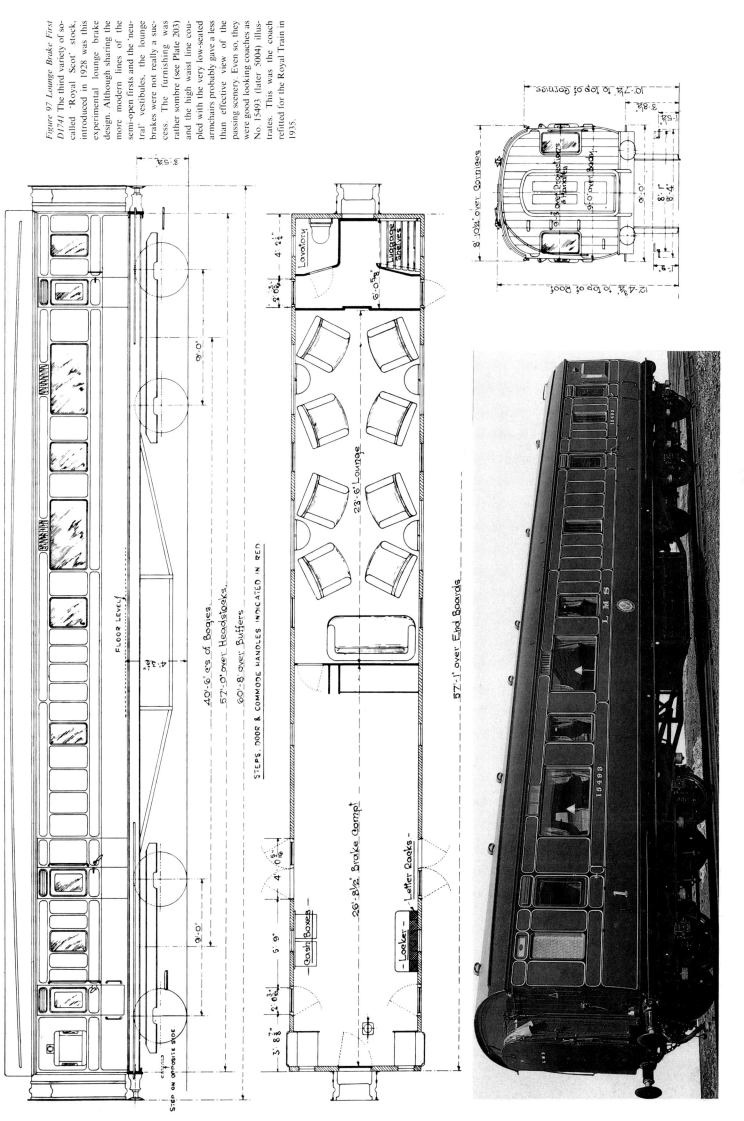

Figure 97 Lounge Brake First D1741 The third variety of so-called 'Royal Scot' stock, introduced in 1928 was this experimental lounge brake design. Although sharing the more modern lines of the semi-open firsts and the 'neutral' vestibules, the lounge brakes were not really a success. The furnishing was rather sombre (see Plate 203) and the high waist line coupled with the very low-seated armchairs probably gave a less than effective view of the passing scenery. Even so, they were good looking coaches as No. 15493 (later 5004) illustrates. This was the coach refitted for the Royal Train in 1935.

STEP ON OPPOSITE SIDE.

FLOOR LEVEL

9'·0"

4'·3½"

40'·6" c's of Bogies.

57'·0" over Headstocks.

60'·8" over Buffers

9'·0"

3'·8⅛" 2'·0⅝" 5'·9" 4'·0⅝"

Lavatory

2'·3⅜" 2'·0½" 4'·2½"

Luggage Shelves

6'·0⅝"

23'·6" Lounge

STEPS, DOOR & COMMODE HANDLES INDICATED IN RED.

26'·8½" Brake Compt

Cash Boxes

Locker

Letter Racks

57'·1" over End Boards

10'·7¾" to top of Cornice

3'·8⅜"
1'·5¾"
8'·10¼" over Cornices
9'·3 over Projectors & Handles
9'·0" over Body.
6'·0"
1'·9"
8'·4"

12'·4¾" to top of Roof.

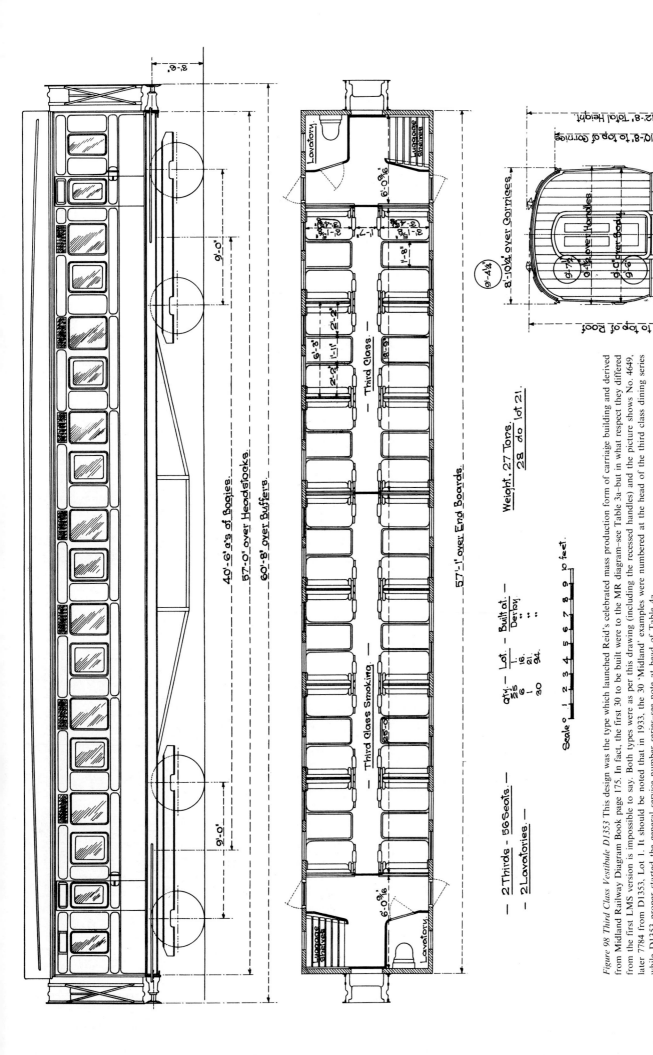

— 2 Thirds - 56 Seats. —

— 2 Lavatories. —

Weight. 27 Tons.

Qty.	Lot.	Built at.
55	7.	Derby.
6	16.	"
	21.	"
94.		
30		

28 do lot 21.

Scale 0 1 2 3 4 5 6 7 8 9 10 feet.

Figure 98 Third Class Vestibule D1353 This design was the type which launched Reid's celebrated mass production form of carriage building and derived from Midland Railway Diagram Book page 175. In fact, the first 30 to be built were to the MR diagram—see Table 3a—but in what respect they differed from the first LMS version is impossible to say. Both types were as per this drawing (including the recessed handles) and the picture shows No. 4649, later 7784 from D1353, Lot 1. It should be noted that in 1933, the 30 'Midland' examples were numbered at the head of the third class dining series while D1353 proper started the general service number series—see note at head of Table 4a.

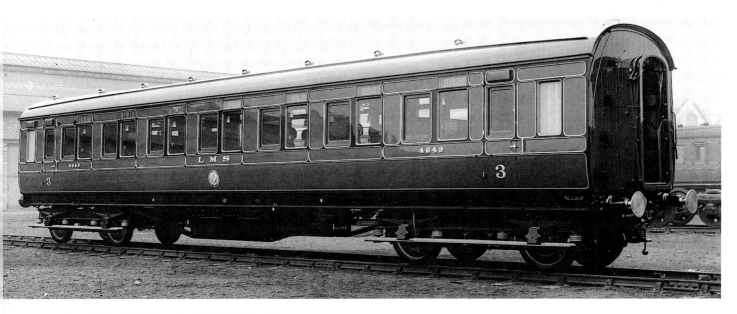

Figure 98 Cont. Third class Vestibule D1353 No. 4649

Plate 203. This, the only other known official view of any type of 'twin window' open third (save for the all-steel examples), shows No. 1078, later 7611, one of 30 examples put onto the MR diagram and not even allocated an LMS lot number. We cannot see any significant difference between this carriage and that shown at Figure 98; even the weight plates (MR pattern) are identical.

Plate 204. The 'Grandad' of them all–pioneer open third No. M7600M in BR red and cream livery at an unknown location c.1953. It was built as No. 139 on MR diagram page 175 and, apart from the removal of door top ventilators, it seems largely unaltered. (*The late Gavin Wilson collection*).

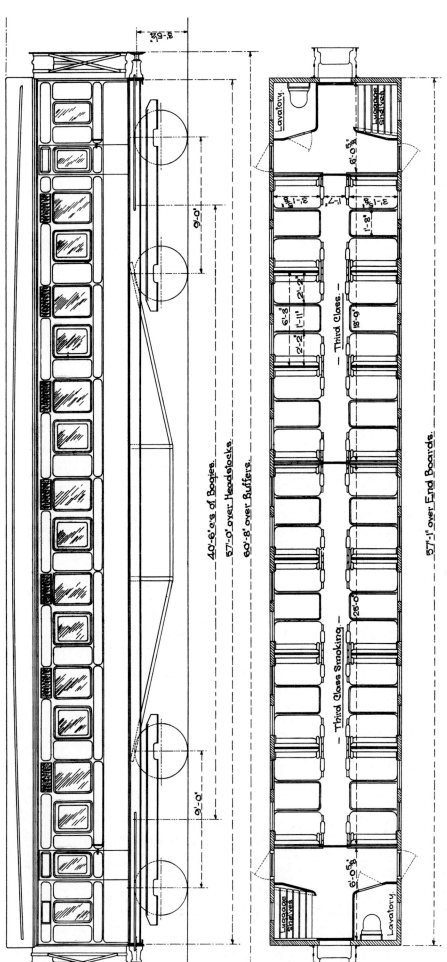

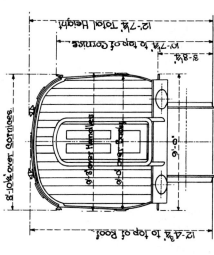

Figure 99 Third Class Vestibule D1692 This, the most numerous of all the LMS TO designs, was all but identical to the previous type, save for non-recessed door handles and the use of louvred door top ventilators. Perhaps surprisingly, no official exterior ex-works views of this type have survived, so once again, as in Chapter 3, we must resort to the ambulance train conversions, this time in the shape of No. 5805, photographed officially by the LNER at York in October 1939. Its old number is not known.

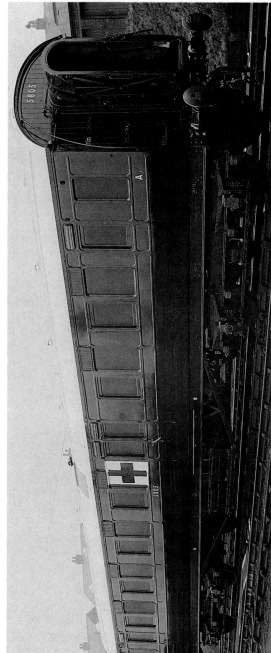

Plates 205-206. Interior views of either D1353 or D1692 are almost as rare as exterior ones but this pair are believed to be from No. 4623 (later 7794) of D1353–certainly that taken looking down the length of the coach–and quite a number of interesting points can be made. Firstly, the luggage rack ends (see also Plate 181) are to the 'pre-LMS' pattern which supports the earlier diagram and secondly, the close-up shot gives clear indication of a 56-seat third in use as a dining car. This was not uncommon in early LMS days and we wonder whether the pictures were taken in association with the introduction in 1925 of the celebrated London–Bradford 'Vestibule Train', one of Britain's first 'fully open' trains in the manner of current (1992) practice. In the publicity surrounding this service, the LMS made the point that although a 42-seat third was provided for dining (see Figure 100): "... if there is sufficient demand the kitchen or car staff will be prepared to serve meals in any part of the train..." Careful examination of the 'long' view reveals that the carriage beyond the far door does have 2 + 1 seating, though its vertical seat ends suggest it is first class for reasons which are explained in the next page.

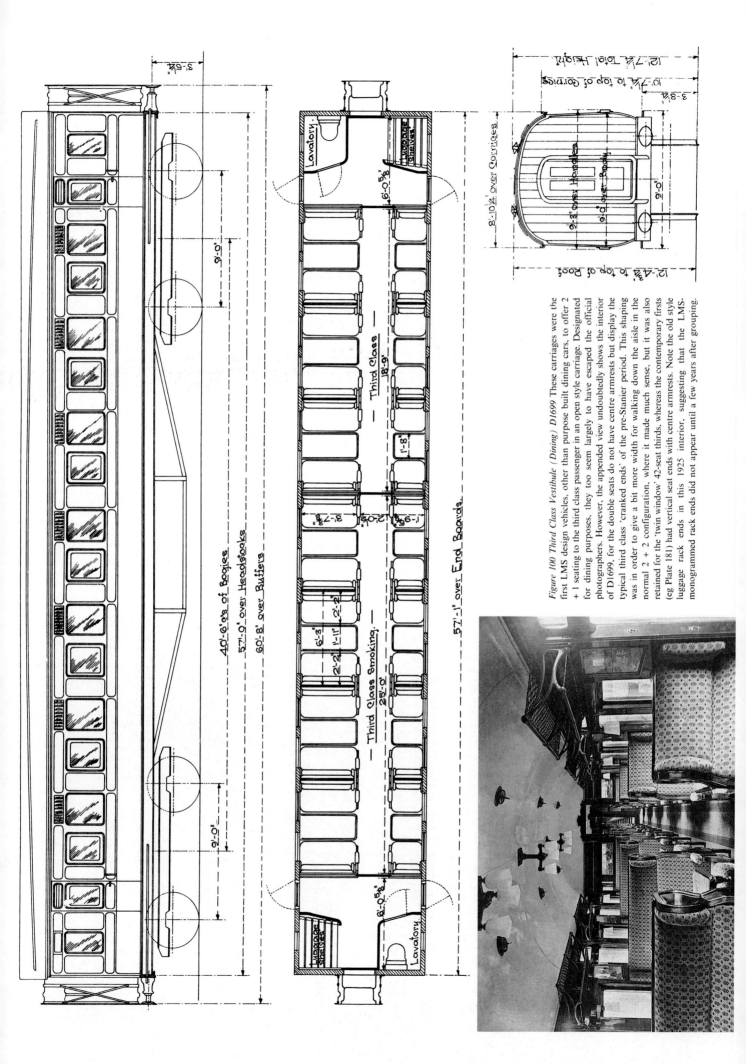

Figure 100 Third Class Vestibule (Dining) D1699 These carriages were the first LMS design vehicles, other than purpose built dining cars, to offer 2 + 1 seating to the third class passenger in an open style carriage. Designated for dining purposes, they too seem largely to have escaped the official photographers. However, the appended view undoubtedly shows the interior of D1699, for the double seats do not have centre armrests but display the typical third class 'cranked ends' of the pre-Stanier period. This shaping was in order to give a bit more width for walking down the aisle in the normal 2 + 2 configuration, where it made much sense, but it was also retained for the 'twin window' 42-seat thirds with centre armrests. Note the old style (eg Plate 181) had vertical seat ends with centre armrests, whereas the contemporary firsts luggage rack ends in this 1925 interior, suggesting that the LMS-monogrammed rack ends did not appear until a few years after grouping.

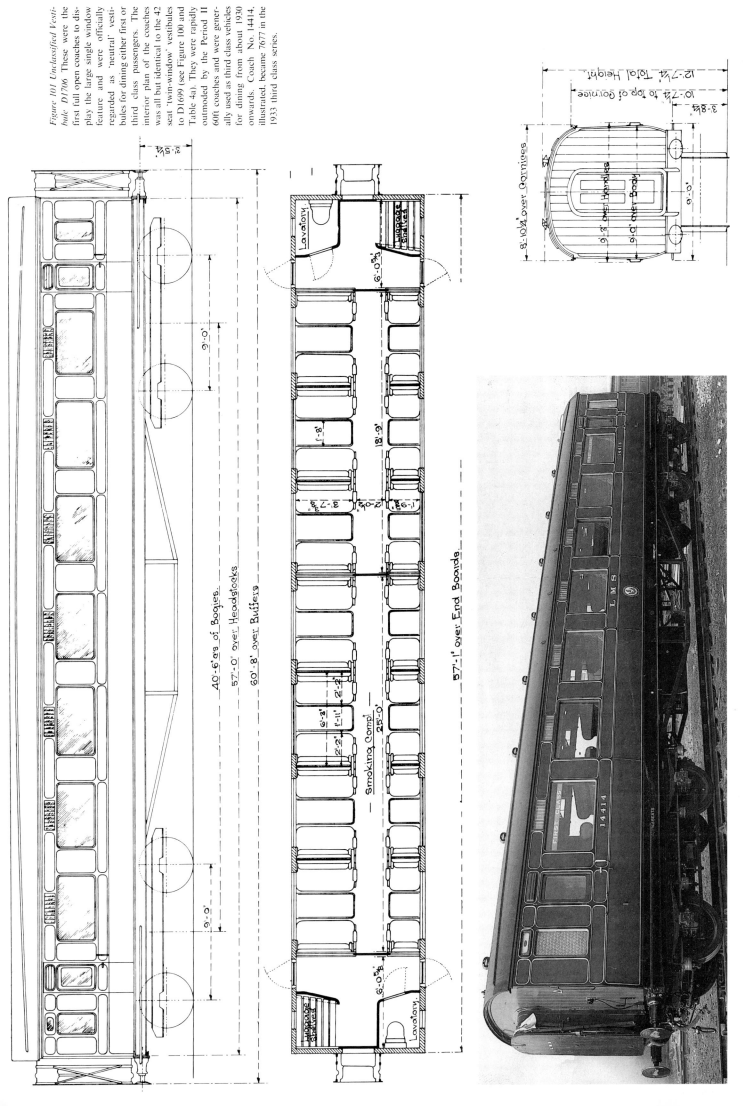

Figure 101 Unclassified Vestibule D1706 These were the first full open coaches to display the large single window feature and were officially regarded as 'neutral' vestibules for dining either first or third class passengers. The interior plan of the coaches was all but identical to the 42 seat 'twin-window' vestibules to D1699 (see Figure 100 and Table 4a). They were rapidly outmoded by the Period II 60ft coaches and were generally used as third class vehicles for dining from about 1930 onwards. Coach No. 14414, illustrated, became 7677 in the 1933 third class series.

12'-7¾' Total Height
10'-7¾' to top of cornice
3'-8¾'
8'-10¼' over cornices
9'-3' over handles
9'-0' over body
6'-0'

3'-5¾'
9'-0'
40'-6' c's of Bogies.
57'-0' over Headstocks.
60'-8' over Buffers.
9'-0'
3'-5¾'

Lavatory
Luggage Shelves
6'-0⅝'
1'-8'
18'-9'
3'-7'
2'-0'
1'-9'
6'-3'
1'-11'
2'-2'
2'-2'
Smoking Comp⁺
25'-0'
57'-1' over End Boards.
6'-0⅝'
Lavatory.
Luggage Shelves

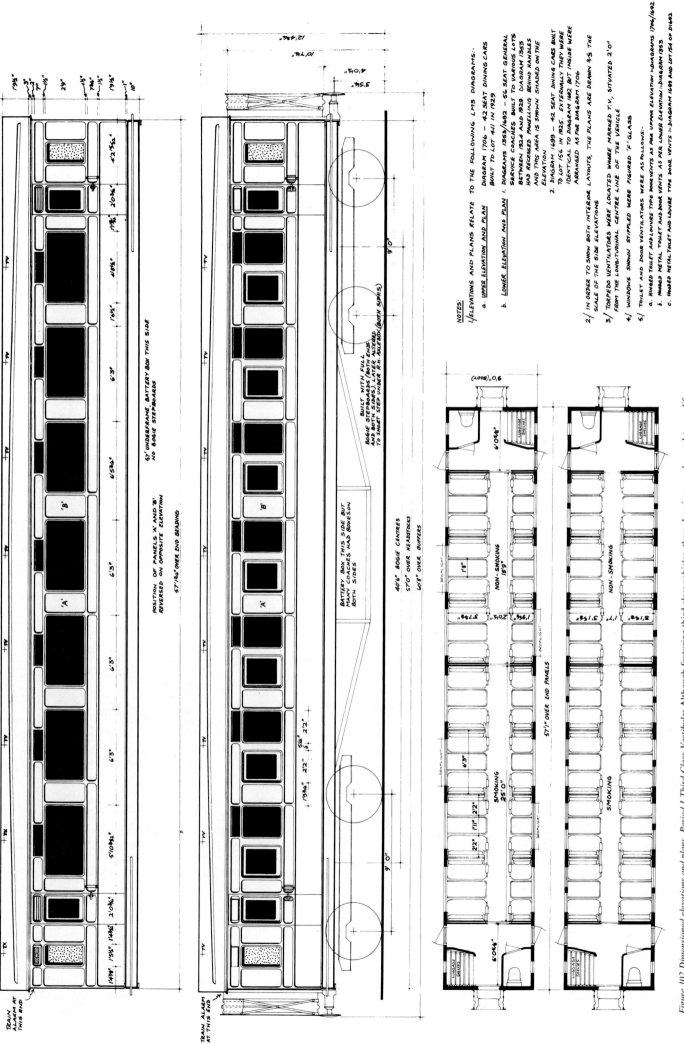

Figure 102 Dimensioned elevations and plans, Period I Third Class Vestibules Although featuring third class vehicles, these drawings can be used to amplify many of the other wooden bodied types of similar period, given that door and window detail was standardised throughout. The panelling detail is valid for the third class brakes to D1693 and very similar, save for 'between window' width to the contemporary first class and composite vestibules.

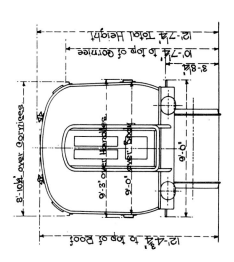

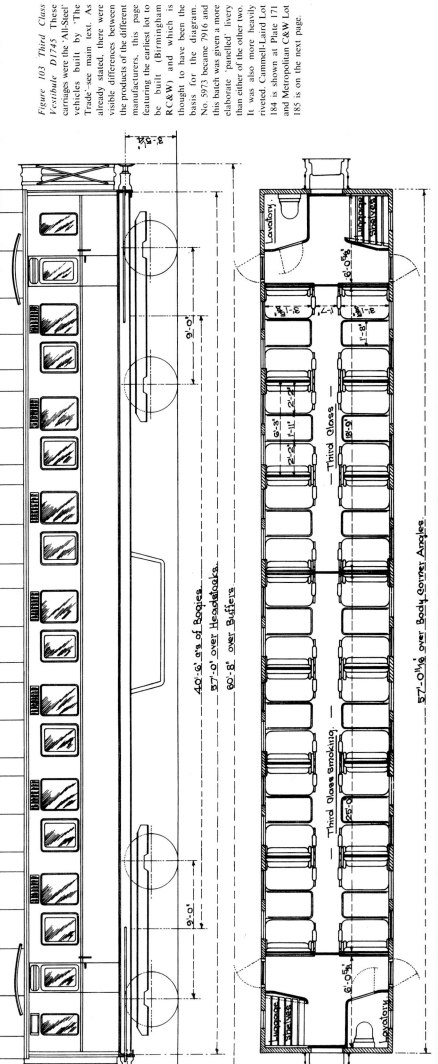

Figure 103 Third Class Vestibule D1745 These carriages were the 'All-Steel' vehicles built by 'The Trade'—see main text. As already stated, there were visible differences between the products of the different manufacturers, this page featuring the earliest lot to be built (Birmingham RC&W) and which is thought to have been the basis for the diagram. No. 5973 became 7916 and this batch was given a more elaborate 'panelled' livery than either of the other two. It was also more heavily riveted. Cammell-Laird Lot 184 is shown at Plate 171 and Metropolitan C&W Lot 185 is on the next page.

Plate 207. No. 6260 became 8071 and was from Lot 185 and waist panels apart, the Metropolitan C&W carriages were given as elaborate a livery as Lot 183. This lot was also distinguished by the 'rounded' corners between sides and ends and represented half the total built to D1745.

Plate 208. Lot 185 was also distinguished by having an all-metal interior finish where wood was normally used. However, no attempt was made to change the traditional LMS seat and shape with its 'cranked' ends. The effect seems to have been rather spartan if this interior of No. 6260 is any guide.

Plate 209. Many of D1745 were converted to BR heating vans during the steam-diesel changeover and this is No. M44420M. Its rounded corners reveal a Lot 185 example but we do not know its LMS identity.

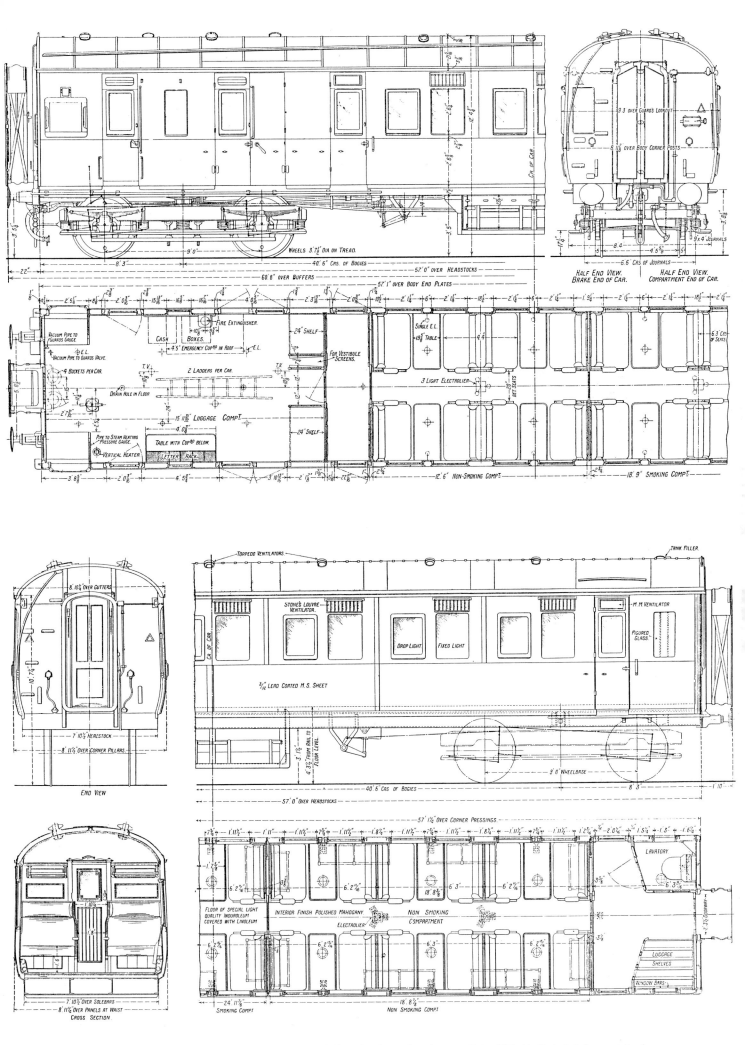

Figure 104 Detailed elevations and sections, 'All-Steel' Vestibule Stock These drawings and sections were first published in the technical press at the time the LMS 'All-Steel' stock was built. The upper elevation/plan actually shows details of the BTO to D1746 (Figure 116) but all are put here for convenience.

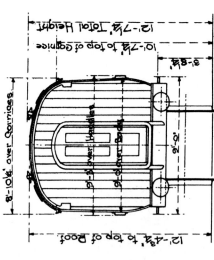

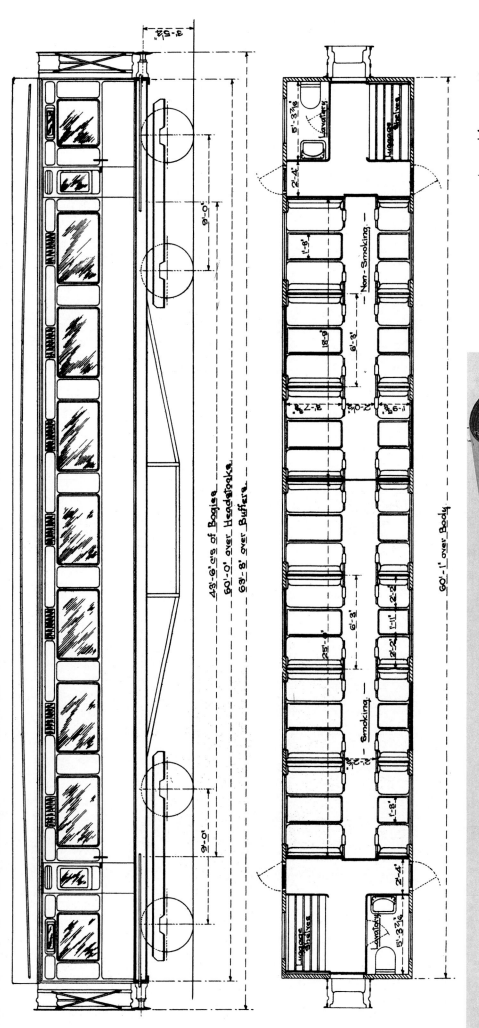

Figure 105 Third Class Vestibule (Dining) D1721 This was the first of three near-identical diagrams raised for the 60ft Period II vestibule stock and is identical to D1722 (Figure 92) already considered. The picture shows No. 1324, later 7711, one of the last of Lot 491 to be built.

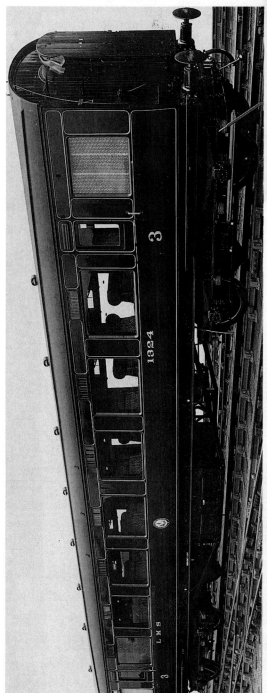

Plate 210. This interior view of D1721 almost certainly shows carriage No. 1324 again. Note that by now, third class seats in the 2 + 1 configuration (see also Figure 100) had been given vertical ends as per first class, but the doubles did not have centre armrests.

Plate 211. This rather spectacular view of the Leighton Buzzard accident in 1931 shows D1721 No. 1325 (later No. 7712) as the middle vehicle of this Period II trio. The left hand carriage straddled across the tracks is No. 14733 of D1795, later 7764 and subsequently rebuilt with steel panels–see page 182–while the right hand coach is an unidentified TK from D1782 (Figure 54).

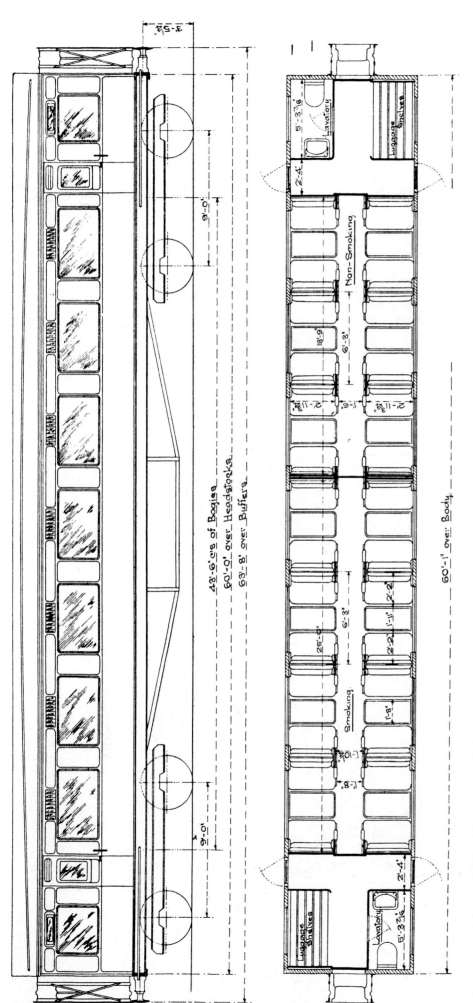

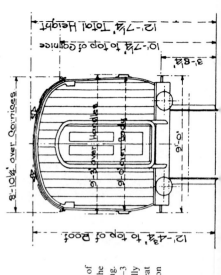

Figure 106 Third Class Vestibule D1738 There is no known official ex-works view of this type, neither have we ever seen any other picture of one; but as can be seen, the coaches were identically styled to all 60ft Period II opens, save for the interior seating. For some reason–see notes to Table 4a–they were renumbered after D1807 in 1932–3 and it may be that this small 56-seat batch in a predominantly 42-seat series was initially forgotten. The appended view shows the general interior style of all Period II 56-seat open carriages but is in fact, the identically styled interior of the 57ft D1807 version No. 8867 (see page 221).

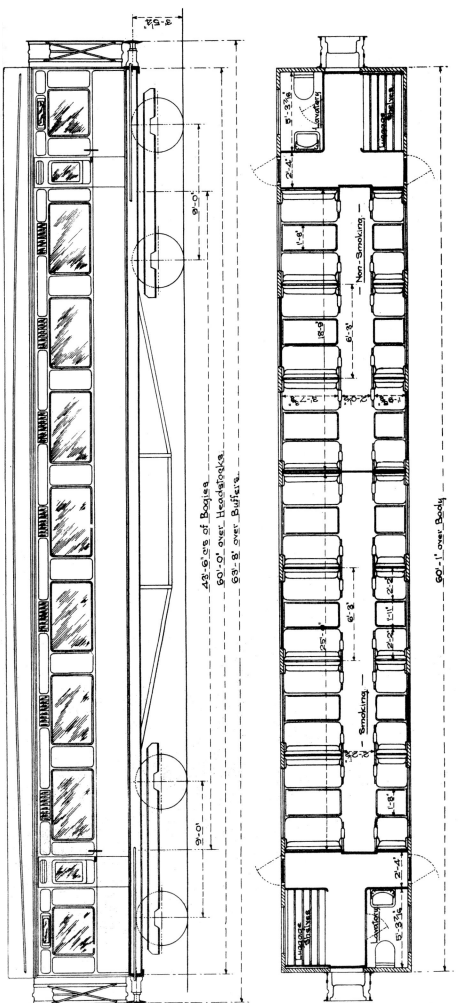

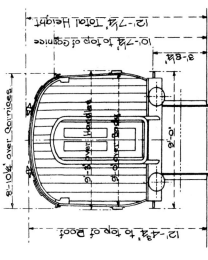

Figure 107 Third Class Vestibule D1795 This was the last of the Period II 60ft open stock and built to the same lot number as the 56-seat version to D1738. Although never officially classed as 'Dining', many were so used and they were given 1933 numbers from the dining series. The picture is especially interesting in that it shows the Lot 628 steel-panelled rebuild of old No. 14733—see Plate 212. The car is being loaded on *SS Beaverdale* in connection with the 1933 'Royal Scot' tour of North America. It carries its new number (7764) in stretched scroll figures and note that the gangways are of the 'suspended' type, introduced by Stanier during the building of the D1807 57ft vestibules (Plate 176).

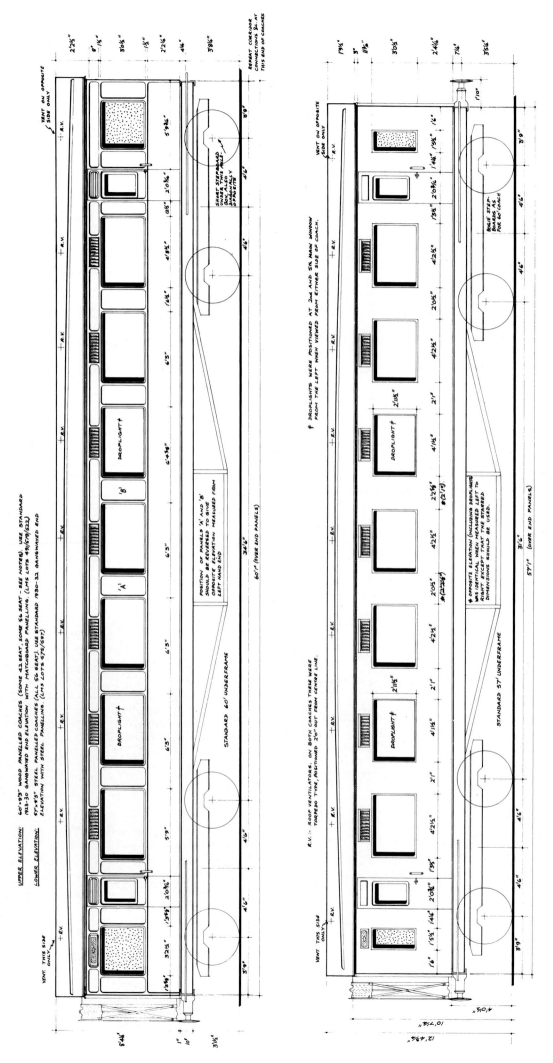

Figure 108 Dimensioned elevations, Period II Vestibule Stock. This drawing should be taken in conjunction with the four 60ft diagrams for the wood panelled stock already considered (one first class, three third class), plus the 57ft steel panelled version to D1807. The latter elevations represent the first 200 examples which had Stones ventilators over the windows.

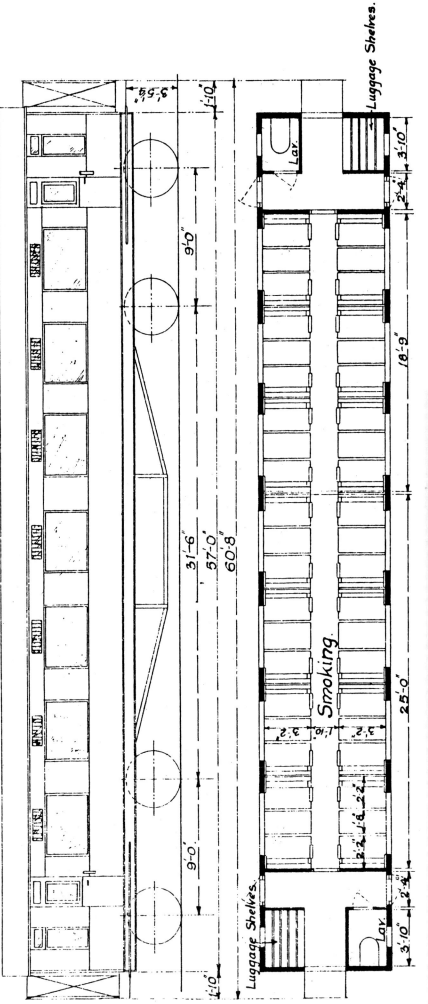

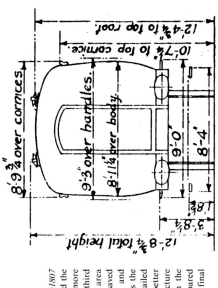

Figure 109 Third Class Vestibule D1807
As can be seen from Figure 108 and the preceding 60ft diagrams, the far more numerous 57ft Period II open third contained the same size passenger area as the earlier vehicles, length being saved by the much smaller lavatories and luggage racks. This diagram marks the changeover from the more detailed diagram drawings but at least is better than many of its successors. The picture shows No. 2744 (later 8737) from the earlier series and should be compared with Plate 176 which shows the final version.

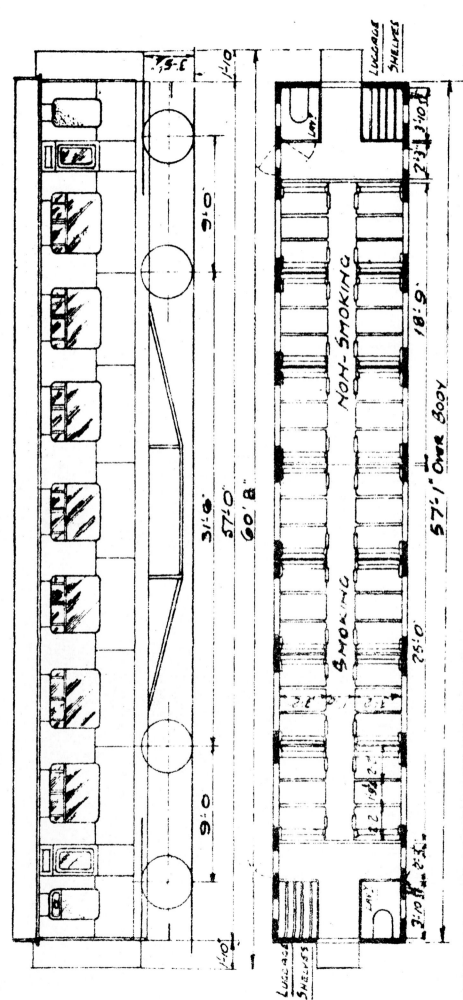

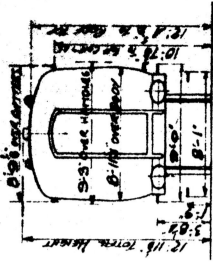

Figure 110 Third Class Vestibule D1904 The general service version of the first Period III open third design was identical in dimensions and layout to the immediately preceding D1807. However, within the carriages, there was a noticeable improvement in quality compared with Period II as can be seen from the appended interior view of No. 8929. The familiar dark wood finish is retained (it too was soon to go) but the seat design is much improved, though whether one could say the same for the modish upholstery is a matter for debate. What was an improvement, however, was a slight inward inclination of the seat ends (to afford extra waist width in the aisles) replacing the old 'cranked' form. As usual, the diagram is poor but combined with D1807 and standard Period III detail dimensions, plus the pictures on the next page, it is thought to be adequate for the type to be interpreted.

Plates 212-213. These views of Nos 8929 and 9004 allow comparison between the first two Period III open third diagrams. No. 8929 was the last of Lot 736 and was built in 1933. This was one of the first batches to receive the deeper sliding windows. The later lots also had the simple livery. No. 9004 shows the effect of the special livery on the nine coaches rebuilt to D1981. They mostly remained unchanged externally, save for the ventilation grill at the lower right hand end and the new ducting along the roof.

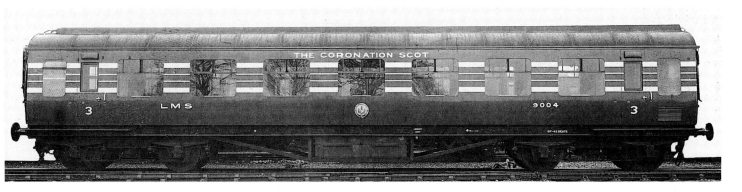

Figure 111 Third Class Vestibule (Dining) D1981 The 42-seat 'Coronation Scot' rebuild of part of D1904 was a heavier vehicle than that from which it was derived, largely because of the extra heating and ventilation provided. The unit was fitted in place of one set of luggage shelves–see Plate 213–and is shown in plan on this diagram. Unfortunately, the poor diagram quality of this period does not give any detail of the roof top ducting, nor have we been able to find any drawings of the feature. Should any further detail be discovered, it will be included in Volume III where we tell the story of this train and should any reader have information, we would be grateful to be advised via the publisher.

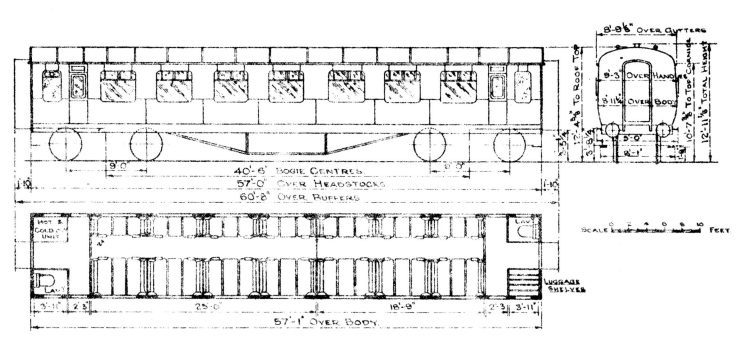

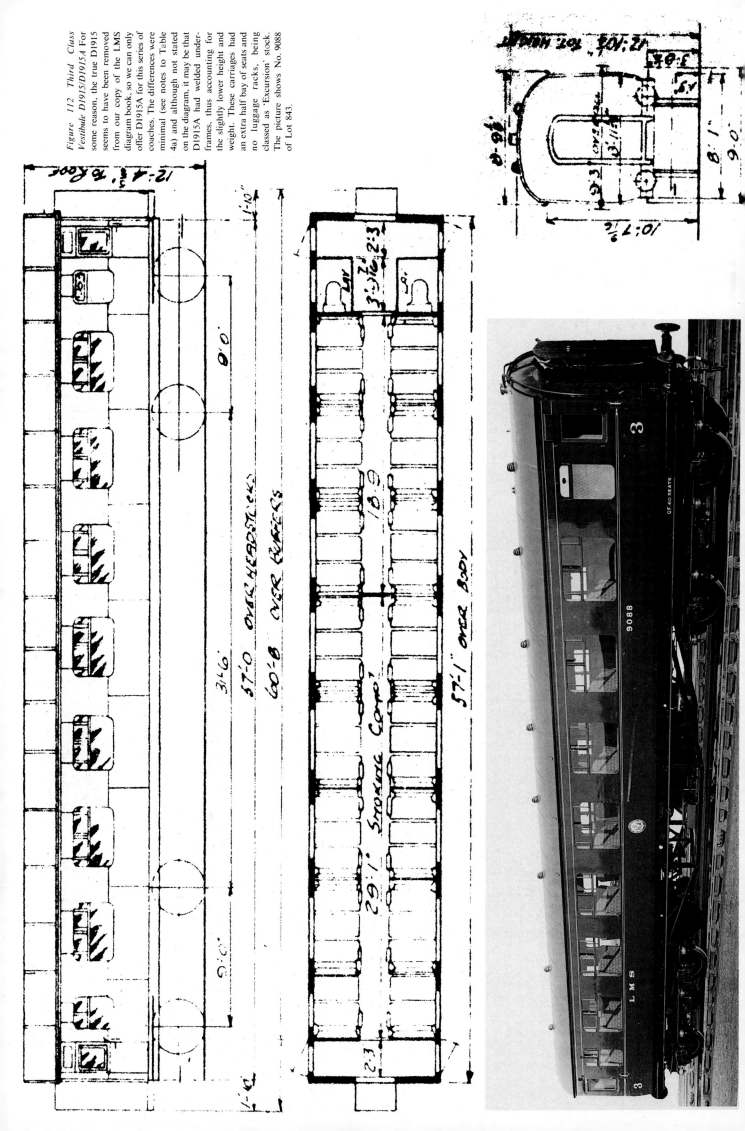

Figure 112 Third Class Vestibule D1915/D1915A For some reason, the true D1915 seems to have been removed from our copy of the LMS diagram book, so we can only offer D1915A for this series of coaches. The differences were minimal (see notes to Table 4a) and although not stated on the diagram, it may be that D1915A had welded underframes, thus accounting for the slightly lower height and weight. These carriages had an extra half bay of seats and no luggage racks, being classed as 'Excursion' stock. The picture shows No. 9088 of Lot 843.

12:4½ TO ROOF

1'-10"

9'-0"

34'-6"

57'-0" OVER HEADSTOCKS

60'-8 OVER BUFFERS

9'-0"

1'-0"

LAV

3'3/16" 2'-3"

29'-1" SMOKING COMP'

10'-9"

57'-1" OVER BODY

2'-3"

12:1¼ TO ROOF

16'-0

3'-0"

2'-3" COV'D'WAY 3'11¾"

8'-1"

9'-0'

10'-7½"

Plate 214. Exterior view of No. 9178, Lot 894, giving rather more detail of the carriage end and underframe.

Plates 215-216. These interior views of Nos 9088 and 9178 (the latter has the monogrammed luggage rack ends) show two further upholstery patterns (colour as usual is unspecified) and a slight lightening of the interior woodwork.

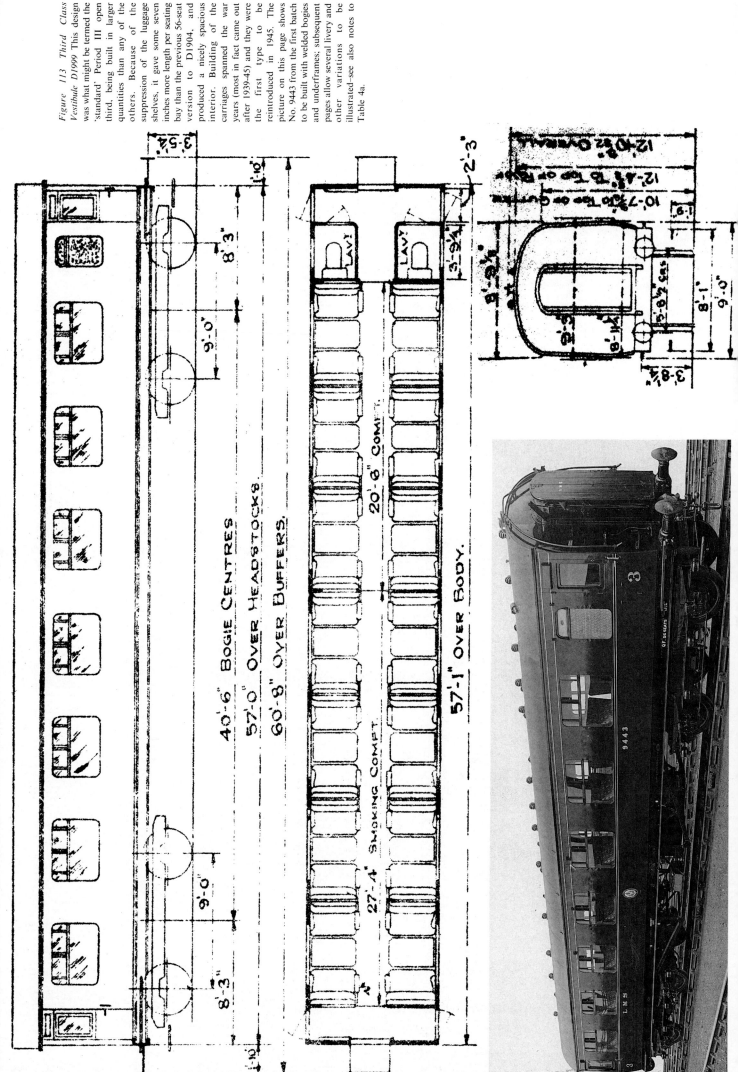

Figure 113 Third Class Vestibule D1999 This design was what might be termed the 'standard' Period III open third, being built in larger quantities than any of the others. Because of the suppression of the luggage shelves, it gave some seven inches more length per seating bay than the previous 56-seat version to D1904, and produced a nicely spacious interior. Building of the carriages spanned the war years (most in fact came out after 1939-45) and they were the first type to be reintroduced in 1945. The picture on this page shows No. 9443 from the first batch to be built with welded bogies and underframes; subsequent pages allow several livery and other variations to be illustrated—see also notes to Table 4a.

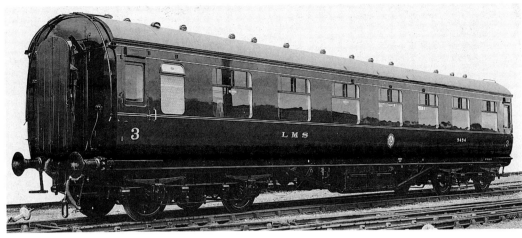

Plate 217. Opposite side view of No. 9494, Lot 1188, with welded bogies and riveted underframes. This is thought to have been the only batch built in this combination, thus explaining the extra weight–see Table 4a.

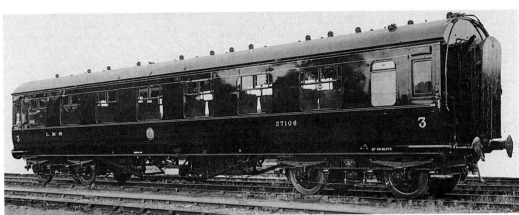

Plate 218. Post-war No. 27106 from Lot 1400, the first new carriages after the war which also reverted to welded underframe construction. The insignia are the common post-1939 standard with a return to scroll pattern running numbers and the introduction of flat topped '3s'. Many carriages were also given the new and darker maroon colour with this style of insignia during final LMS days, probably including all D1999 examples built before BR days.

Plate 219. Most of the D1999 vestibules came out in LMS colours (see also note to Table 4a) but No. M27309 was a late LMS example which soon became repainted in experimental chocolate and cream livery in 1948. The layout of both colours and lining was exactly that of the later red/cream style.

Plate 220. Pre-war No. M9457 in 'Royal Scot' service carrying BR red and cream livery c.1951.

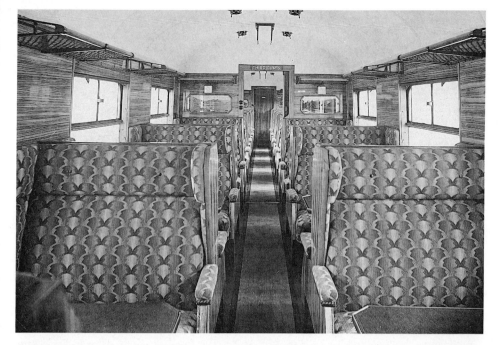

Plates 221-222. The D1999 open thirds continued to see the lightening in tone of the interior decor and the two main pre-war batches were most successful in this respect. Post-war examples were rather more mundane and retrogressive but times were not easy and the carriages builders often had to 'make do'. This pair of views shows the interior of the two pre-war examples already illustrated: No. 9443 has the 'shell' pattern upholstery and No. 9494 displays the very light and airy interior consequent upon pale wood finish and restrained upholstery.

Figure 114 Third Class Vestibule D2021 The survey of open thirds is concluded with the diagram issued for the one-off Period III rebuild of No. 9034 (ex-D1721) on its existing 60ft frames–see note to Table 4a. We have no picture (which is not really surprising) but careful perusal of the diagram dimensions makes it quite clear that the carriage interior was as for D1999 with the addition of luggage shelves to take up the extra length. It was probably a very agreeable vehicle.

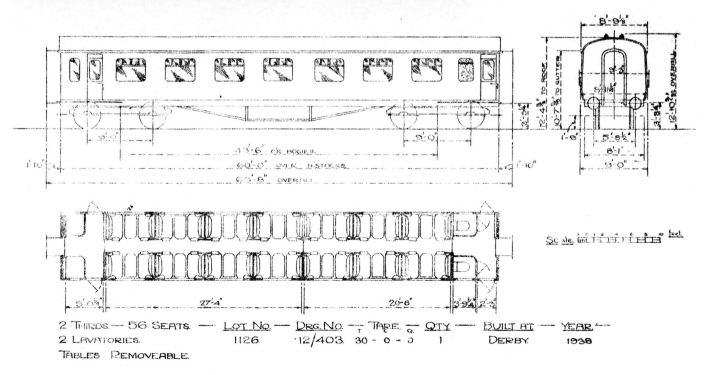

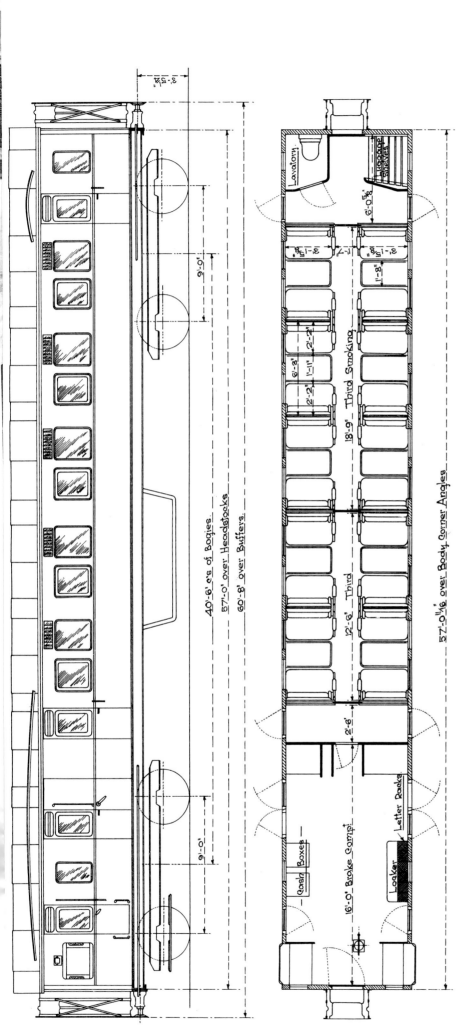

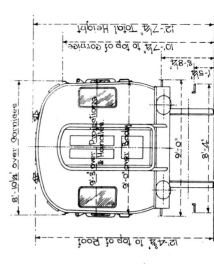

Figure 115 Third Class Vestibule Brake D1746 All things considered, the LMS was slow to introduce a brake ended vestibule coach and the first actually to appear were the 'All-Steel' examples to this diagram in 1925. Indeed, the well known London–Bradford train had to make do with ex-MR clerestory vestibule brakes at first. D1746 brought a new contractor, Leeds Forge, into the 'All-Steel' programme and it is one of their carriages which is shown here (No. 7675, later 9818); note the shallower solebar and even heavier riveting compared with the full thirds. We have no views of the Birmingham RC&W series but imagine they would be much as Lot 183 (Figure 103). Additional detailed drawings of the brake ended type appear on Figure 104.

229

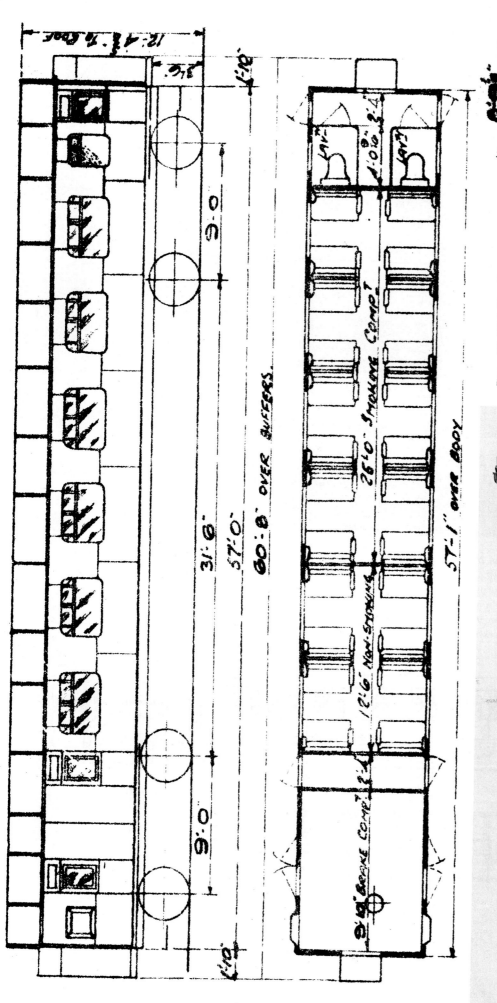

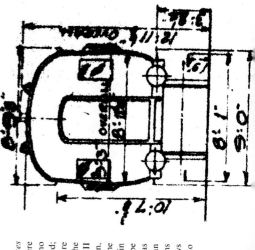

12'-4½" R. Back.

3'-6"

1'-10"

9'-0"

31'-6"

57'-0"

60'-8" OVER BUFFERS.

9'-0"

57'-1" OVER BODY

26'-0" SMOKING COMPT.

12'-6" NON-SMOKING.

9'-9" BRAKE COMP. 2-4.

Figure 118 Third Class Vestibule Brakes D1916/D1946 These six-bay designs were dimensionally identical and we can offer no good reason why two diagrams were issued; so, given the poor diagram quality, we are allowing D1916 to stand for both. Like the full thirds to D1915, this second Period III BTO design was a high capacity design, probably for excursion use. In spite of the seating capacity, the bay length at 6ft 3in was by no means as cramped as might be supposed; the required passenger space was achieved at the expense of restricted van space, conceivably less important in terms of its normal role. The picture shows No. 9933, one of the last to be built to D1916.

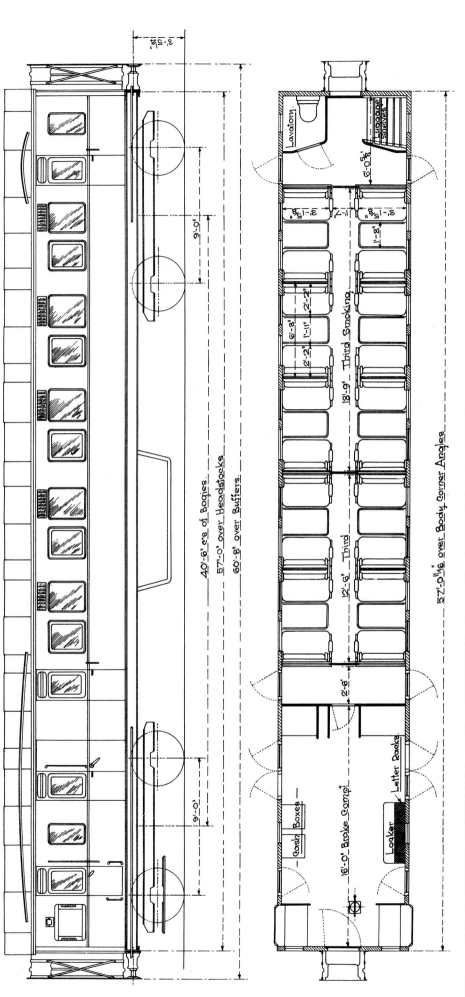

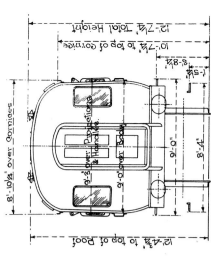

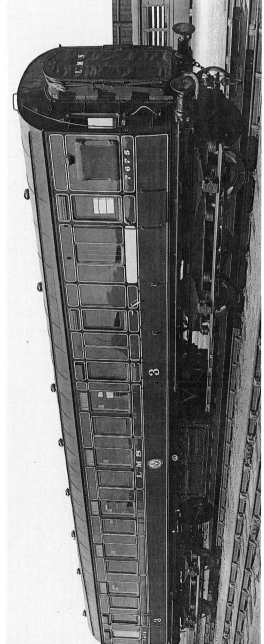

Figure 115 Third Class Vestibule Brake D1746 All things considered, the LMS was slow to introduce a brake ended vestibule coach and the first actually to appear were the 'All-Steel' examples to this diagram in 1925. Indeed, the well known London–Bradford train had to make do with ex-MR clerestory vestibule brakes at first. D1746 brought a new contractor, Leeds Forge, into the 'All-Steel' programme and it is one of their carriages which is shown here (No. 7675, later 9818); note the shallower solebar and even heavier riveting compared with the full thirds. We have no views of the Birmingham RC&W series but imagine they would be much as Lot 183 (Figure 103). Additional detailed drawings of the brake ended type appear on Figure 104.

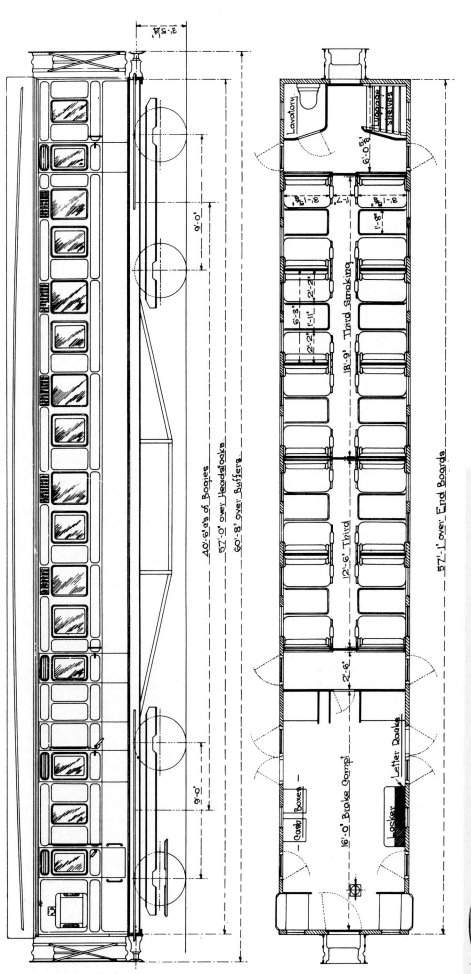

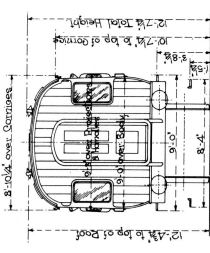

Figure 116 Third Class Vestibule Brake D1693 Vestibule brake coaches were nothing like as numerous as the matching full open coaches on the LMS. This was in contrast to the side corridor style, where there were almost as many brakes as ordinary carriages. The most common of the Period I vestibule brakes is illustrated here. Like all the 'twin-window' designs, it had much Midland Railway atmosphere to it. Number 638, the example illustrated, became 9835 after 1933.

Plate 223. This excellent picture shows the pleasant interior arrangement of BTO No. 638 (Figure 115) and may also be regarded as typical of the whole of the later Period I 'twin window' third class stock. For once, the upholstery colour is known–a pale fawny-pink background with dark coloured motifs. This rather dignified design was a popular third class LMS trim pattern in the later 1920s, and by good fortune it has survived in preservation, where a special length was re-woven for the NRM (from an original sample found at Wolverton–where else?) in order to re-trim the museum's preserved SLT (D1709) which also carried the same material. It was also widely used in Period II stock and may even have appeared on some Period III coaches.

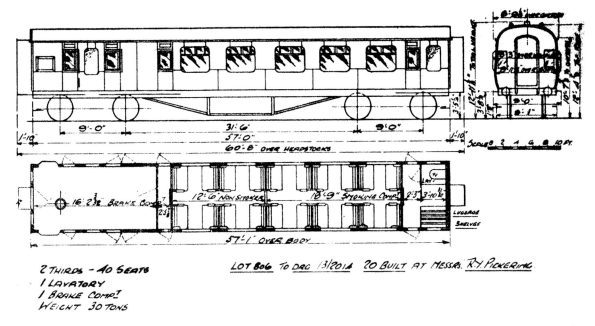

Figure 117 Third Class Vestibule Brake D1913 This was numerically the smallest LMS BTO design and we have no picture of the type, but the diagram reveals that dimensionally, it showed no real difference from its Period I predecessors. It was one of a relatively small number of LMS coaches built by R. Y. Pickering & Co., and if the picture at Plate 225 is any guide, it may well have had slightly non-standard LMS insignia when new.

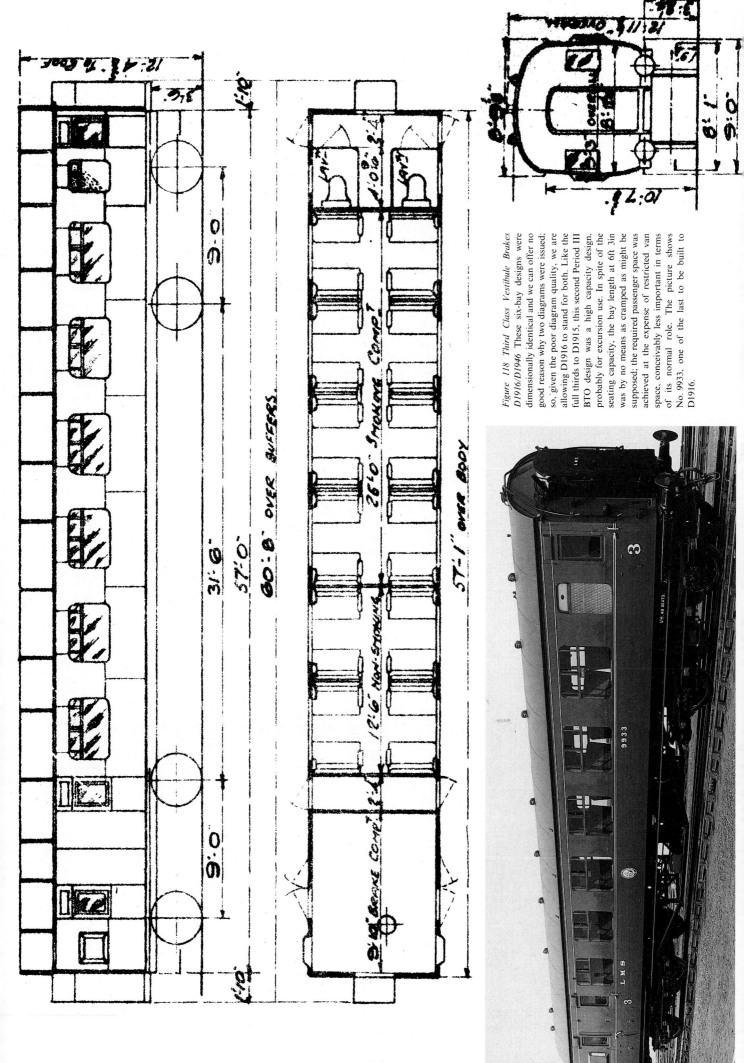

Figure 118 Third Class Vestibule Brakes D1916/D1946 These six-bay designs were dimensionally identical and we can offer no good reason why two diagrams were issued; so, given the poor diagram quality, we are allowing D1916 to stand for both. Like the full thirds to D1915, this second Period III BTO design was a high capacity design, probably for excursion use. In spite of the seating capacity, the bay length at 6ft 3in was by no means as cramped as might be supposed; the required passenger space was achieved at the expense of restricted van space, conceivably less important in terms of its normal role. The picture shows No. 9933, one of the last to be built to D1916.

Plate 224. Interior view of No. 9933 (D1916) looking towards the van end.

Plate 225. This less than perfect official view shows No. 9952 to D1946, one of 50 examples built by R. Y. Pickering & Co. to Lot 955. The main point of interest is the use of non- standard insignia for the running numbers; we do not know if this was typical for this firm—see also Figure 117.

Plate 226. This opposite side view of No. M9954M, another Pickering-built carriage to D1946 and repainted into BR red/cream livery, clearly shows that there was no important difference between these and the D1916 series. (*The late Gavin Wilson collection*).

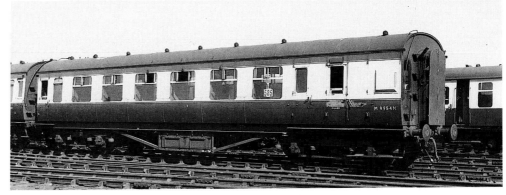

Plate 227 Third Class Vestibule Brake D2008. As with D1915 (Figure 112), our copy of the diagram book is also deficient in this type, but it was the brake ended equivalent of D1999 (Figure 113) and shared its more spacious bay size. This meant that even with a reduction to 5½ bays, the van was even smaller than for D1916/D1946. The appended view of No. 27948 reveals the toilet ends to have been identical to that of D1999, so those who wish should be able to make valid deductions about the remaining linear dimensions. The smoking compartment had four bays and the 1½-bay non-smoking area had the half bay backing onto the cross-lobby at the brake end. Like D1999, the two principal batches displayed similar airy interiors. As far as we can determine, all were built on welded underframes.

Plate 228. This view shows the non-smoking compartment in No. 27948 looking towards the van and indicating how the half bay was arranged. The interiors of this series (Lot 1174) matched D1999 Lot 1188 (Plate 222), while that of the first five carriages (Lot 1085), followed that of D1999 Lot 1084 (Plate 221).

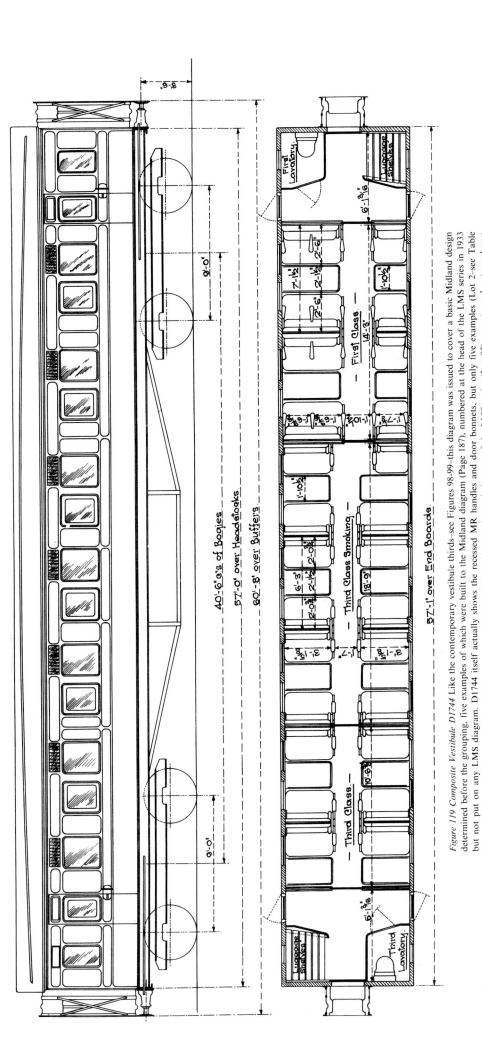

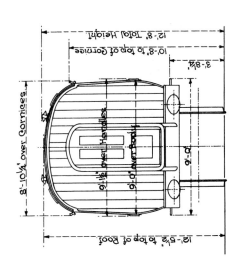

Figure 119 Composite Vestibule D1744 Like the contemporary vestibule thirds—see Figures 98-99—this diagram was issued to cover a basic Midland design determined before the grouping, five examples of which were built to the Midland diagram (Page 187), numbered at the head of the LMS series in 1933 but not put on any LMS diagram. D1744 itself actually shows the recessed MR handles and door bonnets, but only five examples (Lot 2—see Table 4a) were given these features. Plate 170 shows one of the 'non-diagram' examples and the rest of the LMS series (Lot 93) were turned out as shown here by No. 9265, later 9719. It is probable (not confirmed) that Lot 2 may have had the double outside panel between first and third class sections, a minor feature which would distinguish them from their otherwise identical 'non diagram' ancestors.

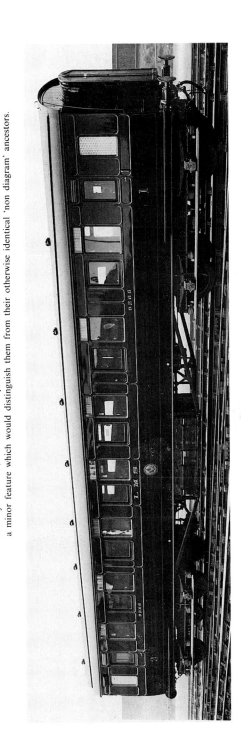

235

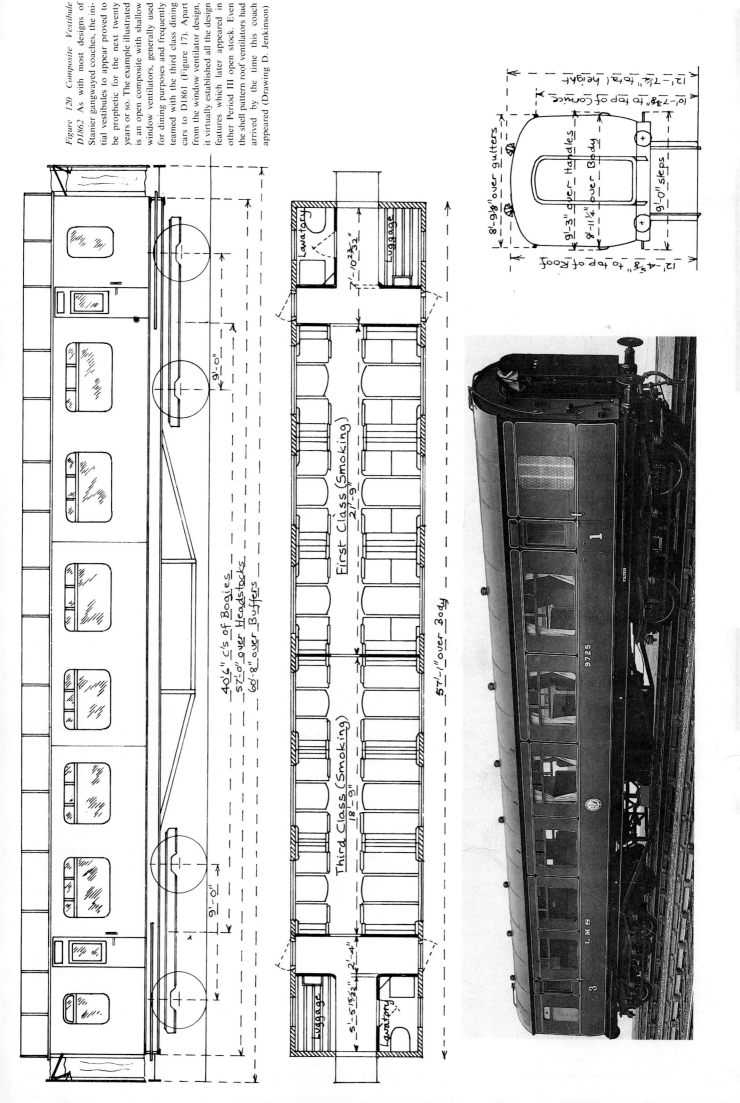

Figure 120 Composite Vestibule D1862 As with most designs of Stanier gangwayed coaches, the initial vestibules to appear proved to be prophetic for the next twenty years or so. The example illustrated is an open composite with shallow window ventilators, generally used for dining purposes and frequently teamed with the third class dining cars to D1861 (Figure 17). Apart from the window ventilator design, it virtually established all the design features which later appeared in other Period III open stock. Even the shell pattern roof ventilators had arrived by the time this coach appeared (Drawing D. Jenkinson)

9'-0"

9'-0"

40'6" C's of Bogies
57'-0" over Headstocks
60'-8" over Buffers

Lavatory

Luggage

7'-10²³⁄₃₂"

First Class (Smoking)
21'-9"

Third Class (Smoking)
18'-9"

57'-1" over Body

5'-5¹⁵⁄₃₂" 2'-4"

Luggage

Lavatory

12'-1⁷⁄₂" total height
10'-7³⁄₈" to top of cornice

8'-9⁷⁄₈" over gutters
9'-3" over Handles
8'-11¼" over Body
9'-0" steps

12'-4⁵⁄₈" to top of Roof

9725

1

3

LMS

Plates 229-230. The first series of Period III composite vestibules, along with their matching first and third class dining cars (see Chapter 2) were to establish most of the interior design parameters for Period III open stock, much as the broadly contemporary brake composites to D1850 (Chapter 3) had done in the side corridor field. These two interior views of D1862 No. 9725 show that a very stylish arrangement was achieved which more than stood the test of time; it certainly yields little or nothing to the BR MkIII and IV interiors of fifty or sixty years later. The woodwork may still have been rather dark, harking back to an earlier era, but the upholstery material in the third class had not yet approached the excessive flights of fancy which it was sometimes to achieve in later Period III vehicles! It is worth noting that the first class double seats no longer had central armrests and that the third class seat ends retained their vertical alignment in a 2 + 1 configuration. It is also an interesting comment on the changing times since then that the whole of this fundamentally *dining* vehicle was designated 'Smoking'!

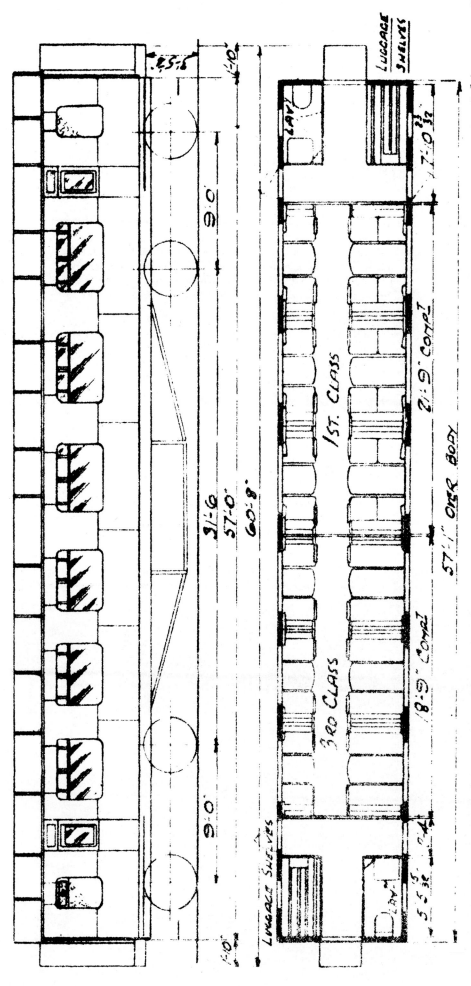

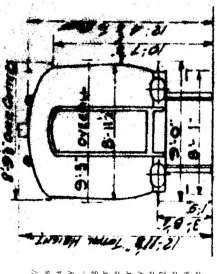

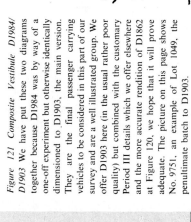

Figure 121 Composite Vestibule D1984/ D1903 We have put these two diagrams together because D1984 was by way of a one-off experiment but otherwise identically dimensioned to D1903, the main version. They are the final passenger carrying vehicles to be considered in this part of our survey and are a well illustrated group. We offer D1903 here (in the usual rather poor quality) but combined with the customary Period III details which we offer elsewhere and the more accurate rendition of D1862 at Figure 120, we hope that it will prove adequate. The picture on this page shows No. 9751, an example of Lot 1049, the penultimate batch to D1903.

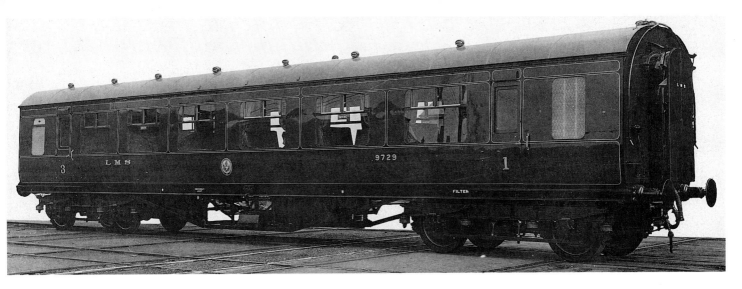

Plate 231. No. 9729 was the one-off Period III composite vestibule to D1984, generally believed to have been diverted from D1862, of which only nine were built. A separate diagram seems to have been raised solely because the carriage was of 'welded construction', but it must be recalled that this was a time when the LMS was actively experimenting in the coach construction field, so what later became standard practice was perhaps understandably regarded as somewhat experimental at this time. In fact, the term 'welded' referred solely to the bogies and underframe and perusal of this picture will reveal that No. 9729 was effectively the prototype for the welded underframe/bogie combination which later became commonplace on the LMS, having established that a modest weight saving of about 3–4% could be achieved. Another view is at Plate 177.

Plate 232. As has been shown at Plate 179, No. 9729 was also made the object of some interior design innovation. This third class section suggests that a rather more conservative approach was adopted at this end of the carriage; a dark wood finish is still dominant and the upholstery is modest compared with the rather more 'jazzy' first class section beyond the partition.

Plate 233. In the event, the rest of the Period III composite vestibules were built to a 'welded bogies plus conventional underframe' formula, a not uncommon LMS compromise at that time. This is No. 9755, taken from the opposite side to No. 9751 at Figure 121.

Plates 234-235. After No. 9729, the Period III composite vestibule interiors reverted to the traditional Stanier style. Several upholstery variations were tried, especially in the third class, some of which were very like those already depicted for TO D1999 and BTO D2008, others being as shown here in the third class end of No. 9751. First class interiors seemed rather more consistent and are represented here by the first class section of the same vehicle which had much the same trim as all examples of D1903.